HIP HOP HITS
The Producers Speak
by Jake Brown

The TMG Firm

New York

The TMG Firm, LLC
112 W. 34th Street
17th and 18th Floors
New York, NY 10120
www.thetmgfirm.com

ISBN: 978-0-99879-931-5
Library of Congress Control Number: 2017954844
All rights reserved

First The TMG Firm Trade Paperback Edition October 2017
Printed in the United States of America

This is a work of nonfiction. The events are portrayed to Jake Brown to the
best of the producers' memories. The conversations in this book all come from
the producers' recollections, though they are not written to represent word-for-
word transcripts. Rather, the producers have retold them in a way that evokes
the feeling and meaning of what was said and in all instances, the essence of the
dialogue is accurate. While all of the stories in this book are true, some names
and identifying details have been changed to protect the privacy of the people
involved.

Cover Concept by Jake Brown
Cover Design by Cesar A. Torres

This book is dedicated to the fourth and fith grade, Captain Elementary School 'Licensed to Ill' generation that I first discovered the Beastie Boys, Run-D.M.C., and hip hop with: Sam Horrell, Nicholas Barrios, Dominic Painter, Kevin Dennis, Tim Woolsey, Christian Stahl, Billy Boyd, Jason Player, Cory Cook, Timmy Wilson, Phillip Chu, Brian Carner, Andrew Garner, John McElwain, my younger brother Josh and anyone else I'm forgetting from the good old 80's that I got into rap with!

Thank You(s): I started working on this book back in 2010, and seven years and twenty producers later, here we finally are. I would first very much like to thank the producers who signed onto this project - many for the first time - to share the stories behind your lives and music in this book: N.O. Joe, Easy Mo Bee, Boi-1da, Wyclef Jean, Mario Caldato Jr., Eric B., Patrick Adams, Mannie Fresh, Johnny "J", Sir Mix-a-Lot, Jerome 'J-ROC' Harmon, Tony Hinds, Mike Dean, Afrika Islam, Pete Rock, Drumma Boy, Bangladesh, Jon Conner, Big Smo, Bubba Sparxxx, Jeff Bass, Frequency, Aaron Harmon, Teddy Riley, Sean "Puffy" Combs and the LEGENDARY SCARFACE for giving me the chance to speak with you about your craft, a career highlight! And to my publisher, The TMG Firm, SD Green, Chris Hocking and Ingram Content Group, thank you for taking a chance on this book and its 650 pages, I'll see you on store shelves this fall; and my cover design artist, Cesar A. Torres for helping put together the perfect cover.

Photo courtesy credits: Chapter Three Boi-1da photo courtesy of Myashe Samuels, Chapter Four Teddy Riley photo courtesy of Nat Carter, and Chapter Seven Jerome 'J-ROC' Harmon photo courtesy of Brad Gregory.

Thank you 'Boo,' aka my lovely and loving wife Carrie Brock-Brown and my other constant companion, Little Hannie; my father James P. Brown for taking me at ten years old to buy Beastie Boys' *Licensed to Ill* and Run-D.M.C.'s *Raising Hell* because I was too young to do it myself, and my mom Christina Brown for letting me turn our basement ping pong table into my first drum set at eleven to start playing along, my brother Ret. US Army Sgt. Joshua T. Brown and aunt Heather Thieme for growing up like siblings in the 1980s listening to the hip hop some of these producers made, my in-laws Bill and Susan Brock (RIP Gyps and welcome to the fam Gizmo), the extended Thieme and Brown families; my life-long network of loyal friends, Alex P. Schuchard (and my beautiful Godson Jackson, his sister Willimina and Ellen), Andrew and Sarah McDermott, Cris and Tiana Ellauri, Sean and Megan Fillinich, Bob and Cyanne O'Brien, Richard Kendrick, my longtime engineer Aaron Harmon, Joe Viers *(www.soniclounge.com)*, Adam and Shannon Perri, Paul and Helen Watts, Tony and Yvonne Rose; and everyone else who has helped me personally and professionally throughout my fifteen-year career.

TABLE OF CONTENTS

"I have no concept of formal music training or anything like that. I produced Miles Davis' album and everything that I've ever done in my career all by *ear*." – Easy Mo Bee

CHAPTER ONE

"Yo Mo Bee, Drop That Shit!" – Easy Mo Bee

Close your eyes and imagine that one of your first production jobs in a professional recording studio was producing what would become perhaps jazz's greatest legend's final studio album, one that Downbeat saluted as, "A hell of an exit!" Now, keep your eyes closed and imagine that the same jazz legend was none other than the late great Miles Davis. And he gave you the creative freedom with not only the album's major musical production decisions over how instrumental bed tracks were laid down, but even felt you were substantial enough as a creative partner to entrust you with naming the record's final song titles. Now open your eyes and you'd be sitting where Easy Mo Bee found himself at just twenty-five years old back in 1990:

> I had this idea at that time that I needed a manager, and at the time, everybody upon everybody who was somebody it seemed like, was managed by RUSH, Russell Simmon's management company. So I wanted to be with RUSH so bad that one day I called up Information/411, asked for the number to RUSH, called up, the receptionist comes on and I'm speaking in this little scared, humble voice, and said, "Yeah, I'm Easy Mo Bee, I've done..." I'm explaining my little efforts that I had just recently done, it wasn't much, and said, "I want to find out how to be managed by RUSH?", And because I was a producer, the receptionist told me, "Well, we have RUSH Artist Management and Russell just started a Production Management Company too, it's called RPM (Rush Producers Management). The girl who heads it up, she's out to lunch, but when she comes back, give me your number and I'll have her call you back.
>
> So sure enough, this lady called me back! Her name was Francesca Spero, and I began telling her about the little bit of stuff I had under my belt, speaking all scared and real humble and thinking she doesn't know anything about me.

So, she allowed me to go into this long story and then after that, she says in one short sentence, "I know who you are." (laughs). Just like that, and I was like, "Wow! Yeah?" Is how I replied. And she told me she knew about the Big Daddy Kane songs, and that made me feel a littlemore comfortable. So later, I went over there, and soon started a couple of projects. The first thing I did was I remixed the very last Third Bass record for the *Gladiator* film soundtrack. I was doing other little projects here and there and then one day Francesca called me and said, "Listen, Miles Davis has been hanging out with Russell recently, and he told Russell he wants to get into hip hop. So, what we're doing is we're putting together a bunch of reels from the producers on the roster over here and submitting it to Miles. I want to put together a reel of yours too, so just give me some tracks and I'll take some of your other stuff and put together one big reel and give it to him."

So they sent it out, and Miles listened to everybody's stuff, and when he listened to my reel, for whatever reason he gravitated toward me. I think he liked my drums, the accent on the drums, because my stuff is real punctuated. It really is. And I guess that comes from playing drums and my experience with drums. If you listen to any of my stuff, the drums are always dominant. One thing I remember him telling me was, "I don't want no cursing on my album, I don't like that shit." Those were his exact words, then, he told me, "I like your music, I like what you're doing." You know what inspired him, from what was on the reel? Not only had Francesca sent him instrumentals of mine, but she sent a couple songs I'd done with Kane and GZA. What he really loved was the song "*True Fresh M.C.*" off *Words from the Genius* album. I remember I was bugging out, saying to myself, "The deluxe Bee-Bop master from way back when, one of the innovators of jazz...he likes *True Fresh M.C.*" Fran was the one who had to tell me. She said, "He's crazy about this one song on your reel, that Genius song," and I was like, "What?!"

So, when we finally had a meeting, one of the first things he did was play *True Fresh M.C.* and asked me, "Can you do that for me? Can you do that?", and I was like, "Yeah, yeah." It's like he wasn't even sure. He wanted me to be sure, and asked me like twice, and then again, "Can you do that for me?" And I remember smiling, and reassured him, "Yeah Boss, yeah." Listen man, listen, fresh into the game of producing, and my fourth major project that I'm doing is Miles Davis. That's proof, that if you're not ready, you better get ready! That's what I had to do, I knew everything that I always wanted to do, I just didn't have the equipment back then to do it. Now, I had the equipment. I was perfecting my craft, honing my skill and understanding how to work all my equipment to achieve everything I wanted to in the studio.

That passion is one that stretches as far back into Mo Bee's childhood as his memories do of growing up in his family's church. Flooded with musical exposures that continued in as animated a celebration at home, where the legendary producer recalls, "I grew up in a musical family, my roots are from North Carolina, and my father's father, that is my Grandfather, was a preacher, one of those singing preachers, you know (laughs). And his sons, my uncles, they also preached and played guitar and organ in the church. I always considered Soul to be the next second-descendant of Gospel, and it really is when you think about what Ray Charles did, borrowing from Gospel and kind of turning it in to what we now call Soul. Anyway, whatever you want to classify that as, it was definitely handed down in my family, and then that transfers over into me being born and being a child in the house around my father who was constantly always playing music: Ray Charles of course, and a lot of Gospel, Aretha Franklin, Otis Redding, Sam and Dave, James Brown, all kinds of stuff man, blues, even jazz. So I grew up as a lover of music because my father was a man of many records, 45s stacked up in the corner in the living room and all of that." With such a rich library of derivative influences to weave into his own productions years later, Mo Bee collected records the way most kids his age did baseball cards and comic books:

As a young kid, starting somewhere around seven, eight years old, I just picked up after him and started collecting records, and from there, the loving of the music turned into DJing at around twelve years old. I got on the Turn-Tables as a twelve-year-old boy, and they had what we used to call Jams or Block Parties where the local neighborhood DJs would drag the big speakers and the turntables and mixer, all of their equipment out into the park, and would have a Block Party. I kind of idolized those dudes, I thought what they were doing was so incredible, taking two turn-tables and making sense of two copies of the same record. We have machines to do what we call looping today, but basically that was the beginning concept: two turn-tables and two copies of the same record. You take what you feel is the most important part of that record, and you just find a way to keep it going back to back, back to back. Thus today we have what you call, "the loop." That's where it all came from.

Like so many fellow producers of his generation who first discovered the concept of combining two songs into a new one and the implied possibilities, Easy idolized musicians the way most kids growing up in the inner city might a hustler standing on the corner or a basketball player shooting on the court. Or for that matter a kid like the late great Michael Jackson watching James Brown performing on TV versus spinning in his bedroom mirror. Mo Bee immediately began practicing his moves behind the turn-tables, becoming instantly industrious as he began gathering gear and teaching himself how to operate it, both mechanically and musically:

That's where the inspiration for DJing came from, was standing there out in the park just watching those guys, and at first, I was scrapping up any kind of cheap turn-tables that I could. I was only twelve, thirteen years old, trying to get

it going, and I did. That was the start. I didn't
have the professional equipment that those DJs
out in the park and on the block had, but it was
a good way to practice. And that was the
beginning.

As his creative circuitry began plugging into what Mo Bee
soon discovered was an intrinsic ability for his mind to
mechanically understand its way around the engines of the
machines he was creating with. His identity as a producer was
born. Successfully experimenting with ways to take his limited
equipment and turn it into a musical instrument, he was not
only creating on but simultaneously capturing to tape as Easy
began accelerating his way through an education on the basics of
home recording:

Even back when I was just starting out DJing, I
knew what the process was of recording, but I
didn't have the equipment to do it, and before I
even actually understood the process of multi-
track recording, I was doing it and didn't even
realize what I was doing. You would do what
used to be called a "Pause Tape," where you'd
take the break in a record that you like and keep
putting the needle back and playing it and wait
until you get a break and let that Pause button
go right on the tape deck right on the break,
right on the one, and then you stop it at the end
of the break, on the one, and then you come
back and play the record again, wait for the
break to come up, and then release that Pause
button again, "Boom," perfectly on the one, and

then at the end of the break, out on the one, and you keep doing that over and over and that would create like a loop.

We went through all kinds of things man, using the pause mechanism on the tape deck to create loops. When you get four minutes of that, I had two tape decks, and I play that one loop I created now in one tape deck, and have another tape deck recording the one that's playing. Then, I do another track on top of that. Then, take that tape out, put it back in the deck. And it was like layering tracks. Basically, what I was doing there was multi-tracking and not even realizing it.

By the time Easy had gotten his hands on his first real sampler – in yet another lucky example of how his aspirations had real-timed perfectly with the advent of the technology that would transform hip hop into the ground-breaking art form and revolutionary record-making process it became in the hands of producers like Mo Bee – he felt like he'd arrived at his own next level, confirming that "I think the first real studio I ever went into was at somebody's house, my man from Brownsville named Skiz, and this was around 1987. He had this big Akai rack-mount keyboard sampler, and as I was checking out what he was doing, right around that same time EMU came out with the SP-1200 series. Eventually, I got up enough money to get the SP-1200 and that's where it all started." A revolutionary piece of gear for Mo Bee in his own evolution as a fledgling record producer, the hyper-space leap forward in technology for a mind that was already there on the forefront waiting musically meant he could start building a catalog of original beats immediately:

Before I even got that piece of equipment, I already knew in my head what I wanted to do. See, the SP-1200 is a sampling drum machine, so you have the opportunity to sample drums – whether it's looped drums or you could take individual kicks and snares and put them in a separate track – or tap out drum patterns and sample loops of music, or take small pieces and just kind of arrange things however you want. I think the sampling drum machine is one of the most incredible things that was ever released, andthe guys who were really mastering that machine at that time and who I consider my mentor and one of the biggest influences to me, was Marley Marl. Marley and Ced-Gee, who was responsible for a lot of those early KRS-One/Boogie Down Productions records, but those two cats right there, there's other producers too that I was highly inspired by at the time like Hitman Howie T, Herbie Lovebug, Jazzy J, those were my influences right there, especially as DJing eventually turned into producing by my early twenties.

Needing a name to help brand the sound he was quietly creating in the 80's and that millions of hip hop fans would be blasting at full volume by the early 1990s, Easy had first come up with his professional DJ handle back in his bedroom, inspired by one of his early hip hop heroes, "Kool Moe Dee, who was all that back when. He first started rhyming and was in a group called the Treacherous Three. So I just thought he was one of the most incredible, innovative artists at the time, I was highly influenced by him, so much that I wanted a name like him. So he was Kool, so I said, *I'm going to be a similar adjective like Easy.* He was Moe, so I said, *Drop the E.* And he was Dee, so I said, *Since my family nickname is Boobee, and he was Dee, I'm gonna be Bee.* So, I became Easy Mo Bee."

When he was focusing on the music, Mo Bee was perfecting his first signature sound as a producer, starting with a band he was himself a member of along with childhood friend A.B. Money in R.I.F. (Rappin' is Fundamental). Dubbing the group's sound *Doo Hop*, the title of their debut LP as well, where Billboard would later write about their 1991 release that "there is little to dislike about Rappin' Is Fundamental and their mix of funky beats with breezy acappella breaks and doo-wop harmonies...Influenced by vocal harmony groups like the Flamingos, they were certainly among the more sophisticated members of New York's hip hop culture." Following R.I.F., Mo Bee got to work with GZA on his pre-Wu-Tang *Words from the Genius* album and Big Daddy Kane on the major-label, Gold-selling *It's a Big Daddy Thing*, smiling at the way he flipped "the check I got from doing that first gig with Big Daddy Kane to go out and buy my first SP1200 with. So that gig bought my first equipment, and I still use that same machine to this day. By now, I must have three or four of them, but that first one is like my Lucille."

By the time he'd graduated to the opportunity of a lifetime in working with Miles Davis, Entertainment Weekly reported that the jazz legend had first been drawn to Easy's sound because he felt Mo Bee's beats had the authenticity, "To capture the sound of today's urban streets." *Musician Magazine* meanwhile complimented the producer's success in creating, "A hip hop record...for younger ears weaned on modern beats, an inviting opening into one of the great cornucopias of American music...Like most everything Miles played, the music of DOO-BOP is cool and warm, beautiful and true." Well before the magic amalgam he and Miles were cooking up in the studio together ever hit critics' ears, Mo Bee remembers feeling most inspired by the sheer latitude of the creative freedom Davis had granted him as lead producer to pursue:

> With somebody like him, the possibilities for me to just open up were kind of endless, because in hip hop, you may have certain lines or rules, but in the jazz thing, he was just kind of like free-wheeling it with me. He actually let me just take the project and run with it and do whatever I wanted. We would finish a song, and I would ask him, "Miles, what do you want to call this?", and he would look at me and say, "I don't know, shit, call it whatever you want, I don't give a shit." He would say it just like that, so I ended up titling all the songs on the album, and he even gave me the responsibility of titling the album.

Much in the same extemporaneous vein with which jazz breathes musically, Mo Bee kept a fluid flow at play in the studio as Miles laid down performances on his famous trumpet, bringing fans inside the studio for a front-row recreation of he and Davis' animated rapport as they worked: "When Miles was recording, he would do one whole long full take all the way through, and when it does get to the end and we're rolling the tape back, talking to each other from the booth to the control room, I'm telling him, "Yo, I like that!" And you know what he says? "Nah, bring it back, I want to do it over again." And sometimes I would persist, "I loved that Miles!" And he'd say, "Nah, I can do it better. Bring it back one more time, I'm gonna do it." So he'd go back and do it again. What you thought was so good from the first take, he would do it over. You would understand why he wanted to do it over when you listened back, because you'd be like, "Wow! That one is better."

Highlight rhythm rockers like *Chocolate Chip* showcased what the L.A. Times felt marked the album's "high spots, notably, Davis playing off James Brown-style rhythm guitar licks on *Chip* and *High Speed Chase* and the way Easy Mo Bee skillfully sets him up on *Fantasy* with a melody reminiscent of Sly Stone's *If You Want Me to Stay*. On *Blow*, as Easy Mo Bee delivers a strong rap over a buoyant rhythm track and Davis tailors his phrases to fit the vibrant groove like a glove. It's the best performance on the album, musically substantial and a piece that hip hop and dance club youth can easily embrace." All byproducts of a totally-synched vision where Easy made his instrumentals essentially sound like parties while Miles played the crowd overtop, their creative rapport in the studio is one he reveals here for the first time:

> I'm glad you asked me that, and it's interesting you asked me that because *nobody ever really asked me that question before*. In other words, he didn't play something to me – like a note or a line on his trumpet – and say, "Okay, I want to create something to this." No. He would pick the tracks that he liked ahead of time. The instrumentals, we'd put them on in the studio, and he would just like freewheel to him. In a way, I guess you could call it like a jam session. It's just that instead of jamming to his normal, traditional band structure that would be set up in the studio. He was jamming to my beats.

There's stuff that he would do, right at the last minute on the spot, and you could tell he was making this stuff up as he was going along and then sometimes he would hit a note and nobody upon nobody is going to tell Miles Davis what to do, but I'm in the studio and of course, I wouldn't stop him. I'd wait until it was finished and we'd roll the tape back, but then I would tell him like, "Miles, you know in that second verse part where you was playing, I heard a note that sounded a little...", and he would always be like "Leave it, leave it, I want that, leave it." I sit back and listen to that stuff now, and am like "You know what, he knew what he was talking about. That was him," and if you listen to his other records that he made, he always did the same thing.

For as many hats as he was already wearing as the pair forged toward wrapping recording, the one Mo Bee would add next reflected just how precious the performances he was capturing to tape were. In both in substance and sum, they would prove the final musical statement Miles Davis would ever make after he passed away unexpectedly on September 28, 1991 of pneumonia, respiratory failure and a stroke. Suddenly finding he was sitting behind the console alone, the producer made his bones finishing the record by himself, recalling that "he died somewhere around the sixth song, so to make a complete album, I remixed two more songs from his vaults, and because I had to remix those without him there, just working with the tapes, and that was actually fun though, that was fun, because I'd never, ever heard Miles Davis' horn soloed on a multi-track mixing board where you can listen to just the horn, and when you hear something that uniquely special, all kinds of ideas start coming to you man!" Mo Bee's charmed collaboration with Davis would go on to make fans and Miles proud listening down from above after the first jazz rap album in either genre's history debuted at #1 on the Billboard American Jazz Album Chart, earning both he and Davis a Grammy Award for Best R&B Instrumental Performance. While appreciative for the accolades and appreciation over the album he and Miles made together, for Easy Mo Bee, the greatest honor for the producer came simply with the opportunity to work with the jazz legend at all:

> I was just happy to be in the studio working with him. I had no idea it would even reach that point or that level, we were just in there making music. So the biggest reward to me was I was just happy to be in the studio with somebody as great as him at that point in my career. I hadn't worked with anybody as great as him, all of the people I worked with were up and coming rappers, and the biggest, most well-known name I'd worked with was Big Daddy Kane, that's it.

With his career on a roll, the producer would next transition from working with a legend to a total unknown who would in time become one himself. Mo Bee holds the distinction of being the first producer to ever work with Brooklyn legend the late great Biggie Smalls, aka The Notorious B.I.G., in the studio producing *Party & Bullshit*. His track was a re-invention for New York's hip hop sound that *XXL Magazine* in 2013 crowned, "A classic that continues to remain relevant in pop culture" twenty years after, "The Easy Mo Bee-produced single...(first) appeared on the *Who's the Man?* soundtrack and introduced Biggie to mainstream fame." Taking East Coast hip hop by storm from its opening hits. The beat Mo Bee drummed up for Biggie's debut single was a thundering one where the producer explained that by sonic design:

> The drums are actually brighter than the real music. And I don't know, for some reason, I wanted it to sound that way. When you play the track back, it kind of hums. It's got like a low hum, but it's a good hum because the bass is deep. But there's also some rich mid-range there too. And there's a guitar strum that goes on real low in the song, it's also filtered too. I just thought it would sound better if that sample was a little dull, and for the drums to be brighter than anything in that record. It kind of made him stand out more up front too.
>
> The loop, the sample, was kind of Jazzy, and I did a lot of chopping on the sample, I kind of spliced the sample up, and I know this may sound weird: usually you want the sample to sound really crisp and bright, but I kind of muffled the sample on purpose. I don't know why, it just sounded better that way. You know when you have a filter on a sample, if we're talking about percentages, I would say that sample was filtered about 70%, it just sounded that way. If you listen back to that record and the main music, and you'll be able to hear it.

The track was done first. I was listening to the Last Poets around that time, so it was my idea to use *Party & Bullshit* as a hook. Biggie had never heard of them before, he had never heard of the Last Poets before, I kind of turned him onto something, played him that and was like "What do you think about that? I want to use that some kind of way," and he said, "Alright," and took it and flipped it over instead of me having to sample it, he kind said it over and use it as his own vocal.

With as street as Notorious B.I.G. sounded on tape, once Moe Bee was hired to bring that same energy to Biggie's debut LP, the producer knew his beats had to be as *hard* as the blocks they would be banging on once the record was out. An urban soundscape that *Rolling Stone Magazine* would later describe as a, "Rugged uptempo funk produced by Easy Mo Bee...(where) the music rushes you through B.I.G.'s nihilistic existence and life history like a jolting, uptown subway ride." As he and Smalls got down to business, one of the album's true hood anthems would emerge with the manic *Gimmie the Loot*:

The track was made beforehand, and Biggie wrote to it, came up with the concept for the two voices and the two characters thing, one speaking to the other. It's funny, because a couple people – after the record was made – came to me and said, "Yo, whose that other cat on the song?" And I said, "Yo, you stupid? That's him!" And they said, "Word, for real?", and I was like, "Yeah man, he just did like a high voice and a low voice." He did that on *Warning* too. When we tracked it, we started with the low voice, or as far as the characters go, his voice, and he would lay his voice first, leave the gap spaces where the other character would go, and then after he would do the first character voice, he would come back and fill the gaps on another track with the other voice. As opposed to Pac, Big *did* do punches, if he needed to, he would punch.

The legendary *Source Magazine* would lavish praise on Mo Bee for creating, "Timeless classics from that four and a half micer" including alongside *Gimme The Loot.* The, "back and forth storytelling adventures of *Warning,* and...the eerie title track itself as, "Highlights of this legendary project." BET went a step further, declaring that, "Easy Mo Bee's grimey, blue-collar funk was the backbone of Biggie's classic debut." In decoding the science behind how he found his way to that album-defining sound, the producer pointed to the sonic architecture of the aforementioned *Warning* as among his favorite illustrations:

When you have records that have a lot of space and a lot of room, like *Warning* wasn't a noisy record, it had a lot of room to breathe across it, so on a record like that, it was okay to let that reverb breathe across it. Biggie preferred not a lot of reverb on his voice while he was tracking. If you listen to all of his records, the vocals usually sounded a lot more personal, that's from not using a lot of reverb. If anything, you use a personal one, like a small room reverb, not too much.

I was always heavy into a lot of Issac Hayes, I liked the big orchestra sound that he used to have, which was similar to the same thing that Barry White was doing but it's just that, to me, Issac Hayes had more of a harder, straight-to-the-point, more soulful approach, and I just loved everything that he was doing. Also around that same time right there, the *Dead Presidents* movie was out and *Walk on By* was in that movie, and I'm just looking at this record like, "I wanna do something with that." It's different when you listen to something, but when you get a chance to look at it, it has even more of an effect on you. If you look at how that song was used in that movie, you might have ended up making a beat off of it too like I did (laughs).

Now legendary for the amazing feat of not writing down his lyrics before he laid them down on tape in the studio, Mo Bee still shakes his head marveling back at Small's genius at work, revealing of the word wizard's esoteric process in action. "Biggie, he didn't waste no time putting vocals down. He would sit around on the couch for forty-five minutes, an hour, an hour and a half, two hours. He's sitting there just like mumbling to himself with his two hands clasped together, and you can see him twiddling his thumbs. He's sitting there with those hands grasped like that, twiddling his thumbs on his lap and you come along and try to talk to him. He'd put his hand up, almost like as a signal, like, *Hold on, chill, chill, I'm doing something, I'm writing.* He didn't have to say that, he'd just put the hand up and keep mumbling to himself, because he's writing and didn't want to be interrupted. So even if you don't think he's doing anything, what he's actually doing is writing *in his head.* Biggie was not actually the first person I ever saw do that. The first person I'd ever seen write in their head without writing a single thing down was A.B. Money in R.I.F. Biggie was the second person, and Jay-Z was the third I ever saw do that right there in the studio." Biggie's voice would prove to be the perfect partner in crime for his way with rhymes. One that Mo Bee remembered stood out to his ear first and foremost because:

> Biggie wasn't saying the things other people were saying, it was just different man, his stories. One thing I can say is that his cadence and the accent and a lot of the phrasing was very reminiscent of Big Daddy Kane, Rakim, whathaveyou, some of the best rappers of our day, but his stories and the actual choice of words and how he was putting him together, a lot of the things he was saying, and his flow and the tone that he would use, he just made it all sound so easy. You know how rappers rap where they sound like they're running out of breath because they're trying to say all they're trying to say, he never sounded like that. He just made it sound easy, like the words just rolled off his tongue.

Though credited as the conceptual inventor of the *hip hop soul* sound that defined East Coast radio throughout the mid-1990s and listed as co-producer on album hits including *Juicy, One More Chance, Me & My Bitch, and Big Poppa,* Sean "Puffy" Combs' physical presence and creative contributions to Mo's six tracks on the album were far more hands-off musically, limited strictly to Small's vocal tracking. With being the most easy-going ego in a room full of them a requisite skill for any truly professional record producer, Mo Bee kept a patient bed-side manner has the team worked their way through vocal tracking:

> Puff, a lot of times, what he would do, he would stand back and he's in the control room and me and him are on the board with the engineer, and I'm making suggestions too. But Puff is making even more suggestions: "Yo, bring that back. Yo, give me a little bit more of this," or "Yo, wussup? You sound dead Yo. I'm saying, come on man, give me some more of that." So he was real vocal, he had a lot of vocal input, and Biggie was cool with it. A lot of the times, Puff was right. I would even agree with certain things in the vocal, maybe that he needed to fall back." And as for me, on the tracks, I thought ahead of time when I played the tracks for him at the office or when I would shop the beats. Initially, upon hearing them, after he agreed that he liked or loved that beat, I was able to take that and just run free with it.

XXL Magazine among countless other critics would take care of properly shining the spotlight off of Biggie and on to the fact that if you, "Look at the production credits of Notorious B.I.G.'s *Ready to Die*, Easy Mo Bee's name won't be hard to find. The longtime producer crafted classic Biggie hits such as *Gimme the Loot, Machine Gun Funk, Warning, The What* featuring Method Man, and the album's title track, *Ready to Die*." Establishing a sort of sonic signature for Mo Bee whereafter a fan could hear a one of his beats and know it was produced by Easy without needing to read the back of a record, he breaks his science down as one where:

> That so-called "B.I.G." sound of mine, I want to tell you where that comes from. For every track that I do, I kind of EQ my sounds as I go along. There are a lot of people who will just go ahead and just whatever sample sounds they're using in the keyboard or the sounds they sample from records, or from drum kits, and make the record and say "I'll mix it and EQ later," NO, Easy Mo Bee does not do that – we EQ the sounds along the way. While I'm in the process of sampling and putting the beat together, I EQ my sounds, so the sounds have to be EQ'd before I sample, in other words.
>
> So if I'm beefing these sounds up, right, and I EQ them before I sample them, when you take a song to the studio, usually – especially in hip hop because that's what it's all about, it's all about a big sound and the drums are always supposed to be knocking hard, basses we consider those that they should be deep – if I've already EQ'd these sounds, I'll tell you what normally happens: you have a big sound with sounds that have already been EQ'd before the mix, so you take the track to the studio, and what does the engineer do? What's their job? To make things sound bigger and greater, and it never was planned this way but what you have is this double-EQ thing going on, so in other words, I already made things sound big, then you take it to the studio and it

gets in the engineer's hands, and ends up being one big whopping sound.

Mo Bee's name would ring out again on the heels of the Super Bowl Victory-size success of Biggie's debut album, this time earning him the distinction of being the only producer to work with both the Notorious B.I.G. *AND* Tupac Shakur as rising stars ahead of the fatal East Coast/West Coast rap wars of the mid-1990s. Remembering Pac as the equivalent of a hungry journeyman prizefighter working his way up to a title shot, Mo Bee would find himself working with Shakur right as his star was rocketing through the eye of a hurricane of controversial media attention, making the studio his only sanctuary away from all the noise:

> Pac was here in New York in 1993 filming *Above the Rim*, and while he was here, he did a show with Big Daddy Kane at Madison Square Garden where he appeared on stage with him. So during that night, I met him backstage, we exchanged numbers, and he told me, "I'm out here filming a movie, come out to the set and check me out!"

As a producer - especially one on the rise - there is arguably no greater shout out than to have the artist you're producing reference your beat-making skills on tape in their lyrics, let alone the profile than having that co-sign kick off the song as Tupac did at the top of *Temptations* when he famously exclaimed, "Yo Mo Bee, drop that shit!" Beaming to date over the endorsement, the producer described an instant bond at work as the two got down to theirs in the studio, both because, "I think he was definitely comfortable with my sound, and he felt confident that

I had his back. Obviously, he wouldn't say something like that otherwise, and whenever you hear the artist egg the producer on like that by mentioning their name and everything, he must feel like you got his back." Touching musically on how the hit, where *Rolling Stone* singled out, "Producer extraordinaire Easy Mo Bee for laying the beat low and thick." When it all came together, he proudly points to the fact:

> That whole idea was mine. On that record, that sample, everything that I used up in there, that was my idea. You hear a lot of patches on drums up in there, like patched kicks and snares, a lot of times I'll create fills – there's the kick and the snare, or what we know as the "boom" and the "bap," and then the way real drummers play, in between those booms and baps there are the insertion of fills to make your drums sound funky, make them feel liquid and loose and real. I would do stuff like that. The patches on the drums have always been a big thing for me too.
>
> For the bass, all of my basses – in anything you've ever heard – all of my basslines were always played through the SP1200 drum machine. There's some kind of analog translation that that machine does that I just like: once a signal runs through it, I guess it's just something in the way that it processes the signal. If I can best describe it, what I love about the SP1200 is it has the sound of what I call "that 45 sound." If you've played records before, then you know that thick, round, fat sound you get from playing a fourty-five as opposed to playing

an album, to me, the SP1200 is like that fourty-five sound. Like a fat James Brown forty-five or something that's got a sound like that.

When it came to tracking Tupac's patented multi-tracked vocal style, a signature the rapper had invented and first introduced on tape to hip hop before it became a fad even employed by Mo Bee on Biggie's debut album on tracks like *Gimmie the Loot* and *Machine Gun Funk*, working with the originator was a new experience for the producer and one where he happily credited Pac as a co-producer for the simple truth:

> Yo (laughs), this dude could use sixteen tracks on the board alone on his own just for vocals. You could tell he had it all mapped out, like he was baking a cake with different layers, like, "Okay, my verses are here, my ad-libs...," and he had spaced-out interval ad-libs, and then there was that constant doubling or tripling the voice, making it sound bigger. But on top of there too, sometimes he had certain spots where he would come in and act the main vocal up with an additional an ad-lib or something. Those tracks are really, really complicated.
>
> It was crazy. I was like, "Yo, this is like the Miles thing all over again." I found out Tupac was the same way. What was really important out of what both of them were doing was like when you do that, when you record straight all of the way through, you're moving like a musician. In other words, a bass player – a real bass player – he plays all the way straight through the song,

giving that song a real true, loose feel. Nothing is programmed. It's not where he gets like the first eight bars of the bassline that's good and then even in the days of tape recording, because they could do things like that, where they'd just loop that 8 bars over and over. No, a real bass player plays all the way through the record, and then that's where you get all of these different changes, and the real feel – no loops – you can hear all of the fills, and the real stuff. So that's the similarity between Miles and Tupac.

Not a stretch at all in analogous terms, as Mo Bee delved more deeply into his comparative look back at working with two geniuses who, despite recording in different musical mediums, had similar methods to their madness, such that, "Miles Davis had a process of recording where you cannot stop him. I'm talking about even if there's a verse that he's playing, even after that verse is over, something else is going to happen on the hook. He wants the tape to run from beginning all the way to the end. Here's what's so crazy, I worked with Miles first, right. And maybe like three, almost four years later, I worked with Tupac. And guess what? Come to find out he's the *same way.* He said, 'Put the tape on and just let it roll, don't stop – even at the end of my verses – I'm not finished. Just let it keep running all the way through.' When it would get to the hook parts, that's where Pac would either be quiet or he would hum little ad-lib stuff on the hook, real low. Then he'd come right back in with the second verse and do the same thing for the second hook, then third verse, last verse. But the rule was, 'Do not stop the tape!'" Shakur's rule of the recording road with every producer who had the privilege of recording with him, Mo Bee reveals for fans a look inside the vocal booth at Tupac's fascinating creative process building the body of his vocal performance:

> He would track over himself each time, and with instruments, they call that creating a patch, like when a bass player and a guitar follow each other and play the same note on top. Well, people do that with vocals too, some do what they call "doubling" their vocals, right on top do the same exact thing. Like if the voice could be a wave, just picture two of them following each other – the hills and the valleys – you got two waves right on top of each other. And that's what Pac would do. He would double, and sometimes even triple his vocals. That's why when you listened to Pac's voice, it had that big sound.
>
> Pac, with his lyrics, I guess that's why they always felt so much more real than a lot of other vocalists that I worked with, is because he treated his voice like an instrument. Again, like a bass player that plays all the way through the song, no punches, Pac always told me that, Miles always told me that: "No punches. Don't punch me, just let the tape run all the way through. If I mess up something, I'll come back and get it the next time around or just do it all over. But don't stop me." Like Miles, Tupac would do one long take, and I'm like, "YO! That's knocking, I love that!", and he's like, "Nah, bring me back, I want to do it over. I want to do another one," and again he does it, and you sit back and listen and

you're like, "Yo...yeah, okay, I understand why he does what he does."

One thing Pac would allow me and the engineer to do is, while he didn't want me to do any live punching, what he would allow us to do was, say he did like four tracks of the same vocal all the way through, he would lay three or four different tracks of vocals all the way straight through, and we could comp the vocals.

Imagine sitting in a recording studio working with a rap legend you grew up listening to under the armed supervision of a prison guard standing watch behind you, and that's precisely where Mo Bee found himself working with Slick Rick on a work-release day pass tracking vocals. Fighting the clock in every sense of the word that day, which the producer still counts as among his most surreal studio sessions ever, the rapper still managed to maintain "his edgy wit," *Entertainment Weekly* later concluded, thanks in large part to "several top producers" including Easy, who confirmed:

Indeed the session was somewhere at a remote location in upstate New York not far from the prison, and I just remember all night while we were recording, that guard just standing arms folded, supervising the whole session. Now, as a producer, it was bizarre, and you have to imagine, if I was coming to the studio prepared and didn't really want to waste too much time, then you have to think Rick was probably thinking that too because he only had so many hours to work, and he's in the booth recording while he's being watched over, so he just wanted to get what he had to do done.

I'll just say this much: I do appreciate that they would arrange it so that he could be whizzed out of the jail to the studio with me to record. It wasn't some, "Here's the vocal take on the master tapes and we want you to make a beat to this vocal." Like he'd just done a rhyme on the click track, "Now, make a beat around that." It was organic, live in the studio, and Russell Simmons had gone to the trouble to arrange for him to be together with me in the studio, I have to give them props for that. But I remember at the session, this dude was being supervised by a Dept. of Corrections guard who was present on the scene in the studio, standing arms folded by the door! He was there the whole time, and Rick couldn't leave the studio, he couldn't go nowhere, not even to the bathroom without this guard standing outside of the bathroom waiting for him.

Ironically, right as another of his recent collaborators, Tupac, was shipped off to prison following he and Mo Bee's work together, the producer received a call from Biggie Smalls, who co-incidentally was beginning work on his ambitious follow-up to the wild success of the 4-million-selling *Ready to Die*, which had restored the East Coast's respect within broader hip hop following the near-fatal Kid 'n Play era. With B.I.G. and Puff's eyes set on topping the considerable expectations via a double-LP, Easy was not surprisingly feeding off their energy with his own creative adrenaline pumping, felt in the thumping pulse of the Top 40 hit record he produced for Biggie, which *Rolling Stone* – now a frequent fan of the producer – highlighting as "the hottest track" on the 24-song opus as *Going Back to Cali*. Remembering *RADIO* as the conceptual keyword for he and Smalls were seeking to head with versus staying with the more street sound of his debut, during pre-production meetings, Mo Bee recalled that:

> Puff wanted a totally more refined, brighter, crisper sound. I shopped 80-something beats towards *Life After Death* and Puff turned all of them down, because they were all in the style of and just as gritty as the *Ready to Die* beats. I was thinking, "Hey, we did a wonderful thing. Let's keep it going, let's do more of that," and he was like, "Nah, I want Biggie in the club. I want him on radio. I want chicks loving him. I want people dancing to him. You know?" So if I wanted to be on that album, I had to cater to that perspective, and that's what I did, I said, "Okay, I'm gonna meet them half way."

> With this more refined approach to the choice of tracks and stuff like that, the more club-danceable sound, more radio-friendly, he had a lot of new things going on on that second album that didn't happen on the first. I know for a fact that you didn't know that, number one that *Big Poppa* was the last song recorded for *Ready to Die*, and number two, that Puff has a lot to do with that new, *calmer* voice that you heard from Biggie on *Life After Death* and all the records

after *Big Poppa*. Because if you listen throughout the whole *Ready to Die* album, he's either got the yelling or half-yelling voice. But by the time he got to *Life After Death*, he sounded more confident, more poised, more laid back – not like where he had to yell to make the point or to make you understand. In other words, if there was an emphasis, it was on the words and not necessarily the tone. As you go along, you get to find your own voice and you learn yourself.

As he got down to the work of making a track that sounded like it flew out of the speaker and swooped the listener up along for the ride, Mo Bee's muse for the funk-fueled voyage was an ideal pick: *More Bounce to the Ounce*, that was a track by Zapp and Roger, and that was something that was just my idea altogether. I always wanted to do something with that song, but so many producers had already sampled that record that it almost wasn't gonna happen. But then I said, 'Wait a minute, hold up. You want to sample this record, then you do it like nobody else has ever done it!' and that's what I ended up coming up with. That song had somewhere around fifteen different chopped sample parts, and the approach I took was something like this: when somebody else would sample the full, long straight loop, I don't want the loop. I want all the sounds in those loops so I can play it back myself. (laughs) And if I have that, then I don't have to settle for just the loop. I can play it back and arrange it how I want, so I can have that same sound. But now I have the ability I can take anything in there – a kick, a snare, the bass – and place it where I want and play with it how I want. If I have only the loop, I have only the loop to settle with, right? So why not dissect it, and have the elements for me to have total autonomy over, where I can place them anywhere I want and do what I want them to do. From there, my bass on that song was the SP1200 and Akai S950, those were my weapons of choice. By that time, I was *freaking* the machine!"

Back in the midst of production for *Life After Death*, when Mo Bee found out that he was being given another high-profile assignment with the duet he was charged with producing featuring both Biggie and Jay Z – returning the favor after Smalls had appeared on Marcy's finest's debut LP, *Reasonable Doubt* – Easy knew he had to bring his best game forward. Showcasing arguably New York's two premier emcees of the 1990s trading verses like Jordan and Pippen trading the ball down the court, the producer remembers already having the perfect track in mind, one that ironically:

> I'd already played Puff for the first album, and I guess he wasn't ready for it on the *Ready to Die* album when I'd first offered him the *I Love the Dough* track. I guess it wasn't time yet, so when he spoke of this more refined, crisp, mature sound, I thought about it and told him, "Oh yeah, that's right, you remember the Rene and Angela track? You didn't want it for the first album, this would probably fit now," and he was like, "Alight, hook it up." So I hooked it up, brought it back, and they were like, "Yo, that's poppin', use that!" The original title of the song is *I Love You More*, and Diddy had Angela Wimbush come back into the studio to re-sing the hook. The original hook went, "I love you more, more than you know, gotta let it show, I love you more, hey," and he told her to change the words and sing, "I love the dough" instead.

31

Mo Bee kicked off the millennium by releasing his own solo studio album with *Now or Never: Odyssey 2000*, which *The Source* rewarding with three and a half mics out of five what they celebrated as, "A galactic journey through hip hop's multicultural spectrum," while continuing to rack up credits with an eclectic troupe of the biggest hip hop stars of the day, from Busta Rhymes to Heavy D & the Boyz, Mos Def to Wu-Tang Clan. The producer's sound would continue to bump in the ear-buds and computer speakers of the download/iPhone generation both courtesy of the massive legal and illegal downloading of both Tupac Shakur and Biggie Smalls' respective catalogs. Once Napster and then iTunes came online, even as he remained relevant as ever as a current hit-maker, taking Alicia Keys. Rocketing into the Top 10 with *If I Were Your Woman/Walk on By*, which peaked at #9, the album it was featured on debuted at #1 on the Billboard Top 200 Album Chart, moving over 600,000 copies in its first week of sale. Happy to be back at the top of the charts, Mo Bee would receive a nomination for Best Traditional R&B Vocal Performance at the 2006 Grammy Awards, an icing on the already sweet victory of crossing over successfully into the realm of R&B mainstream.

Spin Magazine would compliment Keys for having a, "Knack for getting producers to shear away many of their (trademarks)...and meet her half way, so that her instinct toward vintage southern-fried 70's R&B pervades every track. On her cover of *If I Was Your Woman/Walk on By*, she gets Easy Mo Bee to back her with a sound that conjures Roberta Flack jamming with the Jackson Five. The track provides an interesting bridge between the old-school Soul influences that dominate this album and the more futuristic hip hop mutations" brought to life by Easy. Speaking on the opportunity to grow as a producer, Mo Bee remembered jumping at the chance:

To work with a female singer, that was exciting to me, because I don't feel like I've done *a lot* of that in my time, just that alone, and again, as far as chameleoning yourself into situations, when you're making a song for a man, you make it a certain way. When you're making a song for a woman, you're thinking another way. You want to cater to people, you want to appeal to them.

First of all, the Issac Hayes sample was her idea. She came to me and she was like, "I wanna rework that again. Could you re-work that for me?" And I was like, "Yeah, cool!" So we ended up working hand-in-hand together in the studio, and you had me on the production side with the track and the beat that I came up with. Then she's matching chords and the piano – which is her key thing, about her – to the track, and making it all make sense. Then Dwayne Wiggins of Tony! Toni! Toné! We were all three in the studio working together: me on the track, her on the piano, and Dwayne on guitar. And three of us were collaborating in the studio, trading ideas, and making that all make sense.

After *Time Magazine* in recent years named *Ready to Die* as one of the most influential albums of the past fifty years, Easy has entered that stage of his career where the words legacy and legend have begun to be tossed around in the same sentence with his name, but he seems to get the biggest kick out of the creative ways his hits show up in modern pop culture:

They used *Flava in Ya Ear* in a 2012 McDonald's Big Mac commercial? I think the commercial is definitely a highlight. Another highlight is when Irv Gotti sampled my *Flava In Your Ear* for Jennifer Lopez's *Ain't It Funny*. I don't know, but I think that says a lot about the longevity of a piece of music that was done by me. I'm from an era where it's important to be yourself, it's important to have something special about you to set yourself apart. That's how I am, and how I always chose to be, and when you're like that, for some reason, people never forget you. To me, it's more about than just blending in with the fabric, I don't want to blend in with the fabric, I want to stand out, I want to be different, I want to be Mo Bee!

As Time Out New York correctly noted, after such a, "Ridiculously storied career in the game," when Easy reflects back in his greatest hits in closing, where some producers posed with the question of favorites veer into the safer, "They're all my babies," territory, Mo Bee – faced with jazz versus hip hop legends – seems proudest to have started his career making the final studio LP with jazz's most preeminent pioneer:

The Miles Davis album, I consider that to be the greatest thing that I ever did over anything. The stuff I did with Biggie, Busta Rhymes, anything that I did – it's all good, it's all cool. But to work with Miles Davis, naw, I'm sorry. I have to regard that as the highest-regarded thing that I ever did in music. I have to, I have to! *Warning* by Biggie is like the perfect union of lyrics and music man. Another one of my favorites is *Everything Remains Raw* by Busta Rhymes. On the Miles Davis album, the song *Mystery*, I really, really like that record man. Really, really like that record. *Jeeps, Lex Coups, Bimaz & Benz* by The Lost Boyz. You know why? That's just another one of those records where there's just something about it. I guess it was all of the things that I did that culminated together in the end to make this one record that. When you hear it, man you just feel so good. I want to do that every time.

https://twitter.com/easy_mo_bee

"The most influential DJ/MC combo in contemporary pop music period." – NPR

"Rakim's cool-and-deadly vocal style, and Eric B.'s DJing and production techniques, both helped bring hip hop of age."
– *Spin Magazine*

CHAPTER TWO
Make 'Em Clap To This – Eric B.

Jazz rap has only a few true founding fathers, and Eric B. is without question the Ben Franklin of the bunch. An inventor whose mind musically married samples together in ways hip hop fans had never heard before he first paired them. A skill honed from his earliest years growing up around the eclectic DJing culture in urban New York in the 1970s when the turn-tables still stood taller than he did in size. Eric took it all in with a wide-eyed fascination that he's clearly still as entertained by today:

> I started out carrying records for a group called King Charles in Queens, Burnin' Vernon was the DJ, and King Charles was the guy who owned the equipment. I was what they used to all back then an E.C., Equipment Carrier, so what they would do is play up at PS1-27 in East Elmhurst, Queens, so they used to rope off an area and only the DJ and essential people like King Charles could be behind the ropes, so I was lucky to be able to carry records and be behind the scenes and watch all that, and then the next day, I was the MAN at school. All the neighborhood kids would say, "We seen you behind the ropes at the show!" and I'd say, "Yes you did." Back then I was just carrying records, but it was my first experiences of getting that endorsement.

Growing up in the New York Public School system in an era when the New York Times reported the city, "Once a national leader in arts education. The country's first high school for the arts, the High School of Music and Art, was created there during the Depression, and many high schools had noted art departments that drew students from throughout the city." For Eric, the exposure to a literal symphony of instruments to play with as he began to display his musical talent was an invaluable resource, agreeing that, "I think the greatest thing for me, is we had band in school, and I had a band teacher by the name of Mr. Grillo, I'll never forget that, because he was determined to teach us the notes. We would play every instrument possible in the classroom, and that's the difference between growing up with my musical background and the kids now, they don't have music in school. We had racks and racks of guitars in our class, probably 100 and they ranged from electric to acoustic, and were ready and available inside the classroom." Surrounded by the same constant influence of sound around his house, Eric B. began familiarizing himself with the very record collection that he would later draw from as a DJ in crafting some of hip hop's first jazz rap instrumentals:

> You had your parents playing music around the house on Saturdays – and mine played some of the best music ever, from your James Brown and Nat King Cole to coming through the Disco era to Barry White and the South Soul Orchestra, Al Green, and there were so many different producers, singers, songwriters working on those records. But we played everything around my house, the Average White Band, if it was a hit, it was played at home, so we went from jazz to blues to pop, rock. I'll never forget having a Frank Sinatra record in the house and playing it.

Occasionally borrowing records from his parents' collection to suggest to Burnin' Vernon as he carried crates to and from shows for years throughout his later grade school, junior high and early high school years, Eric still gets chills sharing his memory of being thirteen years old the first time he got a chance to step into the spotlight behind the turntables and assume the official role of DJ in front of a live crowd. With his heart racing at a million beats per minute, he knew he had only seconds to react:

> The first time Vernon let me get behind the turntables, he was talking to someone, and told me, "Yo Eric, throw on the next record," and I looked at him with shock, *Throw on the next record?!* I remember we were at the park, and the park was PACKED–everybody from school, from the neighborhood was there. Well, he had the GOI mixer and Technic 1100As, and the first record I threw one of the hottest records out at the time, so when I threw it on, the park went crazy. We still laugh about it to this day.

Knowing he had something special, Vernon mentored Eric throughout his teenage years, hipping him to the DJing game and introducing him into the New York DJ scene where his skills behind the turntables soon began to build a buzz that would prove to be, "My start, Vernon gave the opportunity to be a mobile DJ, and from there, I went on and worked at a radio station called WBLS. I was actually on the first street team ever created for a radio station. We went throughout the tri-state area to New Jersey, Connecticut, and New York in these big WBLS vans. We would go from town to town and city to city and play at the parks, at the different festivals, or people would call in who were having block parties. We would be the DJ and bring hats, buttons, fans, T-shirts with the radio station logo on them." Scratching his way around the tri-state hip hop scene, Eric B. began to build a network of connections and fan base that would continue to grow into a following. It was one he loved entertaining with both the outside-the-box choices of records he picked to spin and the mystical ways he then spun them together:

> Magnavox 1180 turntables, those were my first set, and then went to 1200s, which I liked because they were smoother than the rest the belt, because when it came from belt to quartz-lock, the 1200s didn't drag. If you knew how to push them along, it wouldn't drag. As a DJ, it was great because I already had a record collection from my parents, and just added on, our record collections back then were really mental notes, because mentally if you knew what you wanted, you could go down the block to your friend's and get it if you didn't have it. If I didn't have it, my next door neighbor had it, so I would take notes in my mind, "I need this record, I need that record," then go down to the corner to my friends on the block and say, "Yo, I need these records, I'll bring them back." That's how it was back then, people would exchange records and stuff like that.

Promoters were taking equal note of Eric B. as a DJ with his own unique spin on the way he picked and mixed records on the turntables, including local live concert promoter Alvin Toney, who would become yet another emissary on the DJs behalf as he took another sizable step forward in his career, meeting his future co-producer and partner in rhyme, the one and only Rakim versus being paired by a manager or record label, Eric and Rakim organically gravitated to each other immediately upon being introduced, feeling like they were meant to be making music together:

> It was like meeting somebody where you're both on the same page but you don't know why, and so when I went and met him, it was like, "Yo, let's just do something," and was an effortless thought. It wasn't like it was a struggle to talk about music, and I got to talk to his brother Stevie Blass, whose a musical guy - he played piano on one of our songs, *"Put Your Hands Together,"* and talking to him about music. Rakim and Stevie had a musical family and background: his mother sang, his father played, his aunts played music, and to be able to talk about music was refreshing, to be able to communicate with someone with a great musical background like Rakim had.

Eventually, as word of Eric B. & Rakim's promise made its way around the old-head New York DJ gossip network, inevitably that buzz made its way into the ear of DJ Marley Marl. The already locally-legendary DJ/producer had first met Eric working at WBLS, and would wind up playing a major role in translating among arguably his earliest and most important production visions into reality in the studio setting. History was made on one historic afternoon in Marley's basement studio:

> When I was sitting talking to Rakim while we were making *Eric B. is President*, and I had James Brown's *Funky President,* and said, "Yo, I'm going to chop up Fonda Rae's *Over Like a Fat*

Rat and put it on top of it. Rakim spit his beer all over the wall and just started laughing, like it was the funniest shit he'd ever heard in his life. Right then his brother Stevie said, "Eric, don't listen to this stupid motherfucker right here. All he does is write rhymes, do not abandon the plan. Because those are some of the greatest musical compositions I've ever heard in my life. And for somebody to take those two worlds and bring them together, don't abandon the plan." So then I turned to Rakim, and said, "Alright, you're laughing now but when you become paid in full, I wanna see how much you're gonna laugh then!" That's how the album title came about.

Not many producer/DJs become appointed a leader of a new school of sound within hip hop on their first album out, but when *Eric B. is President* dropped, it commanded immediate respect of a royal kind both musically and lyrically, so much so that *Rolling Stone* issued the decree that, "*Eric B. is President* was one of the two or three biggest moments in hip hop, and the revolution it began continued with their debut album." Taking fans back into Marley's studio to recount the actual production of the iconic DJ anthem, Eric singles out Rakim's brother Stevie Blass as another key agent working on behalf of advancing his career, courtesy of his ability to provide the DJ free access to a literal library of vinyl, chuckling as he confirms:

I got the records from Rakim's mother and brother, Stevie Blass for *Eric B. is President!* He worked in a pirate printing place where they back-door pirated and printed records. And he worked in the warehouse. He had every breakbeat or record you could ever think of. He had clear copies, so I went to Stevie and he'd say, "Yo Eric, what you need? I've got this, I've got that." And I'd tell him and he'd bring it home for me the next day.

Once I brought those records in, Marley to me was great because he was an engineer and knew how to use the equipment. We all had the mental notes to what we wanted, but Marley could bring it to fruition and say, "Hey, this is what it is," and that's what happened. You can ask a lot of different people – from Big Daddy Kane to Biz Mark – we all had great ideas but Marley knew how to work all the equipment and was an engineer extraordinaire. So we could bring him the records, and say, "Marley, we want to chop this, we want to do that."

Eric B.'s circle of champions featured another New York hip hop legend who, at the time, was himself coming up on the national Rap map but already was locally an old-head who like Marley mentored many of the newest up and coming talent passing through the scene on their way up. For Eric, having Fresh as a sounding board was something today clearly he still considers as much of a privilege as he did back then. Crediting Doug E. Fresh as being a combination coach/cheerleader whose council he sought out constantly in his early days finding his way around the recording studio for the first time, fondly recalling that, "Doug E. Fresh was really somebody who pushed me musically, so every day I would go to Doug's house with an idea. When you have a guy like Doug to actually sit there and listen to you and push you to the next level, it made me want to deliver a hit record. That only motivated me more, because I couldn't wait to get back to Doug's house to see what he thought about them. He was a great supporter back then."

An instant street classic that landed the group a record deal in 1986 with local indie label Zakia Records. They quickly entered Power Play Studios in Manhattan to continue expanding on the blueprint they'd laid out with *"Eric B. is President."* It was here that the sonics of their sound fully formed thanks to the lucky card the rapper and DJ drew in their engineer, Disco production icon Patrick Adams. A pioneer in his own right who the Red Bull Academy recently singled out for, "His prowess as an arranger and experimental approach. He took boogie to strange new places, pre-figuring house music and providing inspiration to New York's hip hop generation." He would do just that for Eric B. & Rakim when they first showed up with the grand production plan that became *Paid in Full*. Adams recalled exclusively that the dynamic duo happened to be in the right place at the right time for the kind of experimentation they were doing inventing the jazz rap subgenre that their sound gave birth to:

> **Patrick Adams:** By the time Eric B. & Rakim showed up at Power Play, the studio had become a real sort of laboratory. My greatest strength in working with artists is I'm a facilitator, when Eric B. & Rakim walked in and asked, "Would you produce us?" And my answer was, "No, you guys are going to produce yourselves, but I will help you." There were moments where there was

a lot of give and take, and it's the person whose open to new ideas who succeeds, because there should always be a give and take, and with Eric B. & Rakim, it was a beautiful thing to watch because Eric would present his ideas, Rakim would present his ideas, and I sort of became the tie that binds their ideas and then bringing my experience to the situation as a facilitator to figure out a lot of times, "How do you do that which has never been done before?"

Making history on wax indeed, BET would years later affirm that their, "1986 debut, *Paid in Full*, changed the hip hop game forever, with many crafting lengthy arguments as to why the duo are among the most influential DJ-rapper duos of all time." As Eric and Rakim began working side-by-side with their new collaborator, Eric recognized right away that, "Patrick was a great producer and songwriter. He'd done *In the Bush* and iconic records like that. And I remember Nile Rodgers – one of the greatest songwriters of our time told me, 'Hey Eric, I always wanted to be like Patrick Adams, because Patrick to us is one of the greatest songwriters, engineers and producers of all time.' Nile Rodgers is still relevant doing daft punk. And starting out, he wanted to be like Patrick." Adams would arrive at just at the right time in hip hop to know precisely how to help the two artists put their heads – and a song – together as producers:

Patrick Adams: Eric and Rakim back and forth just had these great ideas, and if anything, I was like a seamstress trying to marry this sample with that drum beat. When I was growing up playing in self-contained bands, we played a lot of James Brown, we played a lot of Chicago, so when Eric and Rakim would come in with these samples, I was already very familiar with a lot of the samples and I think that's another thing that helped gelled things because they from an aesthetic point of view might have liked something and my understanding of how rhythm sections are put together and how the sample really needed to sit.

By '85, '86, the studio had grown from the 8-track to 24 tracks, the board was a Trident, and it was a semi-automated board. On the first album, we used mostly the SP-12, and the Emulator 1, which was a sampler. We also used a French sampler called the Publison, and I even at times found a way to use a piece of outboard gear that only had one or two seconds of sampling time. I had sort of perfected certain things by working with Salt-N-Pepa, and even when I did *Tramp* with Herbie, we didn't have samplers yet, so I used the tape loop, because we didn't have sampling time! By the time Eric B. & Rakim came in, we had grown to the Emulator 2, which had sufficient sampling time to do two bars of music, which could be repeated over and over again.

The concept of sampling in hip hop would be advanced by literal light years thanks to the alliance between Eric B.'s ear, Rakim's rhymes, and Adam's ability to tie it all together in the studio. It was a synergy that would lead *Paid in Full*, in the esteemed opinion of *Rolling Stone*, to become, "The first hip hop album to foreground sample drumbeats as the primary rhythm bed instead of using them as drop-ins, stabs and accents." Beyond just switching up this custom within their drum sound, Eric and Co. – in an effort to give record buyers as 3D a listening experience as possible from the jump – pushed hard to build extra bottom into each beat, explaining his ambition as one where "one thing we always did was, I had a vision and remember listening to a couple of records and were great records but they sounded so out of date and didn't have any like bottom to them, because they were recorded during a certain period. So all our records that we started doing, I started lowering the bass, and the bass was so low that you couldn't hear it but if you stood in front of a speaker, you could feel it." Breaking down how this feeling of sound was actually created in the studio, the group's indispensible engineer Patrick Adams recalled:

> Sometimes a live drummer might vary in his playing, so Rakim, Eric and I would sit for maybe an hour and take a drum sample from a break-beat where the first half might be very smooth time-wise, but then the drummer might speed up from the back and we would take the time find maybe a different section of the drum break to put in the back so that it was smooth and you didn't feel that speed up.

This rhythmic shift was an innovation made possible by the expertise and years of experience Eric and Rakim were able to tap into with Patrick Adams, who helped the group become the first in hip hop to begin "sonically tuning records." Eric points to their engineer as "a great teacher, he taught me how to put the bottom in a record, so again, you wouldn't hear the bass if the song was playing on the radio, but if you were in the club, you would feel it." Divulging first-hand that his secret weapon was normalizing good old engineering standards to hip hop, to Adams' ear for recording excellence, Eric B. & Rakim's brand of hip hop deserved no less than this kind of specialized sonic attention:

> **Patrick Adams:** Whenever one of them came in - and sometimes it was Eric and sometimes it was Rakim – with something they wanted to sample, we would sample it, but I had a very specific rule that rooted in my being horrified by a lot of the early rap records where producers were taking samples and throwing them together, but there was no effort to tune the samples. For a musician, especially one like me who loves melody and chord progressions, etc, to play a sample in one key, and then maybe have horns that are in a different key was so disruptive to my mind that I insisted whatever we sampled would be tuned and pitched so they were in the same key or a relative key so that it was more soothing and complimentary to the track.

A true artist behind the turntable whose every scratch was the equivalent of a stroke of paint flowing onto a canvas, in Eric's case, it was analogous to a stylistic collage that once mixed. Leaping off the needle like a b-boy getting wild with his crew on the club floor, after dancing its way across the Billboard Hot Dance Club Play, Hot Dance Music/Maxi-Single, Hot R&B/Hip Hop Songs, and even the UK Singles Charts all at the same time, they were no doubt dancing to the rhythm of Eric B.'s turntable scratching as much as the beat or bassline. Patrick Adams as he recorded the song, remembered looking at, "Eric's turntables at moments as a percussive instrument, and then there were moments when I looked at it as a vocal instrument. I thought it was very brilliant the way he cut, 'Y - Y - Y - Y - Ya got it!' That became a very big part of the record, even though we added the gang vocal in, initially it was just from the record, and I'm quite sure without thinking too much about it, we did the group vocals because it needed to fatten up that moment." Reflecting directly on how he cut his way to another innovation for the group and hip hop at large while playing around on the turn-tables, Eric made the musical discovery that led to the record's creation one day when:

> Here we go again, Rakim is late to the studio, and I had two records and I was in the studio messing around, I'll never forget, and I mixed the two records together and I had them playing on the left side and the right side, and just dropped it. So now everybody's at the studio, and my brother Anthony was really responsible for that song becoming a record because he came in and said, "Yo Eric, what is that?", and I said, "I'm just in here messing around man," and he said, "Naw E, I think it's brilliant, you gotta keep them together, I'm telling you" because I had them originally as two separate records I was doing, and he said, "Eric, you shouldn't waste it, that sounds great." He's the one that kept pushing me all day, "You can't break those records up." So I listened to him, went in and

put the kicks on it, the bass on it, and when I finished it I played it for him and he sat there and said, "Eric, you don't understand how big this record is," and I said, "Yeah, alright."

Eric B. Is On The Cut was the same thing, I was just in the studio messing around on the turntables, playing games, had nothing better to do, only that time I knew tape was running, so I was taking this record out and saying "Hey Pat, record this," and he assembled it.

One of Eric's most dazzling displays of ninja work on the turntables would happen out of a happy accident one day when he recalled, "Rakim was late for the studio. And the funny thing about *Chinese Arithmetic* is I was just sitting there bored, so I was going like I normally do in the morning. I had just finished breakfast with my engineer Patrick Adams, and we're waiting for Rakim. So I went in the live room, got behind the turntables and started scratching records, just fooling around. Now, what I didn't know was that Patrick Adams had pressed record. So I'm scratching, scratching, taking more records out, just messing around, and then went back out into the control room – I remember this like it was yesterday – and by now, it's almost lunchtime. So I went out to order us something to eat. Well, by the time I got back to the studio, Patrick had taken all the records I had just been scratching, put all the scratches together, and the song was already done! He said to me, 'Hey Eric, I came up with something,' and when he played it for me, I said, 'Patrick, you've lost your damn mind!' But he'd taken all my scratches together and made a compilation out of it." Weaving together an exotic tapestry of turntables conversing with a futuristic city of sounds that communicated musically in a way hip hop listeners had never quite heard before – a common feature of the Eric B. DJ listening experience – the adventurous engineer still gets a kick to date out of having pulled off putting such a sophisticated track together:

> **Patrick Adams:** As I remember it, they needed one more cut for the album, and I was in the studio by myself that night and I think it was the last thing I was mixing for the album and there was no rap on it, and so what I did was I went through all the multi-tracks on the 24-track tapes, and grabbed Eric's scratches from different songs and put them through a sampler, the Emulator 2, so *Chinese Arithmetic* is actually a sort of combination of scratches from 5 or 6 different songs. The whole thing was an experiment, we were just in unchartered territory, and I didn't know if anybody had done that at the time.

Included in *Vibe*'s 100 Essential Albums of the 20th Century and, "Heralded as a trailblazing effort and one of the top ten hip hop opuses of all time," in MTV's opinion, *Paid in Full* was as much a breakthrough for hip hop as it was for Eric B. & Rakim professionally. Delivering with their debut what rap pages would years later celebrate as, "Masterfully executed music," their hometown paper *The Village Voice* credited the record with helping to, "Inaugurate hip hop's ballyhooed Golden Era." Reflective of the eager acceptance not on Rap fans but as quickly as they heard it, crossover artists within pop's mainstream, even some who had been previously dismissive of hip hop for the simplicity of it's music and subject matter were now suddenly doing an about-face based on the accessibility the jazz rap genre Eric B. & Rakim invented. Offering an opening to entirely new demographics of potential hip hop fans, it was a transcendence that was driven home for the first time for the group's engineer Patrick Adams:

> After there was an interview in 1986 in *Outpost Magazine* with Paul McCartney, and they asked him what records he was listening to at the time, and he mentioned *Paid in Full* and that blew me away. It was at that moment that I really felt proud, really felt that I had accomplished something important. I'm most proud, #1, of producing music that was musical at a time of great dissonance, because as I said, all of the loops were relatively in key and relative pitch, so as a creative person, I'm very proud of having participated in something which has stood the test of time like that.

Rushing right off the road and back into the studio to keep their momentum rocketing forward at full throttle, Eric B. & Rakim within just twelve months would achieve a position of influence where *XXL Magazine* reported that, "Just two LPs in, Eric B. & Rakim were already considered the faces of Rap's golden age." Proud that the group gained such respect so quickly for their success in taking new musical chances other hip hop groups hadn't before they hit radio, Eric remembered keeping his ears alert and open wide like a radar ready to pull new pieces of musical magic from out of the air to incorporate into the next evolution of the group's sound:

It's all over the place. I can hear some drums here, or hear a bass line here, a snare hear, and come up with an idea. So it's not one formula, like, "Drums, bass line, hook, chorus," because I can find a catchy hook and then build around it. So it was a little bit of everything. There's not one way that I looked at a record.

The New York Times took the lead in revering the fact that, "From the opening, space-age *Follow the Leader* to the chilly funk of the closing *Beats for the Listeners*, Eric B. & Rakim define their own territory." Expanding boundaries as far as he had to fully explore whatever sound his inspiration was pushing him to chase, Eric felt free to explore first and foremost because "it was never a budgetary thing with us, because we had the same thing that was available to us whether we had millions of dollars or didn't have any money, so it wasn't a budgetary thing, it was a state of mind in what we wanted to hear to push the envelope, and *Follow the Leader* was one of those records where you listen and go 'What the hell is this?!' as you listen to it over and over and over again." Hypnotic in what *Rolling Stone* characterized as "a menacing bass throb and spooky special effects," in creating that atmosphere on tape in the console, the duo's Merlin engineer detailed a maze of samples that he's still impressed he, Eric and Rakim made as perfect sonic sense of given the song's sophisticated soundscape:

> **Patrick Adams:** Technologically, *Follow the Leader* to me was an amazing accomplishment because I believe there's eleven or thirteen samples or elements in that record. You've got

the drum tracks, the bass line, the Bob James strings, and that was another thing: a lot of people didn't know that Rakim was a musician. He was a sax player in high school, so those horn licks were something that we built.

Microphone Fiend was the kind of addictive-at-first-listen moment of glory for hip hop both lyrically and musically that inspired a generation of aspiring emcees and producer/DJs alike. Falling to sleep at night listening over and over as it's melodic guitar hook danced with the beat while Rakim's words captured the musical imagination overtop, the dreamy flow of the song's production was a byproduct of Eric's search as a producer to create a musical, "Feel, and for me, that was about something you felt good doing as you were making the record. With using *School Boy Crush* by Average White Band, it goes back again to being a DJ, and playing those kinds of records in the clubs and seeing the reaction of people, and you hear records that are timeless and drum sounds that are timeless that you can play that are forty, fifty years old that people dance to now. But the sounds are so attractive to the ear that you want to be a part of them, you want to make a great composition based around them, and that's what I did with *Microphone Fiend*."

Speaking to other signatures from *Microphone Fiend* that helped make the track as permanent a member of hip hop's greatest hits soundtrack as it remains today, engineer Patrick Adams proudly marvels to date as his contribution to creating' "The big splash on the snare drums, I as a producer believe that a record should start out to capture someone's attention, and once you established what the energy level of a record is – especially when you get to that outro point, sort of the climax point – you CANNOT allow the energy to drop from there out or else you're going to lose the record. Another thing was using a slight room delay, or using a twenty millisecond digital delay on the bass drum to make it sound like it's in the room, it's in the space."

Picking up in their praise for the ground-breaking album right where they'd left off with the title track, *Rolling Stone* seemed equally thrilled with the dependable way, "Eric B. constructs inventive backing tracks that incorporate funk guitar (*Microphone Fiend*), walls of noise (*Lyrics of Fury*), exotic percussion tracks, synthesizers and saxes," adding the special caution that, "His switch-blade scratching (*Musical Massacre*) will make your head spin." Taking the DJ as serious musically behind the turntables as he did any other professional studio musician he'd ever recorded with, the group's engineer admitted in the same time to special attention because the turntables were literally Eric B.'s wheels of his genius at work. Making a new sound for the first time, the engineer had what he still considers the unique privilege of recording it to tape for the first time:

> **Patrick Adams:** From moment to moment, Eric's turntables became a lot of different things, because whether it was the horns coming in at a certain point, or vocal things that were done. For a young man to come in the studio and me ask, "What do you do?" and he says, "I'm a DJ and I do scratches," I didn't say, "Oh God, I have to put up with this shit?" No, I had to look at Eric B. as a musician whose instrument was a turntable and looked at it as an opportunity to experience something different. And my job at that point was to figure out what is his artistic statement and how I could help him present that

statement to the world. So for me it was a learning process understanding what Eric did with his turntables, how he did what he did, and figure out a way to record him doing what he did.

We did D.I., plugged the turntables directly into the board with a little noise gate, which I used to limit the amount of any possible noise between the actual signal, because a slight hum would be a very annoying on any track. This was back in the days where anything below sixty cycles really was an annoyance, so just as a general practice, I used to do a very hard shelf at fifty cycles, which is probably what led me to want to use that sixty-cycle Keypex addition to the bass drum on the other side. But the noise gate was always just to try and cut down on the ambient noise.

Racing around the wheels of steel like an NBA superstar down the court toward the net with only seconds left on the clock in the final quarter of a championship game, Eric described the headspace for fans where when, "Creating on the turntables, say on a track like *Never Scared*, I'm in the studio and I just get into a zone, it's like when you ask Michael Jordan, 'How do you score fifty, sixty points?' You just get into a zone and get engulfed by the music where you're just in the middle of it, just working on it. It's something you really can't explain, because once you get into that zone and are really set and locked in, it can translate into a hit record." The New York Times would again jump in their stellar review to turn the applause up to ten for, "Eric B.'s mixes, spare and skeletal, all the better to notice the colors he drops into the beats. He's a minimalist virtuoso, and with Rakim he's defining one of the musical sounds of the 80's."

In 1990, the NUCLEAR assault that dropped when the opening stereo kicks of *Let the Rhythm Hit 'Em* struck hit harder sonically than hip hop had ever heard before, a literal explosion of energy rushing from the speakers that blew listeners away to another musical dimension! Pulsating with such power it sounded literally like the heart of the drum beating, *Spin Magazine* described the dangerous thrill that hit with the, "Wavy, nervous undercurrents of the title track, the intricate orchestrations." It was a bold experiment in layering Eric B. reveals was inspired by a desire to push the boundaries of sound for hip hop in the vein of, "Producers like Phil Spector and Quincy Jones. The way they went in the studio and layered records, and felt sounds and put this and that in, these were some of the greatest composers in the world. Being able to have the opportunity be in the studio and try to emulate those guys to me was great. So now it was just my twist on being a Quincy or Spector, because these guys really pushed music to what it is today."

Strapping in for what he knew was going to be a phonic ride into deep space when he first heard Eric lay out the sound he was chasing, engineer Patrick Adams pulled the curtain back on his own studio tricks pushing the console to its maximum to expand the beat's depth:

> **Patrick Adams:** I wanted the drums to be centered to the conversation, and one of the tricks that I learned early on was adding bottom to a bass drum by using maybe a 60-cycle tone,

so imagine this: you have a 6-cycle tone, then you're putting it through a noise gate, the noise gate is keeping the tone silent, and the only time you want to hear that 60-cycle tone is when the bass drum kicks, and using the Keypex, the bass drum would open that gate when it hit. What this does is, whatever bass drum sound you have, you've now superimposed the 60-cycle-tone to the bottom of that bass drum, and that was one of the tricks we used to make the bass drum bigger.

Eric B.: We used everything, samples, live sounds, with that record we did so many things and Patrick Adams again brought so much to the table. For that song in particular, we did like a 360 pan, where we had 360 sounds going on all around you, and we were the first to be able to do that. Patrick was phasing this sound in and that sound out, and I think as an engineer, he really did an amazing job of pushing the record to the next level sonically. One thing about Patrick, you could bring in a new keyboard, a new drum machine, and in fifteen, twenty minutes he'd dissected and figured it out, even if he'd never seen it before.

Hitting #2 on the Billboard Hot R&B/Hip Hop Songs Chart, a position Patrick Adams was personally most thrilled to see the song reach than any of the many other charts he'd seen his studio work sit atop over the years. As he watched his sound filter in such an influential way into a new genre and generation of music fans, Adams was thrilled to be able to bring the culmination of his knowledge to bear in making the single what is still considered one of rap's most powerful punches ever to hit the ears of fans, the engineer proudly mused that, "I engineered *Let the Rhythm Hit 'Em*, and at this point, I had fifteen, twenty years of experience as a mixing engineer. We had one gold, one platinum album. They had just made a million dollar deal with Universal and by that point, we had certainly worked out certain formulaic ways of doing things. Plus at the time, I'd been working with Teddy Riley too. Teddy was one of these guys who got me into using multiple snares and multiple bass drums. I had been studying records from the time I was seventeen. So here we were, twenty years later and I had forgotten in Motown Records how on *I Heard It Through the Grape Vine* there's two bass drums, or two snares on A LOT of Motown stuff. So it was around that period, by time we got to *Let the Rhythm Hit 'Em*, and me working other nights with Teddy or R. Kelly. That layering process was influencing me."

Once listeners had recovered from the amazed daze the title track blew them away into, excited critics like *The Source* gave the album its deserved five mics. The *L.A. Times* in exploring the rest of the futuristic album praised the DJ/producer for his consistency of innovation across the record's entire planet of sound, celebrating the way, "Eric B. takes simple snatches of beat and melody, shifts them ten degrees, and fills the spaces with grunts, saxophone wails and washes of sound. He keeps it on the brink of anarchy, just unpredictable enough to rivet your attention, regular enough to dance to. They scratch in beats, they repeat the old rap formula, they incorporate jazz and soul songs and surface noise...they do what everybody else does, but better. Call them hip hop classicists. This, their third LP, might be the first mature rap masterwork." Comfortable by this point with taking any creative chance that his muse dared him to try, Eric was aware of the cutting edge he was riding toward his next wave of innovation for hip hop itself. When it came crashing down, the producer is proud of the fact looking back that it did so with the power of a heavyweight champ:

> It's a comfortable zone, like Mike Tyson or Floyd Mayweather were comfortable inside the ring in their day, and when you get into the music, that's your comfort zone, and you shut everything and everybody else out, and for me, the studio was the comfort zone, music blasting, challenging myself and push myself to do something better than what I did yesterday, or find some more sounds that yesterday I didn't have, and how do I push myself to the next level?

Hitting so hard that the album's power reverberated all the way into the musical mainstream, with Entertainment Weekly seeming most blown away by the consistent fact that, "Eric B.'s beats are densely woven, usually from three or four kinds of musical thread – a drum pattern, maybe a bass riff, perhaps a tickling keyboard or big-band horns – all pulling in different directions." It's a result the DJ/producer blames on the freedom that he and Rakim felt to make, "*EVERYTHING* an influence on that record. We would come into the studio and Rakim would come up with an idea, 'Eric, I have an idea for a sound. How do we take this to the next level?' I'd come up with a beat, and Rakim would have one to go under it."

By the dawn of the 1990s, the jazz rap sub-genre that Eric B. & Rakim had invented was in full swing, with offspring like De La Soul, A Tribe Called Quest, and Digable Planets had taken their creative cues from the bold direction the two had set. On *Don't Sweat the Technique*, *The Village Voice* became an instant fan of another master class they concluded sounded like, "A jazzy minimalist funk trailing uncentered horn hooks--relaxing with pep." Seeking as always to not only raise the ceiling with their sound, but blow the roof off entirely as they lifted off for the next level riding a new wave of technology they brought to bear like rocket scientists in the studio:

> With that record, we were in technical mode. There was new equipment coming out, and we were pushing it to the limit. *Don't Sweat the Technique* was Eric B. & Rakim pushing the envelope with sounds and sonic. Every time you listen to that record in total, you'll hear something different. It was just something we did that felt right at the time. Music was changing, and we took pride in seeing the curve coming. So a lot of the records we did were years ahead of their time and people would look at us like, "What the hell was that?" Then, when they listened to it again, now they're like, "Hold up a second, this is a brilliant composition!" But again, we did it because it felt good, not because we were trying to prove a point to anybody.

Proving himself once again one of the sharpest ears for a catchy hook in the business he chased what iTunes a generation later would salute as "a vision of hard-edged New York City jazz rap," Eric B. proudly points to the album's title track as one such savvy example where he knew he had a hit on his hands, "As soon as I heard that opening bass hook! I could have played that all day long. Then the drop, *Don't Sweat the Technique.* When you hear that in the studio, we knew that was a dangerous record." *Rolling Stone Magazine* would pay Eric a similar praise for the "majestic album" where, "Rakim is sustained with thick, kill-crazy beats that display a moody, cinematic quality." Arguably no more vivid a musical definition of that than another of the legendary album's biggest hits, *What's On Your Mind,* whose instantly infectious hook first hit Eric's ear:

> Riding down the West Side Highway, I had just bought a Range Rover and I'm not a speed demon, I didn't have a bunch of speeding tickets or none of that, I drive with a seatbelt on and do the speed limit because I'm not going to give the police a free shot at me. But this day, I'm driving down the highway and *What's On Your Mind* is on the system in the truck, and I remember flying, looked up and I was doing one hundred fifteen miles per hour going down the West Side Highway! So I slowed down and remember making a left off the highway, going straight to the record store and then straight to the Hit Factory and we looped the record up, and then Rakim came in, heard that, and said, "Eric, I got an idea for some drums I want to put under it," and that's how we made that record. That record to me is one of the greatest I've ever made, I love and could listen to that record all day. If you asked me what was my favorite record, that would be it.

Blowing critics like *JET* away with, "High energy tracks." The album was packed full, like a bomb of sound waiting to go off as soon as the listener pressed play, and Rakim's favorite musical munition his DJ revealed was, *The Punisher*! "Rakim lyrically pushed himself on that record, and that's his favorite all-time movie. So that song was his brainchild, and he wanted to pay homage to the Punisher." Meanwhile, from Eric's side of glass sitting behind the console, his most potent pick from the records' rougher soundscapes was *Pass the Hand Grenade*, which remains among his favorite bangers to date. Because of the anthem he's been told by so many fans throughout the years that the song became for what was happening, "Out in the streets, which were changing from the crack era and the war on crack. We were just really the eyes and ears to things that were happening in the streets, and that's where songs like *Pass the Hand Grenade* came from." *Don't Sweat the Technique* would become a soundtrack for soldiers fighting in the Desert Storm war, helping soldiers stay sane through the horrors of war. As Eric shares one such survival story that still hits his heart hard every time he recounts it:

> I remember a sister telling me she was in the Desert Storm war in a trench and she had her headphones on listening to Eric B. & Rakim while rockets and bullets were flying over her head. She told me, "The only thing that didn't get me to stand up and try to run away was listening to your music, because it kept me calm and saved my life!" I didn't know what to say, except, "Wow!" And that right there made me feel good about what I've done all these years. That made it worth all the sacrifices Rakim and I

went through to make those records. Being away from our families, listening to those kinds of conversations makes it all worth it.

The Source's 5 mic review would, "Salute Rakim Allah and Eric B. for this classic album," upon release, and years later, hip hop historians still study and marvel at as a masterpiece whose artist himself agrees succeeded in, "Taking you on a visual journey. With Don't Sweat the Technique, we wanted to take you on a trip. And that's what we did musically and lyrically, was give you riding music to take you on that trip."

Always as exciting as when a new Eric B. & Rakim album dropped was the live tour that followed, and when word went viral that the duo would be reuniting for the first tour in decades in 2017, the frenzy within the buzz of excitement among fans and critics alike, who made front page headlines like Ebony Magazine's that, "It's been a long time and Eric B. & Rakim did leave us without fresh rhymes and dope beats to step to for twenty-four years to be exact. However, the essence of their music hasn't left the culture and Rakim is still on the scene rocking shows. But come 2017, the dynamic duo will connect with an abundance of overjoyed hip hop fans when they reunite for a tour...Their legacy continues!" Confirming he's looking forward to returning to the stage with Rakim, Eric highlights what he hopes to bring back in living color for fans is what the legendary DJ still regards as the greatest aspect of playing live was the stage show itself:

When Eric B. & Rakim goes out, we take these elaborate stages and have lasers and different changes on the stage, and to be able to give a crowd a show and be able to take somebody's dollar value and say, "We're going to match it with the performance."

And for you to be able to say, "Man, I had a great time, I've never seen anything like this before," I think we took pride in being ground-breaking and doing things other people hadn't done. I'm looking forward to the 2017 Eric B. & Rakim 30th Anniversary to be able to get back out on that stage and do amazing set changes with all 21st century technology that really wows the crowd. I don't want to go to a show just to see somebody walk back and forth across the stage. And that's what is about: having the consumer leave saying, "Man that was a great show!"

For those millennial fans coming out to see the group – many for the first time – when asked what advice he'd dispense to those among them who he might inspire to hop behind the turntables for the first time, especially in a day and age of the industry declaration that "the DJ is the new rock star," Eric points them straight past the limelight of the stage and back to the old-school, pre-digital basics of the craft, beginning by hammering home the importance of:

> PRACTICE! Practice is important in anything and everything you do. I don't care how much you know or what you've done over the past thirty years. There's always something new – a new technique, a new sound. And you have to stay on the cutting edge of what's out there or you'll make yourself look like a dinosaur.

> Other advice I'd give, first is, if you ask everybody else in this book, I bet they'll feel the same way: It's great for me to wake up and say, "Oh, I'm going to make a hit record," but it don't work like that all the time. You do records

that you feel in your heart are great, and hope that people embrace them the same way. The second thing is, research everything, and with the internet, research everything: every producer, what records they made, what it came from. The best thing about research is by studying the history, you know what came before you. It's what made Mike Tyson great, studying the fighters that came before him. As a producer, you have to understand your craft, and you don't know anything till you know your history and where you came from. You have to be able to be well versed in your history. To be a well-rounded producer, you have to know where all these records came from. I tell people all the time, "You've got to do your homework about this business." And with the internet for the millennial generation, is where you can find out about each producer and where their records originated, so you don't make yourself look like a fool.

With Spotify streams alone on 10 of the group's most classic tracks, including *Don't Sweat the Technique* (7,244,255), *Paid in Full* (5,579,699), *I Ain't No Joke* (3,386,897), *I Know You Got Soul* (5,163,894), *Juice (Know the Ledge)* (2,137,856), *Microphone Fiend* (1,739,228), *Eric B. is President* (1,432,596), *Paid in Full (7 Min Mix)* (1,351,753), *Follow the Leader* (1,709,115) adding up to over 30 MILLION streams and counting on that listening platform alone. Eric B. & Rakim's sound has stayed as relevant as ever as an influence in hip hop simply because what they pulled off thirty years ago is still ahead of its time today. Whether it's a new fan catching up getting to know their catalog or an old-head whose never stopped nodding his head to records that will likely be as studied and celebrated in 100 years as they are today. For the DJ/producer of it all, he takes as the greatest compliment of all:

> When somebody comes up to acknowledge what you've done, that is great for me. Because I like them all, it doesn't make a difference to me. Just don't leave me out of the equation. I feel great about listening to any record we do, because the greatest reward of it all is to be able to inspire people to be great. Some of these guys who are great producers who come up and say, "Hey Eric, you inspired me..."
> *https://twitter.com/ericb*

CHAPTER THREE
Not Afraid – Boi-1da

Triumph is precisely what Eminem needed in 2009 when he returned to the studio after a near-crippling – personally and professionally – prescription medication addiction that had taken hold following the death of his best friend Proof. Marshall Mathers' therapy sessions not surprisingly would take place in the vocal booth, and while Eminem's victory march would begin when he stepped up to the mic, it wouldn't be complete until he topped the charts with his first #1 hit in seven years, *Not Afraid*. Debuting atop the Billboard Hot 100 Singles Chart in the summer of 2010, the comeback smash earned him a diamond award for moving ten million unit's as one of the millennium's biggest-selling singles ever, even bringing Mathers a Grammy Award for Best Rap Solo Performance. Behind the beat was a Jamaican-born/Toronto-raised Matthew Jehu Samuels, a 30-year-old self-taught prodigy who became one of the digital generation's first true in-the-box superstar record producers, proudly revealing:

> I made the *Not Afraid* beat using FL Studio, and the funny thing is I produced that beat with these two young producers who went to my high school that I was mentoring, and they kind of brought an idea to me, and it was a dance beat originally, as funny as it is. The thing about me when I do beats, if you listen to the process of me making a beat, the beat will change about like nine times before I finish it, into completely different stuff. So it started out as a dance beat, and I zoned out and it became that, my boy played the chords on it, and then I slapped some drums on it, and those were 808s, but the way I used the 808s was the way someone would use East Coast drums. I was feeling like at the time, if the drums were not 808s, they just weren't poppin', because the 808 just sounded so good. So I was like, "I'm going to make this into an 808 bounce, but not southern at all." Then I used a lot of virtual instruments including a Midi keyboard called Hypersonic. When I think

music, it's all about feeling, and when I heard those chords, I thought, "This gives me a nice, triumphant feeling," so I tried to keep it as simple as possible and give it some knock, put the bass on it, arranged it, and took out the dance elements because it didn't work with.

The crazy story on how that came about is, I had gotten new management and my management was very tight with Eminem, had worked at Interscope back in the day and was good friends with Marshall, and one of the first things he said to me was, "Yo, Em's working on a new project and he really liked that *Forever* beat, and he wants to get a batch of your beats." So I said "Cool," and packed up a batch of beats, maybe like 15 beats, and sent it to my manager, and he sent them right over to Marshall. So then not long after that I was at dinner with him, and he said, "Yo man, I just got a text from Paul Rosenberg and he said Eminem slaughtered two of your beats!" I was just like in shock, like "No way," and then come to find out that I had the first single, I can't explain how it felt, I was just thanking God because these were like my dreams coming true, my dreams manifesting into reality.

In an era when many beat-makers pass along a cache of material that never allows them the expectation of interfacing directly with the artist recording overtop, let alone someone of Eminem's stature compared to the newbee Boi-1da. In a brilliant strategy to keep his sound fresh with the millennials, the legendary rapper had smartly aligned himself with a new generation of up and coming producers to keep his finger on the pulse of the street, a move that allowed their collaboration and the surreal moment when, "He first finished the song and called me and said, 'I made an amazing song, it's a contender for the first single,' and just thanked me for sending him that record because he really loved it, and that it meant something to him and whatnot. I love that he's so unpredictable, and the fact that he's the greatest lyricist of all time. I don't care what anybody says, Eminem is the greatest ever, so you can always expect the wittiest lines, and I love that about him. He has fun, and his beat selection is always good, he always has some crazy beats." Among the chain reaction of good fortune that would come the producer's way from the song's international success, one of the highest honors for the then 24-year-old Samuels was the opportunity to share a production credit *with* Eminem. After Mathers added his own musical flavoring overtop Boi-1da's mix in the studio as he worked on the song, the producer shared his memory of being blown away:

> When he arranged the way the music, I think it's great, and his mixes are amazing as well too, and the things that he adds, for instance, a lot of people don't know that he added some of the piano parts to *Forever*, that was all Em. So you think that Eminem's going to get on your song and just rap, but he always adds a little something, a little more than you think he's going to do.

A product of the laptop era where the genesis of aspiring producers like a young Matthew's discovery of their own creative potential began online versus in the music room at school, a cyber-child who stays loyal to his roots, "To this day, I still use Fruit Loops," Boi-1da remembered he first got his taste for after "somebody told me about FL Studio in eigth grade. It took me like a year to look for it and actually get it, and in ninth grade, I actually got it on my computer and that's when I started learning about how to make music and do hot beats. The first one I ever had was Fruity Loops 3, and I didn't know anything about it really, but I was so in love with the process, and the fact that I could actually make my own music was like a drug to me. I would not stop doing it." Instantly addicted to the beat, he quickly began marching to its hypnotic rhythm full-time, becoming so central to his free-time:

> When I would get in trouble at school and get suspended or something, I used to use that program so much that if I was grounded, my parents would say, "No computer," I'd be allowed to watch TV or go outside, but I would be pissed because I wasn't allowed to make music. I was allowed to do anything else, play video games, go outside and hang out with my friends, but I couldn't make beats, that was my punishment, that's how much I loved it!

> In high school, all my friends wanted to go out and party and hang out with girls, and I was just in my basement using Fruity Loops, I did not care about anything else. I just wanted to be a great producer. I was inspired by Dr. Dre and when I was in high school, I came up on the whole 50 Cent/Dipset era, early Kanye West,

and music was just so fascinating to me that I really didn't care about anything else, other than the process of making music. I'm kind of a late bloomer with things in my life because of that: I feel like I just started going out and hanging out with friends and having a good time because I was so engulfed in music. I loved it so much.

Keeping his Jamaican roots alive and reverberating authentically within his sound, *Esquire Magazine* recently declared the 2016 #1 hit *Work* Boi-1da co-produced, "An icy, futuristic re-imagining of a dancehall beat that...is just the beginning of a Dancehall revolution." Certain to continue being one of its pioneers, the derivative celebration of his homeland is a full-circle journey from the early point in his life where, "I was born in Jamaica in a section called Shrilani, and then we moved to Kingston when I was three, and then ended up moving to Canada shortly after that, because Jamaica was not the nicest place to live at the time and my parents just wanted to get out. So we ended up in the Silver Springs area of Toronto, Ontario." Reinforcing just how rich his record collection growing up was with the sounds of his homeland, Samuels found his experience unique in how this music affected him as a listener:

Because the crazy thing is my dad is a huge music-head when it comes to listening to music, but nobody in my family was *ever* musical, so I'm the first person in my family to ever try to actually do music. Everybody else was just listening, but my dad was a big influence on my music, my dad and my mom because they just listened to music all day, it was always around the house. My parents listened to a lot of dance hall, especially my dad. That was all he played was dance hall, dance hall, dance hall. My Mom was more the one who would be listening to C+C Music Factory, Tony Braxton, R&B stuff. But my dad would always be pumping Beenie Man around the house. So just a lot of dance hall growing up.

I actually didn't start listening to hip hop until the late 90's, and I always the person who was intrigued by the beat. If the beat wasn't good, I couldn't really listen to the song, where for some other listeners, it's all about the words. So I would always pay attention in detail to everything that was going on in the beat, like the little tiny things that people wouldn't notice I would always pick up, versus how it was arranged, it was all about the beat to me.

With the rhythm already banging around his head, his talent began to beat down the door in physical expression, "When I was younger. My mom told me I would literally bang on the wall making beats. We didn't come up with a lot, my parents didn't come from any sort of money, so growing up, we had to suffice with small things to keep our entertainment. My parents would work very hard, but it wasn't enough, because we'd just come from Jamaica, so I would be beating on walls and hitting pencils on pots, and I begged my mom and she finally bought me my first Casio keyboard at age eight." Feeling his way around the keyboard, Matthew soon found himself happily stuck, "In the percussion section! I would use the pianos and other sounds, but I loved playing the drums." Gaining his first early exposure to producing after word soon got around the playground that the prodigious Boi-1da could actually make the beats he and his friends were hearing blasting out of the boom boxes around their urban neighborhood, he soon set up his very first recording studio in his own basement, all before he'd even begun Junior high:

> I would have my friends come over and rap while I played percussion on the keyboard, and we'd record it on the tape deck. It was really interesting, because we used to take an empty tape and I had a radio where you could put it on auxiliary, press record, and you could record your own voice. So that's the first set of recordings I ever did when I was ten. Me and my friends would record songs like that, but it was all live, there were no tracks or anything, we just did it all live. It was fun man. When I was in high school, I started hanging out with friends who had the same interests as me, and for some strange reason, I wanted to be a rapper at the same time as well.

By the time Matthew had graduated into his teenage years, his reputation as a producer had become socialized around his high school, making him something akin to a star basketball player everyone knew was going to NBA years before they even graduated. As the go-to guy to see about tracks for any teenage rapper with the ambition to take their first studio dive, Boi-1da could keep the beat going on the street just as live with his own two hands, recalling that "back in high school, I beat-boxed, and anytime friends of mine were having a freestyle battle, they would call me to come beat-box, I was the beats guy at school and would always be walking around the halls playing people my beats." His proverbial foot-in-the-door would come knocking one day:

> When my friend came by and told me about this competition, Battle of the Beatmakers, which was actually a country-wide competition where anyone could enter. I'd actually heard it about it from a friend in high school whose cousin had told him about it. A lot of my friends had told me my beats were good, but your friends can tell you stuff all the time, but they can just be, "Yes men." So I went, and was actually the youngest person in the competition, and let me tell you, I was so scared, because they put all the competing producers in a room backstage together before we each would come out in front of the crowd and everything.
>
> I was seventeen at the time where there were guys that were like twenty-five, twenty-six, so I was literally like the baby in the room. And I remember everyone was talking about the equipment they use, like, "Yo, I use this, this combobulator, and compression," and I was hearing all this stuff that I had no idea about. So when they asked me what I used and I said Fruity Loops, everybody kind of gave me that look, "Oh, this guy must suck." So when I ended up going out on stage, I had a crazy crowd

reaction to my first beat, and I'm not trying to sound cocky or anything, but I just like slaughtered everybody, and won that competition three or four times.

A networking nerve-center where Boi-1da made the kind of introductions and connections on a city-wide and even regional basis with a whole new scene that ensured his sound would be heard beyond the halls of his high school in the months to come, and sure enough, "After I won the competition the first time, word started getting out and a lot of people started reaching out. I started meeting up with a lot of people, and met someone who wanted to manage me, which was perfect at that time. He actually introducing me to a guy who I started producing with named D-10." A fated encounter that would prove the catalyst for Samuels to first get in the ear of a child actor who would soon break out overtop Matthew's beats. Becoming the biggest hip hop sensation to EVER come out of Canada to take over the world, the producer recounts of the happy accident:

> It turned out that D-10 and Drake were very good friends, worked together at a restaurant and happened to be in a group together where D-10 did the music and would play the keys while Drake rapped. Even before I'd met Drake personally, D would tell me about him all the time, and be like, "Yo man, you gotta hear my boy. You probably know who he is, he's on that TV show Degrassi High, but he's really sick at rapping, you should take in his stuff." And I was very skeptical about it, because I'd seen him on Degrassi High and thought, "That guy doesn't

really look like a rapper," and at the time, hard
core rap was popular: 50 Cent, Dipset, etc. So I
was kind of skeptical. But D ended up
introducing me to Drake, who sent me a song
through email, and I was impressed and as soon
as I heard the song, I understood his vision and
everything.

His primary job as a producer in giving Drake what he
needed in musical compliment, Boi-1da would confirm at their
very first recording session that he was right where he was
supposed to be sitting after the emcee proved he was the genuine
article on, "The very first record me and Drake ever recorded
together, it was called *Do What You Do* and leading up to that,
there had been a few times when I was supposed to get in the
studio with him. But he didn't end up showing because his TV
shoots had gone over time. So one night he actually came
through the studio while I was making this beat. We met, talked
for a bit, I played him that beat, and he went outside the room,
came back in about thirty minutes later and said, "Yo, I got a
crazy verse to this. Can I spit you my verse?" So he spit the
whole verse, and I couldn't believe it. I'd worked with so many
people locally at that time, but was so impressed by what he was
doing on the beat. It was like, I'd never had this sort of privilege
ever to have my beat blessed like this. So that was kind of the
first step to me working with him." A moment of musical
enlightenment that would itself become the birth of a new sound
for hip hop altogether, it was one that would be raised from the
underground up on the infamous EP *So Far Gone*, which Boi-1da
proudly points to as:

One of the most downloaded, if not the most downloaded mixtapes of all time. When we first put that mixtape out and seen the response it was getting and when Drake when on his *So Far Gone* tour. I'd never been on any kind of tour before, and I remember seeing him doing a soundcheck somewhere at twleve in the afternoon. There were people already lined up, and his show wasn't until like ten that night. Then, when I came back later that night closer to the show's start time, that line was wrapped around the building like eight times. I remember thinking *I can't believe this is happening!* We dreamed of this, me, Drake, D-10. There were some days before he blew up where we sat around sad, like, "Yo man, I wonder if this music shit is ever gonna work?" So that was literally our dream manifesting right in front of our faces.

Setting new precedents for the kind of mainstream success a mixtape could reach in the Digital age of record sales. The dynamic duo would actually break the mold entirely when the fans pushed *Best I Ever Had* onto the Billboard Hot 100 Singles Chart before Drake even had a record deal. Keeping the smash there for twenty-four weeks, it climbed all the way to #2, selling over two million copies and putting Boi-1da on the radio for the first time. A song that happened as serendipitously as any other aspect of he and Drake's success has, the producer remembered first pulling a rabbit out of a hat:

When I was just looking through samples, found the sample for that beat, and thought the beat

was relatively unfinished when I spoke to Drake
while he was touring with Lil Wayne, and he
said, "Yo, I'm near the end of my mix-tape, I
really need you." I ended up sending him that
beat and the beat for *Uptown*. He ended up
recording *Best I Ever Had* in a few hours on the
road and sent it back to me. And I was just like,
"Oh My God, this is amazing! This is a smash."
We've done a lot of music in the studio together.
But I've also sent him a lot of music that he's just
liked and just done his thing on, where I didn't
have any input on the vocals. So for those songs,
I just sent him the beat and he'd call or email
back saying, "This is crazy! I have a crazy idea to
this." And laid his vocals down at his own
studio.

Rolling Stone praised *So Far Gone* as, "The dark and
sometimes moody narrative of Drake's journey into adulthood
that's been powered by the upbeat *Best I Ever Had*, where he not
only raps on the track but sings on the song's chorus." A skill
that came as, "The Canadian producer was...helping Drake shape
his sound." The famed music mag would add, Boi-1da was
among the first producers to have hits with Drake singing, a
voice he helped the star find:

> After first discovering he was a hybrid artist: he
> sings, raps, he's amazing man. He just does
> everything. I like everything about it. He's just
> so melodic. But at the same time, it's not really
> singing. But it's still lyrical. Everything is always
> lyrical with him. And he has this voice and

things that he says just paint such a picture. He has the ability as an emcee to paint pictures. He can rock his ass off, he can spit, he has bars, and he can come with fun music.

Drake's voice would soar into the Top 10 of the Billboard Hot 100 Singles Chart for the second time with 1da the next year in 2009 when Boi's stomping beat to *Forever* took the charts by storm, landing at #1 on the US Hot Rap Singles Chart and #2 on the Hot R&B/Hip Hop Songs Chart. Not only taking Drake to new commercial heights, but re-launching Eminem as a star for a new generation of fans at the dawn of the millennium's second decade. The track would prove too hot for both Kanye West and Lil Wayne to ignore, hopping aboard the kind of thrill ride for listeners that only came around once. Its phenomenon was made that much more exciting with MTV's observation that, "*Forever* is especially impressive because it came about without any prior warning. No Twitter updates from the studio session – just a little heads-up from Mack Maine and boom, the song appeared." Delivering the kind of Jordan, Kobe, Dr. J and Lebron-level lyrical performances. The friendly competition on the track led MTV to add their opinion that, "Eminem came back with a vengeance, using a machine-gun flow to have the hottest appearance on...perhaps the biggest all-star hip hop collaboration."

Little did the producer know that was just the beginning the helping hand he would give Em in reclaiming his throne, long before the track made its way into the stratosphere, like so many other hits Samuels first created back before he took off for the stars:

I started that one in my basement one day by myself. I usually start my beats with the drums first, because I like to get a little groove going. I'm a rhythm guy and I just love having the rhythm first before anything else on it, but that song actually started from the melody. I was just goofing around with my keyboard, and playing the main melody of the song. It kind of just inspired me to put some drums to it. I started off with that part in the chorus where it has a southern bounce to it, with the quick hi-hats and what-not. I started with that, and at first the whole beat was going to be like that. But then I just felt like, "Naw, something needs to be different on the verses," so I ended up looping one part of the horns that created that repetitive pattern you hear from the top of the song.

Then I was like, "Let me try something brand new on this." I wound up making that drum pattern that drops when the verses kick in. Both the kick and snare on that part have a lot of layering. So the kick drum on that beat is literally like about four kicks together with a little, tiny bit of reverb effect on it. It gave me this kick that sounds like you're kicking a bathtub or something. Those kick drums are really Timbaland-inspired to me. And with the snare, I went through like one-hundred snares in a minute, just clicking the button really fast and listening to everything until I heard these two snares. I thought it would be perfect because it was really boom-bappish. The snare in the chorus is just a regular like 808 snare. I wanted to bring a southern element to the beat because the south was pretty hot at the time. And also bring it back to the boom-bap because I never stopped loving boom-bap. So I figured out to just fuse the two sounds into one, and it satisfied everyone.

That was one of those beats where you just know it's a hit. You just know sometimes, and with that one, I said, "Yeah, someone's going to do something real serious on this beat." My first instinct is always to send my beats to Drake first. He never fails to me, so he got that beat first. I sent it to him and then when I heard Lil Wayne and Kanye West was going to be on it, it was a super-trip. Especially when I heard Eminem was going to be on it too! The first album I ever bought was *The Slim Shady LP*, and Eminem is one of my favorite rappers. When they told me he was going to be on the song, I almost thought I was gonna cry, and thought, "This is not even real right now..." I didn't really know how to feel because I was still on the come-up and living in my Mom's basement, so I was really trippin.'

Heading straight into the studio to record a proper debut to follow-up the smash success of hip hop's best-selling breakout mix tape, *Thank Me Later*, would reflect the rapid pace at which Drake had not only become a star, but the pressures that fell upon his core team of producers to keep feeding him the same kind of musical mojo that had gotten him this far this fast.

Opting to stay loyal to the same ears that had gotten him here, Drake enlisted Boi-1da to produce hits off the album including the Grammy-nominated *Over*. The #1 Hot Rap Singles Chart smash won Boi-1da the ASCAP Pop Music Award for Songwriter of the Year and inspired Billboard to declare that the team had succeeded in proving, "He's worth the hype." He was responsible on the same album for the Top 20 Hot Singles Chart hit *Miss Me*, which the producer remembered working on during a sleepless studio marathon, he was already all too familiar with. Revealing that as a casualty and consequence of his creativity:

> My sleeping is terrible. Sometimes I just can't sleep because I'm so excited about everything. So sleeping has become difficult because I always hear music in my head too. The song *Miss Me* by Drake and Lil Wayne, I actually dreamt about that beat. I had a sample and the way I chopped that sample up was in a dream of mine. I woke up, went and did it the same way. Then went to the studio and played it for Drake and he loved it, wrote the verse, and I sent the files to Drake's engineer 40. He's responsible for a lot of the reason why Drake sounds so amazing vocally on everything. He ended up adding a chorus section to the beat and it worked out perfect. This stuff is a gift from God man. Because I can't fathom how I literally dreamt that, ended up waking up, and making it. And it was a song that was very popular and people loved it.
>
> When I made the music for *Over*, I produced that with a guy named Nick Brongers. He makes

real actual samples, and his thing that he does is make orchestrated stuff. He doesn't really make beats, but he makes a lot of orchestrated things. I worked with him for quite a while. The day he sent me that sample, I remember I was in the office at a meeting, listened to it on my headphones, and I just left the meeting and went to the studio immediately to go make the beat. Sometimes when I hear things, I need to just go. It's like when you need to use the washroom or something like that. Because I heard that and I was like, "I need to get out of here and go make this beat right now." I sent it to Drake, and the first time I sent it to him he didn't like it. I think because he was at the airport and listened to it on his laptop. But then he went into a studio when he landed, played it on the big speakers, and was like, "Oh my God!" He called me right up and shut that beat down, and told me, "Don't send it to anybody."

A request he laughs about now having heard over and over so many times over the last few years has become habitual. Both out of a mix of loyalty and logic as the emcee's voice continues to compliment his sound to successfully, Boi-1da confirms that, "Anything that I think is good, I send to Drake first because that's my brother. We literally came up from nothing together and started from the bottom, so he's always going to get that love. Me and him came up together, so I never want to break that bond. So anything I make, he's always got first dibs on. I trust Drake completely, because he's never failed me ever, he knows what he wants to do and it's never wack. He's just good what he does." Following the success of *Thank Me Later*, which took Boi-1da to #1 on the Billboard Top 200 Album Chart, moving 447,000 its first week, the two million copies the album sold allowed Matthew the financial freedom to move out of his parent's house and open his own studio. Using the opportunity to begin mentoring young producers as well as he stepped fully into the role of hit record producer, *Take Care* would keep the team in the *Headlines* after the hit reached #1 on the U.S. Hot R&B/Hip Hop Songs, US Hot Rap Songs, and U.S. Rhythmic charts, moving an astonishing four million single unit's along the way. Recounting a similar frenzy to the song's creation, the producer points to it as one of those songs that fell into the classic "wrote itself" category:

> That one was crazy, I tell a lot of people, because I made that beat in like ten minutes. I had a lot of stuff going on at the time so I was stressed, I had a brand new daughter and was sending a lot of music to Drake, and he wasn't taking anything. I was just in one of those times when I had downtime with producing and was just frustrated, and ended up just slapping together that beat and sending it to him, thinking, "Let's just see if he likes it," and he ended up flipping out over it. I was like, "No way," because that was the quickest beat I'd ever made in my life. So after that, I started trying to time myself and see if I could make beats in like less than ten minutes and see if people would like it. In terms of other artists doing freestyles over the instrumental – I think I like Meeks' the best.

Catching Drake in the eye of the whirlwind his career was moving at that point. He and Boi-1da broke another rule and record for hip hop. Proving its ever-commercial presence in the market no longer had to rely on traditional release date with advanced promotion. Dropping the surprise mixtape-album *If You're Reading This It's Too Late* on February 13, 2015, the record sold an astonishing 495,000 copies in its limited three-day reporting window for first week Soundscan. Crowned #1 as it sat atop the Billboard Top 200 Album Chart the following week, Drake and Co. broke their own Spotify first-week streaming record, racking up just over 17 million streams versus 2013's *Nothing Was the Same*'s 15 million total. Keeping fans as freshly on their toes as Drake kept his producers in the studio, Matthews remembered keeping the usual round-the-clock schedule as the team raced to finish up work on this bold sneak-attack model of record releasing they were helping to pioneer:

> It was definitely the plan to drop it like that by surprise. At this point, everything should be because you catch people off guard, especially with that caliber of artist. I think every major artist should be doing it like that, because they're just so big. You can't have fans anticipating it because people will try to leak your stuff and whatnot. It worked for Beyoncé as well, and artists like her and Drake. They can drop an album and the whole world is going to end up knowing about it. Twitter's going to spread it through social media like wildfire, so it's a better idea to catch them off guard.

Receiving the usual rave reviews all around that Drake's constant output of content was used to being showered with, Boi-1da's two-million-selling single *Energy* was one of the highlights for listeners, hailed as an, "Anthemic stomper," by the *L.A. Times,* which earned Samuels' another Grammy Award nomination for Best Rap Song. An example of the multi-platinum producer's savvy entrepreneurial side was working with up-and-coming producers, acting as a mentor on this specific hit when, "I was working on some beats with my boy O.B. O'Brien. With the vibe we were on, we were on some old-school Three 6 Mafia, really simple beats that just get the point across, and I just found a cool little, simplistic melody on the piano – which was actually a virtual instrument called Addictive Keys. We were listening to some old Three 6 classics and just tried to make my drums sound like some old Juicy J/Project Pat drum patterns, and it ended up being that. We were kind of rocking it in the studio and the speakers were really loud. And you know, that beat's very raw. There's not many effects or anything really on that beat. It was just straight raw, and it turned out being great. When Drake heard it, he was like, 'Yeah, I need that.' The day he recorded it, Drake had been having kind of a crazy week. He kind of just put his crazy week on tape, and all the energy that he had of frustrations in that song. He just let it go. I was very proud of that song, because he painted such a bigger picture with it that the song was amazing when he was finished with it."

Imagine if you got to the point in your career where you produced a beat that was so good it had two of hip hop's top entertainers literally fighting over it? *0 to 100*, Drake's 2015 Grammy nominated hit hypnotized the summer clubs and radio rotation playlists. It elicited precisely that kind of storm when old-head legend Sean "Puffy" Combs and millennial superstar

Drake got into it over who had proper claim on the instantly-catchy instrumental track Boi-1da had produced. In a drama that reinforced the beatmaker's consistent demand among the top emcees in the game, Billboard reported Combs' accusation directly when they quoted him on stage confirming the accusation: "Hey yo, I want to play this next beat, and I want somebody to get this shit on tape. I'm gonna play this next beat. This n#$$a stole this shit from me. But at the end of the day, the beat is still hard." The kind of competitive demand that means job security for a record producer. Even at Samuels' level, he remembered being taken back-in-the-day when the inspiration to make the song first hit his creative radar:

> I was going through this phase where I was listening to a lot of late 90's hip hop, early 2000s hip hop, a lot of Wu-Tang, and a lot of Mobb Deep, Queensbridge. And basically, I heard a sample that this producer Frank Dukes had sent me and just decided I would flip it in like an East Coast dungeon kind-of style. So that is a chop of a sample Frank made. As soon as I heard that sample, I knew it would be something because it just sounded really different. Like reminiscent of old-school, but had kind of a twist to it. Then I added the drums and bass to it, and I sped it up as well, which gives you the way it swings. The sample wasn't going that quickly before, it was actually really slow. The beat was made in FL Studios, and I have a weird way of doing things as I make beats where I have source banks of kits, but I purposely scatter all my sounds all over the place and actually not organize them

because I like to just be surprised. So I go to the scattered folders, scan through them and find new things every time.

I actually made that beat really quick, that one took maybe half an hour, forty minutes to be completely finished with. Usually, the ones that are really special, they always come quick. And I knew that was a special beat. I was in the studio with Drake when he heard the track for the first time, and he just gave me that look, and was like, "Yo, drop that one in my email, because I'm about to work on that tonight." I trusted him with it because he always kills everything send him. When I heard the finished track with his vocals on it, it was just like dope from the jump. I knew it was going to be a hit immediately, and that it was going to be really great for the clubs.

The year 2015 would prove a busy year for Boi-1da indeed, where, along with the phenomenon of *0 to 100*, he would get a call from a new superstar-on-the-rise in the same position Drake had been when he and the producer had first shot to the top together. This time, the phone came ringing from the West Coast, where Kendrick Lamar was working on the go-to project for the millennial generation's biggest newbies and vets alike. The producer described the competitive atmosphere as akin to something like an Olympic All-star team behind the boards that to no one's surprise had Boi on the production roster! The critically-extolled masterpiece would include a portrait of Matthew's hanging prominently in its gallery with the single *The Blacker the Berry*, where in crafting the hypnotic head bobbing instrumental that *Rolling Stone* singled out for its, "Engulfing, layered production by Boi-1da." The producer agreed with the critics, singling out the provocative track:

> Actually, one of my favorite beats I've ever made in my life. I was working with another producer named KOZ, a very talented guy from Toronto. He had another beat where that guitar riff you hear in the Kendrick song was going on throughout the entire track. I told him to solo everything and remove everything but the guitar. Then I created the drum pattern. It just rocked so crazy on those guitars. It was just so aggressive. So we ended up just building around that. Just the straight drum pattern and guitars, and then we created the little hook section.
>
> I remember playing it for the first time for Kendrick and his reaction was so crazy. It was like, "Nigga, nigga, nigga, naw, nobody can hear this beat!" He staked his claim on it early, as soon as he heard it, he said, "This is mine." And I'm just so happy he picked that up because he destroyed it! The concept, and everything he said on that beat is amazing. It was such a beautiful song. It felt old school but current at the same time.

Coming off the heels of two Grammy nominations for his work on *To Pimp a Butterfly*, the producer refocused on advancing his ambition to, "Bring dance hall back to the masses." His greatest success in that endeavor would arrive with

Rihanna's #1 worldwide smash *Work*. A call-to-clubbers everywhere to hit the floor that hit the top spot on the US Hot 100 Singles Chart – it was Boi-1da's first return to the top of the charts since Eminem's *Not Afraid* seven years earlier in 2009 – owningthe throne at #1 in Brazil, Austria, Canada, Belgium, Denmark, France, the Netherlands, Portugal, the U.K. and all the way across the globe in South Africa, while just missing the mark in Mexico, Slovakia, Ireland, and Sweden, peaking at #2. A salute to both superstar singer and producer's shared Island roots, Billboard hailed the hit as a, "Proud, powerful reminder of the Barbados-born singer's...roots - and a milestone for dancehall: The last song in the genre to hit #1 on the Billboard Hot 100 was Sean Paul's *Temperature* in 2006." As he set about bringing the pulse of the song to life, for inspiration the producer turned back the clock in his own memories:

> Growing up on dance hall music, that's mainly what that song was inspired by. When I first moved to Canada, that was the first music I was ever introduced to. Whether it was Beenie Man, or Sean Paul...a lot of those artists. So I was listening to dance hall before I was even listening to hip hop. I just remembered how good dance hall used to make me feel. And certain songs, when I would hear them, they would give me a certain vibe; a certain energy. And made me wanna dance.

Getting out there more, I've been going out a lot. Going to parties, just seeing people and the reaction to a lot of the music. And it's like, nobody's dancing, everybody's just doing these dance moves, so I kind of wanted to bring that whole feel back of people dancing again. I don't know if you've been in a club when *Work* or *Controlla* comes on, but those records really make the ladies want to dance. They really make ladies want to gyrate. So I was kind of just trying to bring that whole thing back with it, and I took a chance and it worked. No pun intended! (laughs) Breaking down the production of a sound that the *Chicago Tribune* in 2015 eloquently described as, "The musical language created by (producer)...Boi-1da." The beat-smith begins with a rhythmic flow that he lets guide his creative compass, revealing that, "For me, it usually always starts with the cadence. I know it's not the most important part of the song, but to me, the cadence is always my first thing. Just because sometimes I like to rap myself, and figure out how somebody would rap on something like this. So I figure the cadence out, like, 'Okay, there's going to have to be a lot of room for a person to rap on it,' so you can't put too much. My thing is not putting too much, but putting just enough. So it's always the cadence first. I used to rap unfortunately, and I wasn't good, but I understand patterns and cadences and room. You have to have room in your beats for people to get off, so that's where it starts with me." Even while he's happy to be identified as one of the sonic designers of Drake's sound, and typically sends those beats he feels have the biggest potential to be hits to the superstar to hear first, the producer discloses that he usually likes to begin work on new music with a blank canvas:

> For the most part, I never try to tailor anything towards anybody, because you never know what anybody wants. When you think you know what they want, it's never what they want, so I always just try to make what comes to my head. So I just free my mind and might start out

thinking, "I'm going to make a rap beat." I wind up making an R&B beat, or some dub-step sounding, or just a weird beat. So even though I send everything usually to Drake to check out first, I don't even make beats with him in mind specifically. It's just all so random with anyone that picks anything.

Few producers hit #1 on the Billboard Hot 100 Chart even once, let alone with superstars like Eminem and Rihanna. So when Boi-1da got word his beat had banged all the way to the top nearly a decade after he'd first hit the peak, even though he'd returned to the Top 10 with Drake and other artists countless times in between the two, it was still a confidence booster he admitted he needed in a way:

> It feels great, just because it wasn't just a fluke, and it really gave me reassurance of my talent and my ideas. A lot of times, my ideas used to get shut down. But when I get an idea that actually worked and the whole world loved it, it was a big confidence booster more than anything. The fact that I got my mom - who's a fan of Rihanna - got a chance to go to her concert and told me she knew *Work* was a big song, but never realized how big it was and that so many people loved it. She said when Rihanna was performing it, the whole stadium went crazy! So that was cool to have a song with that kind of magnitude again.

Boi-1da would stay sitting atop the summit when Drake shocked the system again with a now-trademarked unannounced record release in the summer of 2016 with *Views*, which kept its penthouse panorama debuting at #1 on the Billboard Top 200 Album Chart, selling an astonishing-as-always 852,000 copies in its first week of sale. Blowing the theory out of the water that kids don't buy records anymore, Drake's millennial fan base logged 245 million streams, and 4 million copies sold in the U.S. alone to date. Once again, Drake would throw a stranglehold on the summer radio, club and streaming rotations as hit after hit smacked down the competition, beginning with the predictive *Summer Sixteen*, a promo teaser single that dropped at the top of 2016, immediately rocketing to #6 on the Billboard Hot 100 Singles Chart, and letting the world know just how hot the rhythm of hits coming would be blazing. One of those write-themselves kind of moments that demonstrated just how at home the superstar felt bouncing off of Boi-1da's beats into his cosmos of confidence as an emcee, delivering the kind of spit that lit his fans up out of their seats, as the he brought the heat to the beat in the studio, the producer revealed:

> The crazy thing about *Summer 16* is I did both of the beats on that song! The second beat that the song turns into, I made that actually teaching somebody how to make a beat. I wasn't really even taking it seriously, to be honest, and the first one was a very fast beat as well, I made it very quickly from a sample of *Glass Tubes* my homie CuBeatz sent me, they create samples and whatnot, and I kind of just reversed it and threw some drums on it. Drake was in a mood, like, "I'm trying to get something off, I've got a lot of

energy tonight, when I get in the studio, I want something energetic," and that track had a whole lot of energy to it. Then 40 ended up combining the two together and working his magic with Drake's vocals, and that's how that song came about.

Drake's choke-hold on radio would continue with he kicked off summer with *Controlla*, where Boi-1da's flirting hi-hat rolls dancing with one another as the listener was sucked into another celebration of his dance hall roots revival. Hometown Canadian Broadcasting Network noting that, as a consequence of the producer's commercial success with reinventing that sound into pop radio, "The influence of dancehall on mainstream music seems to have reached a tipping point this summer." Fulfilling a revelation he first heard in his head as a literal part of his beat-making process, the producer remains respectful of and humble to the musical medium at work inside:

> That allows me to have a vision any time I'm making a track of how I want it – especially the drums – to sound, and I just kind of replicated that. I was beat-boxing how I wanted it to sound, but I wanted to make it sound as modern as possible and not just like an old-school dance hall beat. So I put in some hi-hat rolls at the beginning, and just wanted to make it move. There's a certain cadence you can use to make feel dance, and that was one of the ones I decided to use. Dance hall is very good for that too. They have very good cadences where basically, when you hear drums in a certain cadence and you

want to move a certain way to it. So that's what
I was trying to replicate.

Giving back to his hometown by giving aspiring producers
dreaming of the same success he's had a shot, Boi-1da considers –
even above all the monster hits he's co-produced with them –
among his highest honors has been the shot to share the
producer by-line with a new generation of stars he's helping to
mold. Admitting that versus trying to build a pool of prodigies
stable from a financial motivation, "I just feel obligated, I come
from Toronto, and there's not a lot of musical opportunities in
Toronto. Myself and a few other people I feel are like
gatekeepers within the music industry up there. The city is very
small, and a lot of people don't have a lot of outlets. I just
remember coming up as a producer and I didn't have a mentor. I
never had anyone on the come-up to really do anything for me. I
feel like there's so many talented young producers and I have so
much opportunity. There's so much work, that it's unrealistic to
think I'm going to sit here and produce everything myself."
That spirit of generosity is one he spreads around today with as
open-door a policy for giving every one of the thousands of
aspiring producers who hit him up on social media each year
asking him to check out their demos. Proudly pointing to his
track record:

> I signed a lot of producers to give them a chance
> to work and make something of themselves. I'm
> not the guy that signs people and puts my names
> on their beats and sends them out. I'm really
> giving guys a chance to do their own thing. For
> instance, the producer T-Minus, he was a
> younger kid at my high school that I mentored

and literally taught him how to make beats. I took him under my wing, introduced him to Drake, and he took off. And it was so amazing to see because he's such a talented kid. He's gone on to produce songs including *How Low* for Ludacris, *I'm on One* for DJ Khaled, which featured Drake, Rick Ross and Lil Wayne, *She Will* by Lil Wayne featuring Drake, *Make Me Proud* by Drake featuring Nicki Minaj, and *Heartbreaker* by Justin Bieber among others. I'm a fan as well of Sven Thomas, the Finals, Alan Ritter, Frank Dukes – so many guys – there's so many guys to plug, but those are the main guys I think are really dope.

Alongside the feedback he values from his protégés and peers, Boi-1da has another set of ears he relies on for reaction to the newest beats he's banging out from the newest generation of millennial music fans; his daughter Shayla, who has grown up playing at his feet in the studio: "Oh yeah, I'll be making beats, and I have a Triton that I set up and she bangs on it and makes noise in my ear. So I'll be driving, and when a song I did comes on, I'll tell her, 'Daddy made that beat.' Then when the next song comes on the radio, she'll say, 'I made that beat.' She knows the stuff that I've done, recognizes it and will say, 'Daddy made that beat,' so it's pretty funny." The applause he received from another fan would come with an impossible-to-resist offer by Kanye West to collaborate on his 2016 studio album, *Life of Pablo*. West's studio retreats working with multiple groups of producers at once had become one of the hottest invitations in the game, and when Boi-1da finally received the call, he leapt at the opportunity, painting a producer's paradise:

I actually went to Paris to work with Kanye. That was a crazy trip! I spent the weekend in Paris with Kanye working on the *Life of Pablo* album. It was me and a bunch of producers like Charlie Heat and artists. It was a cool trip man, because Kanye's like one of my favorite artists *ever*. I'd first gotten to meet him a couple weeks prior and I was playing tracks for him in the studio for almost FOUR hours, and it was a real cool vibe. He's such a nice guy, a very funny guy. We had a really good time and he told me personally, "I love the colors you're painting within your music. I want you to come out to Paris and help me with this album. See if there are songs you can fix up for me, or create something from scratch."

Fired up to take it back to the old school 'Ye days, The Huffington Post would later argue he succeeded after concluding upon listen to the song West collaborated on with the producer that when, "'Ye released his newest song, *Real Friends*,...everyone (agreed)... the 'old' Kanye is back. Bringing back a sound that fans would recognize from earlier albums," a mission the producer was proud to accomplish: "I was so happy with the song because it just reminded me of the old *College Dropout* Kanye because he really like told a story on there and it was amazing."

With several world-wide radio play and streaming records already under his belt for international song sensations like Eminem's 10,000,000 selling #1 *Not Afraid*, Rihanna's *Work*, which broke and now holds the single week streaming record with 2.056 million streams in one week. Though he doesn't say so to sound like he takes it for granted, Boi-1da admits that "I think I've gotten used to it. Still, when I see a song go over with the crowd in a club, that's really the reaction that I live for because I see it and that's an honest reaction: everybody's in the club and they're having a good time, they're intoxicated, and when a song like *0 to 100* drops, everybody starts going crazy, so that's a good feeling."

Setting his sights to the next decade of number ones, Samuels' forecast is brighter than ever as his bold aims include an aspiration to, "Be known as one of the producers who are mentioned among the greatest ever." Along with continuing to open the door for a new generation of kids growing up on his sound now, indulging his love of, "Giving other people opportunities" to be put on. When pointing to a hip hop Godfather he follows the example of in pursuit of such grand ambitions, Boi-1da looks not surprisingly to Dr. Dre:

> I'd love to follow in his footsteps, and branch off out of music to something else, because Dr. Dre is a huge inspiration to me. I just want to be like Andre. I've met him a few times, and got to kick it with him for a few hours at his studio. Just the way he conducts his business and conducts himself is just amazing to me. I always try to model myself after him and the way he took over eras. He had artists that just took over eras: he had N.W.A., he had Snoop Dogg, he had himself, and he had Eminem. They took over eras of music. I just want to be like that.

With his phone continually blowing up with calls from everybody in the business wanting to work with him, one name remains on the producer's wishlist: "Justin Timberlake, I'm a big fan of JT, I'd love to do a big song with him." After *Vice Magazine* correctly noted in 2016 that his was, "The rare name who can generate as much interest in a track as the artist," and Forbes hoisted him profile even higher when they featured Matthew on their coveted *30 Under 30* 2016 List in recognition for his knack for, "Constructing hit after hit." Boi-1da remains as fearless as ever as he pushes the next boundary out of his way, confessing that:

> I feel obligated – not speaking highly of myself – but I feel like I'm one of the best doing what I do, and I feel very obligated to keep pushing the envelope, so I'm just continuing to look for new sounds, new grooves, new vibes for people to enjoy themselves to, and a lot of it comes from nostalgia, like with *0 for 100* and the way Mobb Deep and Wu Tang made me feel, I tried to bring that back with that track. So I'm just doing the same thing with this Island-flavored music.

Founder of his own label and production house, OVO Sound, Boi-1da may very well have the makings of an *Aftermath* on his hands. Following in the footsteps of hip hop legend Andre Young, Matthew Samuels – while aware of the impact his sound has already had upon the culture he continues to shape – keeps his head in the music and out of the clouds as he moves forward starting work on *Volume II* of his Greatest Hits Collection:

> It trips me out a little bit to be on such big records. But the most important part to me is

keeping the music alive. A lot of producers now, they're throwing tags on their beats, and that's cool for themselves. But I feel like the music industry and a lot of producers are looking at things the wrong way. They find a sound and keep repeating the same formula. I just believe at the end of the day, I don't want my music to ever become something with a brand on it that you can just buy. People always ask me, "How come your shit never sounds the same?" And I always say, "It's art man." You might hear one of ones from me, or two of twos, but you'll never hear the same thing from me like ten times in a row. I'm painting different pictures every day. I never want to paint the same picture. You have to reinvent yourself and your sound constantly. Look at the greats like Timbaland and Dre, they keep reinventing themselves every time!
www.boi1da.net

"His era-defining sound represented a cultural touchstone."
– *Vibe Magazine*

"Music gets me out of stress, drama, and complications. It gets me away from everything. Even at a time in my career when I thought I was going to lose everything...music got me out of it."
– Teddy Riley

CHAPTER FOUR
"You can't hate on a classic" – Teddy Riley

For much of 2017, Teddy Riley has been working on an album of classical music. But his head isn't any busier musically than when he's producing hip hop or R&B, an extension of a power of projection where, "When I make a beat, my mind is so cluttered I hear everything at once. I know what my keyboard parts are going to be and I know what my bass is going to be. Music never stops in me...I'm always doing it." His first musical vision arrived as a toddler with the realization that he wanted to be a performer when he grew up, years before ever discovering his gift as a record producer:

> I was just five years old the first time I ever got up before a big crowd when my baby sitter had taken me to the Apollo Theatre for the first time to see Gladys Knight singing *Neither One of Us Wants to Be the First to Say Goodbye*. It must have been fate, because we were sitting in the front row and Gladys actually had them pick me up and put me on the stage with her! I remember I was dancing around and the crowd went wild!
> That was the first time I said to myself, *I want to be a star*. Hearing the way that audience lit up for me, I knew that I wanted to be on that stage!

GENIUS is a word thrown around often in the entertainment business, so much so that the music industry has had its share of "one hit wonders," hit-makers who were declared "brilliant" during their fifteen minutes of fame never to be heard from again. It also had its rare share of real geniuses. Those with a musical talent exceptional enough to make timeless hit record after hit record for any artist they're teamed up with. Michael Jackson would say as much at the Grammy Awards when – accepting the Legend Award – he declared from the stage: "Teddy Riley, you're a genius." True words for a man who invented his own genre of music and played a key role in shaping much of the mainstream of hip hop and R&B for the last three decades.

Hailed as the one true *King of New Jack Swing* and, "The true definition of a super-producer" by BET, Teddy has been a wunderkind since his early teen years. A musical prodigy who grew up in real time with the genre of hip hop itself, Riley produced some of its earliest and most ground-breaking-and-dance floor-shaking hits, including Doug E. Fresh's legendary *The Show*, Kool Mo Dee's *How Ya Like Me Now*, *Wild Wild West*, and *I Go to Work*, Big Daddy Kane's *I Get the Job Done* among other highlights. In 1989, his sound broke down the barriers built up between the genres of hip hop & R&B at radio, crossing over into the kingdom of mainstream success with Bobby Brown's *My Prerogative*, Teddy's first #1 hit by the time he was barely out of his teens.

Going back to the beginning of Riley's prodigious musical childhood growing up in Harlem in the mid-1970s quite literally in the shadow of the famed Apollo, as fate would have it, the theatre's back parking lot sat across the street from Teddy's elementary school playground. Instead of spending his lunchtimes playing kickball, Riley and his friends would sit star-struck watching the behind-the-scenes activity day in and out of the biggest soul, R&B and Motown acts of the day. With these stars now not nearly as far away, suddenly, his dream of becoming one of them seemed possible:

> I attended Harriet Tubman PS 154 elementary school in Harlem from pre-K, kindergarten, first grade, all the way up through the fifth grade. And through all of those years, we had lunchtime in the same school yard, which happened to face the back parking lot of the legendary Apollo Theatre. It was like getting two educations, because it seemed like every time we

would be playing out there, I'd see people coming in and out of this building, loading musical instruments and gear in and out, and I didn't know exactly what they were coming in and going out for, but I remember being instantly mesmerized with curiosity because of my own fascination with music.

The big "a ha" moment as a kid came for me one day when I recognized among those people walking in and out of the Apollo was James Brown! Then I started recognizing other faces I'd seen on TV and it all clicked for me. So guys like Johnny Taylor and B.B. King, who even at that young age I knew distinctly, and then one day we saw the Temptations, who all dressed alike. After that, it instantly became a hobby for me and my friends to sit at lunch and after school every day across the street from that parking lot and people watch everyone walking in and out of that building, trying to see who could recognize them first, and though it was kind of a game between me and my friends, at the same time, I'd started dreaming of becoming a star myself when I grew up. During this same time as a grade-schooler, I remember my friends would talk about wanting to become a hustler, or fireman, or astronaut when they grew up, I always said I wanted to be a star.

When I was a young kid, I was not popular. I was just a kid that didn't really stand out until I started doing music, which was age nine when I made an imaginary friend that I called 'The Music Man.' A lot of kids have that imaginary friend you never see, that invisible friend, that's what music was to me. As I turned six, seven, eight, music kept pulling me deeper and deeper in as a passion.

Like so many of his contemporaries who grew up attending houses of worship every Sunday, Teddy's first exposure to what would become his principle instrument in a career to come happened "when I turned nine, my mom began pushing me to play piano in our church. So after I first played for that church, soon after that, I started attending a church where I was the *only* piano player. Still, I felt like I wasn't even getting what I needed to know, I was playing while everybody was singing, but we went to this Church Anniversary celebration one weekend, where there were different singers and musicians would come up and I'm there playing piano for my church. Then this other church came up, and they had a drummer, and I said 'You know what, I need to find a church like that closer to my church!', and wound up attending Universal Temple, where Jazzy J from Africa Bambatta was the *drummer*, and their DJ Red Alert was the DJ for the church! You couldn't ask to have nothing more than the DJ and the drummer from Africa Bambaattaa!"

Raised against the urban backdrop of Harlem that would prove to be an ideal training camp for the toughness of the record business where push and shove competed with one another at every turn, Teddy was challenged from the first shot he got after approaching a group of hustlers on his block who doubled as an R&B quartet about joining their group. Though he was twelve years their junior at the time, Teddy's passion pushed him past any pausing, recalling a daring move he made that would have robbed him - literally - of his musical equipment if he didn't pull off the audition:

> When I was twelve, I got my first keyboard. A Casio, and it was like my best friend because I never rolled anywhere without it: in school, on the street, everywhere. Across the street from my projects, I went to Universal Temple church until I was fourteen. As great a training experience as it had been to play keyboards in the church band, I was ready for something a little more challenging musically. And boy did I know how to pick one. I was actually on my way uptown one day on 7th Avenue headed up to 125th Street on my way to go to the Barbershop, and I heard this band rehearsing. The funny thing is I used to see and hear the band, Total Climax, across the street from my projects every day practicing. Until one day, I decided I *needed to be* in that band.

> So one day, I gathered up enough heart and say to them after watching them for five or six months, "I play piano," and took my little Casio over there. They said, "Shorty, you don't play. Get out of here." So I went home, and then came back again the next week, again I said, "I told you I play piano, I could play your keyboards. I know how to play and want you guys to give me a shot." So he said, "Alright shorty, we're gonna give you a shot. We got this piano down here,

but if you can't play, we taking your Casio!" So now the stage was set, and I knew I had a lot riding on this audition because that keyboard was everything to me at that time. But I was confident, and said, "Alright, try me out." Thank God, they voted the old keyboard player out and me in *unanimously*. Which as you can imagine gave me a *huge* confidence boost being only twelve years old. These guys were in their late teens, and might as well have been grownups to me at my age. It felt good that before I was even a teenager, I was already being taken seriously by professional musicians, club owners, and most importantly, the audiences that were listening to me play.

Catching the ear of local music manager Gene Griffin, whose reputation on the streets preceded itself as one to be taken seriously, by both musicians and labels alike, Teddy took the shot when he and the boys in the band signed, "To our first record contract as part of Total Climax and Kids at Work with Gene when I was fourteen with Gene's Sounds of New York imprint. Then that same year, I left Total Climax entirely to join Kids at Work and signed with CBS Records, which Gene was managing. Our first and only studio album was eponymously titled *Kids At Work*, and was released in 1984, and featured singles like *Sugar Baby, Singing Hey Yea*." A kid at work was a precise way to describe Teddy's momentum at an age when most kids were playing video games, by playing music instead, he was granted an *almost* emancipated minor status where his mother allowed him to perform as the only teenager in a band full of adults at nightclubs during both school night and weekend gigs.

As Riley entertained the city's most ruthless gangsters at the height of the 1980s crack epidemic at Harlem's hottest hustler hang-out spots, including the legendary Roof Top, he was already studying what made the New Jacks swing, taking his mental notes upstairs after shows to his very own recording studio the club's owners had built especially for him to continue working on his new sound:

> My ground-zero headquarters back then as a teenager was a studio my uncle Willie had built for me in the upstairs office of his famed Harlem club The Roof Top. This was actually the first club I ever performed in as a member of Total Climax. My studio at The Roof Top was where we would go every night after we'd finished performing, when we'd take our instruments upstairs to the studio and continue working on music. It was against this backdrop that I'd first started experimenting with making hip hop beats. At The Roof Top studio is when it first came on to me hard, the whole concept of what hip hop meant as a lifestyle, which musically just drew me in that much deeper.
>
> At this age, like every other kid in the inner city, I also hustled a little on the side as a member of The SHACK Crew. That's actually where I had a little art-imitating-life moment when the idea for one of my earliest new jack hits, *Just Got Paid* by Johnny Kemp. Friday was the night when we had the most customers, and I came up with that in my head while I was out there hustling. That's

what I called a *corner record*. *Go See the Doctor* was a corner record as well. I got the idea for that one because when we were out there on the corner, there were girls who would come around because they wanted to be a part of the SHACK Crew. There would be girls sometimes who would mess around with everybody in the crew, and we would basically share her. Well, in that case, some unlucky guy from the crew was going to wind up catching a VD. And he was the guy who had to go see the doctor. I always used protection back then, even with my girlfriend, because I was conscious of that, but *Go See the Doctor* was inspired by that.

As word of his whiz-kid talents quickly spread throughout the projects, it inspired both admirers and jealousy among some of his peers, and Teddy was given protection by Harlem's most violent, feared, and revered gangsters, who were so impressed by his talent that they warned around the neighborhood: "Nobody touch shorty." A ghetto pass that was reserved only for an elite of rising sports stars and entertainers whose shot was so rare it inspired everyone to root for them, in Riley's case. That prodigal celebrity would quite literally save his life one night when a ski-masked stick-up crew burst into The Roof Top after hours in a strong-arm robbery with guns and dark intentions only calling off an execution after one of the stick-up crew recognized Riley. As the producer still recalls with a touch of eeriness after seeing his life quite literally, "Flash before my eyes. I was working out of The Roof Top recording studio, and one night they showed up when we were all there working: me, Timmy Gatlin, Lavaba Malison, and Greg G. These guys came in with guns out and made us all lay face-down on the ground! This was the first time in real life I'd seen someone get pistol-whipped in the head with a gun. Then while we were all lying on the ground, and I had turned my head to the side so they could actually see my face, thinking maybe they'd have some sympathy for me as I prayed. This scene felt right out of a movie looking back on it now. Music saved my life that night because suddenly, one of the masked gangsters cut in and blurted out, "YO, THAT'S SHORTY!" As soon as I heard those words, I felt an instant rush of relief run over me, and just then another of the masked gunmen said, "What are you talking about?" And this guy yelled back to him – this time in an even more forceful voice, "Don't do nothing to shorty, that's that little music motherfucker! Don't do nothing to shorty..." Quickly relocating his studio back to the ironically safer turf of his mother's apartment in the St. Nicholas Projects, some of New York hip hop's biggest early hits would thereafter wind up being created in his mother's living room:

> After that experience, I moved all my equipment out and set up shop full-time back at my apartment because I no longer felt safe recording at The Roof Top, and my mother's living room became ground zero. I still shake my head that my mother allowed me to take it over like that, but it was yet another reflection of her belief in my growing talents, and after hearing about my near-death experience, she was happy to have me somewhere safe. My studio-set up back then centered around a very classy-looking wooden Jukebox that had been in our living room since I was a small child. In fact, I believe we were the

first family in my projects – probably the only family – that owned a real Jukebox, and I remember it had a top so you could close it, and I would set my keyboard, drum machine and tape machine on top of it while I worked.

Back then, by the time I was in my teens, I'd gotten a hold of a TEAC tape machine, and this all came from the soundman Newbie – who we called 'Mr. Nubulus' – from Total Climax, who'd first loaned it to me until I'd gotten the money together to buy it from him. He was the first one who ever introduced me to the art of recording and taught me how to engineer and recording to tape. It was funny, because for as many kids as might have been jealous of the music I was making, I had equal numbers of fans in my neighborhood, so much so that I lived on the first floor in the projects, and my bedroom was my studio, so people would see me in the window, playing and making records, and kids would come to the window just to listen because I would always keep it open while I was working on songs.

The year was 1985 when hip hop history would be made by a group of Harlem high schoolers who became the first to create hybrid of live beat-boxing holding down the pocket with a programmed drum machine while the theme to the *Inspector Gadget* cartoon cleverly and playfully danced around a now-legendary synthesizer line. Played by a 16-year-old Teddy Riley, whose idea it had been to add the Gadget theme, he remembered,

"By that age, I had started producing tracks for everybody locally around the neighborhood, making songs for F.A.M.E., Total Climax, Kool Moe Dee, Schoolly D, Busy B, and then one day Doug E. Fresh came to my house and everything changed forever! I first met Doug after I'd wound up being kicked out of Martin Luther King High School for getting in a fight with a guy in a class of mine. After that, they sent me to a tougher school. Park East High School, where kids went who'd gotten kicked out of their regular high school, thinking it would be too wild for me. It just so happened that Doug E. Fresh went to that school! I didn't know who he was at first, and he didn't know who I was. But everything happens for a reason, because we wound up making *The Show* together, which played a huge role in launching both our careers. Once we were classmates, even before we'd recorded together, I started hanging out with Doug E. and the Get Fresh Crew, and Slick Rick."

Now singularly legendary to hip hop's underground explosion, *The Show* would put Teddy in the position locally, "Even before he became a star," of being a kid who had already achieved the reputation among urban lure as, "Something of a legend" around Harlem and the burgeoning New York hip hop scene, according to *The Guardian*. Headlining the extraordinary accomplishment that while still, "A teenager, he helped Doug E. Fresh turn *The Show* from a string of good hooks into a hit," Britain's biggest news service – like many media outlets around the world – would go on to celebrate the paramount moment in hip hop history that Riley remembered helping build the foundational hip hop hit from the ground up:

> I initially came up with the beat you hear on *The Show* after Doug had played me a demo he'd made in the music teacher's classroom, which

had the concept for *The Show*. But I felt they had too many commercials crammed in there together, so along with the beat, I added the Inspector Gadget theme music to the song as well. Luckily, back then, they didn't have all the interpolation copyright infringement laws in place yet, so you were a lot freer to use samples in songs. So once I added that to what they already had with Doug E.'s beat-boxing. To top it all off, I pulled off my Oberheim DX -7 drum machine, and added those low shakers you hear in that instrumental, which was actually the birth of the New Jack Swing sound.

Teddy's next hit with the hustlers would gain both he and the song's emcee instant street fame when Riley's name began ringing out even louder after *Go See the Doctor* dropped in 1986. An underground anthem for the neighborhood player that Teddy reveals, "Was the moment I started to see New Jack Swing first taking form as a fuller sound building on what I'd done with Doug E. Fresh," the song inspired *Rolling Stone Magazine* to spotlight, "A young Teddy Riley's irresistible electro-funk production." Knowing he was on to something big in the way his music so naturally synchronized with Kool Moe Dee's flows, Teddy breaks down the making of the classic cautionary tale thirty years later beginning with his memory of:

> I made that song at a friend's house that played for Confunktion. The guy owned a studio in Jersey, and he had an 808 drum machine there, and that 808 was the instrument that I'd say 99, 100% of the music industry uses today. And I

used it back when I made *Go See the Doctor*. That was all I had to work on at the studio. Along with the little Yamaha DX-100 keyboard, which is what I played the bassline on [starts humming the bass line]. Now that's church right there, *church in rap*. Another funny moment in that song came when you hear me going, "Skeeza, ungh, come on, Skeeza!" When it was released, that was the biggest street record for every neighborhood, and every ghetto. Everybody was singing *Go See the Doctor* when that came out in '85. Between that and Doug E. Fresh coming out with *The Show* the same year, my beats were ringing ears all over Harlem!

That was the first time where I heard my music really influencing the streets, and knew this music had so much of an edge on it, because the streets – especially my streets – was loving it, especially at The Roof Top, where *Go See the Doctor* was an anthem. We'd first released the single on Roof Top Records, which was our record label. Then Jive Records picked it up, and Kool Moe Dee got signed. After that, *Go See the Doctor* started getting played on the radio. I remember feeling proud that it got from the streets to the radio. And I remember the first day I ever heard it and yelled out, "Mom, my record's on the radio!" This was all back while I was still in high school too.

It was on Moe Dee and Riley's next collaboration where Teddy – at the astonishingly young age of just nineteen – would fly to London, England for a magic carpet ride that would inspire their next album. Still considered among the gold standards of 1980s hip hop, while at the same time, *Record Collector Magazine* noted that Moe Dee as an artist was moving Teddy's sound, "Further down the New Jack Swing route on 1987s superior *How Ya Like Me Now?!*" Teddy utilized rap as a laboratory of sorts while he experimented with and refined the fundamental elements of the new sound he was inventing. *Soul Train* would acknowledge the history he was making years later when they rightly recognized him as, "A standard-bearer in production since a teenager...Teddy Riley is considered the catalyst of modern soul, R&B, hip hop, and pop. He shaped the sound of a generation, creating a sonic foundation that current trends have since been built upon." Knowing he was on his way to somewhere special the minute he lifted off from JFK Airport in Queens on a flight bound for the United Kingdom, Teddy even back at the age of eighteen remembered feeding off of the pressure that came from the responsibility of being named the album's lead producer by Kool Moe Dee personally:

> By 1987, just based on the success of my first collaboration with Kool Moe Dee, I was whisked off to London to work at Battery. I was excited personally because this was my first time ever leaving New York City, let alone the country. And professionally, because I was being flown to England and paid to do what I'd been doing in my project living room only months earlier. At that time, they rented an Akai MPC-60 and I didn't know nothing about it. But once I got my

hands on it, they were amazed because I taught myself how to use the drum machine in less than an hour. I had all of my sounds on floppy discs, which I used with my DDD-1, and actually started working on the *How Ya Like Me Now?!* album until I learned how to use the MPC-60, and then took all my sounds from the DDD-1 and imported them into the MPC.

So my preference was getting the sounds on there, all the hits, because I didn't play that on the keyboards. Because then they didn't have a keyboard that could sample that long. So I was making those sounds on the drums, processing the bass drum, and then next thing you know, I got all these kick samples – like one shot hit samples from James Brown – so those were the sounds that I put in the drum machine, and that's how *How Ya Like Me Now* came about. And then I added the horn sounds are from the Yamaha DX-7. It was done with just those two pieces of equipment, the MPC, and DX-7.

An amazing hotbed of talent back in the 1980s, Harlem would prove to have crucial proximity to Riley's career not only by how many up and coming hip hop stars that were hurled into his universe during these years, but R&B stars as well. It was Teddy's ground-breaking work with a new generation of crooners who would provide the true synthesis for his New Jack sound to fully take hold after the producer cracked the code and, "Spearheaded the R&B fusion offshoot," *Billboard* wrote as they began to take note of the young prodigy and the sound he was slowly sneaking up their charts. Keith Sweat's soaring voice would prove the springboard for that sound to truly make its high-profile debut when his debut LP, *Make it Last Forever*, debuted at #1 on the Billboard Top R&B/Hip Hop Albums Chart and cracked the Top 20 of the Top 200 Album Chart upon release in November, 1987. Just twenty years old, Teddy had first met Sweat on the local Harlem teen-boy band circuit years before:

> Back when I was still in Kids at Work in the early 80's, we did things as a band other than just make records: we performed and were even in a competition against Keith Sweat's group, Jamilah, and Johnny Kemp's group, called KiKi Fox. It was a small world, and that's how Keith and I started making music together is because he lived around the block, and growing up, was always that kid from around the block that was making music like I was. So one day he came to my projects, and said "I wanna work with you, and get some of that music from you." And I said, "Man, I don't make R&B music, I make rap music," which was easy for me. That was easy money. I made quick money with that. It was like the street game: I made a beat and I got twenty-five dollars at first. BUT, by the time I finally agreed to work on the Keith Sweat album, it worked out being in my musical and financial interest because I suddenly started making one thousand dollars a song!

By 1987 just as hip hop was being born, many were arguing that R&B was dying a slow, sappy death courtesy of endless FM love ballads that saturated radio before BET argued that, "Riley...singlehandedly breathed life back in R&B, crafting anthems for...crooner Keith Sweat." *Vibe*, meanwhile, captured the contagious nature of the fever Riley and Sweat's new sound was spreading when they mused that, "Anyone who blasted Keith Sweat's debut album during the winter of 1987 understood that the best way to kick it to this R&B classic was to let it run till track eight. Which means, it's damn near impossible to pick an underrated song given that radio seemingly embraced every cut on this highly influential release which doubles as Teddy Riley's production breakthrough."

With the new generation of R&B artists Teddy was recording overtop his New Jack Swing template – one *AllHipHop.com* explained as a formula where, "Riley blended soul vocals with hip hop beats, single handedly creating one of the most popular sounds in R&B history." He was running a literal hit factory out of the St. Nicholas Projects while adding a naturally gritty edge to his brand of R&B that played well with both the ladies and the hustlers as he wrote them a weekend soundtrack with hits like Sweat's *I Wanna* and Johnny Kemp's *Just Got Paid*. Riley's second New Jack Swing hit at R&B radio – reaching #1 on the Billboard Hot Black Singles and Hot Dance Club Party charts as well as cracking the Top 10 of the Hot 100 Singles Chart – as Teddy introduced his sound to a mainstream pop audience for the first time, he marvels to date at the fact that he had by the age most kids were just getting their driving license accomplished so much with so little:

When I was working with Keith Sweat, I made *I Wanna* and *Just Got Paid* by Johnny Kemp using that same drum machine, my very first, the DDD-1, which was a Korg drum machine. And back then, we were recording vocals using a Shure mic that looked just like the ones they use at radio stations. I had to leave Keith bare because when you add an effect like symphonic or chorus, with a voice like his, that sounds so vibrato. Those kind of effects don't sound right. So with Keith, I used reverb, something that's a small-voice plate. And that makes him sound a little wider.

Back in the day, we didn't have that many tracks, and you couldn't do so much a lot of times, so I would comp it, and do the next part. Most of the time, how we did it, was go in and do one take. Then do a lot of punching, if the singer didn't have it right away, or he's reading the lines and I want it to sound natural like he's not reading. That's where I'll punch it. I'll say "Remember that line. Let's punch." So for instance, with somebody like Bobby Brown, I didn't do a lot of punching, I let him record it straight down a couple times, and then that's when I would pick, "Okay, this line is the best, this is the best," and comp together a performance from the best takes. There are exceptions to that though, because when I worked with Johnny Kemp, that was one take, the whole record. That was a one-take. And working with Johnny, I didn't have to do much. I didn't apply anything effects-wise on his voice.

And there's only certain singers you work with like that, where you don't have to do that. Working with Keith was a big deal because it marked my first success at writing and producing an R&B record. It opened my mind to the realization that there were so many musical opportunities out there for me to be working in multiple styles, from the hip hop to the R&B to the pop charts.

Teeing up for the Grand Slam hit that would take New Jack Swing to #1 on the Hot 100 Singles Chart for the first time, *My Prerogative* would turn its star hitter, Bobby Brown – and producer Teddy Riley – into household names. This recognition came courtesy in part of a now-legendary shout-out during the chart-topping song's breakdown where Brown boastfully proclaims: "What is this, a business where I can't have money in my pocket and people not talk about me...I made this money, you didn't. Right Ted? We outta here!" An infectious pop soundscape where nothing is missed in the master ingredients for what makes a #1 hit, *My Prerogative* would instantly become New Jack Swing's official anthem, and *Rolling Stone* agreed, proclaiming the chart-topper, "A masterpiece, the pinnacle of New Jack Swing," while *Spin* celebrated, "Harlem wunderkind Teddy Riley's brand new funk," as his name became instantly synonymous with inventing the genre in real time with its rise up the charts. With the Bobby Brown recording session, Riley - who contrary to GROSS misreporting by Wikipedia and other historical annals that Gene Griffin had any musical involvement in the song's creation of any kind - produced *My Prerogative* entirely by himself and co-wrote the hit with future GUY bandmate Aaron Hall, revealed of the song's roots that:

My Prerogative was actually a song I did *way* before. It was supposed to go on a GUY album, but we were too late because we were already mastering the first GUY record. I wrote that song with Aaron Hall, and I remember I'd come up with the beat, played it for him, and said, "I've got this hook." I ran it down for him, and then Aaron started singing that verse melody, "Everybody's talkin', all this stuff about me, Why don't they just let me live?" So he was singing it just like you hear in the song. Once he sang that first verse, I then answered him with, "They say I'm crazy, I really don't care, that's my prerogative..."

Aaron and I co-wrote the lyrics, but I wrote all of the music for that song. I played the signature bass line you hear in the opening of that song on a DX-100, which was my main keyboard by then, and then the D-50 as well. So Aaron and I were originally supposed to sing that right before the GUY album, and our manager Gene Griffin told us, "It's too late bro." So when Bobby Brown came through the projects looking for me after that to work together, we had this record already finished, tailor-made. We handed it to him on a platter (or so you would have thought).

For many record producers, the single most uncomfortable part of their process comes when they have to push an artist they're recording to go somewhere they don't want to for the greater good of the song. A dynamic Riley ran into head on with an initially headstrong Brown once the two were face to face in the studio, Teddy behind the boards and Bobby in the booth, he recalled that, "As it worked out, though he loved the original demo, once Bobby and I were in the studio tracking his vocals, I gave him the way to sing it which was the same way we'd done it for him back at the house. Well, once we got to the studio, when he was trying to sing it. He wasn't comfortable at first and wasn't delivering with the attitude we needed him to. So I told him at one point, 'Bobby, you want people to know you as something different,' and then I said, 'If you can't do it this way, then it's not gonna work,' and he actually said, 'Alright, I'm outta here,' and walked out of the studio on me!" Knowing precisely the type of attitude the song's vocal performance needed to keep up with the rebellious rodeo of music blasting underneath, when the producer started giving Brown direction toward that end and got pushback. He worked fast to use the singer's aggression to the song's advantage:

> He was really mad at me. And in spite of his initial protests to the record company, they told him, "If you don't get your ass back in the studio, we're going to shut your project down! You need to get in the studio with that New Jack swinger. Do you understand? Anything he touches turns to gold. So you need to get your butt back in the studio." That's what Lou Silas, the label head said. So a couple days later, he came back in the studio, and sung it the way I told him. But I could still tell he wasn't totally feeling it, and things finally came to a head. I remember distinctively, it was when it came time to record that bridge vocal rap. Bobby had sung

all the way through the song and I did the solo. What happened was, when we got to that bridge part where we launches into, "What is this a bizzit that I can't have money in my pocket and people not talk about me? I don't know what's going on these days, Got this person over here talking about me, this person..." Initially, he didn't say my name like he eventually ended the vocal rap with: "I made this money, you didn't. Right Ted? We outta here..." We didn't get that on the first run-down because he didn't want to say my name, he was still mad at me.

So at that point, I put my psychologist hat on, brought him in the control room to hear his singing, and I said, "You need to listen to this," and when he came in and listened, everybody looked at him and said, "He was right, this is the new you." And then something switched on in his head right there because he started believing in himself. He started believing what everybody was telling him, and that sparked an extra moment of inspiration that helped make the song. The next thing Bobby said was, "Alright, I got something else." So first he went outside and smoked a joint, and when he came back in, he said, "I wanna sing it down. I just want to do some things and throw some stuff in there. Like ad-libs and whatnot." So he did the whole song straight down in one take. And that's where I got that, "Yo Teddy, kick it like this, oh oh oh, I can do what I wanna do, me and you..." and then, "I made this money, you didn't. Right Ted?" All of that came out in his ad-libbing, and it brought even more life to the song. "It's my prerogative, can't you see baby doll?" And, "Why you wanna talk about me? Tell me, tell me..." near the end of the song. All of that was Bobby.

Proof that his instinct to push Brown into a more cocky headspace paid off handsomely, Teddy walked away with a lesson that has stuck with him throughout his entire production career, reasoning that, "The session with Bobby was a lesson in the importance of being firm and fearless as a producer no matter the stature of the star you're working with in the studio. Because usually the tension turning within the creative back-and-forth will produce something truly inspired that helps make a song into a hit. As an interesting footnote to that song, that's also one place where I can say Michael Jackson followed Bobby with *Remember the Time*. When he nears the end of the song he ad-libs, 'Remember the times? Do you remember girl?' He only did that because of Bobby doing, 'Why you wanna talk about me?' Michael said, 'I want my ending to be like that!'" Once Bobby Brown was fired up on the mic bringing the heat Teddy wanted from him, the producer remembered:

Recording Bobby on that one with an old Neumann vocal microphone the studio had, the Shure wasn't available at the studio. They had a C-12 and an AKG 414, but I wanted the Neumann. It was nice and big and wide. And I felt like it would work with his voice, because I wanted all that picked up. Effects-wise, I added the symphonic vocal effect from the Yamaha outboard SPX-90, which had chorus, and a flanger. But the symphonic one is the one I wanted on him because that's what I had on my voice for *Fantasy*, and I used that on Bobby.

Teddy's decision as a producer to push Brown paid off in platinum dividends, hitting #1 on the Billboard Hot 100 Singles Chart – Teddy's first #1 – and crowned with nominated for a Grammy Nomination for Best R&B Urban Contemporary Single as *The Village Voice* would later credit Riley for, "(Propelling) soul into the digital age...Teddy invented it." A phenomenon that was spreading like wildfire by 1988 as Riley remembered, "My New Jack Swing sound was starting to tear across not just the nightclub scene but Urban radio and video as well, putting me in a position to start – alongside hip hop – to start producing hit singles and albums before I was even out of my teens for Keith Sweat with *Just Got Paid* and Bobby Brown's *My Prerogative*, and *that* was the song that really put my sound on the map!"

While Keith Sweat, Johnny Kemp and Bobby Brown are widely credited with being the first SOLO R&B stars to take New Jack Swing mainstream vocally, in the esteemed opinion of the *BBC*, it wasn't until the genre's first group, GUY, dropped their self-titled 1988 debut that the genre fully matured with, "The first New Jack Swing or Swing Beat album ever made. The album's influence and that of its producer Teddy Riley on R&B cannot be understated, as the album single-handedly created both a sub-genre and sound aesthetic which would remain popular through to the mid-nineties." Teddy's history with the group's members dated back to childhood and, "A guy named Timmy Gatling from my neighborhood had grown to be like a big brother to me and a good friend. I was actually working on the Keith Sweat album when Timmy had first come to me with the idea of forming GUY." Not yet sold until on stepping back out from behind the boards given the success he was having as a songwriter and producer, the deal closer came when Riley first heard the voice of lead singer of Aaron Hall:

> I hadn't really thought about being in another group at that point because I had already been there/done that with Kids at Work and felt that my forte was producing, and my goal was to be behind the scenes. Then at the same time, I felt in order for me to be visually known and seen, maybe I should join another group. But I didn't want to force it. So one day, while I'm working on the Keith Sweat album in New Jersey, Timmy Gatling made what turned out to be a fated trip out to the studio with Aaron Hall. When they got to the studio, I immediately took to Aaron's voice, I really dug his voice. At the time, he didn't really say much, but he played the piano and sung.

> Well, when he sung, I immediately said to myself, *I want to work with this guy.* I didn't know that Timmy had brought him with the idea of all three of us being in a group. But that night, Timmy starts talking about starting a group. And he said, "You produce it," and Aaron basically intervened and said, "I don't want to do a group. If I'm gonna do a group, I want him in it," because he heard me play piano as well that

night. He didn't really know who I was yet as a producer, so artistically, there was a mutual respect there. And when that happened, I said, "Cool, I have some connections, and told Timmy: "We should check Gene and see what he's doing. And I know we can also go see Andre Harrell and he'll probably give us a deal because my next projects are Heavy D & The Boyz and Al B. Sure for Uptown." So once I made that hook-up between Gene and an already very excited Andre Harrell, the deal with Uptown was a no-brainer for everyone involved.

Following the usual trends by then with Teddy producing hits that still bring fans to their feet today like *Teddy's Jam, Groove Me,* and *I Like* which reached #5, #8 and #2 respectively on the U.S. Hot R&B/Hip Hop Singles Chart not in a fancy recording studio but instead once again in Teddy's make-shift studio in the living room of his mother's apartment in the St. Nicholas Projects, Aaron Hall revealed exclusively that, "We recorded the vocals for that record in Teddy's mother's bathroom, the whole twelve tracks! I used to be over at Teddy's house all the time, and we used to just be up all night making music in that living room all the time." Used for decades now to a state-of-the-art recording backdrop commensurate with his elite level of record producer, Teddy chuckles looking back as he confirms bandmate Hall's memory that:

> We didn't even make the first GUY album in a professional studio, believe it or not. It was made back in my mother's apartment where I was still living at the time in the living room, with the

bathroom acting as a vocal booth! The first song we actually came up with for the project was *I Like*. Timmy had come in with the first part of the verse, and then Aaron started elaborating and I was basically playing the keys. Once again, every song on that album was written by myself, Timmy and Aaron solely. Even though Gene added himself as a co-writer, he didn't contribute a musical note to that album! Usually, Aaron would come in with a melody or a piano part and I would broaden it, and take it to the next level.

Once we'd wrapped recording, we took the album down to a studio called Sound Works, right next to the original Studio 54. Then upstairs in that same building at another studio called AXIS, is where we were comped a lot of free studio time from the studio owner, Uncle Charlie. The funniest part of the making of the album was once we took everything we'd been recording at my mother's apartment studio and tried to re-cut it in the studio, we couldn't get anything to sound the same sonically or instrumentally. So we then had to transfer from an AKAI 12 Track all the original tracks, because there was just no way to duplicate that sound. So we took the 12-track to the studio, and individually transferred all those records from 12-track to the 24-track so we could stack more background vocals, make it sound bigger, and

that's how we did it. We kept the authenticity of
our music raw.

Even though their album had debuted at #1 on the Billboard
Top R&B Albums chart, it wasn't until the next year in 1989
that the group would hit with their first #1 on the U.S. Hot
R&B/Hip Hop Singles Chart with *My Fantasy*. A single featured
on the Spike Lee *Do The Right Thing* motion picture soundtrack,
a reflection of just how big the group was blowing up, it was so
hot in fact that Teddy remembered, "It got to the point during
the height of the first tour when we couldn't even get in the
building of our own show, that's how crazy it was for us. We
were it!" GUY – who Soul Train would in later years credit for
having, "Revolutionized the slow jam"– would achieve an even
greater cinematic profile when they were rightly approached to
write and record the theme to another film bearing the title of
the music genre Teddy had invented, *New Jack City*:

> We had the honor that year of recording the title
> track from *New Jack City* for the motion picture
> soundtrack. And given the film was titled after
> the sound that I was popularizing with my
> productions, and GUY with our sound, it was a
> highlight for me to see my music connected with
> such a ground-breaking gangster film for the
> 1990s. I knew they had to put something from
> me in there, so that the continuity of New Jack
> Swing. You couldn't really put that New Jack
> stamp on the film without it. That soundtrack
> almost feels like a celebration looking back of
> the mainstream cross-over my sound was
> preparing to make heading into the next decade.

In 1990, Teddy would finally shed himself of former manager Gene Griffin's suffocating shadow. For years, Griffin had taken fraudulent credit for Riley's work as both a writer and producer, most egregiously claiming writing and producing credits on Bobby Brown's *My Prerogative* when in reality he'd played no creative role in the song's creation whatsoever, as well as many other signature hits including GUY's entire debut album, where Griffin had claimed songwriting and producer credits though once again had no role in either creative functions. The L.A. Times in a cover story the same year, made clear who the public believed, reporting the fact that, "For more than a decade, Riley's touch has been among the most consistent, and imitated, forces in pop, placing him alongside Babyface and Dr. Dre as the ultimate shapers of contemporary urban sounds."

Finally free to fully breathe in the studio and inhale the sensation of a new generation thriving on his New Jack sound, as he crafted the group's appropriately-titled *The Future* LP. Riley was positioned perfectly to become one of the most influential and trend-inventing producers of the decade in both hip hop and R&B. This status had been earned in part because – as the *Times* continued – "One of Riley's strengths is knowing when to intercede and when to hang back and let his collaborators do their own thing. With Guy, this method allows the voices of brothers and co-members Aaron and Damion Hall to lift *The Future* out of the dance-music record bins to the sanctified level of soul music."

Teddy's talent for keeping things fresh was in full effect with GUY's second LP. With the band almost single-handedly spearheading the genre's continued relevance after *Billboard* noted that by 1990, "New jack swing, a hard-edged, high-tech blend of funk, R&B, and rap/hip hop, has been milked for all it's worth and run into the ground by GUY's numerous imitators in the late 80's and early to mid-90's. But in the hands of its highly influential originators, GUY, it sounds fresh and inspired...lead by the ubiquitous producer/songwriter Teddy Riley, the trio brings a definite urgency to grinding, forceful funk...to such slow jams." Keeping the asses shaking and the speakers rattling required a round-the-clock 24/7 work ethic from Teddy. When he wasn't off shooting a video or playing a sold-out live gig, he was in the studio, where the hustle-a-holic producer remembered:

> I spent the better part of 1990 completing work on *The Future*, GUY's second album and the first post Gene Griffin, which for me marked something of a creative triumph. And to finally be reading my name properly acknowledged as a writer and a producer without Gene riding my credit coattails anymore. We also had big hits with *Wanna Get With You* and *Let's Chill*, which went to #4 and #3 on the Billboard Hot R&B/Hip Hop Songs Chart respectively. Along with *Do Me Right*, which peaked at #2, and *D-O-G Me Out*, our fourth single to crack the Top 10 at #8.

The launch of the 1990s was an even crazier whirl-wind for Riley, taking him to even bigger heights than he'd ever dreamed when the newly-dubbed King of New Jack Swing received a call from out West from the King of Pop, Michael Jackson, requesting Teddy's immediate presence in the studio. A master marketer seeking to modernize his sound by aligning with the hottest hip hop/R&B producer on the charts, Jackson and

Riley's creative marriage was one made in heaven for both – creatively and personally – forming a bond that would last until the time of Michael's tragic death in 2009.

A full-circle moment for Riley indeed following his pivotal childhood inspiration watching from his grade school playground across the street as Michael and the rest of the Jackson 5 loading in and out of shows at The Apollo, *Vibe Magazine* years later would muse on the true impact that the charmed collaboration between Teddy and Michael had on the world, highlighting that, "MJ's musical alliance with New Jack Swing visionary Teddy Riley should be viewed in an...important context: It ignited R&B's next great run. Before *Dangerous*...New Jack Swing had enjoyed a hugely successful run as America's coolest trend-setting youthful soundtrack...Everyone it seems wanted that Teddy Riley magic, including the biggest entertainer on the planet – Michael Jackson...Jackson had taken Riley's New Jack Swing to new global heights making the newest era of rhythm and blues into the go-to pop sound." Taking fans back to the day the one-in-a-million call came, he remembers experiencing a momentary state of disbelief:

> I first got the call to work with Michael from his manager Sammy, who called my manager at the time, Harvey Austin, and said, "Michael would like to talk to Teddy about working together." The next thing you know, Michael himself hopped on the phone with Harvey, who in turn in his Wolfman Jack voice, said, "Hold on a minute, I got Teddy right here for you." And history was made. I remember being so nervous when I got on the phone, because the first word

out of Michael's mouth was, "Teddy..." and so I replied I'm sure sounding like his number one fan but trying not to, "Hey Michael," like I already knew him. So next he got down to business: "Are you here?" meaning in L.A., and I was back in New York, so I said, "No, was I supposed to be there?" and he said, "Yes, you're supposed to be here working with me, we're working on the record together."

So I'm sitting there in my manager's office in a daze, flabbergasted, and right then, he started asking me a bunch of questions about music and what I was working on at that moment. Then, he surprised me by asking, "Is it for me?" So trying not to sound too eager, I said, "No, I'm actually working on a bunch of things." And soon enough, he cut to the chase and said, "Well, can you be here this Saturday?" and I said, "Oh, no, I can't be there this Saturday, but I can be there the following Saturday." Now, you might think after having Michael Jackson call me to come out to California and work for him, that I'd have been on the first plane out. But the truth was, and I told him, "I'm very excited about coming to be there with you, but I also want to be prepared. I want to be prepared for you because I want to make sure that I have something that will blow your mind."

The try-out of a lifetime with zero room for misses, Teddy brought only hits with him when he flew out a week later to

Neverland to meet Jackson. After a sleepless, week-long studio lockout session, he revealed came courtesy of A Tribe Called Quest, confirming that, "What saved me making the Michael Jackson deadline was actually Q-Tip letting me use his studio to do the preproduction for *Remember the Time* and all of those tracks I made for Michael. It's funny, because we call it pre-production in the industry, but to me, it's really more like creating *for the creator* before the creation." Racing to finish up other pending deadlines for other major-label artists - reflecting the constant demand his production was in at that point - Riley remembered the crazy whirlwind of, "Working on the Jane Child *I Don't Wanna Fall In Love* remix, *Why You Wanna Dog Me Out* by GUY, and I was mixing *Make You Sweat* by Keith Sweat." When his attentions were turned to Jackson, along with artistic adrenaline, Teddy spills the secret:

> I had three studios running at the same time. I spent most of that time buried in making beats, but I always had a girl there in the studio with me for inspiration. In the case of getting ready to work with Michael, me and an actress friend of mine were hanging out the whole week keeping songs flowing through me and out of onto tape.

Hearing Jackson as the voice to take his sound global, he introduced the next wave of New Jack Swing with the tracks he produced for the King of Pop, impressing *Rolling Stone Magazine* at the time with how they, "Dramatically illustrate the versatility of his style. Instead of the cocksure strut of a New Jack classic like Bobby Brown's *My Prerogative*, the stacked layers of keyboards on *Dangerous* shift and percolate, varying textures over insistent, thumping rhythm tracks. The aggressive yet fluid dance grooves Riley helped construct – and his emphasis is on writing grooves, not traditional songs – prove a perfect match for Jackson's clipped, breathy uptempo voice...Teddy Riley replaces Quincy Jones as Jackson's primary collaborator on *Dangerous*, an inspired selection that is the key to the album's finest moments." He naturally hoped Jackson would wind up including at least one – let alone the seven Riley-produced tracks that made the final record, including Top 10 hits *In the Closet* and the worldwide smash *Remember the Time* – the producer confessed:

> Even if I didn't make the album, the point of the matter was: I got to meet Michael! That's the thing that was like the gravy. All the stuff he said about me, it was just something that: unless you were there you would never believe. I couldn't tell my friends, "Michael did this for me," or "Michael bought me a Rolex watch," or "He bought me a whole new set-up for my studio out in California, so when I come out there, I have a set-up."

> By then, I was very wealthy, so I had all of my stuff: I had like three racks of S-3000s, S-950's and 900s, about four MPC-3000S and MPC-60's, and I had Logic on an Otari computer, and I had bought seven Otari computers because they would go out on you, and I didn't want that to happen with me and Michael. So when Michael gave us our budget, he gave us a deposit of like $100,000. It was like, "WOW! Okay, what are we gonna do now? We're going to go get the

right equipment," and then I had this guy make me a rack system that connected everything through Midi and Man. It was just crazy!

A bedroom is in fact exactly what Jackson had custom-built for Teddy at the Hit Factory when they returned home from California to continue work in New York City, shaking his head as he affirms that, "He really built me a bedroom in the Hit Factory studios in New York, and had it done in twelve days, with the studio. They built a brand new studio, including bedrooms for Michael and I." The notoriously private Jackson's desire to lock down Teddy's undivided attention for the better part of a year and a half spoke volumes about the trust the biggest star in pop had placed in his new producer, a chemistry that Riley described this way:

> It was almost like when he used to work with Randy, that's what he used to always say, "You remind me so much of Randy, he would just come up with these grooves, and sometimes he didn't even know what he had," and he felt the same way about me, because he used to always say, "Do you know what this is?" And I'd say, "No, it's a track, it's a track for you," and he'd say, "No, this is genius." Vocally, on that song and others, Michael and his vocal arrangements are amazing. He would go in and try stuff, different background stuff, and when he goes to do his leads, he's amazing. We would go back and forth.

Michael possessed this beautiful presence in the studio as both a person and a musical genius, and it was constantly inspiring. He really was a special kind of star: I'd been discovering and shaping stars my whole career, but with Michael, it wasn't just like working on a whole other level, it was like operating in a whole other universe. He was the biggest star in the world at that point, and could have picked any producer in the business to work with, and he chose me, so I knew I had to deliver the strongest songs of my career. It was a great time in my life, because I was free of everything, and wound up spending fifteen months out in California working day and night in the studio with Michael and his engineer Bruce Sweden, locked down making music. We had all three studios running at once and we wound up locking out the entire Larrabee Studio complex for that whole year!

The moment many would argue was the album's finest, *Remember the Time,* was the kind of pure pop gold with a melody anyone could get stuck in their head, and after five weeks stomping all over radio, conquered it's way to #3 on the Billboard Hot 100 Singles Chart and #1 on the Hot Hip Hop/R&B Singles Chart. Simultaneously, it would reach the Top 10 around the world, including Spain, Australia, Italy, Canada, Belgium, France, Germany, Ireland, Norway, the Netherlands, the United Kingdom, New Zealand, Switzerland, and Sweden among other countries. Taking New Jack Swing global as Teddy's sound was exposed to millions of new listeners and the producer became a household name internationally,

Jackson was the first to recognize the song as an instant smash immediately after first hearing Riley's demo:

> I remember when he pulled me out of the room while I was working on the demo for *Remember the Time*, and this is after I'd just finished working in the studio on sixty or seventy tracks for him to listen through. That was the fifth track I played for him, and he loved all five. I played him *Joy*, which eventually went to Blackstreet, but he got to hear everything first to see if he wanted it. With that one, he just felt like, "This is not me," and all I could say was, "I can't tell you that you should have this on the album, because I already have seven songs," and he would say, "I trust your opinion," but he loved *Remember the Time* from the first time he heard it.

> It was important to give him something that will shock the world, where people just have no choice where it's undeniable, and *Remember the Time* – the hard drums, he just wanted stuff that would hurt you on the dance floor. That's what he would always say, "I need you to hurt me with this record. The mix, I need it to hurt me, I need to be laying on the floor from the kick drum, banging the room out!" That's the one thing about Michael, he loved his music so loud that the engineer Bruce Swedien and I had to leave the room sometimes! Ear plugs still didn't help, so Bruce would say, "Okay Michael, I'm

going to start the tape up and then leave the room," and the song's opening chords would come on while he was running out, and then as soon as those drums kicked in, Michael and Emanuel Lewis would just get down and dance all day!

Following the wildly-successful 35-million copies *Dangerous* sold around the globe, Teddy next opened his own Future Records Recording studio. An appropriately-named HIT factory based in Virginia Beach, here Teddy would not only produce hits like Blackstreet's signature #1 smash *No Diggity*, SWV's wildly popular at radio *Right Here (Human Nature Remix),* which reigned at #1 on the Billboard Hot R&B Singles Chart for a record seven weeks in 1993. More uniquely, the single featured an almost unheard-of Michael Jackson-authorized sample of *Human Nature* as a key hook to Teddy's brilliant flip of the hit for a new generation - and the early 90's classic *Rump Shaker,* which took his brother Markel Riley's group Wrecks-n-Effect to #2 on the Billboard Hot 100 Singles Chart.

It was here that his gifts as an A&R man for recognizing and mentoring young talent also led to the discovery of superstar recording artist/producer Pharrell Williams, giving the teenager still in high school the opportunity to ghost-write his rap verse on the song. Beginning a studio mentorship where Pharrell would show up at Future Sound after school to apprentice under Riley's guiding hand, recalling firsthand how blown away he was to find himself suddenly sitting next to his hero:

Pharrell Williams to NPR, 2015: "(Teddy's) one of the greatest producers. We got discovered at a talent show and then we were like trying to meet him, but it was the toughest thing because he was like super busy. I think he was like working on Michael's album. So when we finally met him, he was like, "I heard about you," and I was like, "What did you hear about me?" He's like, "I'm going to give you a shot. I got this song, I want you to write my verse." I was like, "OK!" So I wrote his verse for *Rumpshaker*.

That was like mind-blowing to be in a studio for the first time. We were all like, you know, Chad, Shay, myself and Mike, who was a fourth member at the time, we were all like tripping out. We were like, wow, this is like crazy. And I watched him like make so many records and also do like a ton of remixes. And he just had this style that was just unbelievable. And he's still such a huge influence mix-wise, too. But just watching his like his process was just like it was crazy. He just was meticulous about everything, like he would spend like an hour on a snare, just mixing a snare. I'm like, what is he listening to? You know, but for him it was crazy because he could just make everything pop, you know. And we were there for a while, we got signed as a group. And it was crazy... in the process, we got a chance to like write and produce songs for other people because that's how he had it.

Following in the tradition of all great record producers of giving the next generation a shot when it was obvious they deserved one, for Teddy, whether teaching an aspiring producer how to put a record together or producing an aspiring talent, he admits to almost always getting a bigger kick out of working with new artists than established artists, confirming that, "I'm always on the lookout to help out new talent, that's how you got a lot of the artists that are still doing things today just because I gave them a word or an opportunity. It's my calling."

Keeping the hits coming, after banging out a comeback single for M.C. Hammer after he signed to Death Row Records in 1994 with the Top 40 hit *Pumps and a Bump*, before launching his next supergroup the same year when Blackstreet's self-titled debut album produced the hit singles including *Before I Let You Go*. A Top 10 smash reaching #7 on the Hot 100 Singles Chart, *Joy*, which Riley co-wrote with Michael Jackson, the album also produced the hit single *Booty Call*. *The Source* - giving the group instant street credibility for a new generation of listeners - celebrated the album's success in playing, "Like a fat blend tape and it is consistently enjoyable...Blackstreet's debut is one of the better total R&B packages to come out recently."

After a million-selling warm-up, Teddy would head back in to the studio to take the group to *Another Level*, the title of the sophomore LP that would produce the biggest R&B anthem of 1996. "*No Diggity*" would send Teddy rocketing back to the top of the Hot 100 Singles Chart and earning the superstar producer-performer a Grammy Award for Best R&B Performance by a duo or group with Vocals in 1998. Instantly addictive from its now-legendary opening piano notes, Teddy takes fans back to the moment his hands first found them on the piano, knowing immediately he was on to something BIG:

> I had that hit, that piano hit that opens the song,
> I got it from the Roland 770 samples, and it's a
> piano hit and I didn't know what to do with it,

but I said, "You know what, I'm going to save that hit for something special, it's going to be something special that his is going to belong, and it happened to be *No Diggity*. The part just reminded me so much of when a show ends, that little cartoon melody they always played at the end of the credits. That's what I was thinking when I heard, "Shorty get down, good Lord, Baby got 'em open all over town, Strictly biz, she don't play around, Cover much grounds, Got game by the pound," (insert piano) then, "Getting paid is her forte..." Well, to me, that was sort of my rendition of what they'd do back in the day, where a comedian would say something, then would have the drum hit. So that's the things I do, I apply those things to my music, and I'm really good with doing that, so don't give me an idea, because if you give me an idea, I'ma make that idea blossom, I'm gonna bring it out. I programmed that whole song on the MPC-60, and still use that to date. I'm on the MP Renaissance right now.

Singing the infectious chorus and first and best known verse of the massive hit, Teddy's decision to feature fellow contemporary Dr. Dre, the West's equivalent of Riley in both the timing of their respective rise as influences in shaping their respective coast's hip hop scene over the ten years prior. A nod of mutual respect and benefit that Dre chose as his first post-Death Row Records single appearance which in the same time gave Blackstreet instant props with West Coast rap and R&B audiences alike, Riley credits visionary Interscope head Jimmy

Iovine – who coincidentally had both pioneers signed to his label – with making their crucial introduction: "Dre came to us because when he heard the song, before it had been released to radio yet, he told Jimmy, "Tell Teddy that I want to be in the video when he do this song, because I want to be able to dance on this song!" and I said, "No, if he's gonna do anything, he's gonna give me sixteen bars, because I don't want it to look like he's just in my video,' and that's how we did it."

Teddy would play a key hand in ushering in another new genre on the other side of the world literally when he shot to the top of the charts in 2012 as a co-producer on K-POP sensation Girls' Generation (SNSD)'s smash single *Boys*. A Top 20 hit on the Japan Hot 100 Singles Chart and a #1 hit on the South Korea (Gaon) Singles Chart, the world-wide smash sold a record-setting-for-the-genre 3+ million digital downloads and #1 on the Billboard K-Pop Hot 100, reflective of how hot the genre was that it commanded it's very own chart, where hits by EXO and SHINee landed too. With over a staggering 156 MILLION YouTube views to date, longtime Riley fan *Rolling Stone* in noted of the group's sensation that as, "The nine-member group recently unveiled their first international single titled *The Boys* produced by Teddy Riley...Girls' Generation have proven to be one of the top acts in Asia topping the charts in both South Korea and Japan."

Declared, "An icon in his own right" by BET 2016, that same year, the *Soul Train Awards* crowned the King of New Jack Swing with their Legend Award, which CNN – covering the show – argued was long overdue because, "There are few artists in the industry who have not worked with Teddy Riley. The super producer earned the Soul Train Legend Award and showed us why." The legendary producer has been showered in recent years by peers he influenced over multiple generations, starting with fellow hip hop mogul Sean "Puffy" Combs - who would go on to discover Notorious B.I.G. and pioneer the hip hop soul genre - exclusively credits Teddy with being, "The teacher: of Devante Swing from Jodeci, whose a student of Teddy Riley. Puff Daddy is a student of Teddy Riley. Rodney Jerkins is a student of Teddy Riley – he gave birth to all our sounds. It's evident. It's not even like we're trying to hide it, it's obvious."

With his D.N.A. now permanently a part of hip hop's own after thirty plus years, Riley's offspring have started to filter into the culture as his three daughters - Deja, Taja and Bobbie - came into their own as stars as members of the R&B vocal trio *R I L E Y*. Carrying on the legendary family name on the popular television show *Love & Hip Hop: Hollywood*. While Teddy has maintained a relevant force in shaping the millennial generation not only by default of his massive catalog of hits that are constantly sampled – either stylistically or outright – and fused into modern music, it's a reminder that New Jack Swing continues to reverberate throughout the ages. A point of pride Teddy in closing emphasizes as:

> Very important, because that helps you find out where you're going to have your longevity. Where are you going? You have to constantly think about the future in this business, because I've seen producers come and go. But I planted my seeds early, so early, and achieved everything I wanted to musically. And I'm still doing it today. I got people still enjoying everything that's musical about me, saying, "Please, release another one." And that's the stuff I love right there. That's from me being musical and

innovative, and trying different things that people had never heard before.

https://twitter.com/TeddyRiley1

"I've always said that when I stop having fun, I'll stop doing this." – Mannie Fresh

CHAPTER FIVE
GO DJ – Mannie Fresh

Every region of hip hop geographically has had a producer-prodigy that pioneered the key sound signatures that region of the country is stylistically identified with: for California, it's Dr. Dre with G-Funk; in New York, Teddy Riley with New Jack Swing and DJ Marley Marl with the art of break-beats; and in the south, more than any other, credit for the birth of bounce goes hands-down to the one and only Mannie Fresh, who admits twenty-five years later that he's fought the title a bit over his stylistically-varied career: "I've never been a producer who created one thing. I get it, I am the dude who tripled the hi-hats and the snare-rolls and all of that, but that's just one thing, because I've got so many crazy musical personalities listening to me that it's nuts. So it's really a playground for me to explore everything." Long before he took on a mentoring role with Lil Wayne similar to that Dre did with Snoop Dogg or produced #1 hits like *Go DJ* and *Back That Azz Up*, Mannie had already found his calling behind the turn tables as a DJ, confessing:

> To date, it's kind of hard for me to wear that title of "producer" because my first love is DJing, and the producing thing is kind of like I do it for fun. I'm the type of guy, I like to look up and see the crowd all in unity and moving as one, that's a good feeling that music brings to me, even producing. If I go somewhere and they put on one of my songs, and for a second it makes people forget about everything else in the world, that's what I want to accomplish, that's the feeling that I love.

Born with the wheels of steel turning in his DNA, a young Mannie grew up in the shadow of his father's turntable stands and stacks of record crates, watching and listening to his father's every move like every young child does until one day, curiosity got the best of him:

> I kind of mimicked what I saw around my house because my dad was a DJ, and I felt like this was my calling, because I remember like yesterday

the first two records I that I mixed, *Good Times* by Chic, and it took me all of like fifteen minutes to figure out how to back-spin, how to make a rub, how to cue the record and all of that. I was like, "Wow, this is meant for me," it was like hearing somebody do that and you already got an idea of how it goes, and then when you get a chance to do it, you're like, "Wow, I've already figured this out." Then when you fall in love with something, you're gonna be there all day, so I took those two records and I mean, for twenty-four hours literally, dissected that record from every point of the record you could possibly have or do.

After that, I started remixing records, just kind of copying what I heard, and it just turned into producing. I grew up on Disco records and old Soulful R&B songs, that was the era that my dad was playing, Marvin Gaye, Chaka Khan, and *Good Times* by Chic was one of my favorite songs, The Freak, Ring My Bell, those type of songs – I grew up in that era.

While Mannie kept two fingers scratching on the record, he had another constantly on the pulse of the crowd, honing arguably the most basic tenant of record production and DJing: putting his own original spin on the records he was playing, recalling that, "Once I started DJing at local house parties around New Orleans, whenever a song would come out, I would kind of change it around myself to make my own new version of it. So it really started out with me copying everything else just to make my own personal remix. That gradually turned into, 'okay, if you can do this, you can have your own little original beats and music.' But I really wasn't even setting out to be a producer, I was just a DJ that just started making my own unique little remixes of songs. Like I would add a bass line on top of something, or say like find an acapella version and put another beat down, and at that time, I didn't realize that's really what a producer does, because I was a street DJ just doing my little remixes."

Though he didn't know it then, in years to come, other aspiring DJ/producers in the same position Mannie was in the early 80's would be spinning *his* records as they were going through similar learning stages. Still, back then, because the south still was hip hop's wild frontier and largely unknown on the national scene and still finding its own voice as a sound, Fresh found an unusual freedom creatively to inject anything that grabbed his ear stylistically into his remixes:

> This was around the early 80's, New York was like the mecca of hip hop, so we really were on all the records that New York cats were putting out, and we were trying to mimic what they were doing. Before Run RMC, you had Rapper's Delight, which was big from the Sugar Hill Gang, and Grandmaster Flash and what they were doing. You had all these songs that were cool songs they were just remaking and rapping over, so right then and there was the birth of hip hop. It just woke you up to like, "Wow, it's incredible, what they can do if they dissect the doing and do their thing to it," and what was a super-change for me was, I was in love with all

the Grandmaster Flash songs and Sugar Hill songs, but when Run-D.M.C. came, I was like, "Okay, this is it," because this was the era of the drum machine.

When I first started, there weren't any samplers around. So I first started on a Roland 808, Moog keyboard, and just like a 4-track, and I was lucky enough to have some 1200 turntables. Like I said, my dad was a DJ, and he was able to pass his old turntables down to me, and back then, I didn't even know how serious 1200 turntables were back in the G, but I had those along with this big club mixer that was probably huge. At the time, all mixers were probably the size of an album cover in length, and I just started out taking all of these cool songs that I got from my dad's record collection, and I got to dissect them and take all of these bits and pieces from them and make my own crazy little remixes.

Mannie's professional moniker would reflect the blind-faith support level he'd had from his proud parents from day one, including his father naming him out of an organic love and belief in his son that began ironically not with music but with the fashion that came with it:

My dad nick-named me Mannie, so that was already there, and Fresh came from tennis shoes, kicks. A lot of people don't know that, but everybody in the neighborhood where I was like, "Man, dude just loves tennis shoes," like to this day, so everybody would say, "He always got fresh kicks on," and most people called me 'Fresh,' and it's ironic, because you had Doug E. Fresh in that era, but I had two nick-names: it was either Fresh or Mannie, so I decided to put both of them together.

Soon gaining the ear of not only house partygoers but other prominent local DJs around the city, MTV later reported that, as a consequence, "The New Orleans native got his start in 1984 as a member of New York Incorporated, arguably New Orleans' first hip hop crew." As his reputation grew with the size of the parties he was now DJing around the crescent city, rather than having to seek out voices to rap overtop his tracks, they would find him and in 1987, Fresh's foot into the door to producing his first professional records would arrive:

When I first hooked up with Greg, this record company that was in New Orleans recording had actually hired me to do some scratches on the record, and they asked me, "Do you know any rappers, any emcees?" I told them I knew one guy, MC Gregory D, who I knew from rocking house parties and wound up finding him, bringing him to the studio, he auditioned for them, and they were just like, "Well, can y'all put a record together?" and we were like, "When?" and they said, "Tonight," and we said, "Oh, we'll do it right now!" So we put that record together and from there, stayed together as a duo for the next ten years or so.

My first drum machine before I got the 808 was the Boss DR-55 Dr. Rhythm drum machine, but once I got the 808, it was like the basics of hip hop, we would make all the beats at my house on my 4-track recorder, and then all those early DJ Mannie Fresh and MC Gregory D records, like *Freddie's Back* and *Buck Jump Time*, those were songs we did in the studio when we had the opportunity to go in a real one.

The technical side of the process would come as naturally to Fresh as musical ideas did, the prodigious producer could keep physical pace with every creative invention and innovation his mind was throwing at him, "Because I grew up in the era where my dad was a DJ, and he was big on knowing what you're doing. He used to tell me, 'Don't get nowhere and don't know how to hook your own stuff up,' and from the process of how it was explained to me – input, output, etc – I was pretty much already there by the time we were sitting in a real studio, so it was easy to figure it out, once somebody was like, 'Hey, this is the patch bay, this one goes with one, this one goes with two, and vice versa...So I feel like, in that sense, I was blessed because I was already prepared for that."

Whether or not Fresh was consciously aware of just how big of an untapped boom-to-come he was sitting on with bounce at the time or not. Its natural evolution made perfect sense to Mannie as he invented it in the studio. Breaking the science of his sound down to its purest definition and one he's been guided by throughout his entire 30+ year career, the producer proudly explained that, "Bounce to me, the definition of it is *the essence* of hip hop. It's the beginning of hip hop: it's just about call-and-response and a beat, and it had to grow."

Experimenting with that formula through the old-school, tried-and-true creative trick of throwing everything at the wall to see what stuck, Mannie's open-minded approach led to some of bounce's earliest local dance crazes as the infectious new sound found its footing in the hottest clubs around the city. Creating the kind of buzz necessary for a social culture and scene to sew and grow around the sound as it quickly caught on, the producer reminisces fondly on some of his favorite homegrown byproducts inspired by fan reactions before bounce began to break nationally:

> When I was making bounce beats back then, I would try all kinds of stuff. It's funny, right now we have this term called "yacht bounce." Yacht bounce is like 80's songs mixed with a bounce beat, but we were really doing that a long time ago. I was trying to force anything that I could that would go with a bounce beat. And the crazy thing that bounce did for New Orleans and a lot of cats around New Orleans really don't realize this, is it kind of bridged the gap because it brought culture to some street kids who'd never, ever heard these songs before. As long as you had that bounce beat behind it, you could pretty much force anything in there, you could have an Elton John with a bounce beat behind it and the next thing you knew, the whole club was singing it. And then when you tell somebody it's Elton John. They're just like, "Man, who is Elton John?" I remember we used to run Kenny Rodgers' *The Gambler* with a bounce beat and

the whole club would sing that song, but nobody knew it was Kenny Rogers. They just knew it had that banging beat to it, and the words were simple enough to follow.

By the dawn of the 1990s, Fresh's beats were beginning to creatively converse with the raps of a new troupe of homegrown emcees, and well before he linked up with Bryan and Ronald Williams, his sound was already ringing out around the underground, recalling that, "I was a couple of albums in before I even hooked up with Cash Money Records. Even with the U.N.L.V. stuff and the volume of music that I was putting out, it was never, ever hard to do it because I was just having fun. I was just doing what felt natural to do. Before U.N.L.V., there was this artist Pimp Daddy, and before him, you had Lil Slim. The first thing I ever produced was the Lil Slim record *The Game is Cold*, and it was a local hit in New Orleans, and that kind of gave me and Cash Money this relationship. When I did Lil Slim's record, it took every bit of probably five minutes to do it, and they were like, 'Damn! That's it?' And I was like, 'Yeah, I know what's going on out there. I'm DJing everywhere in the city, this's gonna work.' So the popularity of that made U.N.L.V. come in. When they came in we did *6th & Baronne*. It was the same little scenario with my little 4-track recorder, two Realistic Radio Shack mics and it was magic. Because nobody had really just done bounce and just put a little bit of elements to it."

Deconstructing the genius of Fresh's sound from the heart of how his DJing exposure to live audiences large and small throughout New Orleans had given him an invaluable education on the appetites of the city's music fans. Seeing what they were reacting to on the dance floor from the old school and new school, and most importantly, how they mixed with his own original spin, the *New York Times* – who hailed Fresh as "the city's greatest hip hop producer" – qualified crowning him so by correctly noting that Mannie "pulled the musical legacy of New Orleans into the 21st century...(perfecting) an exuberant electronic sound...that helped make their city an indispensable part of the hip hop world...Whereas Timbaland, another great southern hip hop producer, loves the spooky precision of computer music, Mannie Fresh has always been more gregarious. Gravitating toward shiny synthesizer lines and rippling drum-machine rolls that evoke the exuberance of New Orleans brass bands...you could hear brass bands in the synthesizers, drum lines in the rattling beats. And Mardi Gras Indians in the sing-song lyrics."

Recognizing the untapped mine waiting in Mannie's head to be turned into gold and platinum hits, versus most DJs who would have leapt at the opportunity to become an in-house producer for a local label on the rise, Fresh ironically was happy as a solo act working behind the turntables. Already making plenty of money and a name for himself doing what he loved, the producer confessed that initially, "The thing of it was, I wasn't really looking for anybody to do this with, I'm gonna keep it a hundred with you, I wasn't going 'Well, if I do this song, we're going to have a long history,' because like I said, I was still focusing on DJing. I was happy with what was going on with me in my city, because basically I had every club that I ever wanted to DJ and every house party I wanted, and at that age, I kind of felt like I was successful at what I was doing. I was making nice money, so I wasn't really setting out to become the in-house producer for Cash Money, but then every time we put out a project after that first UNLV record, which just showed a little bit of elevation, it just got bigger and bigger and took on a life of its own."

Still, Fresh recognized in the same time the irresistable opportunity to act as a talent scout developing a roster of talent around his own sound with the label's owners deferring almost entirely to Fresh to make virtually all of the musical decisions for those acts' albums in the process. It was incredible freedom for any producer, and a meeting of the minds was struck after Mannie found himself impressed with basically the way Cash Money picked their artists back then, which was based from a DJ perspective of what was going on in the streets:

> Like if I said, "Hey, I did this party last night in the projects and this kid came and he rocked it, he got this song that people are starting to gravitate to," so they went solely on my word, like what I thought was hot, because I was out there in the streets DJing. One important discovery made that way was when I first heard Juvenile, and told the label, "Hey, bust this dude Juvenile, y'all need to get with him. He's nice right now." I'd bumped into Juvi at a couple of gigs and he'd started rapping these songs to me, and I was like, "Oh my goodness, dude!" So he pretty much had that whole first album, *Solja Rags*, done. He just didn't have any beats for it, and I told Cash Money, "This dude Juvenile, he's nice, he got everything that y'all could possibly want to bring y'all to the next level." And even when we did the B.G.'s, the B.G.'s originally were Lil Wayne and B.G. I was like, "You know what? The little dude B.G. himself, his subject matter is so different from what Lil Wayne is

doing, you kinda gotta let him go on his own because they don't really mix."

Moving at a hustler's speed in the studio, where Fresh expected his artists to show up ready to work from the moment they stepped inside the vocal booth. Cash Money recruited hungry emcees looking for a soundtrack to rap and rep over. Mannie was happy to oblige, knocking entire albums out in the time it took most recording artists to track a song or two. Inviting fans inside his hit factory for an up-close look at just how tight a ship he ran, the producer ran his studio with Military precision, proving that performing under pressure can pull the best creative results out of competitive artists like Juvenile and B.G. and future superstar Lil Wayne with the talent to rise to the occasion. Moving at the speed of the genius inside Mannie's mind churning out multiple instrumentals at a time, he reveals of the hypersonic work atmosphere that:

> We made entire records in two days at most, and all of that stuff we made up on the spot because we only had one rule, which was *stick to the subject*. Because early on, we had this problem with just rambling, and I'd have to say like, "Dude, if we're going to do this in a professional manner, we gotta stuck to the subject," because it's not just you, you've got to outdo the next dude, and that extended to the way the Hot Boys worked in the studio as well, all the Cash Money groups that I produced.

Fresh's sound would first take on regional fame with B.G.'s *True Story*, bringing Cash Money Records a level of visibility outside the city that allowed a buzz to start building as Mannie's bounce sound started to take over night club and strip club dance floors all over the south. Drawing both the ladies who wanted to dance and the hustlers from the block due to the combination of his beats and what the producer felt was a lyrical authenticity because, "B.G. was the raw street. The crazy thing is, both them and Wayne started out as bounce artists, and it was just more or less saying, "Hey dude, let's try another format with them," and B.G. did that and went crazy with *True Story*. That was a break-out record for Cash Money regionally, but what made it even more crazy is his lyrics on it because people weren't used to nobody over a bounce beat doing lyrics. It was more of call-and-response or some chant. But now you got this record *True Story*, and it's like, "Okay, it got a little music to it, it's got a little swang to it. And he's saying something,' and then we followed it right up with *Chopper City*."

Still considered a southern classic, in 1996, where national critics first took note not only of the new sound bubbling up from the Bayou, but the mad scientist behind its creation, as reflected in the *L.A. Times'* observation that, "As enjoyable and polished as B.G.'s raps are, it's the powerful production of Mannie Fresh that drives the album. Using rapid-fire drum tracks, stunning synthesizers and gripping guitars, Fresh creates a hip hop aural utopia." By the time they got to the third B.G. album in three years with *Chopper City in the Ghetto*, which *XXL Magazine* noted was, "Entirely Mannie Fresh-produced." And, "A landmark release for Cash Money," the producer was ambitiously evolving his bounce sound from its basics into a more sophisticated soundscape. This musical evolution was reflective of his desire to grow artistically in real time with as the label's popularity as both prepared to step onto the national stage:

By the time B.G.'s *Chopper City in the Ghetto* came along, they said, "Well, you know, Manny, his bounce thing, that's his baby, he got bounce on lock, if you're looking for something that's a bounce beat in any kind of way, go to Manny Fresh, he got it." And I was like, "Well, you know what, I appreciate this. Bounce is going to be around forever but, I got so much more in me," and was ready to move on to the next level, and so *Chopper City* was just to show that, "Hey, wow, I have growth in me, I can be a musician, and I can show you some different things I can do, as far as musically, my drum patterns and all of that."

Around then, I'd started to move toward musicians more, like I was still on my SP-1200, which was probably a six second sampler or whatever, but it's the greatest – to me – drum sampler in the world, to this day, because of the gritty sound it puts out. It samples at such a low bit-rate that it's nuts. It makes the drums sound so gritty and nice, once you sample them and slow them down, you can't duplicate that no kinda way.

I was still using the same mics, but every time I did something, I was learning something, so by the time we'd gotten around to *Chopper City*, I'd met some engineers and was always asking questions, "Okay, this is how this goes," so what I was doing was I would take internships at studios at whatever and do stuff just for free, just to kind of ask questions or whatever, because I wanted to know, "How do you EQ this, how do you make this work?" And when I had people explaining that to me, it brung our production to a whole other level, and it brung our mixing skills to a whole other level.

Feeding the demand that kept coming from regional record stores, clubs and radio as he went about creating a new generation of hip hop. *Rolling Stone Magazine* would later argue the label did so as quickly as it did in large part based on the momentum of, "The extraordinary futuristic productions of Mannie Fresh. Fresh, in codifying the southern bounce sound, effectively became the most significant rhythmic innovator out of New Orleans since the Meters' legendary Porter/Modeliste rhythm section." Mannie's instinct for how to musically compliment Juvenile's vocal cadences and styles of delivery had a rhythm that moved as smooth between them and in the way it played for fans as Michael Jordan and Phil Jackson's, with the producer proudly elaborating in reflection:

> Your job as a producer too is to create the identity with whoever you're working with, especially if you're working with different people and you do albums, so it was like, "Okay, how do you create this identity for Juvenile and how do you keep it Juvenile? How do you make sure his album is a little bit different from what you're doing with Wayne?" So personally, you've gotta know something about them, because you kind of know what they feed off

and what's going to be the best music for him? What could possibly be the best single? Juvenile was always ready to go like I was, so we had a great working relationship in the studio. I think Juvi is at his greatest when he knows his song. So if it was a song he already knew and he had perfected it by the time we got into the studio, then it was great.

Twenty years later, iTunes would highlight *400 Degreez* as a record that has stood the test of time, "Not just as Juvenile's shining moment but also as the album that forced everyone to suddenly take this dirty south collective very seriously," highlighting as the primary conduit, "Producer Mannie Fresh's seemingly bottomless well of hot beats." *Back That Azz Up* would send Juvenile into orbit as a star would simultaneously launch Cash Money as a national record label and its in-house "super-group" featured on the song, starring a colorful cast of personalities including Lil Wayne and Mannie as an emcee in his own right. Ironically, the latter two appearances turned out to be the kind of studio happy accidents that often make up music's most classic moments. Both for introducing the world to Wayne, along with what would go on to become one of the millennium's most popular hip hop culture keywords to describe success, with Fresh revealing that:

> *Bling* was actually popular on Cash Money before anyone else ever heard it, that was just something that we always said, and on top of that – this is what's so cool about Wayne, you gotta know this – Wayne was *not slated* to be on that song. Wayne kind of forced his way on that

song. Because he was in the studio the whole time when we were doing the song, just sitting around. Even though he was like, "Listen dude, I got a part for the end of that record. I know this is gonna be a big song. There ain't no way in the world I'm not getting on this song," and I was like, "You know what dude? Go ahead, finish it off." Because he'd told me, "Yo, come on dude, I need to be on this song!" And once I told him, "Go ahead dude, let me hear what you gotta say." And the part that he put on there, he did in *one take*! So he already knew what he was going to say. How he was gonna do it, everything. Wayne was this whiz-kid and he had this wordplay. He was smart at doing creative sound effects, and whatever he could do to get your attention.

With the smash single's international success, Mannie would introduce classical music elements prominently into bounce for the first time. Laying strings overtop a hip hop beat in a stroke of new musical discovery for the genre at large that would become widely imitated in the years to come, it was one that he remembered first occurring to him as he was pushing himself creatively to keep it as *fresh* as possible, recalling the moment of clarity as one that arrived after he asked himself, *How can we do something that's gonna make it creative?* Bounce was just more 808 drums, it wasn't no music or nothing like that, so I was like, *Well, how can we take bounce music on the level where it's just gonna be worldwide? Where everybody's gonna hear it and enjoy it.* So I was thinking *What would make black culture and white culture come together?* Well, if the beat is bounce then it's gonna be crazy! But I could put some classical music on top of it, and we're gonna win people who we never, ever thought we could touch! Building the song's musical architecture around an acapella vocal skeleton following the same blueprint he and Juvenile had previously, Mannie remembered a sketch of the song coming to life in his mind instantly:

> When Juvi first rapped me the song, I kind of already knew the elements of what I wanted to do with it: how I wanted it to go, how I wanted it to move, how I wanted it to start off. Juvi had a different idea in mind, and the crazy thing is when he first did the song, I did the last verse on it, and the pattern I did on the last verse, he went back and re-wrote it and said, "Well, you know what, I gotta do my pattern just like yours, the same rhyme scheme of what you did because it feels a whole lot better." The original way he was doing the song was more straight, it didn't have no swag to it, it was just like a regular rap, so when he told me that, I said, "Dude, just put a little twist to it or something." When he's saying, "Yeah" after every word, the only reason why he changed it is because I did the last verse and I was doing the flow of that. And then he was like, "You know what? I need to change my two verses to have the same flow of how you're saying it. I gotta say something where it will make sense for people to answer back." And I was like, "That would be a better way of doing it, versus regular rapping." And Juv was like,

"Yeah, I felt like the way you did the third verse."

This is what was already said, and you probably could interview some of them and they would say it. With my production style, they would say, "Dude, you always knew how to compliment your own raps," and I was like, "Well, I'm not a rapper." So I knew how to put breaks and beats around my raps that will create extra things for the listener, and I try to do the same for any rapper. So I'm like, "Hey dude, it's gonna be something that's gonna enhance your words, there's gonna be some breaks and all of that." So when I was doing *Back That Azz Up*, I was thinking about this part right here where the breaks goes into these big old massive hits. That's where the girls are gonna go crazy, and all of that.

Go crazy they would for both the song and its orators, making an overnight sensation out of Juvenile, and launching the Hot Boys on their way, as *Vibe* would later affirm, to creating, "Their own international movement...with producer Mannie Fresh." With an album already under their belt following the release of the regionally-successful *Get It How You Live* album in 1997, with 1999s *Guerilla Warfare* – released on the heels of Juvenile's 400 Degreez album ascending all the way to #9, cracking the Top 10 on the Billboard Top 200 Album Chart - the Hot Boyz would rocket even higher when their sophomore LP debuted at #5. Crossing over into the hip hop mainstream, *The Source* would hand the album 4.5 mics out of 5 mics in a stellar review that complimented both lyricists and producer for, "(Rewriting) the game over a steady stream of crushing beats" upon release in the summer of 1999. The Oz behind the board directing virtually every musical aspect of the songs he was creating in the studio, versus slaving away for hours on end searching for his next new sound, Fresh's talent accelerated at such a sonic speed:

It was kind of easy because when I came to the studio, I already had these songs designed, and the later I got into production, the more organized I got. By the time we got to that point, I was to the point where I'd already written the song in my head, and already knew the hook, and I did the beat around the hook so it could be totally a marriage when you hear it, and I knew exactly whose voice was going to go where in the song. So it was totally orchestrated before I even got to the studio, and then once we were recording the song, I would tell whoever was performing on it, "Hey dude, I just done this beat last night, I already put the hook on it, you gonna do this part, you're gonna do this part."

Like when we did the Hot Boys, I was thinking of old Grandmaster Flash and the Furious Five because I was like, "You know what, nobody has ever been able to do like four emcees, and come in and out and blend since then," and thought it would be a breath of fresh air because it hadn't been done in a long time. I always reverted back to listening to older music, like, "What made this

song great?" or "What made an album great?",
and I was like, "Well, let's listen to this and
figure this out, and kind of put our own twist to
it."

By then, gear-wise, everything was still basically
the same: I was still with my SP-1200, and just
kind of dabbling in different keyboards. I play
keyboards, but I don't read music, and it got to
be something that I wanted to do that was
different parts, like bridges, I would always go
find myself a player and tell them, "I know
exactly what it is, and I'm gonna tell you the
notes," which would always make the recording
process go faster. I guess that's what made me –
to a certain degree – a different producer from a
lot of people, because I can tell you exactly what
it is, what sounds creative, and I find this: the
people who read and are the greatest musicians in
the world, they're horrible producers because
they think with theory.

Transporting fans back into the studio as he transposed his
mental symphony out onto the keyboards with his futuristic
chordal innovations, Fresh revealed that, "What I did a lot of
times in creating chords is I would layer sounds, and it would
sound like I just played a whole bunch of notes to create the
chords, and my chords kind of always went around whatever the
bass note was on. If I hit a C for the bassline, then I would hit
maybe three Cs in a higher octave or whatever, and that would
be the chord for whatever the bassline down below was, or if I
moved up to a G, then I would do the same thing at a higher

register, and hit three Gs and make the chord. So if you have somebody who does music and they're telling you, 'Well dude, that's not really a chord,' I was always like 'It sounds cool to me, and everybody else is great with it.'"

That included the fans, who mattered most, and as Cash Money rang up millions of dollars in record sales around the country, Fresh was their secret weapon behind the boards and all of the hits. A unique distinction for a producer to have no competition as an in-house producer, his contributions didn't go unnoticed by the national press starting to take notice of what Forbes described to the masses as, "An indigenous-to-New-Orleans brand of hip hop called bounce," appraising as the label's, "Most valuable asset: in-house producer Mannie Fresh," as "Cash Money releases quickly took off and were selling big numbers in New Orleans and throughout the south. Many of the artists took the popular bounce style with its call-and-response, often very raunchy chants, and combined it with streetwise lyrics to create a strain of 'gangster bounce' that proved incredibly popular."

Working round-the-clock to keep pace with all the music that was naturally flooding out of his mind at any given time. Mannie's dedication to his craft was that of a perfectionist, reasoning that the video shoots and stage shows were the real work as, "I'm just a studio dude, I never really leave my environment. That's where I am all day every day, till we get tired, that was always my process: let's put in work till we get tired. We were always programmed to say, 'Shit, it doesn't take us no more than a week to do an album,' and the next week we were mixing it. A lot of times, I was just making beats up in the studio right then and there, and I tell people all the time, I've got tons and tons of songs that are already done that I've saved, and a lot of the songs that have always been good songs for me, great songs, I made them up right there on the spot."

Banging out albums at an astonishingly prolific rate for any of his production peers at the time, between 1995 and 2005, Mannie Fresh produced a staggering 30+ albums! This catalog would encompass every hit that Cash Money and its stable of artists racked up, including his own group, Big Tymers *I Got That Work*, which moved 1.5 million copies, and the platinum-selling follow-up *Hood Rich*. Achieving a peak based in large part on the strength of Mannie's own fan base, *The Village Voice* reported that, "The Big Tymers briefly became the biggest act on Cash Money, scoring the Billboard 200-topping album *Hood Rich* and the smash single *Still Fly*, which peaked at #11 and became the biggest Hot 100 song to feature Williams. The several other minor hits the Big Tymers scored in 2002 and 2003, pretty much all featured Mannie Fresh more prominently, with Baby playing the stoic straight man to the goofy, charismatic producer." Not the first producer to rap over his own beats, it's still a rare club in hip hop. In contrasting the process of producing himself versus recording other rappers, Fresh's secret has always been to never take himself too seriously:

> The thing of it is, I always was that dude who had my own little stuff that rocked the party, but I never took it serious. So I was just like, "Okay, I'll try," but I never looked at it like: this is something serious. I just was always like, "I gotta have some kinda skills to keep my parties going, I've got a little something," but I never took it serious. But this is what kind of made it take on a whole face of its own: I would say things with shock value. So people would be

like, "Dude, for some strange reason, your timing ain't always correct when you're rapping, you rhyme, but at the same time, what people do love about you is they like your shock value. They've really never heard nobody say some of the things that you would say!" So I was like, "Well, you know what? I'm gonna keep doing what I do!" And on top of that, it was great therapy for me. I think because it was like, "Okay, I get to express something that I really been wanting to say, and how I want to say it. And I don't have nobody to tell me: 'You can't do that.'"

Big Tymers offered the music media an opportunity to lavish a new wave of praise on Mannie, now one of the most talked-about producers in the hip hop and mainstream music press, with *Spin* highlighting Fresh as, "The driving creative force behind the Big Tymers." The magazine would also celebrate his colorful ability throughout record after record to, "Create a zanily incongruous sound-world where electro B-lines bounce beneath classical melodies played on g-funk synths, and house vamps and techno stabs chitter alongside cocaine-crisp guitar fills." Rapping overtop alongside Mannie was perhaps Cash Money's least-naturally-talented emcee, but one who got as much tape time as he wanted on the label's projects since he was its co-owner, Bryan "Birdman" Williams. The equivalent of Eazy E to Fresh's Dr. Dre in terms of how much work went into producing and developing Birdman as an artist by the time he was co-starring on the cover of Big Tymers' debut album, *How You Luv That* LP:

The thing of it was, Baby (a.k.a. Birdman) was looking for popularity, so if you got your artists and see what's going on, and there was a second where he felt in the beginning like, "Okay, I like what's going on, and I'm the head behind this, the money man," but he wanted the popularity. He was like, *"How do I get that going?"* There was a huge learning curve there, because you're taking somebody who has no concept of rap and how do you figure this out. So what we decided to do was, I was like, "Listen, this is what we're gonna do: you're not a rapper, I'm not a rapper, we gonna make up a whole other term: Gang-spin. It don't matter if you don't rhyme or whatever, whatever you flow at or whatever, you're just gonna tell it like it is, say what you know," and it was successful to a degree because nobody never took that concept.

So that was the gimmick with the Big Tymers, because it would have took a miracle if I'd taught Baby how to rap, and said, "Hey dude, this is what a rhyme scheme is, and this is the pattern we doing..." That concept never went over easy with him, so it was just like, "Listen dude, this is what you do, say what you know, that's all you do."

Testing Mannie's editing skills to the fullest back in the pre-digital days of recording, Fresh developed a process for coaching Birdman through his verses for each of the album's tracks, sometimes line by line, with the producer confirming that,

"Most of recording Baby was punching in or it would be moreso of, "Hey, this is what we're gonna do, I'll give you the lines, you just flow back behind me and you say it, or vice versa." You had Wayne who did a lot of his stuff as well. So Wayne would write some of it, I would write some of it, and then Baby would follow behind whatever we said. He was cool with it because he understood the concept that this wasn't what he naturally did."

Legendary hip hop bible *The Source* was clearly impressed with what Mannie had pulled off, concluding that, "(Fresh's) nimble and ingenious talents on the boards make (the album) an overall success...(His) talents lie on making head-bangin' funk music...the infectious rhythms will make you wanna drip yourself in platinum pieces and head Uptown." Convincing enough to take the duo into the Top 20 on the Billboard Hot 100 Singles Chart when they rose all the way to #11 with *Still Fly*, the producer seems to still shake his head in a little bit of surprise at how successful the side-project became, musing that, "I guess what made the Big Tymers so creative to people was the shock value, because it was like, 'Man, these dudes will say things that are so far out of reach but it sounds so cool.'"

One of Fresh's talents as a producer was spotting the diamond in the rough that was Lil Wayne, working with him to craft a concentrated collection of albums as Mannie worked hands-on helping Wayne develop what became the signatures of his rapping style and sound. Identifying what shined brightest in Wayne's potential to make him feel he was worth the creative investment of time, the producer remembered being most impressed by how badly he wanted it:

> I always felt this way: if you worked hard and did your thing, everybody on the label was gonna have their turn, and Wayne was ready. He

was always hungry, first one there, last one to leave. He always had something for a song, like if it was a dead spot where it was like, "Damn, what do you we do, we've only got 6 more bars?" Wayne would be like, "I got it." That was always him, or if somebody didn't have a verse, he had it. And I was like, "Dude, this dude is always ready," and on top of that, with him being ready too meant he didn't have to always go back to his tablet. He would just be like, "Man, turn the track on, I got something for you." He kept that work ethic, like, "This is my job." Everybody now talks about how he puts out records out every other day. Man, he's been doing that since I first knew him in the 90's.

So the observations I made from that was, "This dude is real serious about this, he don't write down too much and he knows these songs, and I've never heard it before!" That always impressed me, because Wayne was the type of artist who every time he said something, you'd never heard it before, and there was originality in it from his swagger with it, to his tone and his wordplay...all of that. And what made him super-unique when he was young is he kind of figured out a way to get his point across without going gutter on you, without cursing, and it was just as hard as anybody else on the song.

Seeing that Wayne was a star with crossover potential to become the world-wide icon he ascended to over the first decade of the millennium, Mannie decided to try something different with the album's production. It was a risk versus staying with the standard label sound that the *Chicago Tribune* would later validate as paying off with their note that, "This set stands out from other Cash Money releases because producer Mannie Fresh, for the most part, strays from the bounce rhythms that are his signature. The album is more theatrical and sparer than his previous work, and its sound-beds will be embraced by the streets." Introducing futuristic soundscapes that were a leap forward for Mannie into the new century, standouts like the title track to Wayne's debut solo LP, *The Block is Hot,* elevated both artist and producer to the same level of comparison that Dre and Eminem were garnering as trail-blazers leading a new generation of fans into the hip hop's next dimension. Remembering that the album went down like it was meant to happen, Mannie to date regards Wayne as among his favorite production collaborations, first and foremost because the emcee made his life easier by the simple fact:

> Wayne always came ready, out of everybody, he was like, "Dude, I know all of my records." So it was a pleasure to work with Wayne, and I can't ever remember a time working with him where it took long and it was pressure, and I remember when we were doing *The Block is Hot* album, by the time dude was done with the second verse, he was talking about the next song, like, "Man, I got this other song, I'm going to run the verses down to you." The crazy thing was he didn't have to go to his notepad, he would just say, "This is going to be the next song," and would just be

rambling on, and I'd be like, "Dude, let's finish this one first!" (laughs)

Wayne's hero was Missy Elliott back in the day, and Missy had like this crazy word-play with her and sound effects, and I kind of think what I liked about him was he had no problems with saying that, even though Cash Money kept this whole little thing about, "This is inside, we don't want nobody to have nothing to do with this, no kind of influence, none of that." But in reality, all of us were influenced by somebody, but just for street cred, they always wanted Cash Money to look like they weren't influenced by nobody but what's here.

After maturing Wayne's sound through 2000's platinum-selling *Lights Out*, where critics like *Rolling Stone Magazine* sounding almost relieved to hear that, "Mannie Fresh is at the board once again, and the beats here are staccato and jittery, suited to Wayne's precariously controlled persona." 2002's *500 Degreez*, inspired *USA Today* to note that, "Luckily, Manny Fresh is still cranking out the beats that make your body move." Mannie knew he needed to force a reinvention of the Cash Money sound in order to ensure both its and Wayne's future by reclaiming their musical relevance in the present-tense. To that end, producer and protégé would return to the studio as a duo, blocking out any other noise than that they were creating alone together on what would become Wayne's first true classic, the opening volume of his franchise album series *Tha Carter*.

Heading back to the drawing board sonically three years after he'd debuted the next era of his sound on *The Block is Hot* single, Mannie had a producer's heart-to-heart with his artist prior to heading back into the studio, sharing for the first time with fans highlights from the pivotal pep talk that, "When we were getting ready to do that record, I remember we talked about it at a concert in Dallas or somewhere, right before we were going into the studio, and I was just like, "Hey dude, we gotta bring it on this one. We've gotta do something that's gonna make people talk about you, that's gonna show them that you've arrived! That you're that dude. It's your turn, it's your shot right now.' And from hearing some of the stuff he was spitting to me, I was like, 'Wow, this dude really got something to say." And right before *Tha Carter*, Wayne was becoming big in New Orleans because he was doing mix-tapes and everyone was like, "Wow, you got all of this bottled up." I was paying attention to some of what he was doing and how creative it was."

Keeping his finger to the pulse of the street the way Mannie had with his DJing, Lil Wayne was truly the millennium's first mixtape phenomenon. Helping to usher the underground street staple of hip hop into a mainstream norm, *Rolling Stone* reported that, "As he moved into his twenties, Wayne was hardly a household name, and he began to feel as if his record label wasn't doing all it could to promote his music. So he came up with a plan of his own — in a blatant violation of the economic law of scarcity, he began working nonstop, recording and releasing countless mixtape tracks, generally available for free on the internet." An outlet no doubt for Wayne's genius to grow and a clear sign he was itching to break out artistically in the same way Mannie was from what had up to that point been the Cash Money mold. To that end, the producer stepped up on both their behalf to fight against the Williams' brothers' initial pushback, underscoring the importance of the role a good producer should always play in standing up for their artist's right to push boundaries creatively even at the risk of commerce:

> What we did completely different about that album was we left out the business aspect, so anybody who could have disagreed with something wasn't allowed to come to the studio. Nobody really liked it because you got the record company, Baby and Ronald, like, "What's going on?" I was like, "Listen dude, Wayne's gonna have his people there, I'm gonna have my people there, and we're gonna give it to y'all when we're finished." I'd told Wayne, "Let's make this easy on both of us man, bring your A-game and I'll bring my A-game. We're going to do something phenomenal. But we're gonna leave all of the stress out of it, we're gonna keep that element completely out of it.
>
> Because, on *Tha Carter*, what Wayne wanted to show more than anything was that he was grown up. He said, "I can live with Lil Wayne being the name, but I'm tired of this whole image of Lil Wayne being a young, innocent rapper dude. I'm trying to show that I have arrived, I'm an adult," and I said, "Okay, that makes sense." So before anybody can shut that down, we decided to do that just me and him, so we wouldn't have no slack from nobody, and we had to fight to get that done too because when we were turning in songs, it was exactly how we predicted: "Dude, come on man, this ain't Wayne, this record's just

kind of all over the place." And my proud response was, "Yes it is dude," but we weren't paying attention to him. If you listen to the mix tapes he was doing, we weren't paying attention to this, but the public was paying attention. This is what they want from him right now. They want to see growth in him.

Graduating out of his artistic adolescence just as he turned twenty-one, MTV would congratulate Wayne's musical maturation "over Mannie Fresh's Bayou space-bounce" as "the boy from *Bling Bling* became *Tha Carter*." Spotlighting Mannie's success in stretching out once again into a new sonic realm with Billboard instantly hooked on the, "Addictive soundscapes courtesy of Mannie Fresh." *Tha Carter*'s music would prove a crucial portal for Wayne to step through with what the producer proudly felt, "Was the beginning of his creative freedom, and I think I really had to push for it to say, "'Hey, I'm gonna have to work the Trump card, I don't ask y'all for much, but I think this is gonna be the one, this is it.' By then, we were full-on studio, and we cut the whole *Tha Carter I* album at Patchwork Studios in Atlanta, which gave us a little bit of geographical breathing room too. I still was using my SP-1200, just kind of finding kicks and snares off of old records, whatever I could find to make different kits. By then, I had met this guy, Leslie Brathwaite, who was a great mixer. I just got to focus on producing, thinking, *With this dude mixing, I'm gonna be straight*. So Cash Money had said, "You know what? If you really see it that way, then we're gonna let it slide." Then when it came out, it came out slow, that's what's so crazy about it. At first, it was like, "Okay... man, damn, maybe...then all of a sudden, it just hit with *Go DJ*."

An ode of sorts in the classic vein of emcees shouting out their DJs on record, Mannie opens the track with an introductory declaration of his own over a futuristic-sounding beat, "Right about now, it's yo boy, ya heard, back again, D-J Mannie Fre' fresh err fresh, fre' fresh...Go D-J, that's my D-J, go D-J, it's my D-J," before Wayne launches into his signature hook. Giving Wayne an instrumental as imaginative as the lyrics he was dropping over top, looking back over a decade later, Fresh feels the song has stood the test of time simply for the fact:

> There are songs where going back and listening to them, I think, "Okay, this was *way* before it's time, nobody thought they were ready for this." Ironically, the instrumental for *Go DJ* was actually an old U.N.L.V. song that had been done for years, but had never shown up on an album, and Wayne wanted to use it on his record.

> By that point, the writing pad was completely gone. That was amazing to me. I was like, "God damn dude! How many songs we gonna go through? And you know all of them off your head?" Because he would just rap them to me off his head, and then he'd go into another song. You gotta look at Wayne like this, and some people use the word genius, but to me, it's perfection. It's more of, "If you keep on practicing your craft, you're gonna get good at it." And he took his craft seriously and perfected it.

Following the break-out cross-over success of *Go DJ*, the Williams' brothers finally began to heed Mannie's advice, seeking to break outside of the Cash-Money box and begin working in collaboration with artists not within the immediate camp, leading Fresh to the opportunity to produce for mainstream R&B artists like Toni Braxton and R. Kelly. The producer was finally starting to broaden his Coastal collaborations beyond the Gulf to work with superstar rappers like Ice Cube, an extension he felt was made possible both because of Wayne's convincing move toward the middle as well as the lucky timing:

> By 2004-2005, I felt like Cash Money was fishing, they were just like, "You know what, we're looking for whatever's gonna work. Whatever we gotta do to make this work," and an example of that was signing Petey Pablo, and what was so great about that album from critics and everybody, they were like, "Mannie Fresh surprises me yet again." I would even say it was challenging, but the cool thing was like, with Mack 10, by the time he got to the studio I was like, "Dude, I know all your music, and I know what Cube has done with you." It wasn't hard to work with West Coast artists versus producing southern rap artists because I'm a DJ, and so I told both of them, "I'm not that far from what you've done, I'm gonna try to leave you in the realm right where you at with what you do." On top of that, the song I did with Mack 10, Ice Cube and WC, *Connected for Life* on the *Bang or Ball* LP, that was one of the biggest songs on the

West Coast today and it was a song that came together in all of ten minutes in the studio.

Entering his fifteenth year as a working record producer whose reputation preceded him among critics and fans alike where expectations were involved. When he decided to let listeners inside *The Mind of Mannie Fresh* on his first solo album, USA Today mused that, "Not surprisingly, the music is banging," while Billboard predicted that fans, "Are going to be revisiting this album for years," complimenting the concept album as, "A rare journey through a busy producer's mind" versus being a passion project he'd been slaving over in the studio for years. Mannie revealed that he actually only delivered the album under pressure from his label. Now in need of hits like never before with Lil Wayne and Fresh as their only flagship acts – and obliged out of loyalty to the mothership, confirming:

> It was more the record company, Baby and Ronald saying, "Man, we need you to do an album," because whatever stipulations they had with Universal, they had to put out a certain amount of records, and so I was like, "Okay, cool, no problem." The crazy is, you put somebody who do all these records in a studio, and I'm used to – if I'm doing an album for somebody – doing twelve songs, thirteen songs, but you put me in the studio alone and I'm in DJ mode as well, that's why I had so many records on there. I was like, "Dude, this is what I do, so you gotta stop me somewhere and say, 'Hey, you're cutting too many records,' because I could keep doing this every day." So what I

decided to do with that album was because I had
too many records. I was going to make it
something like a day in the life of what would go
on with me, from the phone messages and skits I
had and all of that. So I had to figure out some
kind of way to make the album personal to me.
So everything that was actually going on that
week that I was making that record is what I
made the album sound like. I haven't met too
many people that don't like that album, because
people say like, "Dude, it's the bright point in
my day, still to this day. If I want to have a good
day, that's all I need to do is put that on. It's a
story that will make you laugh," and it played
like a story.

Rated as "grade-A production" as always by the *L.A. Times*,
who concluded that Mannie as an artist delivered "a wide range
of moods, styles and tempos throughout the 17-cut collection."
After a decade spent creating a catalog full of literally hundreds
of masters for Cash Money Records, Mannie felt the label had an
exclusive on his sound for long enough. Desiring to branch out
on his own creatively, he had a financial motivation as well after
arriving at the conclusion that, "Nothing to bad mouth them or
whatever, but financially, Cash Money could never give me what
the owe me. That's not what I'm built on, I'm more of a
comfort person. I'm not tripping on millions of dollars, if I'm
comfortable, and I'm happy with that, I love doing music and I
feel like it's going to take care of me. I had some shit that was
going on between me and them that I really couldn't believe, like
I had somebody point out to me, "Hey bruh, here's a publishing
check they cashed, you never got it. And when you're seeing

things like that, you're like, 'Wow, I never thought they would have did this,' but once you see it, you can't get around it. It was in black and white right here in front of my face, and that was an awakening to me, where I looked up out of my drum machine and saw what was going on around me, and was like, 'Well, everybody got a couple of houses and a few cars and all of this, and I'm just doing music and not really getting paid for what I'm doing, and everybody else is just living a lavish life.' It was time."

As soon as word hit the wire that Mannie was a free agent, to no surprise, his phone started ringing off of the hook from artists who'd wanted to work with him for years, as well as new comers from a generation just coming up into the southern rap game who jumped at the chance to work with the legendary producer. For Mannie, the *fresh* start came with doing what he'd always loved, just on his own terms:

> I was in an environment where I felt like I could breathe, I just was doing what I normally do, but there was no pressure, and whenever I was doing sessions with other people, it was so enjoyable because I just showed up, we talked, we vibed, and we did some good music. And I was like, "That's what's been missing for a long time, this is what I missed about this."

Keeping the hits coming with *And Then What*, the debut single off Young Jeezy's debut album, *Let's Get It: Thug Motivation 101*, Fresh's next collaboration with another ATL-superstar would earn him another Billboard Hot 100 Singles Chart Top 10 Hit with *Big Shit Poppin' (Do It)* peaked at #9. Digging into his crates whenever he's needed inspiration for the next hit throughout his career, Mannie drew as a muse on the classics, confirming that, "I was always listening to music, and if I felt like I had got stuck somewhere, I would just go back to listen to old music, Marvin Gaye, just to get me influenced and motivated about doing it. All I had to do was revert back to listening to music and go hang and talk with my dad and I'm good. We'd brainstorm or whatever, because I always asked my dad what he thought about certain songs, and he was a big influence, because he'd be the person to tell me, 'Okay, you did that already, that sounds like that, figure out something else.' Or he would give me songs that was cool songs and say, 'Okay, make this one your own, turn it into something else.'" Bridging the two generations and genres as masterfully as any producer of Mannie's age who'd brought the music they were reared as an influence into the music he was making now, Fresh proudly points to the legendary lineage of the Big Easy's own Meters as one such influence who opened his ears for the first time to new sounds:

> I used to always ask my dad, "Hey, give me a bunch of cool songs to listen to," and even growing up in New Orleans, I didn't know anything about The Meters till my dad turned me onto them. I remember the first time I heard all The Meters songs, and was like, "Wow, these dudes are from New Orleans? This is incredible," and after you listen to that for maybe a week or go, you're filled with ideas. They're just so raw and funky, it's nuts, from the kick and way the snare sounds on those songs. The bass lines, the organs, that music is like nothing else, and on top of that, you've never heard anybody come close to The Meters in that era. It's like, "What

were they thinking?" It was so funky, and they've been sampled by so many people. We have no idea, "Okay. That's The Meters," until you're actually listening to The Meters' Greatest Hits, and then you could pick out like forty songs that hip hop hits have used in their music.

Arriving at another recent collaborator, Kanye West in recent times recruited Fresh to join his G.O.O.D. Music production team, a think-tank of the industry's finest musical minds that Mannie confirms, "Is based on so many different people it's crazy, there's just artists and a bunch of producers, and the cool concept of G.O.O.D is: you can really branch off and do your own thing. It's more of a co-sign, basically saying, "'You belong to this family, and you do a couple of songs with this family, but nobody's holding you here, you can do whatever you want to do.' We don't have any time limits, we just got bunch of songs, and have been just building this whole arsenal." A full-circle journey for a relationship that began with Fresh acting in something of a Big Brother capacity to Kanye when he was starting out in the business, MTV noted of the signing that, "West doesn't forget where he came from" as Mannie reminisced on fond memories of seeing him come up when Cash Money was in its early 2000s heyday:

And like I've always said, it's so good to be nice to people in this business because you never know when you're gonna see that person again. So one night, we were reminiscing on back when Kanye came through Cash Money when he was just starting but he didn't sign with us, and I remember telling him and the label when he'd played us some beats back then, like, "Hey bruh, that dude got something, what he's doing is so creative!"

This was when Kanye was just starting out, when nobody knew him yet, and he'd asked me when he'd rolled through New Orleans to work on something, "Hey, I need some equipment," and I was just like, "Hey, you can borrow my drum machine, keyboard, whatever you need..." I remember he called home, and told his mom and everything right there, and was like, "Hey, you'll never believe this: I'm using Mannie Fresh's equipment right now!" And I'd told him at the time to use whatever he needed for as long as he needed, and it's always been nothing but mutual respect between us ever since.

Linking up years after Fresh had departed the Cash Money fold at a chance encounter after a concert right as West happened to be launching his G.O.O.D. record label. Tapping the aforementioned braintrust to collaborate as a super-group of sorts, Mannie reveals he essentially joined by happy accident, "After I went to his shows a couple of times, and the crazy thing is – and if you got a chance to talk to him, he'd tell you – we never even really talked about music, and afterward, he just put me on the spot, and was like, 'Man, play me some tracks,' and I was so far in DJ mode that I wasn't even going say, 'Well dude, if I get a chance to play you some songs...' I had a bunch right there, and once I started playing him tracks, he was just like, "Damn, how many songs do you have?" So I told him, 'Well, this is just one of my little phones or whatever, but I got about

200 beats on here...', and he was actually surprised, like, "No way in the world," so we started going through all of these songs and I remember he was tripping out a little, like, "*This dude literally has 200 songs on his phone!*" Recognizing that Fresh could keep pace with his own constantly-racing musical mind, Mannie decided to turn the volume of praise up a little:

> I asked him, "Well, you want to hear something else? I got my iPad with me, and I got like probably 100 on there..." Then his eyes got even wider and he asked me, "What do you do?", and I was like, "Dude, I do this every day," and he was impressed, like, "Damn! This man is playing bangers to me." And for him to acknowledge that, that's cool. He was like, "I love what's going on right now in southern hip hop, but the reason why I signed you to this deal is: I'll go get the source. I'll go get the dude who created all of this, rather than go get a bunch of copy cats."

> **Kanye West:** I was thinking when Mannie was playing them joints, I was like, "Man, he's definitely the best producer. He created this shit, and to this day, the shit is just on that level. He could do soul, he did all the Cash Money albums, like for real, like RZA. Let's really think about it man, motherfuckers don't do that shit man. He did twenty albums, and it didn't have nine songs on it, it was like eighteen songs. That's fucking amazing man, motherfuckers don't do that now!"

Mannie Fresh: Dude is very quick in the studio, and is challenging because he always wants to do new things, he wants to go against the grain. He told me in the beginning, "Hey dude, I don't want you to just feel like you belong to me, go to whatever it is you do to make money. The only thing you're obligated to do is: "If I say, we're going to meet in Hawaii and do some music. And then from there, you can go back to your life and whatever it is that you doing, and on top of that, if you wanna do a deal outside of me, you have my blessing." If you're a producer, the definition of your job is to make music and not to limit it.

Speaking on his other teammates, who took the field together on the *Cruel Summer* album, which debuted at #2 on the Billboard Top 200 Album Chart, Mannie shook his head at the dizzying roster of talent who worked on the project, confirming that, "Everything that's on G.O.O.D is crazy, look at who they're affiliated with: you got Kid Cudi, Big Sean, Common, and of course you have Kanye. When I was in London working with them, Will.I.am came by, and I was just like, 'Wow, this whole G.O.O.D family is just so nuts, it reaches out to all kinds of artists stylistically!' When I start talking to a lot of cats, most people kind of put me on the urban side. There's so many other producers that I love. And would love to sit down with and just pick their brains. Will.I.am is one of those dudes, and I was like, 'Oh my goodness, to be in here with cats like that, I don't even know... this is nuts to me.'"

Returning to the spotlight in recent years with his second solo LP, *Return of the Ballin'*, *Spin Magazine* hailed the record as,

"A testament to the craftsman-like creativity of legendary Cash Money beat maker Mannie Fresh." And, "An unadulterated dive back into the NOLA sonic architect's boinging stripper joints and dirty mind." The producer remembered utilizing the old-school sounding board of his live spinning as a barometer for what was and what wasn't keeper material as he put the project together:

> You know what inspires me, to go DJ a gig? And I know that's where I get my inspiration. I still love what I do, and I think about all the people who go to work who hate what they do, that's enough inspiration right there for me to keep doing what I do. And don't get me wrong, I'll have those times where there's a whole month where I'm in a funk, and I'll force myself to listen to some music, and then say, "Well, you know, that doesn't really sound like anything you'd want to put out." But, you know how you get back in that mood? Go DJ If I go DJ and have got back in touch with the crowd, and let me see the people and I'm feeling them, that's makes me feel like, "Okay, it's all relevant again," because I was having fun, and on top of that, you get paid for it! That's the biggest honor in the world, but as I've always said, "When I stop having fun, I'll stop doing this."

> Right now, I feel like this is a rebirth of me anyway, I'm starting from scratch – which I don't mind, because it's cool to get to know another generation and everything that they feel,

and what's going on with them. So it's Homework for me, and I'm going around and DJing for people, seeing what they react to, what they love, what they don't love, and then I'm like "Okay, now I will return back to the studio."

Mannie did just that in 2016 when he and country songwriting superstar Dallas Davidson – responsible for penning some 22 #1 hits on the Billboard Hot Country Songs chart over the past decade – reached out to the producer for the same reason Kanye did, to go directly to the source, with *Rolling Stone Magazine* reporting that the success of the collaboration that, "Built on breezy strums of acoustic guitar, ornate piano filigrees, and a loping breakbeat, *Laid Back* shows Davidson to be a capable singer in addition his mastery of chart-ready hooks." Seeking Mannie out to tap into a different artistic voice than he was used to writing or singing in, Davidson – already known as a vivid storyteller – painted a picture for fans of their creative back-and-forth in the studio that illustrates just how much a master producer Fresh has become by this point in his twenty-five year career:

> **Dallas Davidson:** The single we released was named *Laid Back*, and the album will be called *Country Boy Swagger*. I'm not a rapper, and I'm not even going to attempt to be a rapper – but I am a singer and a songwriter, and I wanted to put my voice on some stuff and have some features on there, and do it over a true hip hop beat. I'm not trying to insult any Nashville track guys, but I wanted the best of the best, which is

Mannie Fresh, and using a hip hop sound and then writing on top of it. And that's what we did.

I had to call him and he said he'd do it. And I just was like, "Oh my God! He's actually going to do it," and then when we got together it was magic, it just all clicked. He got what I wanted to do and it was just easy. We wrote some songs pretty quick, and then they had Big Boi from Outkast come in there on *Laid Back*, which also features Mannie and Maggie Rose, and now Mannie's producing the whole album, which all started from this country boy swagger idea.

I can tell you what was out of the box was going into a vocal booth how Mannie approaches it, and freestyling, where I'm literally going into the vocal booth, on the mic, and writing a song as I sing it and it became comfortable really quick because he's just super chill and it's almost like, I wanted to do so good, I wanted to impress him almost. So he got the best out of me and made me really on my A-game as a writer and coming up with cool melodies and lyrics just from staring at me in the vocal booth. He hit record and has this beat that's a masterpiece that he's done, and it's up to me to write the lyric and the melody, so that certainly was out of my comfort zone, but I wound up that now, starting to write more like that because it's a lot more freeing, so to speak.

Arguably among the most prolific producers in hip hop history, *AllHipHop.com* recently revealed that the "Louisiana legend...has over 600 published works according to BMI," an astonishing catalog reflective of the constant channeling of genius at work that shows no signs of stopping as Mannie agrees in closing that:

> The crazy thing is, I really don't think I've done my best record yet. I really haven't because I've never been able to really pinpoint something where I can say, 'That one right there.' I don't think I've done it yet. You know what's kind of scary to me? Is when I do it, I kind of got a feeling that it won't be the song that everybody's thinking. It won't be based on the numbers or what it did. It will be something that I just felt good about. At the end of the day, that I did my best is what's most important to me, my very best. And I've come to the conclusion that you're not gonna win all the time, because you could do a good song and nobody buys it. As long as you know you did what you were supposed to do, you can live with that. I just want to be remembered for music that unified people.
> *www.djmanniefresh.com*

"Just try to get the sing-song line 'Mario C likes to keep it clean' out of your head." - Entertainment Weekly, '98

"The greatest musical quality of Yauch's voice was that it evoked an urgency: even when he was being offhand, the sound of his voice made you feel alive." - LA Times

CHAPTER SIX

"Mario C Just Puttin' It On Wax!" – Mario Caldato Jr.

Any fan of the Beastie Boys' is a fan of Mario Caldato Jr., who – as *Tape Op Magazine* quipped – is that "guy who's mentioned and raved about on just about every fifth song on any Beastie Boys' album." Even when you don't hear his name being shouted out by Ad-Rock, Mike D or MCA, you've heard them for years rapping overtop his co-productions on hits like *Sabotage, Intergalactic, So What'cha Want, Root Down, Body*

HIP HOP HITS

Movin', The Skills to Pay the Bills, Sure Shot, Gratitude, Pass the Mic, and *Just a Test* among *others!* Mario's awakening to the unique way his ear heard music began decades earlier when his father bought a Sears Silvertone organ for the house:

> That was the first thing that got me drawn into music a couple hundred dollar organ. I was five years old, and it was a relatively big deal to have this machine that made sounds around the house. Even though I didn't know how to play it, just hitting notes and changing the buttons to violins and trumpet sounds or whatever, and horsing around with my sister, it was a gas, and that kind of really first got me into pushing buttons and messing with the sounds.
>
> Eventually I got into piano and took lessons when I think I was nine or ten when we got a piano, and did the classical thing, but I enjoyed the organ more than the piano, that was always fun so I had both, and would end up horsing more around with the organ. Then starting to get into the popular music and Rock – Deep Purple – and stuff that was going on. I eventually started playing in bands in eighth grade, at twelve, thirteen years old. We had a little school band and I was the only one who had a keyboard, so I got to join the band playing keyboards, and that kind of got it all started. We started doing a couple recordings on 8-track back then, the drummer's dad was a jazz drummer who had an 8-track player that recorded, so we

would set up two mics and record on this little portable thing.

Versus hip hop because the genre hadn't been invented yet, growing up a child of 70's rock radio, Mario remembered "listening to AM radio every day going to school in the mornings, I'd hear the Stones and pop songs and everything constantly." By the time high school rolled around, he would begin making connections with other musicians who shared his interest both in playing and experimenting with home recording, first meeting his muse, Mark Ramos Nishita in his mid-teens, who he credits with really getting him into recording:

> My friend Money Mark, we were in high school and he was two grades ahead and going to a Junior College, and working in our Theatre Dept. doing some music for a play. He decided to do his own music, and went out and bought a 4-track, a reel-to-reel Kiak 3440, and learned how to record his own stuff. He'd play a drum beat, and then a guitar and a bass and a vocal with a little four channel mixer, figured it out, and made his own music, and I was blown away by it, saw the stuff, and was like, "Wow, this is really cool, this is something else." I'd been doing the band thing live for a long time and hadn't thought about the recording side of it – actually making recordings – and he had his set-up at home, and would have to set up in the living room and would always have to tear it down, because he lived in a small house with his family and there was not a lot of room.

Well, as luck would have it, I had just moved out of my house and was living in a back house, and had two rooms – my bedroom and a spare room – and the spare room was like open, and he said, "Hey, can I bring my stuff over and we can set up?", and I was like "Yeah," and he brought over his studio – the 4-track and little Yamaha P.A. mixer with built-in reverb and E.Q. – and left it there. He'd come over in his spare time and on the weekends, and say "Hey, I got a song here, I wanna record it," and he'd show me how to be an engineer: "Keep an eye on the levels here; keep this close to 0; don't let it go too hot or too low; and adjust the volume here; turn up this channel; make this one a little brighter..." He really got me into the recording process.

Finding that the operational mechanics of capturing sounds paired up perfectly with his curiosity about creating them, Mario and Mark began applying the "learning by doing" philosophy to their craft, getting their hands on every new piece of recording gear they could, "just building up an archive of songs and equipment. From our years of 4-track recording, we did that for four or five years regularly, so one week Mark would show up with a dynamic microphone, and then with a condenser microphone, then an echo unit, then a reverb unit, and a fazer, and slowly worked on these skills to the point that it started sounding kind of edgy and cool."

In a demonstration of just how far back Mario C goes in the game, he first encountered his future long-term collaborators the Beastie Boys by luck in the mid-1980s, "Hanging out at Power

Tools regularly. After going there for about a year, one night there was going to be a performance, and they had set up a turntable and some microphones. The Beastie Boys were in town, I think they were touring with Madonna at the time. They only had like a single out, *Hold It Now, Hit It*, and they were going to perform at that club. They basically had a small sound system for a pretty big club that held like 1200 people, and I remember it was a really exciting atmosphere that night. The music stopped suddenly at one point, and these crazy white kids from New York get up on stage, and grab the mics. DJ Hurricane was on the turn-table, does some scratches, they're getting ready to launch into the song and there's this big 808 that comes on and the sound system shuts off! Then the mics all died, and they were like, "Hello, hello." They throw the mics down and walk off-stage pissed off." Seizing the opportunity to put his audio talents to work in a demonstration of what has always been one of the central requirements of a true producer – the ability to find a way around any technical difficulty to keep the artist working – Caldato Jr. recalls coming to the rescue:

> I was in the audience with them, and was thinking, *God, these guys need like a sound guy, this is embarrassing them.* So I went back and talked to one of the club managers and said, "Hey, you guys need a sound man? This is embarrassing, the sound system doesn't work." And he says, "Tell me about it! What do you know about sound?" So I told him I was a sound man, and he invited me up to the DJ booth to have a look at their equipment. So I saw the problem, told them, "This is way underpowered." So next I said, "It's not set up

properly, I know what you need. I've got power amps, cross-overs, and all this stuff." Next he says, "Well cool man, come back next week and bring your stuff." The following week I came back, set up the stuff, and the sound system was 100 times better. And they were like, "Woah!" I brought subwoofers, raised speakers off of the ground, and we had Go-Go dancers dancing on the subwoofers all excited – it really changed the sound and the atmosphere. And the DJ was really excited about it! This was Matt Dyke, and we hung out every week and slowly built a friendship. I'd come out and watch him play records, and when he had to go to the bathroom, he'd let me sit in for him on the turn tables, and say, "Play this record here." I'd be helping him select some songs sometimes, so we struck up a musical connection.

Having made himself Dyke's go-to soundman, Mario carved out a confidence within his connection with Matt that eventually led full-circle back to Caldato Jr. and Money Mark's studio, laying the foundation for what would become arguably among the most successful D.I.Y. production house in West Coast hip hop history. Even while it doesn't ever get the credit in this respect it deserves, Delicious Vinyl – versus the sort of fancy, "proper" recording studio that many of their competitors had access to produce the caliber of hit that Mario, Matt and Co. succeeded in doing:

He worked out of a studio in his living room! After a few months or so, he'd said to me, "Man,

I really want to make my own music," I have a 4-track machine and recorded my friend playing drums, and I said "Bring it down, we'll hook it up," which he did, and we hooked it up and tested it out, and then queued it up, dialed it in and EQ'd it up, and then he goes, "This is going to be cool." So in the middle of the night when he had set going, this was going to be the drum break-down section and we were going to play the 4-track recording, and he was so excited. So he says, "Wow, this is great, I gotta make my own music, I can do this." And I was like, "Yeah! Recording's pretty easy, I've been doing this for a long time, recording, I made a record, a 7-inch." So this inspired him enough to say, "Dude, I've got some money, I wanna buy a machine, an 8-track recorder and a sampler and drum machine so I can make some hip hop stuff."

So I said, "Great, I'll go with you," and we met up and went to the music store, picked out a 388 8-track reel-to-reel recorder, which was like a mixer/recorder all in one that came out in the mid-80's. Then he got an SB-12 sampler/drum machine when it first came out, and started learning how to use that. The SB-12 was the one that had a 5-second sample, and all these hip hop guys started using them, it was just a kick, snare, and a one-bar loop and a half, and they'd have to speed up the record and then slow it down to get more time on it. Matt obviously already had all the records as a DJ, and was sampling all the breaks and beats, and started putting it all together and mastering the drum machine. We were both learning the SB-12 at the same time, but Matt mastered it, and would call me up to come over and record him, and that was basically the beginning of Delicious Vinyl.

Industriously, the label actually began mining for artists out of the throw-aways from major label demo trash-heaps back in 1987, proving the adage, "One A&R's trash is another's platinum record." This proved to be true after, "He partnered up with Mike Roth, who was working at a label as an A&R assistant going through demo tapes. So his department would get these tapes, and it would be like, "No, next, No, next," filtering out shit and throwing most of it in the trash. He'd go, "Wait a minute. That guy was cool, I'm taking this one home." So he brought one home one day that had Tone Loc written on it, and happened to have his home phone number on it. Then, within a short period of time, he found another one in the trash. "Hmmm. Whose this guy Young MC? I'm taking this one too." Mike was crucial in picking up these tapes, taking them home and showing them to Matt. Matt would be like, "Dude, that guy's voice is dope. Let's use him!" So they called these guys up, and said, "Hey, we're making a record, do you want to rap on it?" And these guys would be like, "Hell yeah!" So we'd literally go and pick these guys up, because Tone Loc didn't have a car back then. I drove down and picked him up in the Crenshaw district. Then, drove him back to the studio, play him the track, and have him throw down."

The first song Mario C and Matt Dyke ever recorded with Tone Loc wound up becoming one of the great cult classic hip hop pot classics the West Coast ever produced, and the debut of what *The Source* highlighted as, "A sound unlike what was poppin' at the time in LA." versus *Wild Thing* or *Funky Cold Medina*, where the production team tapped Marvin Young, aka Young MC to ghost-write Tone's lyrics. Caldato Jr. credited another of the album's highlight tracks, *Cheeba Cheeba*, as, "Something that Loc just came off the dome. Actually, Matt has a record that we sampled called *Cheeba Cheeba* by George Benson that we used in that song. It was a theme, and so they went to Loc and said, "Hey, we've got this song, this cheeba loop, maybe you could rhyme about cheeba," and then Loc went from there. So they sampled up some of it, programmed some beats, and let Loc do his thing." Once *Cheeba Cheeba*, which Billboard importantly noted, "Made waves at the time as one of the earliest pro-marijuana raps on record (of course, this was before Cypress Hill, and Nancy Reagan's '*Just Say No*' campaign was still fresh in the public's mind)," became an underground hit in dance clubs locally around L.A.:

> After we did the *Cheeba, Cheeba* single, which actually got a lot of attention, they sent it out to local DJs, and these guys at Claremont College – E.Z. Mike and John King – at the time had a show, and back then weren't yet the Dust Brothers, they were just E.Z. Mike and John King, who had a radio show together. They did a hip hop show, and they played *Cheeba Cheeba*, and loved that thing, and this guy we knew at the station Orlando gave us the feedback of, "Yo, these guys man, they love this track, they play it all the time." Then he brought back to us some demo tapes these guys had going, Mike and John,

and these guys had learned how to synch up loops with Sympti and time-code through a little box, a PPS unit, and a Midi sequencer, through an IBM computer that was running vision. They had a Roland S-10, and they created these really incredible songs with these loops, and they were all synched up to time. See, we didn't know how to synch up, we just programmed the drum machine, hit play and let it go, and they had a grid on the computer and laid down loops and turned stuff on and off, and it was a different technique. Well, once we heard the tapes, we said, "Dude, we gotta meet these guys." They had their local friends rapping on the tracks. They were okay, not incredible, but the tracks they were rhyming on were incredible.

So after we met the guys they came down and were excited to check out our studio, and were like, "Wow, this is where you guys did *Cheeba Cheeba*?!!", and saw our drum machines and said "We've got this other way of doing stuff," and they kind of showed us this other science. Then Matt was just like, "Dude, these guys are on the next level," kind of like Bomb Factory, because they could layer stuff: they'd have four kick drums going, or three snares, and all these multiple loops going. So Matt said, "Why don't you guys help us produce a couple tracks for Tone Loc and Young MC? And they ended up doing three tracks on the Loc record, *Loc-ed*

After Dark, and two tracks on the Young MC record, *Stone Cold Rhymin.*

As Delicious Vinyl's in-house engineer, Mario sat in the pilot's chair of the creative nerve center that by then had become quite an innovative studio set-up where, "We had this Tascam 8-track that was a mixer-recorder, and it was really kind of nifty: it had an 8-track quarter-inch recorder with a mixer built in. It was all in-house so you'd have no wiring or nothing, plug a mic in, mix and out, and I think we made *Cheeba Cheeba* on that, so our studio at the time had grown."

Investing in a different type of machinery, Mario went all-in after he remembered bravely walking, "Into my boss to put in my notice, and told my boss I didn't want to do this job anymore." He said, "Are you sure? Do you want to take a day off and think about it?" I had seven years in this company, and you get severance pay. So I told him, "Yeah, I want to leave," and I sold my tools to my co-workers. And then when I quit. I got a check for my severance pay that I was contributing toward some kind of retirement fund, and it was almost $10,000.00. I wasn't expecting that, and I was like, 'You know what, I'm going to take this money,' and I went and got The Recycler. Back then it was this paper you could buy musical equipment out of, and I bought a Tascam MS-16 track tape machine, one-inch tape machine, and was like, "We're going to update the studio." So next, I bought an Allen & Heath CMC24 Mixing board, which had automation, which was one of the first early Midi-automation boards that hooks up to a little Apple 64, like the first one they had, the Commodore 64. So I looked up in the Recycler and this guy had a whole system: the 16 track with the board, and I went and checked it out and bought it." Surprising his producing partner Matt Dyke that night when he showed up like Santa Clause in the summer time, Caldato Jr. remembered the Delicious Vinyl owner's eyes go wide at the upgrade their studio was about to get just as work was beginning on Tone Loc's *Loc-ed After Dark* album:

> When I showed up at Matt's house and was like, "Matt, I got sixteen tracks, let's hook this up!" He got all excited, like, "Oh shit! Now we can lay more loops and more tracks." And the timing of it was just incredible. I spent all of that money in one shot and bought the whole thing and dove into it. That was a big chance, a big risk at that moment, but it was the best thing I did, quitting that job and investing in the studio. Then, just laboring hours and hours, and then it was like full-on, twelve hours, fourteen hours a day: recording, recording, recording. It was my equipment, my studio basically in Matt's house, and then Matt programmed and did all of the sampling. Eventually, I started chiming in with some samples and ideas, because I was a record collector just like him. So I'd bring in a few things, "Hey, let's add that kick there; look here's a beat here, there's a break here on this record," and he'd usually say, "Cool, let's use that." Then playing them tracks, and saying, "Hey, this track would be good for you. Do you want to try it and do a verse?" And they'd record, and it was like, "I like this one, I like that one." We mixed and matched, and just started making a bunch of songs that turned into

albums. So I was co-producing a little bit on those records.

The hotbed of talent working away in the tiny studio was analogous to something along the lines of a lab full of Silicon Valley start-up kids in their early twenties working on the next big smartphone app phenomenon. The chemistry between Delicious Vinyl co-founder and head producer Matt Dyke and his new engineer Mario was one that produced a pair of hits that would storm the clubs and radio over 1989 and 1990 as the world met Tone Loc and his *Wild Thing* phenomenon was born. Much like a hot stock blowing up the DOW, it raced up the charts as demographics ranging from junior high kids at school danced the floor all the way to forty and fifty something year old crowds at thousands of wedding receptions each weekend demanded the song to be played with the same youthful fervor. As one of the sonic architect of this new sensation, as Caldato Jr. chuckles looking back at the irony that even as he was being embraced by the suburbs, Tone Loc was still an active gang member, and reveals that during recording of the album's other monster smash, *Funky Cold Medina*:

> While we were recording his vocals, he'd always say, "Hurry up man, I gotta get out of here, I gotta go take care of some shit," and he was pretty serious, because I remember going to pick him up for a session and he wasn't around. Then he showed like a week later at the studio and took his shirt off, pulled the sleeve back, and you could see under a bandage that he had a bullet hole that went in and came out of his arm. Loc had never been in a studio before making that

album, and he liked to sit down when he tracked his vocals, he'd sit down, smoke a joint, drinking a beer, farting in there, and he just laid it down. He didn't do a lot of takes. It was funny, because he always had something to do.

As word started getting around that any and all unsigned artists were welcome at Delicious Vinyl studios, the team began building a catalog that reflected the rich stylistic diversity of Los Angeles' underground music scene flocking to the studio as, "We'd make tracks, and we didn't even have all the artists, but people started showing up. Tone Loc was the first guy, then Young, then Def Jef, Body & Soul, and then the Dust Brothers brought in G Love E. and then a bunch of other people were showing up, and we had a little Motown-like hit factory going making all these tracks." With an animated fusion of personalities coloring the backdrop to all the music that was going down on tape, Mario shakes his head to date reflecting back on just how crazy a work environment it was to the traditional recording studio:

> It was funny with so many artists coming in and out of this studio which, remember wasn't even in a house, but the living room of Matt's apartment, with a sofa and some chairs, records, the mixing board and then the vocal booth in the closet. Then the bathroom was down at the end of the hall, and Matt was always getting pissed because everyone always had to use his bathroom, which was next to his bedroom, and he'd even lock the bathroom door sometimes. So if you had to go out this window to a little

balcony and piss off the balcony, it was pretty hilarious.

It was a blast, we were all young and just excited about music, making music, and it just came together man. Producing all really comes down to taste, right? What you're used to listening to, and what you reference as good, and at that time, what we were listening to was our favorite records – the standards of what we'd like it to sound like. So we were just emulating that, and we knew what we wanted it to sound like, and would just try to achieve it with whatever equipment we had. Like if I didn't have a compressor, then we'd just use EQs, or if we had a compressor, we tried to use it by accident, hitting buttons and saying, "Okay, that sounds cool, that feels right." It basically is a feel thing, and if it makes you dance, okay!

That thinking was precisely what led Delicious Vinyl to their first national radio take-over when *Wild Thing* became the biggest thing in pop and hip hop in the spring of 1989 and *Entertainment Weekly* argued that the label's, "Brand of hip hop helped the genre hop across color lines." Back in the studio, the art of sampling was on display, with Caldato Jr. revealing from behind the boards that Eddie Van Halen actually played a key role in creating the song's signature rock hook, "When we were making the track for *Wild Thing* specifically, the signature guitar loop is a sample we took from Van Halen from *Jamie's Crying*. The whole thing! The beat was composed of samples from Bizzy B." While Young MC is credited with writing the song's lyrics,

Mario divulges other secrets within the song's making, beginning with the fact that:

> Matt Dyke actually came up with that hook. He was like, "I've come up with this song, it's going to be catchy." The Spike Lee movie *She's Gotta Have It* was out, and the girl in the movie says, "Hey, this is a wild thing." And he knew Fab 5 Freddy and all these guys. He was like, "We've got to get a hooky kind of thing, this song is going to be about the wild thing." So he asked Young MC – who was a clever writer – he said, "Young, write a song about Wild Thing," and kind of gave him the theme and direction. Then, Young wrote the lyrics and Loc performed it.
>
> When he was recording the vocal for *Wild Thing*, I remember we were giving him a little bit of direction on the chorus, like Matt said, "Say *wild thing*." And he only said it *one* time the way we liked it, so it's actually sampled. They cut it up in samplers, because we didn't want to keep asking him to say it over and over again because he'd get pissed. You hear the same *Wild Thing* throughout the entire song!

After the New York Times reported in December of 1989 that, "Rap music continued to make inroads into the pop mainstream" thanks to, "The year's most successful rap record, Tone Loc's two-million-selling *Loc-ed After Dark*." The label was ready to blow up even larger with their next star. Young MC offered the perfect contrast to Loc's gravely vocal tone with the silky smooth opposite, one that flowed perfectly over *Bust a Move*, the label's second sensation-starting smash hit single. *Rolling Stone Magazine* correctly described the #1 in their 4.5 star review as an, Inescapable funk bomb," when it hit radio in the summer of 1989. Chronicling the impact that the song would have upon hip hop at large, RS credited the song's stunning success as, "Integral to hip hop's eventual mainstream acceptance. Fueled by a sample-heavy production, Flea's popping bassline, and infectious rhymes...(it) helped usher in the era of pop-rap...(and) broke down barriers on radio and MTV playlists, while its corresponding album, *Stone Cold Rhymin'* was a rap record that many adults still remember as the first their parents let them play."

Integrally involved in the recording of this revolutionary leap forward for hip hop into the mainstream, Mario proudly certifies that, "I recorded that one! Matt produced it, and we gave the Dust Brothers an extra production on that one because they helped us link up some extra loops on it that we didn't know how to do." Personally picking Young up from his dorm to head to the album's recording sessions, Mario brought the kind of all-hands-on-deck attitude to his role as engineer/producer that he recommends any up-and-comer have to show they're a team member at whatever studio they're starting out working at:

> At the time Young MC recorded *Bust a Move*, Young was going to college downtown at USC and he didn't have a car. So either Mike or myself would go and pick him up from the door and bring him to the studio. He was witty, he had his book of rhymes, and would say, "I'm ready. Here we go. Boom!" And he'd lay it out,

and the music was always ready – he just had to rhyme over it. He'd pick a theme, and then we'd arrange it to where the chorus comes in after eight or twelve or sixteen bars. Then he was good to go.

On that song, I used the Yamaha F-7 reverb on his vocal, and then I got the SBX-90, which I used for other effects, but mainly the Yamaha F-7, and it was standard that I'd put it on the mic a little bit in the mix, it would be just like a little, a little echo, but that was the set-up for all those Delicious Vinyl hits. On *Stone Cold Vinyl* and *Loc-Ed After Dark*, I had one reverb, a Yamaha F7, and I remember using a short hall or small hall setting, and then you could copy the settings, and I saved it on #23 I remember, I think I still have the unit. But it was one setting I used, kind of a tight reverb, and then I had some Ibanez digital delays – a 1,000 or 2,000, and then a 1,500 – simple delays, I had one short delay and then one long delay.

It was all manual, and those were the main effects we used. I had a compressor, a Yamaha 2020. It's a little one-space cheap stereo compressor, which I would make barely compress it a little bit. So there wasn't heavy compression on the vocals. I used the Senheisser 421 vocal mic, which was mounted on the wall with one of those stretchy arms, and we'd converted the coat closet into a vocal booth, carpeted it up to deaden it up, and then wall-mounted the mic so it stayed stationary, and then the artist stand up in the booth and record.

MTV would play a huge helping hand with an almost constant-rotation in introducing Young MC to the masses, complete with a stand-out guest appearance by Red Hot Chili Peppers' bassist Flea, whose galloping bass line rode funk wild overtop a rhythm track that Mario remembered the team creating with, "Two drum machines, the SB-12 and a Roland S-50, which we used on all those records, and on *Bust a Move* there's a Roland 808 that's programmed in there as well." Caldato Jr. – who personally recorded the now-legendary performance at the Delicious Vinyl studio – credits co-producer Matt Dyke with adding the bass legend and his irreplaceably frenetic energy into the song's mix:

> Flea was friends with Matt, he knew everybody. His club was the spot where everybody would go there – musicians, artists – he knew everybody. So we were like, "Let's get a bass line," and he came down and knocked it out in one hour, he wrote the bass line right there and recorded directly into the board, line-in. He had a bass that had a hot level, it had pre-amps with those pick-ups on it that were really hot, and there was plenty of gain on the line. We boosted the bass as loud as we could go, to where it sounded right with the club reference that we had in the room, and it worked!

Arguably Mario's most significant contribution to shaping the song's sound would come with the new sonic dimensions he introduced to the world of hip hop when he supervised the mixing of all of Delicious Vinyl's biggest hits, including *Bust a Move*, *Wild Thing*, *Funky Cold Medina*, and *Principal's Office*, proudly confirming that, "I did the mixing on all of those records." Bringing the club environment to live on tape, Caldato drew on his years of experience running live sound and watching the way the dance floor reacted to specific fundamental elements like the bass and drums that have long driven hip hop:

> We were going for what we knew sounded good in the clubs. I had the club systems – our speakers back then were the standard that all the clubs had. So at the house, we had a pair of the same speakers you would hear at the club. We also did a lot of mixing reel-to-reel and then put those mixes on cassettes. Which were our reference tapes, so I'd make a cassette mix and then we'd play on this ghetto blaster that Matt had that he'd set in his kitchen, and that was our reference. We'd listen to the radio, and play the cassette, and compare, "The kick needs to be a little bit louder," so he kind of guided it, and I was the engineer and listen to them, and say, "Oh yeah, let's make this a little bit brighter," or "Let's make this a little bit more bumpin' on the low-end." We would play a record, and then play our song. It kind of was just in the park – you know what I mean? So between the Ghetto Blasters, which were the reference in the 80's, everybody listened to them, and then the club

speakers we had in the room, we made it sound
good, the way it was supposed to sound.

That new sound would reverberate across the landscape of
hip hop's cutting edge, where the Beastie Boys happened to be
sitting listening for a new sound that *Rolling Stone* would later
argue, "Pioneered psychedelic hip hop, which was mind-
expanding in text and texture." Mario's talent for organizing
those textures as the album's lead engineer and making sonic
sense out of the group's visionary voyage in sampling that *Spin
Magazine* celebrated as, "Dense, arty, and with enough
production highjinks to fill a junkshop. It honored hip hop
history while predicting the future." This was an opportunity
that first came knocking:

> Matt got wind after the Beastie Boys had massive
> success on their first album that they were suing
> Def Jam and leaving them because they weren't
> being paid their royalties, they were searching
> for a new direction, and Matt all of a sudden
> decides he wants to be their producer. So very
> confidently, he says, "We've got to send them
> some songs, let's send them some of the Dust
> Brothers instrumentals." They were just demos,
> but Matt was like, "Dude, we gotta send them
> some songs to get their attention!" And he had a
> friend up in New York who new Ad-Rock, and
> got him a cassette with a few songs. Well, when
> they heard the shit, they bugged out and that's
> what planned the seeds for *Paul's Boutique*.

Impressed with Mario's skill at keeping up with the whirlwind of creative ideas racing around the room as he tracked them all to tape, along with those he himself contributed, the Beastie Boys and Dust Brothers decided to make Caldato Jr. a permanent member of the production team, beaming as he confirms, "I engineered that entire record and have a co-production on a track. That opened up a whole new thing, once they got excited and wanted to work with us. So next they asked us, "So how do you make your records?" Matt showed them around, and replied, "Well, we have our studio here, and Mario's our engineer." They were like, "Cool. We'll take Mario too. How much do you make?" And I was making fifteen dollars an hour. They said, "Alright, we'll give you twenty-five dollars an hour. Just roll with us." And we basically started the process of making *Paul's Boutique*."

Likening himself to something of a Han Solo-like adventurer sitting in the pilot seat flying through light speed as he sat behind the console capturing everything the creative cosmos was throwing at him, he highlighted *High Plains Drifter* as among his favorite engineering leaps forward. Beginning with his stand-out effects treatment on the trio's vocals, sharing his memory, "That was more reverb and maybe some echoes on the vocals. I remember just messing around, turning stuff on and off, just kind of random. We'd keep it fresh sometimes. And turn stuff on and off, hit some reverb bombs occasionally. Like the 808 when we were working on it, trying to get the right sound. I was on the compressor I'd never used before, trying to figure it out. So I started hitting all of the buttons and I hit this one button. All of a sudden, it started making the right sound, and somebody would say, "That's it, don't touch anything!" We were all really focused and all into it. We had good taste I think as a group. If something wasn't so banging, someone would say, "Oh man, that's weak. Come on man, we can't go out like that." Everybody would have to agree unanimously, it was a real group effort. I gotta say that. And everybody was open, it was cool."

Making many of those decisions during the mixing stage, where he again played a central role in making a masterpiece out of the album's final sound, one that, "Announced that the Beasties were an innovative force." *Time Magazine* would later add their esteemed opinion that there, "Will never be another record like *Paul's Boutique.*" It was as if it added to their all-time 100 albums list, Caldato Jr. recalled that:

> Everything was mixed at The Record Plant, so I used their equipment there, and their reverbs were much better than mine – AMS Reverbs I believe that we used. On *Car Thief*, we treated all the voices, where we processed the voice, ran it through the effect, and then recorded it on another track so they're printed, and we did that with all three voices. Then we'd take each voice and run it through these delays with square-wave modulation, where it was constantly changing with a lot of feedback, so that's a bug-out effect. That's actually one of my signature effects. It's a square-wave modulation on the delay where the delay time is constantly changing, and through the whole song! We would go through and did it manually, but it sounds like it's dusted. It was a Lexicon PCM 41 or 42 that we used, because there's not many delays that do square-wave modulation, they're always sign-wave modulation, and you need square-wave.

Taking sampling into new frontiers hip hop hadn't heard before, when the Beastie Boys released *Paul's Boutique*, they were so far out ahead of their time that when they took a break in 1990 where they wanted to head next, the group decided to go 360 in the opposite direction. Abandoning sampling for live instrumentation they would perform themselves, the only part of the previous production team the group opted to keep in place was Mario C behind the boards, elevating him from engineer to the official position of co-producer. Having proven himself an indispensible technical translator for the group's ideas, Caldato Jr. would soon be given the additional title of head architect put in charge of designing and building the group's new studio from the ground up:

> Heading into the next record *Check Your Head*, the group thinking was one of: "You know what? We spent $100,000 on the last record, we can just buy a tape machine and a board and rent a place and start our own studio." They had signed a two-record minimum deal with Capitol, so they had to make another record. About a year after *Paul's Boutique* had been out, they said, "Let's go work on the next one. We got the money, we got the budget, let's do it."

> We found a building in Atwater Village in LA, near the Los Feliz area and Hollywood, it had been a community center or ball room previously, had a wood parquet floor, and a half-curved, cylinder half-pipe-type ceiling. So the guy who had been there before we took it over had a studio space and used part of it for

rehearsal, but the problem was, the downstairs was a drug store and so you couldn't make any noise till after six o'clock until they closed. Perfect, so we'd start our day at six and go home at two in the morning.

Bringing the man who he'd built his first studio with back as teenagers, Mark Ramos Nishita, in on the project, Mario and Money Mark got down to work on this once-in-a-lifetime opportunity. Building a space around a sound concept centered in live playing among the band, it proved a perfect direction given the size of the space they'd found: "It was a big-room, and already had a wall built but there was no door, so Money Mark—who was a carpenter by trade—said, "Let's put a door here so we can make a control room with a window so we can see out into the big room, which would be the recording room." So we set up shop with a Tascam two-inch 24 track tape machine, and a Neo-tech Elan mixing console, which was a 32-channel with 24 buss, three band EQ, and then I had all the outboard gear and all the mics. The outboard gear included reverbs—the Yamaha Rev 7, the SBX, and three Ibanez delays: the HD 1000, HD2000, and HD 1500 with the harmonizer. Then I had a Yamaha compressor, and had bought a pair of blackface 1176s, which was the first time I had some real nice compressors. Then I had some DBX 160's with the VU." Once the studio was up and running, the Beasties made the wise decision– in the context of time– to take themselves off any kind of outside clock, moving only at the pace of the music they had quietly begun making together *as a band*. An artistic shift in tempo that producer Mario C stated:

The band had reached in reaction to being totally burnt out on the sampling at the time. So once the studio was set up, they had started horsing around and jamming together, and previous to that, Mike was playing drums in a local band called Big Fat Love, Yauch had a band called Brooklyn where he played fuzz bass, and Ad-Rock played everything. So we'd set up the live room with instruments, added Money Mark in on keyboards, and this band was born.

Most fans of the band would argue a new sound had been born as well, one that the band took literally years to let develop, such that, as Mario recalled, "that album took three years to make. We started at the end of '89, six months after *Paul's Boutique*, and recorded up through 1992. For the first couple years, we only focused on instrumental stuff, so there was no there was no vocals, just jamming." Necessary to both find their groove as a band along with being taken seriously down the road by fans as part of their rebirth as an authentic live group of real musicians who played their own instruments, the shift in musical direction put to bed forever the notion that the Beasties were a novelty rap act, with Caldato Jr. revealing:

> This was such an intense focus among the band that with the jamming thing, that went on for a *year and a half* before the rapping started. It brought up the musical level of the band because the guys were playing together every day. Mark was helping them construct instrumentals, and showing them changes and new chords. It was all building up. It was a special thing, to take three

years, which nobody does nowadays, to be on the clock, and slowly make a record that we had no idea at the time how it would turn out as a finished product, it was an amazing experience to come together and be part of it.

Spin Magazine would later hail that finished product as a, "Collection of funky instrumentals, fuzz-bass rock, hardcore, progresso psychedelia, and 21st century schizoid hip hop that is the brilliant new Beasties album." In breaking down that blend into the individual stylistic derivative influences the group was absorbing as they found their sound through live jamming. Mario recalled a library of reference points as varied as *Paul's Boutique* had incorporated, appreciating the open-door policy the band welcomed on input from everyone involved in making the album:

> We'd go in and listen to The Meters, Sly and the Family Stone, James Brown, and just jam and play basketball, because there was enough room for a half-court. Everybody contributed. We were all record collectors, and every day we'd show up, and it might have been something we picked up from the thrift shop, and so we'd be listening to records for a couple hours for inspiration. Then we'd weed out the best of the best, and go out there and try to play something you heard, and maybe even come up with something else. That happened a lot, it was a real collaboration, and so we all brought in little shit – I brought in some stuff, and on that record everybody contributed and we became a real

family over the course of making that record, hanging out every day for three years Monday thru Friday, and sometimes on the weekends too. We definitely bonded, hung out and had a good time, were creative, and the outcome was great.

With their evolution toward live instrumentation, Billboard later argued the band had successfully "repositioned themselves as a lo-fi, alt-rock groove band." Over the course of the Beastie's musical re-invention, Caldato Jr. – who documented every one of its notes to tape – as a rule recorded, "All of their ideas. Which is something I ALWAYS recommend to any engineer or producer. Even if it's in the rehearsal room, because you never know what the band will come up with." Personally designing what was essentially a fixed positioning for the band's instrument micing during basic tracking so he could hit record at a moment's notice without technical concerns getting in the way of the band's creativity, Mario diagrams his micing masterpiece for fans, modestly offering his memory:

It was pretty basic. On Mike's kit, mainly Senheisser 421s on the kick and toms, a 57 on the top of the snare, overheads were 451s, and the hi-hat was a 460. There were eight mics on the drums, which stayed stationary, and then there were times I'd throw a 414 room mic in the middle of the room. MCA's stand-up bass—for that thing, I used a 414 condenser mic, which was my best acoustic mic. For keys, Money Mark had a Wurlitzer we used quite a bit. We did have a Rhodes, but he mainly used the

Wurly, and we ended up using a Korg through the Leslie on some stuff, which sounded very close to the Hammond. He rocked that quite a bit, and then there was also an acoustic upright there.

As the group learned the language of being a live band through communicating exclusively musically, they amassed a vault of original instrumental jams that Caldato Jr. estimated to be "up into the hundreds because we recorded everything over that three year period." Once it came time to begin mining for booty, impressively, Mario revealed that the Beastie Boys favored a group consensus, reflecting how implicitly they trusted him to wear his producer's hat and give unfettered feedback for the sake of the songs first:

We worked together listening back and clearing out and picking out the keepers, like, "This one's got potential." So there was a lot of reviewing and analyzing, and we had time to do it. It didn't put any pressure on anybody, so nobody was afraid to try a wacky song or something nutty. Then, we'd live with it for a while and see how long you were into it. The stuff that stuck made it to the record. So everything you hear on the final *Check your Head* LP, everybody in the group was really pleased with, and happy as a whole on the record. It was like it passed the test of time after three years of making and listening to it. It still sounded good when we finished.

Clearly focused on making sure they had their musical chops down before they picked the mic back up, the band's return to rhyming wouldn't come until "one random day after a year and a half, two years of just jamming!" In what would prove to be a revolving routine throughout the years where different group members came in with different original song ideas that were inspiring enough to spark a healthy competition of creative contributions of the others, Mario shined the spotlight squarely on M.C.A. as the synergist who got the band fired up about rapping again:

> Yauch came in one day and said, 'I have this idea, I want to record it and surprise the guys.' He didn't want to do it at the studio, so he came to my house in South LA and we demoed it there. That song was *Jimmy James*. He'd found the Hendrix loop, the Turtle beat, and we looped it up at my house, arranged it, and did a demo with Yauch doing the vocals himself. Then we brought it back to the guys and they loved it. "Aw shit, I want to rhyme on that!" And all of a sudden, they were all hyped and all wanted to start rhyming. So that set it off.

Taking their creative cues from each others' muse as much as from their own internal inspirational processes as the album's rhyme-schemes were hatched, Caldato Jr. broke down how he organized the Beastie's vocal microphone placements in the studio around the trio's signature rap-trading style in such a way that they could see each other throughout recording:

As far as the arrangement of mics, it was odd, because I'd set up three mics, and one guy would be in the big studio room, one guy would be in the control room, and in between the big room and control room was a little cubbie hole– literally a foot and a half wide– to where you could just fit in it because it was a double-door. So I rigged up a mic in there so the three of them could all see each other and be close, but the voices would be separated. When they recorded vocals on any given song, we would try it out and actually have all three of them recording at the same time, and they would break verses up between them.

With their live-wire energy bouncing off of the walls of the studio throughout recording, the BBC during this period would highlight the thrill of listening to the Beasties, "Trading lines with such liquidity that, at times, the three vocals blend into a perfectly unprecedented stew of consciousness, our protagonists were promptly re-established as both a rap force." From his front-row seat in the audience sitting behind the console, Mario remembered that versus any one secret studio leader among the three, "It was definitely a group effort, and everybody contributed equally." Still, in offering his own observations on the individual strengths of each personality in this color-wheel, beginning with the self-declared "original nasal kid," Adam "Ad-Rock" Horovitz – who NPR argued had, "The most memorable voice." And alongside his unique high-pitched vocal tone:

Behind the scenes: he was very talented in programming, selecting loops, scratching, and coming up with nutty rhymes. A lot of his rhymes he would make up at the moment, he was definitely the best at that, so sometimes he would have two words written down, or one line, and then the rest he'd make up as the song was going. So he might be inspired through hearing Mike D say something, and just add onto it, he was very much more free-style in that sense that the other guys, and definitely a major force in the creative-musical part of it. Lyrically, he was also an artist who could say something you'd never think of, and just do it at the moment, and was so original in his rhyming.

By contrast, Yauch would be a little bit more thought out, and liked to know what he was saying ahead of stepping to the mic, and was more precise on that. Him having the coolest voice in the delivery, and that low end, it really sounded great when you heard his voice come on, it was like butter. It just sounded beautiful. He was also very musical, and had great taste with picking loops and writing his own bass lines. Mike D was more like the character of the group, so when he was writing, he would kick into comic mode and come up with some funny rhymes and you just couldn't help but laugh. He was almost like the cheer leader for the band, so he would be like, "Alright, let's do this," and would get everybody hyped up when it was time to record: "It's showtime!" He would come in with musical ideas too, he was a big record collector, and would bring in stuff to check out and we definitely used a lot of what he brought in.

Filtering their vocals through some wild experiments in effect processing that fused alternative rock experimental norms into hip hop for the first time throughout the album, Caldato Jr. and the Beasties pushed this production principle to the unconventional extreme of applying even to the microphone itself that they were recording with. Showcased boldly and brilliantly on the album's biggest hit, *So What'cha Want,* which would prove a portal of sorts for the group to step more fully into this new dimension of discovery as they tracked:

> When we got into *So What'cha Want,* we had this B-studio, which was for when one of the Beasties had another idea and wanted to go work on it. So in that smaller room, we had a four-track set up with the instrumental music, and a little cheap Sony Karaoke mic that featured a built-in distortion, and had an octave thing where you could make your voice sound like a Martian, and a computer scrambler effect– just some weird effects all built into the mic. So at first, they would use that to demo stuff on, and that little mic sounded cool because it kind of overloaded when you cupped it, and it sounded pretty awesome, so we kind of got used to that– the demos with this sound.

Infectious not only to the fans but to the band first and foremost as they decided to make the distorted vocal effect a sonic hallmark of the album at large, Mario seems still impressed to date with the daring nature of the group's record making in terms of the risks they took, which became bigger and braver as "it grew on the guys to the point where they started saying 'I want to use this mic to do the real version on the record,' because when they would do it on the 58, it sounded too clean and didn't have that intensity. *So What'cha Want* – a smash hit – was recorded on that twenty-nine dollar Sony karaoke mic. That microphone was the effect. There's no other effects of any kind. That was the sound. They wound up using that on the record, any time you would hear a distorted voice. From that technique, I would try out some other hand-mics, like a hand-radio mic and cheap mics I would plug in and distort with the pres, but that Sony karaoke mic was the main go-to, with no extra distortion or nothing. So from there, we used that on everything, it was the primary effect on songs like, *Jimmy James, So What'cha Want*. All the songs that have distorted vocals on them. The rest of the records' vocals were recorded with 58s, and on *Check Your Head*, we did everything on hand-held mic. So they never used mic stands during vocal tracking." Long a storied tool in helping recording artists feel more comfortable in the creation of a vocal performance, the effects helped the Beasties both slip into the personality of their voices and equally in exciting spontaneous inspiration that added new character to that performance in real time with its recording, Caldato Jr. confirmed its constant presence:

> When they were tracking, they all loved effects on their voices. The more effects the better. So they'd always be like, 'Yo turn that shit up, give me more echo,' in terms of what they had going in their headphones while they recorded. What

we kept of that we played by ear, sometimes we would record it when the shit was just banging, like if it was tape delay, then we'd record that, Yauch on one song was really into that, and wanted to record it exactly like that and commit to it. For the vocals, we mainly used short delay and long delay, and I would just adjust them accordingly to the song. So like a short delay to get it tight and kind of fatten it up, and then a long delay for the echoes and that kind of part. Then we'd do panning sometimes on the echoes, and as far as reverbs, I had the Yamaha Rev 7 digital reverb, which I used as a basic reverb, and then would use the SPX 90 more for special effects, like when I wanted a gated reverb or reverse, or flanging or phasing, or auto-panning – any kind of weird stuff. That was basically it.

Celebrating the fusion of vocal and musical personalities that, in sum, produced what Playboy would later reason was, "A record, in retrospect, only they could have created: a 70's groove oriented, lo-fi, fuzz-toned, punk jazz album," Mario as its technical curator sought to stretch the group's creative freedom as far out as he could over twenty-four tracks. Detailing that with the stylistic range of territories the group was exploring and in some cases pioneering throughout *Check Your Head*, the producer described a template where, "We'd basically fill it up and leave three tracks for vocals, and one for Simpti. So that left us like twenty tracks for music. Typically, we'd add a bunch of loops, beats, kicks and snares, scratching. On *Check Your Head*, Ad-Rock did all of the scratching, except for Yauch did all of the terminating. Like the stuff at the beginning of *Jimmy James* – pretty much the rest of the album was Ad-Rock."

Though they'd broadened their horizons musically beyond sampling by the dawn of this next wave of the band's artistic evolution, as pure hip hop heads, they stayed loyal to utilizing the art form as an instrument selectively throughout the album. Demonstrating when they did an ever-fresh instinct as tastemasters for where to flip an clip from something classic in such an original way that it sounded brand new to the ear, the group treated the presence of samples throughout the album as a tool to color the personality of songs rather than define or dictate their overall direction as they had much more prevalently throughout *Paul's Boutique*. From Bob Dylan's *Just Like Tom Thumb's Blues* to The Fearless Four's b-boy classic *Rockin It*, NPR would glowingly compliment *Check Your Head* as "yet another reinvention...that practically served as a template for later bands to follow," and employed the cutting edge as they did so:

> We were using the Akai MPC 60. That was the main one. At the time, that was the new shit, and allowed you to do like thirty seconds of sampling, you had multiple pads, at the time it was just the popular sampling drum machine out there so all four of us had one, except Marc. That way we could work, and if somebody got an idea at home, they could bring it into the studio, so it was interchangeable, you could bring the discs and it was easy to use. We also used the EMU SB1200, which is what Ad-Rock used, he mainly worked on that one. Then we had an 808 that was linked up as well.

Still, for as fast as the technology curve was churning out machines with expanded sample rate times, broadening the creative possibilities therein, Caldato Jr. recalled that it wasn't an exact science yet, rather a guessing game of sorts where, "As far as the timing and the synching up, back then, you didn't break down every single hit or beat, you just kind of took a loop and massaged it into the rough BPM, and it wasn't quite perfect, but you got it as close as you could to where it felt right, which made the stuff really funky." One of the album's most celebrated tapestries of samples from every corner of the stylistic universe being woven together in a new song where they all felt like they belonged, from the audio clip from Willie Henderson and the Soul Explosions' *Loose Booty* that starts the song to borrowing its main chorus beat from Jimmy Smith's *I'm Gonna Love You Just a Little More, Baby* alongside key interpolations from Kool & The Gang's *Give It Up*, Freddie Hubbard's *Uncle Albert/Admiral Halsey*, and *Let Your Lovelight Shine* by Buddy Miles Express. Proving themselves as eclectic as ever, Mario still regards *Professor Booty* as one of the finest b-boy salutes the group ever mashed up:

> The samples on that one came from all kinds of sources, I think the movie *Wild Style* was sampled, Ad-Rock brought in some elements. Those guys had a lot of b-boy background, and they tried to utilize that as much as possible – a lot of old school stuff. That's got a bunch of different loops on there.

Mario C would be branded the, "Beastie studio whiz" by *Rolling Stone* following his work co-producing and mixing what became not only the Beastie Boys' comeback record, cracking the Top 10 on the Billboard Top 200 Album Chart, and in the esteemed opinion of *The Source*, "cemented the Beastie Boys name in hip hop history for sure!" Tuning his ears in to what is in some respects the most important stage of record-making given it's finality, when Caldato Jr. began mixing *Check Your Head*, he described an all-hands-on-deck effort due in part to the pre Pro Tools reality:

> It was a manual operation. So while I would generally take the lead on most of mixing, we'd all help turn stuff up and down, off, hit the delay, and occasionally one of the Beasties would get in and work some of the echoes. We had some automation, the mute automation, because the tracks were constantly looped for like four minutes, and then we'd turn stuff on and off as we needed it. Then we had a Midi-sequencer that was actually hooked up to the MPC60, the drum machine, that also worked as a Midi on-and-off note controller for the automation. So it would read the Simpti, and we'd program the verse, chorus, the break or bridge, and then we would ride the faders manually – that was all done manually!

When the group arrived at the point many recording artists – especially the prolific ones like the Beastie Boys – dread the most about finishing an album, the painful but necessary moment where decisions about the final track listing are made. Ranging from which songs make the final cut to the order they appear in from start to finish, Mario remembered the group facing the challenge after three years of uninterrupted work, not surprisingly, of deciding:

> On the album's final twenty songs because there were probably about fifty total ideas for the record. There were a lot of little things that turned into other things, and on the bonus CD they put out, *Skills to Pay the Bills,* a lot of that stuff surfaced later. But at the time, it was difficult, because every one of those fifty cuts the band considered their babies.

> After we released the album, we went right back to work recording too, because the band went on tour immediately, which was needed because they'd been off the road for three years. So we toured for the whole year, maybe a year and a half, and as we were on tour, in between sound checks, they'd get ideas and I'd record them as they popped up. Well, out of that process, some ideas started forming for the next record.

With *Check Your Head,* the Beastie Boys didn't just rebound, they reinvented themselves, in the esteemed opinion of *Rolling Stone Magazine,* "As a total cultural experience." Ranked #5 in *The Village Voice*'s list of the 40 Best Albums Of 1992, *Entertainment Weekly* would later argue that the Beasties' comeback LP had successfully, "Left a much bigger bootprint on pop than *Licensed to Ill,*" large enough that *Billboard* would declare the record, "An alt-rock touchstone of the 90's." Twenty years later, the *BBC* would conclude that the record, "Remains to this day the quintessential Beastie Boys collection." It's an assessment that – on a personal level – producer Mario C concurs with, sharing that, "*Check Your Head* is still a very special record for me, being the first step into that world, and having three years to work on it. The friendship and everything just building and being created naturally was really wonderful."

Writing much of their next album on the road versus in the fixed space they'd created *Check Your Head*. As ideas for *Ill Communication* started to come together, they did so courtesy of a scavenger hunt of sorts. The band undertook mining for vinyl in record stores the world over on their days off on tour. Laughing as he shared his treasured memory of, "Buying records on tour, it was the best – almost like a competition whenever we rolled into a new town." We'd hurry up and check into the hotel, and then get the phone book, or look around and spot the local record store, and none of us would tell the others, instead we'd be like, "Well, I'm going go rest and kick back and bit." Then usually more than one of us would sneak out and hit the record store, and wind up a lot of times saying, "Hey, what are you doing here?!" When we did wind up at the same store, or head there together, we had this thing where one of us would say, "I call Rock," and another would say, "I call soul. I call jazz." And if we wound up hitting the same genre, it was funny, because sometimes we'd both be after the same thing. We would wind up saying, "Aw man, I was looking for that record." We found some real gold sometimes.

The *LA Times* would later hail the Beasties as, "Masters of the fun part of hip hop that many artists have forgotten– the art of swiping bits of music from hundreds of obscure old records and stitching them together into something resembling art." As they raided Mom and pop record shops around the globe, Caldato Jr. remembered a team spirit at work throughout where, "There were three heads with the Beasties, and then Marc and myself, so five heads just listening and adding ideas, "Hey, check this out etc." Then when we were on tour for Lollapalooza, we were out on the road with A Tribe Called Quest. And we'd run into Q-Tip and the DJ at stores sometimes. So we'd scoop up the records, fill up the bus or sometimes I'd send them home via FedEx because I had so many and didn't want to keep lugging them around. So we traveled all over the country and world and had bought records all over the place, and were really excited from being on tour, because we got back with all these records and ideas for the new album. We were focused on getting back in the studio to do another record – we were ready." As they completed pre-production on tour, along with the sample-and-live-sound-check-jam sides of their writing process, the beatsmiths were also busy banging out their own original rhythm ideas on the bus:

> While we'd been on the road, we had the drum machine on tour, and were already actually sampling some stuff, and kind of getting some homework already done. I think all we had was the drum machine and a four-track DAT, and so whenever they would get an idea at sound check, I would run a stereo mix while they were jamming, just keeping the ideas flowing.

Returning back East to their hometown roots following the completion of the wildly successful *Check Your Head* tour and set up shop in the Big Apple to begin sessions for *Ill Communication*. Re-creating the same kind of organic vibe they had back at G-Son exploring the usual broad range of soundscapes from acid jazz to classic wah wah funk to blues to soul to psychedelic, as the band jammed their way through a by-then signature side of their sound that *Rolling Stone Magazine* would later observe successfully continued "the formula established on *Check–* home-grown jams powered by live instruments...buried under the warm hiss of vintage analog studio equipment." As they prepared to re-enter the studio, Mario remembered an excitement in the air:

> During the first four weeks of recording when we were in Manhattan, and we spent a month in New York recording all the jamming material that became all the basic instrumental material for the record – like *Ricky's Theme, Sabotage, Bobo on the Corner, Sabrosa, Futtermen's Rule, Shambala, Transition,* and *Eugene's Lament* – the basic tracking for those were all done in New York. By this point, Bobo, the percussionist, was now part of the band. Along with Money Mark on keyboards, and of course, Ad-Rock on guitar, Yauch on bass, and Mike on drums. So that first month was great. A change of scenery, and it turned out to be a great idea. We were tracking on an old custom console, a tube board that had a lot of TubePre's.

Even though the live format may have been the same, in drawing sonic contrasts between *Check Your Head* and *Ill Communication,* Caldato Jr. explained that the sound going down on tape was altered, "For those New York sessions because everyone basically played together in these very tight quarters, which give a tight sensibility to the sound. By contrast, the G-Son studio in LA had a big stage, it was a big room, and felt much more spacious, where this space was opposite, again, a little tighter – so the band could see each other and play off each other, plus the musicianship had improved after touring for so long and just playing a lot. I remember Yauch always being very motivated and creative in the studio, always working on his bass sound. He was playing on a fuzz bass and a stand-up bass. So the confidence in the room was high." Once the troupe returned to L.A. to continue working on the record at G-Son, focusing more on unpacking those sample-based song ideas from the road and plugging them into a formal production structure, Mario once again recognized Adam Horovitz as an especially skilled Samauri in the way he cut up samples in the MPC, noting:

> Ad-Rock had a great instinct and talent for putting beats with loops, and for taking a chance, and through that, discovering different avenues musically for the albums by putting different styles together—he really enjoyed doing that.

Pointing to the album's opening track, *Sure Shot* – which *Rolling Stone Magazine* ranked one of the 50 Best Songs of the Nineties – as a master class of sorts on how the art of sampling worked at the level where, "Ad-Rock came up with that flute loop from *Howlin' for Judy* by Jeremy Steig, added a slamming beat, and the track was done." Mario still marvels to this day at that fact that, "I don't even think it was a whole bar – the beat. He found the kick and snare, and he sampled it. I don't even think it was separated, it was together, it was a noisy beat, a noise kick-snare. We added some 808 on top of it, and there was two elements of the beat and loop and that thing was done. We added a couple other sneaky elements on the chorus, and that was it."

Ad-Rock would be in the driving seat as the creative force behind what was by far the *oldest-school* hit off the album when *Root Down* and its instantly addictive bass line dropped. Taking Rap back to its b-boy glory days in a way only the Beastie Boys could while synchronously representing the new school of hip hop with competing credibility, Mario offers fansa rare look inside the song's actual conception and creation as he sat side-by-side with Horovitz for both, beginning with the memory of standing with Ad-Rock:

> When he bought the record on tour – a live Jimmy Smith album – and we listened to it in the car, heard that bass line, and he was like, "Oh My God, I gotta loop that shit up," so he called it. It was so fat that they just used the hook. "I kick it root down." There you go, it's done. So that loop was basically the record, I just re-edited it. We took four or five different loops, and put them in different orders with the guitar and all that shit. I don't think there were any instruments added to it– that's Jimmy Smith, straight up, re-edited in a different order with some scratching. *Do It* was another slamming Ad-Rock track. It's super-funky, I think that one was Bob Dylan song. And as that loop comes in and you hear all that scratching, that's Ad-Rock scratching as well.

Along with *Sure Shot*, *Root Down*, and *Do It*, Mario remembered the band was on fire once, "We came back to G-Son in L.A., that's where we did all the rap joints, including *B Boys*, *Get it Together*, *Update*, *Alright Hear This*, *The Scoop*, and *Fruit*

Loop." While he happily credits Horovitz and the other Beasties for those sample ideas that wound up becoming hits or keeper tracks, two songs that competed just as colorfully with anything the b-boys brought in came with Mario's specific contributions, starting with *Fruit Loop*, which he modestly admits:

> I brought it in. It had a sample of a song called *Flute Thing* by the Blues Project, some 60's shit. I heard that and loved it, looped that shit up, went through my beat pile, and the first record I pull out, the beat fit like a charm. That beat was by Young and Holtz, and it just fit perfect, so I made a demo of that instrumental, brought it in, and Ad-Rock was like, "Oh shit! I love it, give me the mic." And he just started rhyming right away. The guys really liked that one, so I was naturally happy they used it.

An equally-accomplished player and composer on both electric and stand-up acoustic bass, running into the console, Caldato Jr. favored a micing compliment that gave MCA room to breathe as a player, but still captured the personally unique touch he brought to his instrument. Sharing with a clear sense of honor for the privilege of being his producer that, "Yauch's sound came from an acoustic stand-up bass with the big body and he generally used that for recording. At the time we were making that record, I'd just started buying tube mics, and would have had a Neumann U-47 on Yauch's stand-up bass, and sometimes I would use an 87 or a M-49. But on tour, we wound up buying a Z bass, which is an upright bass without the body, and has a small, hallow kind of body that has a little bit of acoustic sound to it also, but was just easier to transport. So sometimes we'd that in the studio as well, mic it up or line in and EQ, but generally always miced and at times processed a little extra."

As practiced a band of musicians as they were by then after playing together night after night on tour, their tongues were equally-sharp as the finest trio of emcees working in hip hop at their height, so much so that the esteemed National Public Radio noted by then that, "I mostly thought of them as a group package rather than an assortment of distinct MCs. Their telltale style was a three-man, tag team weave, where each rapper — MCA, Ad-Rock and Mike D — often finished each other's sentences. To tell the Beasties apart, you needed to focus on their voices." When Mario was doing just that, he remembered that indeed, because the group were so intuitively in synch that in the studio laying down vocals for *Ill Communication*, "Things went very smoothly overall. Occasionally, we'd do an edit if we didn't get it right. We'd go on and record the next part, then punch back in and make an edit. But we generally got it together on the first or second take."

One song that wound up taking the longest to come together of any on the album would turn out to be it's biggest hit, *Sabotage*, which became a MONSTER MTV video hit as well when they recreated a 1970s cop TV show. *Time Magazine* years later would note that "the anarchic energy of Spike Jonez's videos were essential ingredients of 1990s MTV (and later of MTV's *Jackass*), and Jonez pulled off one of his most thrilling stunts for the punk-funk lark *Sabotage*, a 70's goof that cast the Beastie Boys as roof-jumping, suspect-beating, mean-street-sprinting, mustache-rocking hero cops. It will not spoil the video's fun to note its impressive technical precision — the edits are perfectly syncopated to the song's ragged beats, and the doughnut-eating breakdown is sublime in its pacing." Still a radio staple over twenty years later, the song's signature fuzz bass hook was so catchy that it hung around over two years under an alternate title that perfectly captured the band's legendary sense of humor, as Mario reveals:

> At the time, we were into funky, jazzy sounds, and we had an acoustic bass happening where Yauch was really rocking it, going for the exotic sound. So one day we were in the studio fucking around, and Yauch was really jamming—really into his fuzz bass thing—just rocking away on that thing, he came up with *Chris Rock* while he was ripping on that bass. So that lead riff on that song, that's bass, and when he started playing that shit, I remember being in the control room knowing he'd stumbled onto something great, what producers call a gem versus a germ, and I immediately yelled to our percussionist, "Go in there Bobo!" So, Bobo went in there, but didn't know what do to, and started going, "Na-Na, Na-Na." Just like you hear that little part in the final song. Then as this is developing, Mike D walks in, and I was like, "Mike, go in there and follow Bobo," so Mike hopped on the drums, and the two of them brought that start-stop rhythm part to life that the song starts and ends with. So they just jammed it out and created the basic rhythm track that you hear on the record, and is it would turn out, on radio.
>
> The funny shit was, after we did it, the studio owner Chris came walking in, and day after day

leading up to that one, he would routinely say, 'Man, you guys need a hit...' Well, when he walked in that day and heard us playing that track, he said, "Now *that's* what I'm talking about! That's a fuckin' hit right there!" He called it, he knew. And that's why we initially wound up calling the song *CHRIS ROCK*– because he'd bugged out on it so much. In fact, it stayed an instrumental almost up until we were ready to turn in the record, because it was just too challenging, nobody wanted to sing on a rock song, because to them it was going back to *Fight for Your Right to Party* on the first album. They didn't really want to do that. I remember they actually tried doing some vocals on the song. There might have been one attempt in New York, and then when we got back to LA. A few months later, I think Ad-Rock tried something, but it wasn't fitting right.

Chris Rock nearly wound up a casualty of the cutting room floor, but for a burst of last minute brilliance from Ad-Rock that ASCAP would later declare, "Mixed rap and rock in a way that hadn't really been done before!" As Horovitz raged against the paparazzi at full volume, a compositional break-through came that Caldato Jr. remembered crashing down in miraculous form, "Two weeks before we're planning to turn the record in, after the whole album is done. We still hadn't come up with any personality for the song lyrically, so at that point, *Chris Rock* was going to be on the record as an instrumental because it sounded tight. Then Ad-Rock calls me up one day, and says, "Dude, I want to try the vocal one more time," and I go, "Well, okay, the song's already mixed. You want to just do the idea at my house?" So he came to my place, where I had a studio set up, and I just loaded up a two-track pre-mix of the instrumental, gave him a vocal mic, and he nailed it *in a couple takes!* He had the attitude, and the lyrics, and just went off, screamed into it, and when he was done, I remember immediately saying, "Oh shit, that's dope! That's fly dude!" So we had him add some scratching, and the song was done. I bounced it onto my Adat, and added the two vocal tracks he laid down." By far the most multi-instrumental of the group's members, Horovitz fooled fans who thought by how good his chops behind the turn-tables were that it must have been DJ Hurricane on the cut, with Mario confirming of how the song's signature scratching went down:

> The two tracks of scratching, used the pre-mix of the instrumental to mix it, and it was done. It ended up sounding banging, and when Mike and Yauch heard it, they were understandably excited because it had finally come together. The song had to go through all that process for it to be the right moment and the right energy and attitude and Adam nailed it hard! We knew there was something exciting and different about it, but even then, at first the Beasties had some reservations about putting it out as the album's first single because, again, it was a rock song, but they eventually embraced it as part of the record.

When production shifted to mixing, Mario remembered that in line with how smoothly recording had gone down in the studio, because his ear had become so well-tuned to the knowing precisely where to place each of the three Beasties' voices in the mix. The producer successfully balanced what iTunes correctly characterized as, "A signature Beastie Boys aesthetic (it's' too far-ranging...to be pegged as a signature sound) with the group sticking to a blend of old school Rap, Pop culture, lo-fi Funk, soulful jazz instrumentals, Latin rhythms, and punk, often seamlessly integrated into a rolling, pan-cultural, multi-cultural groove." Weaving those seams sonically, Caldato Jr. remembered that the group was again greatly aided by their lock-out luxury owning their own studio, enabling the producer to essentially freeze time any time he stepped away from the board for a break:

> When I'd finish mixing one day, and if it wasn't right, you'd get in the next day and the board is exactly where you left it, so I could do a couple more sweeps, and sit with it. That was the thing, when you have your own studio, you had the luxury of time and could do that. You had your quality control, so it wasn't like 'Hurry up,' and that lock-out element was essential—it wouldn't work quite the same way if we had to hurry up and tear down.

> We were working on the same board, outboard and everything for mixing *Ill Communication* as we'd used for *Check Your Head*, except now we were all a little bit more on our chops, so mixing was always a snap. The whole record we'd completed recording in six months: the first month we spent recording in New York, then the next five months building and mixing as we'd

go, so we recorded song by song and I would mix as we finished recording each song. So we'd work on a song for weeks sometimes, keep working till we get it right and can't do anymore, then go on to the next one, and then go back and revisit or remix. The board, the way it was set up, you couldn't just fly around, so we did it one song at a time.

Entertainment Weekly would celebrate the album's final sound as "the most tantalizing ear candy in year," as Mario – putting on his tech head for a moment – highlighted as his favorite new toy in the effects arena as one that wound up influencing the direction of the finished product: "The one new thing we did buy from the studio we recorded at in New York, this EMT plate reverb that sounded great that I started using a lot. It was one of those great Beatles, German EMT reverbs. When we finished up in the studio, we asked Chris, the owner, if he wanted to sell it, and he said, "Yeah, sure!" So we shipped it out to LA to G-Son, and that was something I used on the mixing, not on all the songs. But on quite a few of the jam songs, I used it."

Three years later, the Beasties would return with 1998s *Hello Nasty*, reminding remind critics and fans alike that the release of a new *Beastie Boys* LP served not only to celebrate hip hop's past, but also show where it was heading before anyone else in the genre had quite gotten there. Each new Beastie Boys' release by this point had come to be regarded by fans and critics in kind as guide posts, and *Billboard Magazine* would reinforce the power of the visionary production team's creative instinct in this respect with their assertion that throughout the group's career, they had consistently released records, "That both set trends and predicted them."

As a consequence, as the group continued to elevate hip hop's commercial and pop cultural relevance in the alt-rock universe, the *LA Times* would add that, "None of the Beasties' peers enjoy the contemporary relevance that Ad-Rock and his bandmates Mike D and MCA carry." Reminding fans that it was not just cool, but also inspiring to take chances where those new directions were concerned, for many Beasties' fans and critics alike, in that spirit, *Hello Nasty* marked their bravest effort yet, and Caldato Jr. credits Ad-Rock as the musical mastermind behind the adventurous, ambitious and simply amazing-sounding leap into the future:

> Ad-Rock was really on top of his game, and was responsible for 85–90% of the music on that record. He was really on fire, and had a backlog of a lot of tracks and ideas, and he was just ready to go. He had a little studio in his house, in the back room, and he came in with this box full of discs, and they're all little songs and ideas, and he'd just pull them out, like, "Let's review this," "Let's review this. That's a good one. So is that. Hey, maybe we can put those two together?" Adam's taste in music was very eclectic, and he wasn't shy to try nutty things. He'd show up just thrilled because he had four new songs he'd done on the SB12 the night prior when he'd gotten home from the studio, and he'd show up with all these ideas. And the guys would be like, "Oh shit, that's dope! That one's even better," and that was really his strength: his ideas, and for

him to be able to do that so easily and focused. The only tricky part came once Adam brought all these ideas in was making it all work and putting it together, and that's where the group came in as a great filter to decide what worked.

The guys were very proud of him. When I recorded with him in the studio, Adam was always *very* quick and he would get his parts in a couple takes – that was it. That's the thing, his attention and his time was short, so he'd go in and nail parts and it would be done. That means we would just move onto something else at the studio once he had that track done. He *loved* being in the studio, loved the creative process, and to him, it was like: "Beats, music, what more do you need?"

Having danced on technology's cutting edge without missing a beat for years in the course of their record-making master-craft, with the advent of digital technology, the Beasties were provided that much more of an opportunity to excel at just that, with Mario confirming that because, "The Beasties were always into the new stuff, especially for the kind of music we were doing, which was always innovative, we embraced digital right off because it just allowed us more tools. Working for the first time in the digital recording realm was definitely exciting and opened up more possibilities by having everything in one computer, and being able to manipulate it, like tuning was much easier, truncating, trimming, just working with it was a lot easier than working with the drum machine. So from my process, it made things easier."

Teaching yet another master class in re-inventive sampling where Mario helped Ad-Rock and company assemble each song's tapestry of interpolated and original band compositional contributions, the producer had a leg up throughout production courtesy of the innovative-for-the-era fact that:

> Basically, I was using the computer as the recording unit. I had sixteen tracks of Pro Tools, analog outputs, and then I had an 8-track called a Sample Cell Card, which was basically a sampler with eight outputs, and the sampling time was endless. So instead of on the drum machines, I was now sampling in the computer. Ad-Rock was still using the SB1200, and so he'd work on that, and then I'd transfer what he did into the computer, and then we'd re-program it on Studio Vision. So I was using Studio Vision, the sequencer program, at the time, and I was using Pro Tools hardware to record the album.

> By then, because we were basically recording everything to digital, going directly to the computer, the writing process for the record was much easier and more streamlined technically than on previous albums because we all had D-88, the digital 8-tracks at home, that way somebody could take the music home on a stereo track, and that way, they'd have six tracks they could add vocals on at home. That was a medium we used for vocals, so the vocals you hear on the final album got recorded on those D-88s a lot of times.

A record where MTV noted the band musically "immerses itself in a variety of styles (salsa, acoustic songs and futuristic dub, for example), without returning to the alternating hardcore and funk dynamic that characterized its last two albums." They headed back to New York City once again at the top of recording. Following a routine that had worked so successfully for the group on *Ill Communication*, Mario drew the important contrast that when the group had set up shop last time, the focus had been on instrumental jamming where this time around, they were returning to their hometown to celebrate their b-boy roots:

> The focus of *Hello Nasty* was mainly making a rap album. They wanted to come back hard, we were going back to New York and wanted to make a hip hop record, so that was the vibe. The New York City backdrop was hugely important in crafting that vibe too, because it was like a home coming, almost ten years after *License to Ill*. We did the two records previous where there was jamming and playing and screwing around, and I think they realized that they maximized that kind of as far as they could with their abilities at the time – musically and with their talents. So the attitude was one of: "We had fun doing this, and have done everything we wanted to do: our Sly Stone, our Meters," and all these influences we were listening to. All these different elements were done, and now it was like, rap was at a stage where it was kind of needed a revitalization, and they were amped to do this.

The digital realm the group was creating in would prove a great assistant technically and inspirationally when their energies were focused on crafting vocal performances wherein Rap Pages would conclude the Beasties, "Deliver their made-for-concert verses in perfect unison." In the spirit of and in synch with their signature style of synergized rhyming, Mario C diagramed a close-knit recording set-up where, "When we were in the studio, we set up three booths so the guys could see each other, and had all the mics up so they could do it at the same time. They liked to track simultaneously whenever possible. Throughout the recording of vocals, it was just basically: Let's capture what they feel at the moment, and we didn't even have to say thing, it was just like, "Alright, let's do this and see what happens." From there, we'd do a couple takes, and would go with the flow, and I could tell if like somebody wasn't feeling it, they would just stop, and say, "Let's not push this," because there was no need to push anything. Everything happened when it was supposed to happen." Feeding off each other's creative energies as they vibed ideas around the room, Mario remembered a chain reaction that, not surprisingly, commonly began with Ad-Rock:

> He would have or two ideas ahead of time, and then from there totally go off his head and feel from the moment and just come up with a rhyme. Yauch, by contrast, would definitely have his thing thought out more and written-you knew what he liked to say, and he'd already have that in mind and figure out to finalize it. Mike was also 50/50, he'd have some ideas and then come off the cuff sometimes too with some crazy rhymes, because he'd hear Ad-Rock say something silly, and then he'd come back with

something ridiculous. He liked to be as silly as possible with his rhymes, and it worked- it was just very normal.

For vocal mics on this album, we used Senheisser 421s, which had a tighter sound. With *Check Your Head*, they used hand-held and were mainly 58s and the Karaoke mic, and the other radio hand mics and all that stuff, and on *Ill Communication*, it was a similar set-up. So by the time we got to *Hello Nasty*, we went to the 421s to change it up, and sometimes it would be hand-held, but a lot of times it would sit on the mic stand–so it went back to a more precise kind of performance.

Decorating the album with a dizzying array of vocal effects all manipulated in entirely original ways from one another to not just enhance vocal and instrumental performances, but take them on, "sonic adventures" in the esteemed opinion of Billboard. The Beasties definitely loved the creative rocket fuel that was provided by what Mario identified as, "The first thing they'd ask for in the booth, like, 'Yo, give me some verb,' and they didn't even have to ask, I already had the reverbs and delays ready, so once I checked the level, it was just turning on the delays– that was a given. So they definitely all liked a lot of effects." Showing how effects themselves can become an instrument for the band, Mario delved into a treasure chest of effects and related outboard gear that included favorites like:

The Yamaha, the Rev7, and the SBX90, and the Ibanez DM2000 – those were my standards –

that's all I needed was two reverbs and two delays and I can get that sound. Then I had a couple compressors for the vocals, and that's all we really needed to get things done. Because the rest of the stuff was samples, stuff that was already treated, except occasionally where we'd do something special.

As far as plug-ins, I didn't really use much, there was always the basics, where I did some cleaning up, or gating, or some basic EQing, but I wasn't really using any plug-ins. I used everything outboard – at that time I was using outboard reverbs, outboard delays, and stuff like that because it was easier for me. So I just used Pro Tools as a recording medium to replace the tape machine. It was also mobile, which meant I had the convenience of being able to bring it with me, which was genius, so I flew out my whole rig to New York in two road cases – and I had a Mackie 32x8 console, which had eight busses and allowed me to monitor everything and have extra inputs. I was still carrying my reverbs, so it was a package where I had everything together.

When we got to RPM Studio, I utilized a better reverb, I think I used the Lexicon 280, the studio reverb. I think I might have used a plate reverb too, and I used some Spring reverbs as well – I had a Parthesis Spring Reverb that this girl Brooke that we knew showed up with one time. It was awesome and I ended up using it on a few tracks. I used whatever delays they had, like the TC 2290's, because it was a little better quality than the one I had, or stereo delay. I used an Eventide for some special effects and harmonizing, and the rest would be compressors. So we put some stuff through a Fairchild they had, and some Neve compressors, 2264s. I used the GML EQ on the mix– like run the whole bus through a GML and then open up a little bit of top-end air, and a little bit of subs. That was mainly the outboards that I recall using.

With all three Beasties operating with similar technical savvy, they essentially were able to take the studio home with them virtually at night. With everyone as deeply committed to working on the album, the digital Pro Tools paradise for the Beasties privately caused Mario its share of headaches, explaining that, "That benefit for them created more work because for me because there were also more possibilities now, so the guys would be like, "Well let's try this version," or "Let's try this version!" So I'd be copying the song over, and trying different edits, and different versions instantly, which was something we could never do when we were working on tape. You'd have to mix it, and then would have to edit it, so it opened up a lot of channels, and was a great too, everybody was into it and excited, so Yauch could say, "Hey, let's repeat that again,' and it was like, 'Cool, done," and literally took ten seconds as opposed to: Hold on, let me get a half-inch machine, and copy it, and tape it, and edit it."

Displaying the kind of bedside manner he recommends anyone should have when bending over backwards to make it easiest for your artists to create is involved, Mario embraced flexibility with the welcome help of Pro Tools, using the cutting edge software in a groundbreaking way with how he manipulated the album's colorful collection of samples. These ranged from Amral's Trinidad Cavaliers Steel Orchestra *Oye Como Va* which showed up in *Body Movin Prelude In C# Minor* by Les Baxter and jazz crusaders *Love Is Blue* on *Intergalactic*, all the way to old-school classics like Run-D.M.C.'s *Sucker M.C.'s* on *Super Disco Breakin'* and Grandmaster Flash and the Furious Five's *Flash To The Beat* on *The Grasshopper Unit (Keep Movin')*:

> Whether it was with editing vocals or loops, and being able to cut up more stuff. Because our sources are what was mattered – the source of the old record; the source of the old sample, or the dirty beat, or the nasty sounds. That's really where the heart of it is. The editing and the sequencing was just a tool that aided and improved immensely the production part of it, and allowed us to do so many tracks. So many songs, and everybody was a fan of it. Especially now, I could comp vocals as opposed to just having one vocal take, and punching in. We could do a few takes, and take the best ones, and put it together much more easily.

Arguably the most famous effects-driven hit from the record came with the arrival of the global phenomenon, *Intergalactic* which landed like a musical U.F.O. in the ear courtesy of the infectious vocoder-coated chorus. Caldato Jr. remembered its introduction as a happy accident coming after, "I had just bought that vocoder the day before. I was horsing around with it, testing it out, and we tested it out on that mic, so that's Ad-Rock"'s voice you hear on the chorus: Intergalactic Planetary. He's singing into the mic, and I'm controlling the vocoder that's hooked up to a keyboard. So as you trigger the notes, it sends the pitch up and down and that's determined by the key but also by the oscillator on the unit, and I was manually rocking it while he was saying the chorus vocals. So we created the sound together, and we looked at each other as I was recording it, like, "*Oh shit!*" So afterward, we cut it up, and were like, "That's the one!" We knew it was banging, it was just ridiculous. For the other effects in play on the lead verses, I used the Lexicon 280 reverb, and the 2290 PC delay– there's no phasing or chorusing."

For as quickly and easily as they'd discovered the solid gold vocal chorus hook, after three years away from radio, the evolution of the song as a concept was actually as old in its own history, as Mario discloses that "*Intergalactic* began as an idea from *Ill Communication* that never got completely realized. Ad-Rock's brother's girlfriend had mentioned at the time that she liked the concept, 'Oh yeah, that Intergalactic, that's a good idea,' and then he remembered the idea. So it was kind of a weak version that at first had nothing to do with what it sounds like now." When it came time to find the perfect magic carpet ride musically for the group to flow over, Mario was the man with the Ace up his sleeve after following good engineering practice of keeping the recorder going at all time – a tip of the trade Caldato Jr. still recommends today – recalling that the rhythm first hit him:

> When we had a couple friends who'd come by and play us records and give us ideas, and this one kid came by and had us check out this Mexican group that had this fat beat on it. And whatever he was playing on the turntable, I was

just recording it, so I captured it the stuff, and then just put it in our library. For that one there, one day Adam and I were working, and he said, "Oh man, we need a beat." So we started going through the library listening through sounds, and when we heard that one, it was like, "Boom, that's perfect!" So I sent that Mexican group sample out to his sampler, he sampled it then programmed the beat real quick, and boom, that shit was done! For the background stuff that was really cool in the track, Adam found a loop that was this Les Baxter electronic lounge music, and that's what *really* made it come together. Because at first, it was just the beat and the vocoder as I remember, then he found that loop the day after to add to it, which worked out perfect. When we were done, Adam and I were just like, "Damn, that thing is bad!" It was just hot. Later on, when we brought Mix Master in, I'd given him a couple records, and gave him a classical record, and said, "Grab some of these hits." He took these orchestral string hits and cut that up, and that shit sounded like *Planet Rock*, it was just perfect."

Following on the heels of the Grammy winner for Best Rap Performance by a Duo or Group, the Beasties dropped *Body Movin'* on the b-boys and b-girls, causing an international dance craze that popped up on the Top 40 of charts from Britain to Dutchland, New Zealand and Australia. Mario once again shined a spotlight on Ad-Rock as its primary musical inventor, classifying it as, "An Ad-Rock special, that's an SB1200 production. He just whips out the disks, and boom there it is! He's got the loop, kick and snare, some noise, and that's it, it was pretty much done. I EQ'd and compressed it separately, so I'd take the outputs, and say, "Alright, give me the sounds one at a time,' and he'd say, "Here's the loop, here's the kick, here's the snare, here's the beat,' and I'd separate them, put them back in on the grid and re-create it so we could make an arrangement, then I'd run it out through the board. So the kick would be separate, the snare separate, and I'd EQ them with the Neve, add compression, and do whatever else was needed to make it sound like it did." Once Horovitz and his co-producer had assembled the irresistible bounce beneath the instrumental, it proved the invitation to inspiration for Mike D and M.C.A., who joined Ad-Rock as the trio put the hits contagious chorus and sing-along verses:

> When that one came together, it just sparked more interest and more anxiety for those guys to hurry up and get this shit together. It provided for fuel for the fire, and led to *Body Movin.*' I remember when we decided to do *Body Movin'* that day, we were like, "Okay, this is the joint with the steel drum band playing, and Mike was joking. "That will make this like some exercise-type shit, Body Movin'..." So when he went in the booth, I turned on the harmonizer, and that's the effect you hear on his voice for the chorus. When I threw it on there, all of the guys went, "Oh shit, that's perfect!" So it's mainly Mike, but all three of them wound up on that chorus. With a double harmony and a high and a

low one from the SBX90 stereo harmonizer, it was just perfect.

After recording the majority of the album in a studio set-up in Sean Lennon's basement Tribeca rehearsal space in New York City, as the team prepared to embark on the next leg of their voyage creating what *Rolling Stone* later crowned a "psychedelic rap masterpiece," the group moved over to the more traditionally-decked-out RPM Studios to mix *Hello Nasty*. Because of its sheer expanse in tracks, Caldato Jr. employed, "An old Neve that was either thirty-two or thirty-six channels that was hooked up to the computer using sixteen of Pro Tools tracks and eight on the sampler. So that's twenty-four, and then the rest were outboard. We utilized everything on that console."

With his ears working around-the-clock, "Mixing where I was pretty focused on sonically getting things to sound right." Mario slaved over the project day in and out organizing the brilliance that *Rolling Stone* argued was, "Everywhere: the grooves are threaded with spaced-out electronics, turntable scratches, backward-flowing drumbeats and subtle flourishes that bespeak thirty months of off-again, on-again studio tinkering." Having developed a technique by now tailored to balancing all the elements of the Beastie Boys' eclectic sound, Mario recalled that:

> I had a technique and formula I kept with, which meant having the beats tight; making sure the samples sounded a certain way; and then treating the vocals a certain way. There were a lot of little nuances, and a lot of time and focus and energy into making sure the record sounded perfect.

When we got to RPM Studio, I utilized a better reverb, I think I used the Lexicon 280, the studio reverb. I think I might have used a plate reverb too, and I used some Spring reverbs as well – I had a Parthesis Spring Reverb that this girl Brooke that we knew showed up with one time. It was awesome and I ended up using it on a few tracks. I used whatever delays they had, like the TC 2290's, because it was a little better quality than the one I had, or stereo delay. I used an Eventide for some special effects and harmonizing, and the rest would be compressors. So we put some stuff through a Fairchild they had, and some Neve compressors, 2264s. I used the GML EQ on the mix– like run the whole bus through a GML and then open up a little bit of top-end air, and a little bit of subs. That was mainly the outboards that I recall using.

Selling a staggering 681,000 copies in its first week of release as it rocketed to #1 on the Billboard Top 200 Album Chart upon release in the summer of 1998, and logging #1 spots around the world that reflected the sheer stretch of the group's influence, hitting the top of the charts in Australia, the European Albums Chart, Germany, Switzerland, New Zealand, the U.K., and #2 in Austria, Belgium, Canada, Dutchland, Norway, and Sweden. *Hello Nasty* was instantly voted into the Best 50 Albums of the Year charts around the globe, including France's Les Inrockuptibles, Rock Sound, and Technikart, Germany's Musikexpress, the United Kingdom's Melody Maker (#2), NME (#2), Q Select, Uncut, and stateside to no surprise, #9 on *The Village Voice*'s Albums of the Year ranking, #10 on *Spin*'s Best 10

Albums of the Year, #5 on *Mix Magazine*'s Best 10 Albums of the Year, and #2 on *Rolling Stone*'s Best 5 Albums of the Year Chart.

Perhaps the greatest artistic nod would come when the group won Grammy Awards for Best Alternative Music Album and Best Rap Performance by a Group or Duo. Proving their competing credibility in both genres equally among peers, and for Mario, reflecting back in closing on his most rewarding part of the album's release and reception being the completion of the journey itself:

> We all pitched in. I definitely spent and dedicated an entire year of my life in New York working with the Beasties, and realizing this dream that was this record. It was a serious commitment and I'm very proud of it. There was a bit of pressure on *Hello Nasty* to get finished after four years since the last record. And there was a lot of anticipation, but we were very confident. I remember when we finished the record we all felt it was the hottest thing we could come up with. I don't think anything else could have touched it. Just as one of the producers on it, and being the one who recorded all of those songs. When we were actually nominated by the Grammy Awards for *Album of the Year* in 1999 for that LP, we didn't win it, but being nominated alone was just an incredible honor for me.
>
> *www.marioc.com*

"When it passes the musical taste test, so to speak, that's what we work for as producers." –J-ROC

CHAPTER 7

The 20/20 Experience –Jerome "J-ROC" Harmon

Watching co-producers Timbaland and Jerome "J-ROC" Harmon collaborating together in the studio is equivalent in its electric energy to watching Michael Jordan and Scotty Pippen trading the basketball back and forth, working their way down the court back in the Bulls' epic 90's heyday. This is J-ROC's time, and as one of the true all-star players in today's hip hop studio game, the analogy is dead-on right down to the professional moniker, which he reveals he got precisely:

> Because of the fact that I'm always in the gym, always working out, always doing some sports. So we were at church one time and the wife of this friend of mine said, "Damn, your arms look like rocks, they're so hard! What's up J-ROC?!" So then my cousins started calling me J-ROC, so it came about because I always like to stay in shape. So it's all about sports.
>
> Before I graduated high school, I was just like any average guy who played sports and had the ambition of going to college on the football and basketball track. So I thought I was going to be a basketball player, that's what was on my mind. But even while I was still in high school, I was heavily involved with theatre, and was in marching band, concert band, and choir. I was actually band president for a couple of years, and choir president as well. I was heavily involved with all of the activities in high school. The reason why was because my aunt who raised me after my mom passed was a teacher as well. She said, "You should always make yourself as many opportunities in life. Don't limit yourself, and don't feel like just because people say you are this or that, that you have to go for that. You have to go for what's in your heart."

So to me, even though I was really, really musically inclined and received a lot of scholarships all over for music and basketball, I wound up going to University of New Mexico. Because A.) I wanted to get out of Texas, and B.) they gave me three scholarships, for music, academics and basketball – which was the best of all three worlds that I liked. And I wanted to get out of that small town as fast as possible.

Today, a world away from his Brownwood, Texas roots, J-ROC spends his days crafting what have become many of the millennium's biggest world-wide hip hop and R&B hits over the past fifteen years. These read like a greatest hits collection including such #1 radio staples as *Drunk in Love* by Beyoncé, *Suit and Tie* and *Pusher Love Girl*, the Top 5 Grammy-winning hit *Holy Grail* off of Jay Z's multi-platinum *Magna Carter* album. Perhaps most notably, Harmon helped resurrect Michael Jackson to the top of the charts once again courtesy of his work on the posthumous worldwide smash *Xscape* album, which hit #1 in six countries and #2 in twelve countries around the world, re-establishing Jackson's relevance with a new generation of fans. Their dream team is one that is rare by the simple fact that for 99% of hip hop producers, to work with a titan of his legend *once* is a career highlight, but to work side-by-side day in and out as his right-hand man as J-ROC does with Timbaland makes them the equivalent of a dynamic duo:

Because there's no boundaries with us. So we kind of feed off of each other, and we don't have specific roles. Like he doesn't just only do drums and I just don't only take the keys. We both collaborate. That's what collaboration is, when you can do it all and you're not limited. And I think that's what makes us so unique because we're not limited where a lot of people are limited. If there's something he can't do, he knows I'm overly-qualified to make sure it happens. I can write out the charts for the guitar player if I need to, which Tim had probably never had that before working with other producers. And that enhances his style and elongates his career and enhances my style and elongates my career.

It's like being in a band where you have a piano player whose as instrumental as yourself and can do several things. The only thing you need to learn is not to clash or step over something someone is doing. Like, a lot of times, if I have an idea and I have the basics of it, he'll say, "Ooh, let me get them drums!" and I'm like, "Cool."

I make sure I don't overcrowd stuff to where he can't add his own influence, and it's vice versa. If he has an idea that he can't really dissect and get it out, he can hum it and I'll be like, "Oh Hey, I got that," and will play the whole thing, and he'll be like, "Yeah, yeah, let's get it!"

When the team was asked to be part of the contemporizing of Michael Jackson's sound for the millennial generation, the dynamic duo jumped at the opportunity with just such enthusiasm. Treating the responsibility of resurrecting Michael Jackson in a modern era as the great one that it was, especially in light of previous posthumous efforts that had fallen miserably flat, J-ROC remembered feeling especially conscious of the latter history as he moved forward with the project:

> Man, let me tell you...They had a lot of producers who tried to do stuff like that, a posthumous type of project, and they failed. It didn't sound like it was authentic, it sounded like it was enhanced and stuff like that. That's from a consumer's ear, to them, it didn't sound like Michael and critics were saying "Michael never does stuff like that." So you had to be real sensitive to the public's opinion, both out of respect to Michael's fans and because this is our livelihood, and so with this one, first of all, it was so scary because I was like, "Man, I don't want Tim and I to be the laughing stock like Will.I.am when he did it." So at first it was a little unnerving because we were both like, "Damn, if it don't go right...", but I've never been afraid of challenges, and I think that's what motivated me. All the "What ifs..." "What if it doesn't go right? What if people won't accept it?" Those were all the reasons why I did it, because it was out of honor of Michael Jackson because a lot of what past people had done was so terrible, that I felt like it was owed to him.

In the interest of a clean slate, J-ROC and Timbaland started from scratch with literally just Jackson's vocal in their ears as they respectively and collectively channeled every generation of Jackson they'd grown up influenced by – from the Jackson 5 to *Thriller* and beyond – into a brilliant hybrid. Bridging the classic elements of Jackson's Disco *Off the Wall* heyday with the kind of modern dance-floor polish that Billboard would later compliment as "smooth," predicting the song would, "Certainly have a pop-culture impact." That pop prognosis would prove true world-wide as the duet version of the track between Jackson and Justin Timberlake produced by Timbo and ROC blasted off to the top of the charts, re-energizing Jackson's international following who cheered the smash onto #1 in countries as diverse as Israel, South Korea, Germany, South Africa, Denmark, Croatia, and Belgium. The smash rocketed into the Top 10 in France, Hungary, the Netherlands, the Czech Republic, Italy, Lebanon, Spain, the United Kingdom, and the United States as fans and DJs alike welcomed back the King of Pop. Taking fans back behind the scenes into the heart of his creative process building a band for Jackson from the ground up with co-producer Timbaland, J-ROC began with the blank-canvas creatively he and Tim were working on:

> When we agreed to do it, I went as an open book myself, I didn't know what to expect, I didn't know how it was going to come to me, I just remember they said that they had some tunes that he did and the estate had picked out these certain songs that they felt could be not the easiest to re-do, but that was more like Michael from the 70's all the way up through his death.

> With "*Love Never Felt So Good*," we played all of the instruments you hear in the song live, and it

was scary hearing his voice in my headphones while we were working, because sometimes, you forget that he's not around, and when you're hearing just his vocals, the way he was recording, he was talking to the engineer, "Oh, can you turn that down a little bit?", and you forget that he's not around, hear that and say "What the hell?!" And I'd be in the room a lot of times by myself when I was doing pre-production, and there were times I thought Michael was looking over my shoulder (laughs).

Featuring a dazzling rhythm track that J-ROC – a drummer since he could crawl – built around the classic concept of *pocket* that Quincy Jones had so perfectly pioneered with Jackson in their heyday, he made sure to infuse some of his own founding influences into the beat's feel and swing, beginning with the Godfathers of Soul and Funk:

I was taught and have always gone by the principle rules of James Brown and George Clinton when it comes to drums. Drums need to have space but they need to be the driving force for that composition, it's got to be the driving force, but it can't be overbearing, it has to have space. When I'm programming, I have to make sure I'm the drummer. I have to make sure, "Okay, now I'm a drummer, I can't be a programmer. I need to make sure this sounds like an actual guy sitting in that booth playing drums." Steve Gadd is a good example. When he used to play a lot with Joe Sample, I used to look at a lot of his videos. I always saw Steve, and Steve stayed *in the pocket*. But you would have thought he was the feature instrumentalist because he was so in the pocket.

He made you lock in and pay attention to everything around him, so when I was doing Michael Jackson, I had to remember all the influences that were around Michael Jackson – the Johnson Brothers, and a lot of musicians who played with Earth, Wind and Fire, their horn section and stuff like that. Quincy Jones used only a handful of musicians, and it happened that these were all musicians I'd grown up listening to, not just on Michael Jackson, but any album that came out, they were always the session players. So "Pocket" has stayed with me since then, and I believe with Michael Jackson, I had to make sure that the nucleus of his music – the drums – had the space and pocket.

Creating a sound that the L.A. Times declared in its review was, "Shockingly vital, as though the producers charged with re-imagining this work had harnessed dance floor defibrillators." Adding of the team's masterpiece, *Love Never Felt So Good* that they had succeeded not only commercially on Jackson's behalf, but artistically as well, arguing the song's substance, "Confirms that hearing Michael sing 'new' material can still be a mystical experience, and throughout the freshly produced recordings the sound of a still-vital spirit rushes into the present with revived energy." As Timbaland and his sidekick worked away creating the instrumental body of the song around the skeleton of

Michael's voice and J-ROC's beat, the producer remembered musically teleporting himself back into Jackson's late-70's era band of session players:

> For *Love Never Felt So Good*, when that song came in with just a piano and his vocals, I knew exactly what era that was, just by listening to the tone in his voice. In my mind, I went straight to musicians like George Duke, who was all over *Off the Wall*, and I'm a big George Duke lover, so I knew exactly what I was going to have to pull out, and knew exactly who I was going to have to have play hollow-bodied guitar, stuff like that. I grew up on Michael Jackson so I knew every era just by his voice, and it took me back, it did, but I didn't want to just try and clone and mimic that era, I wanted to take the essence of it, and then modernize it. That's what Timbaland and I did, we took the essence of everything out his voice, and said, "Okay, I know that's what was going on during that time," and we modernized it and brought it up to date. It still gave you the real Michael Jackson, but with a twist, because the millennials – those kids who grew up not knowing who Michael Jackson was past his name and had never heard his music – we had to bring them up to speed on who Michael Jackson was. So it was a challenge in that sense, like "How can we take the kids who didn't grow up listening to Michael and The Jacksons and make them just as crazy as we were about it!"

So on "*Xscape*," I programmed that stuff. I have this thing called Easy Drum by Toontrack, and that gives you some real good, natural drum sounds. That's really cool, and I used to be the best table drummer in the world growing up, (laughs), I beat the crap out of tables, and on that record, I used a lot of kits out of Contact, and a lot of times, I can take basic programmed drums and I EQ them – that's the trick, is how I EQ the drums and how I make them sound natural and how to make them sound live.

A skill he first debuted with a make-shift drum kit from his mother's kitchen back when he was still an infant and first began displaying his natural inclination for rhythm and precocious musical curiosity that quickly caught his parents' interest, J-ROC chuckled as he recalled that, "The first instrument I picked up on was the drums, I was two and a half, three years old, and my mom noticed right away because I would sit on the floor and go into her kitchen cabinets and pull out all the pots and pans, get her wooden spoons and use them as my drum sticks!" (laughs) A young Jerome kept banging home the point that this wasn't a passing hobby – not only to his parents – but also his neighbors once he moved from his mother's kitchen to the back yard:

My first actual drum kit came when I was six. This was after two years of me using my second home-made drum kit after the one in my mother's kitchen, (laughs) If you've ever watched Fat Albert, and you see how they made instruments out of trash cans and buckets? Well,

I used to take my sister's Easy Bake Oven and
used that as my snare. Then, I would use the
trash can tops as my cymbals, and then I'd take
some plastic buckets and those would be my
tom-toms and my floor tom. That's what I
would use. I would get up at 5:30 a.m., 6:00 a.m.
in the morning, and would wake up the whole
neighborhood in the back yard playing drums!
To me, I sounded like Alex Van Halen. I used to
love seeing him play drums! I thought I was
doing it, but didn't know I was disturbing the
whole neighborhood and had people hating me
for waking them up. But by 6 o'clock, I was out
back beating the crap out of those drums! My
parents didn't have a lot of money, but my
mother saved up enough money to buy me my
first drum kit when I was six. I can still
remember, it was Christmas morning, and I had
a Pearl drum set!

Being raised in a musical home, as J-ROC hailed from a
family where music had in fact brought his parents together in
the first place, he found himself thereafter surrounded as a child
with a household of multi-generational influences to soak up
courtesy of both his parents and siblings' respective record
collections. A child of the late 1970s and 1980s, Jerome had the
added benefit of growing up in arguably the greatest melting pot
the Billboard Pop Charts ever experienced stylistically. On a
given Top 10 from the Billboard Hot 100 Singles Chart, kids
tuning in would hear everything from disco and dance to pop to
hair metal to rock & roll, country, R&B and hip hop to New

HIP HOP HITS

Wave and synth pop and a brilliant blend of everything in-between:

> My mom and dad did grow up as singers. My mom was a singer, my dad was a singer, and they met in a doo-wop group in Ft. Worth, Texas singing, and going around town doing the talent shows. That's how they got together. From there, they had six kids, and raised us all up in a household with a lot of music. All different genres, all different types. All of my sisters were singers and all picked up different instruments as well. But I think I was the only one who really had the inertia of learning how to play several types of instruments. So it all started at home.
>
> I was influenced heavily by Rick James, Prince, Earth Wind and Fire of course, Zapp & Rogers... My brothers were like eight years older than me, so I hung with them and all the music they listened to, I was right there with them. You remember when you could buy ten records from Columbia House for a penny? So my brothers would always buy records, and everything they would buy, they would make me listen to it and play those songs on the piano, and this being the 70's, I was heavily influenced with the Jacksons of course, Kool and the Gang, a lot of really good soul/R&B. And then my dad was a truck driver, so of course, he listened to a lot of country, so I was really influenced by a lot of what he listened to. He loved Merle Haggard, he

was one of his favorites, and he would make me sit down and play a lot of Country and Western as well. So I was really well-rounded because a lot of people in my life were older and they knew what genres and influences would help me to become a better musician growing up.

Like so many R&B and hip hop producers of his generation who grew up in the church, many of J-ROC's most important instrumental discoveries would come from that holy backdrop. These ranged from his first opportunities to physically handle key instruments within his repertoire as a producer and player like the piano and guitar to building his confidence as with each early flourish of extraordinary talent. Recognized from knee-high as a talent that needed nurturing, as his multi-instrumental nature as a musician continued to be exposed, he remembered it happening almost as a happy accident:

I started playing piano around nine, and it just came out of the blue. I have no clue why it came to me, but I do remember when it happened: we were at a Tuesday night church service, and my mom was the Minister of Music at our church as well, so after service my brother and I were sitting in church, waiting to go home, and were kind of bored, and I remember telling my brother, "Tim, I can play that piano up there," and my brother was like, "Naw man, you can't play that." So I said, "Yeah I can," and he warned me, "You go up there, you're gonna get a whoopin'" but I didn't care at this point because he'd dared me. (laughs)

So I climbed up on the stage, walked over and turned on the Fender Rhodes organ and the first song I ever played in life was *Lean On Me* by Bill Weathers, note for note verbatim, the right key and everything. The funny thing was, I remember my mom screaming and grabbing me, but instead of being in trouble, she was yelling excitedly, "Who taught you how to play that?!", because we didn't have nothing in the house but my drums. So I told her, "I don't know, I just started playing it," and rather than getting spanked, a week later, I woke up one morning, came out into the dining room, and my mom had found me an old, upright piano and there were some keys missing at the lower end – I think an F Sharp and an A Flat – so I had to press down real hard to hit those keys. But that's how I started playing the piano.

His roots in the church would prove an equally as huge asset for young Jerome, who as an accelerated student of music came with his opportunity and exposure to playing with musicians many years his senior, in both age and experience, not only picking up a million valuable tips and tricks on the playing and arranging side. At the same time, other church bands from neighboring denominations and communities traveled through his congregations on a regular basis. This gave Harmon the ability to expand both the number of players he could hone his own evolving skill level as a player against, along with sharing the stage at a young age with A-list musicians from genres ranging from gospel to country to jazz and everything in-between:

The church was heavily instrumental, and I'll tell you why: because I grew up in a predominantly white church here in Texas in a country town of Brownwood, Texas, and we had a Minister who was a world-wide evangelist and he would go from different states and preach at these big Gospel revivals under a tent. So we were exposed to a lot of different musicians that would come to our church, and me being a drummer, I would play with different artists that would come and perform at our church. So we had banjo player and fiddle, guitar and then on the other side, a full blown-blown horn section and a lot of the horn section were black people who came from Georgia, St. Louis, and they moved down to Brownwood, so we had this really great-sounding band at our church.

Our church was pretty big, so me being young and being exposed and recognizing that I had a talent in music, I hung with and played for a lot of seasoned musicians that really worked with me and forced me to learn fast, so I was playing full blown-out music and compositions. Some of the musicians were jazz musicians who had their own little bands outside of church, and they would come to my mom and ask if I could come and practice and play with a lot of these different types of groups that were in town. So I learned how to play that type of music as well. So having those two influences, I didn't know how it was developing me because I was just having

fun, but it became prevalent the older I got how
much I did know and didn't know I knew just
by hanging around with all these seasoned
instrumentalists and vocalists at an early age.

The producer's side of J-ROC's musical mind was alive and
buzzing with curiosity from the time he discovered his
instrumental talents onward. Opening his ears to a world of
home-made experimentalism where he honed record-making
basics like editing splicing together his own mixes of the popular
songs of the day on cassette tapes and arrangement as he decided
on the coolest-sounding song orders. Eager for a sounding board
to see how hot they were or not, Jerome took advantage of
another backdrop where his talents proceeded him, and a far
more appropriate one than the church, to test out his latest
original mixes on the basketball court where hip hop had long
been the preferred soundtrack:

> The first time I ever did any type of recording,
> and this is going to sound crazy, but I used to
> have this AIWA dual cassette player with the
> lights in the middle that flashed, and the first
> time I ever did any kind of splicing was with that
> double-cassette. I was in junior high, and I used
> to play Basketball, and when we'd warm up,
> everybody would have their little warm-up
> mixtape, and I made my own mix-tape with the
> double-cassette. I would sit down, put one tape
> in – maybe Planet Rock by Afrika Bambaataa.
> So first, I would take *Planet Rock* and let it play,
> and I'd catch a little loop, and I would cut it, and
> then put it to the tape I was recording on and

splice it in, and then let it play, let play, catch another loop, cut that part, put it on the other side, get my masking tape, tape it down, then I'd keep recording, keep recording, then stop, grab another cassette of another song, and splice it. I didn't even know at the time I was tape splicing, I was just trying to make my mix-tape. So I started splicing cassettes when I was in sixth, seventh grade.

Growing up with a house full of older brothers and sisters and cousins, I was around when hip hop started, and we were listening to guys like Kurtis Blow and Afrika Bambaataa and the Sugar Hill Gang, and when *Rapper's Delight* came out, I didn't know what was going on! There was Blowfly, he was like the original of nasty rap, he had a song called *Rap Dirty*, that was all when I was young in the early 80's. I graduated high school in '88, and by then, there were almost too many influences to name: Rakim, Public Enemy, KRS-One, and Stetsasonic. That was the golden time of hip hop.

An instant hit with his friends and fellow players on the courts, word of J-ROC's DJing abilities were soon getting around the neighborhood as he expanded his mixing platform from the boom-box cassette decks to the turn-tables. Soon impressing his parents enough to be hired as entertainment for their house parties on the weekend, Jerome recalled that, "After a while, my brothers had started buying turn tables, and we would be the kids in the neighborhood who would open up our windows and put the Peavey speakers out towards the windows and we just played music in our little country town, and when people walked by, they would dance listening to our music. A lot of times, I would make my own little mix and then on top of that, while it was playing, I had my piano miced with the Peavey amp and the mic, so I'd put the mic with the Peavey and played with the music I had mixed. And people would sit out on our front lawn, my dad and company and I would be the guy who would entertain his friends!"

Though he'd become a veteran performer, both behind the drums, piano and turn-tables by his early teens, it wasn't until he put a monetary value on his talent as a musician that it first ever occurred to Jerome that he could make a living from that talent. An aside at the time anyway as Harmon had already set his sights on making a profession out of his athletic talents over his musical ones:

> I just wanted to play basketball and track and do music because it was a hobby of mine. It first occurred to me I could make money playing music when I was playing in the church because they paid me when I played organ for my services. Because I was doing it an early age and was always considered one of the best – even among guys who were fifteen years older than me, to me, as a seasoned musician, I could play what they could play, but it wasn't a competitive thing, I just wanted to have fun. I wasn't thinking beyond the front door. I was a kid, and though I knew I had a gift and was always told that and that I would go far, but I didn't know

what that meant. At that point, I didn't think, "Oh, I'm going to be the top producer in the world, I'm going to be the best musician."

My band director in high school, Dr. Scott Mason, he was a Texas Tech graduate and played all brass instruments, and his wife, Mrs. Judy Mason, was a brass player, and they were a couple of young, progressive teachers coming out of a program that was really progressive, the Texas Tech band. Back then, Marching Band and Drum and Musical Core were things I was really, really heavy into, and when they graduated, they were like 24, so both Scott and Judy Mason were heavily, heavily involved with my life. He taught me *discipline*, then through high school, I met Dr. Bill Wagener, he was a great jazz trombone player, and he taught me so much I thought I would become a Professor myself.

By the time he was setting his sights toward 18, the already musically-seasoned Jerome found himself in the unique position of having competing scholarship opportunities based on how dramatically his talents as both an athlete and musician had impressed Colleges taking a look at his maturity on both fronts. Deciding to split his chances evenly, Harmon took a full-scholarship for basketball at a Texas college while majoring in Music. The opportunity to avoid losing focus on either as he headed out into the world was not a leg up lost on J-ROC, who acknowledges in reflection that:

I was very lucky to have the chance to play basketball and at the same time study music at a school where they had a pretty good jazz program. From there, I transferred to University of Texas – Arlington to study Music Media. From those years, studying Music Theory has stayed a rule of thumb to me, whenever I'm in a jam or am having trouble processing something the way I hear it, I always go back to my basics: I go back to theory and make sure whatever chord progression or whatever I'm trying to do is theoretically correct. In college, Dr. Bill Snodgrass at University at Texas – Arlington was really, really heavily influential on me as far as Composition, Music Business. He taught me all about the music business, and how to compose with freedom. Knowing that even though there are rules in music, you don't have to always abide by the rules. Rules are meant to be broken, especially in music. And he also said, "You've just got to have that passion for music." So he really taught me about passion. That was Dr. Bill.

By the time he graduated, Jerome was ready for the Major Leagues, requiring no AA apprenticeship in learning the ropes on playing in a touring band before a live crowd, having used the cheers of church crowds and those he encountered at the football stadiums as part of the band to let him know he was following the right Piper. The next fan he'd land was a fellow up and coming musician on the fellow Texas Gospel scene, Kirk Franklin, a fellow multi-instrumentalist who would click with J-

ROC like two chords that made a perfect sound together, remarking of their synergy:

> Kirk was like me: we both grew up in the church, and both grew up exposed to all types and all genres of music, and we both had a goal in mind of wanting to be the best in Fort Worth. He got tired of mediocrity, Gospel music had become so traditional, and with me having all this experience playing different types of music, it was exactly what he needed to bring a new sound into Gospel. So me and my boy Bobby Sparks, having a background in hip hop and jazz and funk, fusion, we brought that sound with us when we were playing with Kirk Franklin. So that's how his sound became hip hop-gospel. That was one of the most inspiring times in my life because we were really doing it for the love of the music, and when we started touring, it was fresh and it exploded in the music industry, and that's why it became one of the world's best-selling gospel projects ever.

Getting his start in a genre so true to his musical roots was especially rewarding for J-ROC, who – even though he had far greater commercial successes to come – looking back still holds a fond place in his musical heart for the opportunity, which he took on in part as a campaign to tribute his upbringing. Doing so in the most glorious possible light he could celebrate his family and church's support in given the genre was their favorite at heart, Jerome chuckles looking back:

It may sound crazy, but to me, it was like a mission I had to do first, I had to pay homage to my Mom's prayers and all her hard work and being ill and still trying to raise a family – she raised us up until she passed. So this was something I knew I had to do first, I had to go and pay homage to what she instilled in my life growing up, and doing Gospel was something I knew she would be very proud of, so I wanted to make sure that was the first thing I did, and after that, I did what I wanted to do, but first I fulfilled that mission.

Harmon came full-circle in answering his calling after Franklin rocketed to fame. Resulting in Harmon's first contact with the realization of his dream via the validation of three multi-platinum albums and world tours before international audiences, he additionally achieved the astonishing, record-setting distinction of reaching #1 on the Billboard Top Gospel Albums chart for forty-two weeks with *Kirk Franklin and the Family*! He would subsequently top the mountain again as a player on Franklin's smash *God's Property from Kirk Franklin's Nu Nation*, which hit #1 on the Top R&B/Hip Hop Albums and #3 on the Billboard Top 200 Album Chart, selling 3 million albums and producing the hit *Stomp*. His fist taste of cross-over success raised J-ROC's radar beyond the sub-genre of Gospel, setting his sights on a mainstream breakthrough that would come after catching the ear of super-producer Timbaland in the mid-2000's.

Catapulting Harmon into the comfortable but constantly-challenging position of becoming Timbo's right-hand studio man, he knew he'd found home as the dynamic duo racked up whole new generation of hits for Timbaland, with J-ROC finding he folded into the fabric of the sound he was sewing as naturally as if he was always meant to be there. After a few short years together, the Jordan-Pippin team had been responsible for world-wide smashes that had not just re-shaped the culture, but crushed it into a new platform for Timbaland to re-assert himself as a modern, mainstream force in music production a generation after first doing so with Missy Elliott. Taking firm hold of the nation's dance floors in 2013, Harmon and Timbo would lock down both the clubs and the charts with a string of grand-slams that would take the world by storm, starting with Justin Timberlake's multi-platinum *20/20 Experience*.

No doubt the perspective J-ROC viewed the record-making prism through by this point in his whirl around the merry-go-round, he was knighted a member of the round table after he followed it up with a key contribution to international mega-star Beyoncé's follow-up to #1 smash *Crazy in Love* a decade later with an answer, *Drunk in Love*. Hitting the top of the charts in both the U.S. and South Africa, the song reflected how far Harmon's reach as a producer had traveled by that point in his almost twenty year career in the music business. Able to blend as much as he was able to generate an instantly-recognizable part of a song's construct, J-ROC would give a master's class when he came up with the song's highlight bridge, remembering being blown away in the first place by the fact that:

> First off, she's a monster! When she sings and performs, she's flawless when it comes to disciplining herself as to how to attack songs in the studio. Her process is so ill and can't be

copied, I don't know anybody who is so matter-of-fact when it comes to recording. She can be a one or two take singer, but then she goes back and adds all these different parts you wouldn't even think about. Like, she'll have her basic take down, you'll leave, and when you come back, it's something totally, totally different with all the harmonies, etc. She thinks like a musician. She knows where her harmonies are going to be, and don't get it twisted, she knows her theory, so she can self-correct.

I just remember when we were working on her album, we were mixing Justin's album and working on Jay Z's *Magna Carter* at the same time, and *"Drunk in Love"* kind of came at the end of her recording process and when she got the track and did her verses, she was missing a bridge. So I was over there working with Jay for *Fuck You*, doing my parts, and she came running by, saw me, stopped and said, "Ooh, Jerome, I need a bridge!" So I got over there, heard the track, and it was so hypnotizing, it put you in that mindset of like "Man, I feel like I'm on the moon or something!", so the bridge came to me naturally because it had nothing in it but her vocal, and I built the bridge around her vocal. Then Tim added some stuff to it, and it was just magic, that's all I can say! Some things you really can't explain, it just happens.

That spirit of spontaneity would infect Jay Z's *Magna Carter* with the same motivational mojo that was driving the whole team. Putting the best players in the game together on tape the way the Bulls hit the court in the finals during the 1990s, it created an All-Star atmosphere where J-ROC remembered like Scottie Pippen to Timbo's Jordan with Jay-Z acting as Phil Jackson, driving the momentum of the once-in-a-lifetime studio session as Harmon tried to put into words the reality that when speaking of hip Hhop's Muhammad Ali:

> There's not enough adjectives to describe the effect Jay-Z has on producers and getting them to become their best. He's so inspiring in itself that when he walks in the room, he commands automatically your best. He talks to you, and in conversing, tells you exactly what his mood is that day, and he makes you visualize right then where we're going in the future, so he makes you think so much forward that, in essence, all the other projects you did before then didn't matter (laughs), he's so inspiring – inspiration exudes from him.

> Watching Jay record in the studio is like being in the boxing ring with Floyd Mayweather Jr. or Muhammad Ali! When that bell rings, you're going to get so many flurries of punches coming at your face that you can't even...you're froze, you don't know what to do, you got so much coming at you. Then all of a sudden, boom! It's a song, and you're like, "What the hell just happened?" Jay has a lot of power with his mic.

Turning the page for fans back to another coveted collaboration on any producer's resume, working with Justin Timberlake's *The 20/20 Experience*, co-producing the album's two biggest singles, *Suit & Tie*, which sold 3 million copies in an age where no one goes platinum, and the Grammy winner for 2014's Best R&B Song Award. *Pusher Love Girl* dazzled and dizzied dance floors around the globe 24/7 with the kind of heat that roared out of the track like fire out of a Top Gun F-14 Fighter Jet engine, blazing up the charts to at #3 on the Billboard Hot 100 Singles Chart. Singling out his memories of working with Timberlake in the studio on the track, Harmon paid the singer the compliment:

> When we were in the studio recording *Suit & Tie*, Justin reminded me a lot of people who I grew up with and performed with, and wrote and toured with, because we had a lot of white singers as well. It wasn't just black, but they had such a deep root in Soul Music. When Justin gets around certain producers, it just percolates out of him naturally. There's nothing I influenced, he's just a natural. And God Bless his mom for raising him up around music all of his life because this guy's been performing since he was six or seven. He wasn't just singing some Mickey Mouse songs. He was singing some songs! So that was just natural for him.
>
> With *Pusher Love Girl*, when Timbaland came in the studio, man, they were singing old Doo-Wop and he just started sounding out that opening part he sounds out, and then Justin came in with

that vocal and we were like, "That's kind of cool." So as they were singing, I was actually starting to write the music, while he was humming all his little parts. Tim was a DJ, so he just loved Biz Markie growing up and used to beat box and do all that stuff. So he hummed and I put the music around it, and that was pretty much it.

For Justin's lead vocal, sometimes we used the Sony CA-800 mic, especially for Justin. But it depends on the song and what we're trying to capture. So sometimes we want a mic like the CA-800 that's more smooth. That picks up his soft side and then we go to the Neumann when he's going to use some of his R&B/hip hop/pop vocals. So it just really depends on the song, and the mood that we try and reach.

Most comfortable in the studio sitting behind a rig that features "a lot of different keyboards," the variety allowing Jerome the freedom to stay open to whatever vibe the artists he and Timbaland were collaborating with were feeling that day, such that "I don't know specifically what I'm going to use until I know what I hear, so a lot of times, I just pull up a BFD and I just pick a sound and if it matches what's going on with the mood of that track, that's what I use. Some of my favorite go-tos, I use a Korg Micro, and I got the Stage Vintage, which really gives you the essence of a real Rhodes when I had to have one. I use a lot of Sonic Box, Specialtronics, Veturian, etc. I use a lot of Native Instruments stuff – Kontakt, Guitar Rig, Battery, and Transient. There's no set pattern on how we start creating, I mean, we can be inspired by something on TV, so there's no set pattern that I use, it varies." No matter the spark, once the musical engines of invention were roaring, Harmon likened the feeling that built as a track took shape as one akin to:

> Something euphoric. When you're creating a relationship with someone, when you get to that point, you need to release. There's gotta be a reward at the end. (laughs) So that's what I call it: the musical orgasm!

Still, in spite of the highs he gets in the studio, once his music hits the air waves, Jerome preaches the importance no matter how far up the charts a hit climbs, or how long it stays there, to always keep your feet on the ground as a producer. Considering his Trophy Wall is decorated with Grammy Awards that stretch starting in 2015 for Best R&B Song and Best R&B Performancefor *Drunk in Love,* and Best Contemporary R&B Album for Beyoncé, Best Rap Collaboration in 2014 for his work on Jay-Z's *Holy Grail* and Best R&B Song for *Pusher Love Girl* by Justin Timberlake. All the way back to his Gospel roots with a Best Contemporary Gospel Album for Free to Worship by Fred Hammond, J-ROC has stayed in present touch with the notion throughout his whole career:

> As they say, "Never get high on your own supply." Because people get high off of their own stuff. And feel like they're a virtuoso in their own mind. So they feel like they can't be critiqued, they feel like no one can top them, so they become a legend in their own mind. I tell young producers to humble themselves, you've

got to be humble. Sure awards and accolades matter, but it's not the end-all be-all for me.

For all the high points, for Jerome, the downsides to being such a success in the business have come with a common symptom of working as a musician that most suffer from: missing time with their family, a sacrifice that takes it's toll for Harmon in "having kids and not always being home to see them grow up, not always being there to counsel them when they're having problems at school with other kids. A lot of times, I miss out on that, I miss out on a lot for the sake of making sure that they have a better life, like any other father."

Pressed to pick a favorite out from the considerably tall stack of hits he's helped write, play and produce throughout the past twenty-five years in the game, J-ROC wrestles with the answer for a few understandable moments, acknowledging, "That's a hard one, for real. Before landing on the 20/20 Experience with Justin, of course, was an experience within itself, because it takes you on a musical ride emotionally. Before that, we did Chris Cornell, which was the same way we did Justin, but because Chris is such a rock guy. It wasn't really accepted as much, but if you go back and listen to the complexity of that album, you'd be blown away! It was such a creative high, that even though it wasn't commercially that successful. To me, it was one of the most successful projects personally, so I feel very attached to that." While the secret to some producers' longevity has been to find a niche sound and stick with it, for Harmon, that approach is antithetical to what has long driven him creatively, so forcefully that he consistently works hard to avoid his greatest fear of ever getting caught in doing the same patterns, the same chord progressions, the same types of sounds:

I try to avoid having a signature sound, because sometimes having a signature sound can date you, and it can also plateau you out because there's no ebbs and flows within your own creative process. I write to transcend and I write to be a trend-setter, so I have to challenge myself, not only to do something that hasn't been heard before, but that it's accepted, because some people do shit that isn't accepted, it doesn't translate, but when it does translate and people really connect with it, that's the best part of it for me.

For J-ROC, there's little doubt he'll still be inspiring new generations of music fans and aspiring producers, players and songwriters in another twenty years from now as profoundly as he has already. In dispensing closing advice on what ingredients that make up his special sauce that are worth passing along in a recipe for success as a producer working in today's ultra-competitive record industry, the taste-master starts by recommending:

When you're making music, it's almost like making the best chili: you have to make sure you have the right blend of spices, the right temperature for the meat when you're browning your meat, and you've got to make sure the tomatoes you use are fresh. Because everything is blended, just to come up with this one flavor, this one taste, to make all of those flavors become one. With music, it takes a perfect blend of certain sounds as well. So I see things as if I'm cooking a meal, where you have to have that perfect blend.

www.jeromeharmonproductions.com

"His stats are impressive." – MTV

CHAPTER EIGHT
How Do You Want It – Johnny "J"

Hip hop has given us some truly inspired producer/rapper teamings over the years – Eric B. & Rakim, DJ Premier and Guru, Biggie and Puff Daddy, Boi-1da and Drake, Missy Elliot and Timbaland, and Dr. Dre and N.W.A., The D.O.C., Snoop Dogg, and Eminem. For the late great Tupac Shakur, no one more naturally assumed that title than the one and only *Johnny "J" Jackson*, who *XXL Magazine* recently crowned, "A pioneer of the West Coast rap sound. Tupac's favorite producer…(and) perhaps the *single most influential* musical contributor to Pac's catalog." A prolific pairing that seemed almost fated given both the astounding 150 musical masterpieces they composed together in the final 8 months of Shakur's life, and how quickly the dynamic dup started working together after their first introduction, Jackson first met the hip hop icon:

> Through my work with Big Syke on *Evil Minded Gangstas*, word got around, and when Pac heard the beats I had done on Syke's album, he said, "You gotta introduce me to the dude who did your beats," and Skye was like, "No problem, that ain't but a phone call away." Next thing I know, I get a call, "Tupac wants to meet you, I'ma come pick you up, why don't you bring some beats?!" So, it started right there, that plain and simple. I didn't have to shoot any demos, didn't have to prove shit, he heard my shit on Syke's record, and was like, "I need who did your beats on my shit." So it was funny, they had the funniest chemistry over the whole thing, because Syke was like, "Hey, that's my producer!" Then Tupac was like, "Naw, that's my producer!" They had fun about it.

In the studio, Tupac was the equivalent of a live wire on tape, spitting electric verses around the clock overtop beats by the hottest producers in the business, from Easy Mo Bee on *Temptations*, DJ Daryl on *Keep Ya Head Up, So Many Tears, I Get Around* by Shock G, and *Dear Mama* by Tony Pizarro and DF Master Tee. But it was in his fated introduction to Johnny "J"

that Pac would find his mainstay muse. Collaborating with
Jackson for the most concentrated amount of time he ever spent
in the studio with any one producer in the final 8 months of his
life that he was signed to Death Row Records, the team would
often falling asleep at the console or the lounge couch before
waking up and heading right back to work. Analogizing himself
as something akin to a AA Baseball player practicing 'round the
clock for his shot at the Show, when the call finally came and he
stepped up to the plate, he had a hit ready for any ball Pac threw
at him in the way of a lyrical idea:

> Prior to Pac and I meeting, I was doing a lot of
> instrumentals, but didn't have vocals that were
> meeting the ability of where my music was
> going. It was sad, I felt like I was doing
> instrumentals just to do beats, just entertaining
> myself, just to listen to my own music. But there
> were no lyrics or type of written concepts which
> matched what I was doing- until I met Tupac.
> Then I knew- this is where it all begins. I felt it
> was kindred, like we were definitely meant to
> collaborate together. Without a doubt, it felt so
> good. It's hard to explain, but I know the
> chemistry was meant to be, it was written.
> When the lyrics first touched down on my
> tracks, I felt like I was in heaven, I felt like, "Oh
> my God, what a relief." And I wasn't even
> looking at the fact that he was Tupac, I wasn't
> on this star-struck type of shit, I was just like,
> "Finally, an artist who knows what the fuck to
> do to my beats." And he looked at me like
> 'Finally, a producer who knows how to bring

music to my lyrics.' It was that look in his eye, like "I found what I needed!"

Raised in South Central Los Angeles in the 1980s, Johnny Jackson grew up on 103rd and Budlong. The son of hard working Mexican-American parents John Sr., a mechanic, and Lidia, a school teacher. Who celebrated their eldest son's musical gift once he started banging beats out around the house, buying him his first drum machine for Christmas while still in his teens. Discovering the drums while attending the Washington Preparatory High School, playing in the drum line as a class mate of fellow bedroom producer Sir Jinx, Ice Cube's cousin, and rap artists WC, Yo-Yo, and Candell *Candyman* Manson, who would provide Jackson with his first breakthrough hit at age twenty:

> The first hit song I'd ever produced was Candy Man's *Knockin' Boots*. That whole album I did right out of high school in 1991, for Epic Records. I felt there was a lot of overcrowding in hip hop production at the time, where there was a little too much going on in the music. I didn't like that there were too many overdubs, too much going on in the drum aspect of things. So when *Death Around the Corner* ended up on *Me Against the World* I felt like that was a good transition for me from that over to the type of beats I was doing with Tupac, where I got to show, "Here's some aggressive shit," where I could still lay pretty music. But Pac brought a lot more aggression to it, a lot more realism to the shit. So from that time when I first started

working with Pac until now, when I've been
producing, I've never changed my formula even
to this day, I kept it pretty simple.

A sound scientist who even back before he hooked up with
Tupac was already starting to influence a new generation of
producers who grew up on his sound, including future Cash
Money Records house producer and Lil Wayne hitmaker
Mannie Fresh, who remembered that, "I was in California doing
an internship when I was with Gregory D and Johnny was the
first person that told me about a sequencer, and Johnny brought
me to get an SP-12. He was one of the first dudes I would say to
turn me onto sampling and everything. What's crazy, you know
how you have somebody that's kind of like a mentor and to see
them do amazing things, we kind of lost touch and I remember
thinking, *Man, I wonder what dude's doing?* and all of a sudden,
he pops up doing Tupac's music. And I was like, Wow!"

Pac's voice would first debut on a Johnny "J" track on the
highlight *Pour Out a Little Liquor* off of the *Above the Rim*
Motion Picture Soundtrack. Sitting in the pocket of Jackson's
groove with the natural fit of a three pointer from Jordan
swooshing effortlessly into the net. The collaboration would
continue in 1995 when Johnny produced *Death Around the
Corner*, which showed up near the end of Shakur's multi-
platinum *Me Against the World* album, before ending abruptly
just as it was beginning:

> Once we'd discovered that connection-
> unfortunately- not too long after that, Tupac
> went to jail, and it felt like the world ended on
> me. That's where it felt like walls collapsed. And
> I was asking, "Why did this have to happen?

Why did the chemistry have to stop because of some shit like that?" So when he was inside, that was kind of like a hiatus for me, because I did wait for him. I felt as though the walls had caved in, like, "What happened?" It was like my other musical half had left, he was no longer here. I can't have him in the studio. It put me into a slump, into like a deep depression, because I was like, *Oh, I'm back to doing instrumentals again.* Because wasn't nobody else going to rap on my shit while he was inside. And there was a period during those nine months where I stopped doing music, I stopped creating. I said, "I don't wanna do any music right now, I wanna give it a break." Because I felt as though, without him being there with me at that level, why should I continue doing beats when I don't have the lyrics I need on it?"

The music I made with Tupac elevated the potential for where his artistic ability could go. I really felt that I was the motivational piece that he needed, the missing link. I know I was the missing link that he needed to take his concepts and his vocal styles to another level. And I've been complimented for that, people say to me all the time, "Johnny, when Pac met you, it definitely elevated him to another level that he needed." Because there was a time period- proceeding his incarceration- where he was kind of limited, where he didn't really take it as far as he really should have, or really wanted to because the music wasn't meeting him there. It wasn't hitting where he needed it, and I was the one who brought it to the table, and that's where it all went to the next level.

Thankfully, Johnny had eventually managed to pull himself out of his own depression, finding a therapeutic way to kill time in the studio stacking beats in anticipation of Pac's release, recalling that, "After a while, I just went back to work, and just started creating beat after beat after track after track waiting for him to get out, and it ended up becoming some of the songs you hear on *All Eyes on Me*. Some of those songs were created while Pac was in jail, so they were almost fated to end up on that album. It was therapy, and I needed it. While he was inside, we'd write - always letters, cards with shit like, "I love ya man," and "Can't wait to see you man," and "Stay strong, we gonna keep this going." And that connection ended up, at least musically, keeping his spirit alive from what he told me later. It kept him going, because he got letters from tons of people. I know it touched him that he got regular letters from me because of our musical connection." Rushing to make up for lost time once he'd been sprung by Suge Knight from Clinton Correctional in Upstate New York, shortly after touching down in Los Angeles, Jackson remembered getting the call he'd been waiting nine months:

Then as soon as he was out of jail, it was like a day later. I didn't even know he was out, but Suge bailed him out, and I think his plane had landed. He'd just gotten settled into his suite or wherever Suge had him put up at first. So two days fresh out of jail, I get a call from Big Syke,

saying, "Someone wants to talk to you." And I
was all non-chalantly like, 'Who is it? What's the
fucking joke?' Then here comes this voice, 'I
need you in the studio man, I'm out of jail. Meet
me at the studio, I'm on Death Row.' And I
couldn't believe it, I'm like, 'Who the fuck is
this?' And he's like, 'It's Tupac motherfucker,
get to the studio!' And we just got right back to
work, banging them songs out.

Though Tupac would be seen in the almost constant
company of Death Row Records C.E.O. Suge Knight outside of
the studio, when he was in the lab working, Johnny was the first
to credit Knight in spite of his wild reputation on the street for
being an ideal record executive in respect to the fact:

Once Pac was out, I can say this as a definite
compliment to Suge, he definitely gave me and
Tupac our space. Never interrupted, never tried
to put his opinion in. And I give him that much
respect because he stayed on his side of the fence,
and I stayed on my side of the fence doing my
music. Another thing I know Suge loved was my
and Pac's work ethic, because it matched his. He
would always say, "Man, your work ethics are
unbelievable. You remind me of myself when I
was in school."

I think Death Row even had to make an
adjustment when Pac first came on, because I
don't think they expected such a rapid pace of
music. It was just fast, so quick that we ran it

like it was a factory. You couldn't keep me and Tupac out of the recording studio. So when Pac came to Death Row, it became like that was ours - at least in terms of Can Am, the studio they owned, because Tupac became the best seller overnight, and everyone made adjustments there to just let him do his thing in the Studio. Remember, that dude also fit in 9 videos, shot two motion pictures while he was at Death Row, so he just never stopped working. Their job at Death Row was just to try and keep pace with Pac – from the creation of the music to the retail release. They did a good job overall too.

There were definitely artists on Death Row too who were like, "Oh shit, we better get in the lab, because Tupac and Johnny "J" are dishing out too many hits. We better get our ass on our P's and Q's. Tupac is in here smashing, so we better get our shit together too." I felt as though Tupac and I, we set examples for Death Row. We even opened up new ways of saying, "Get up off your lazy ass and get some work done." I think Pac and I's work ethic motivated all the Death Row artists, including Snoop, Danny Boy, everyone who was there. I thought it elevated their model.

On fire from the minute he was released from his year-long cooling off period behind bars, where it's rumored Shakur didn't write a single rap, his mind had still no doubt been subconsciously bottling a bomb of creativity that was ready to blow by the time the rapper got in the booth. Expecting his collaborators to be able to keep up with his Olympian recording pace, Jackson remembered that while he and the rapper were healthy competitors who worked in a constant state of uninterrupted synergy:

> Whenever there was any little minor technical difficulty, Pac's patience level was very short. Say for instance the tape machine got stuck, or something went out on the board, he would get very highly frustrated. He never got frustrated at me, but he got very hot with the engineer. He would get very upset at the engineer. He had a high standard – if they didn't get shit done in due time, or if an engineer ever erased his vocal by accident, they were fired. When you deal with two-inch analog, you can accidentally hit that record button and erase a vocal. We encountered a couple of those moments. That shit pissed Tupac off, because it was Death Row, and there was a very high standard that was always maintained in the studio. Even amid all of the drama and controversy that happened outside the studio. In the booth, Pac was always the most disciplined. That's how he got so much done.

For Jackson, his collaboration with Shakur offered him the rare freedom as a producer to work in a lock-out environment without concern for the usual hassles of recording on a budget. This allowed he and Pac to avoid scenarios where they might be rushing to finish up a track while another act was breathing down their necks waiting to start the next session, or having to worry about coming back in the next day and having to re-set the console levels, microphones, etc. confirming that, "One thing I will also say for Suge is that there was never any pressure when we were recording from the outside. Like we never heard 'Oh my God, we're on an hourly rate.' Nothing like that, we were just flowing. Death Row definitely gave Tupac the freedom to work without the distractions of worrying about studio costs, or shit like that. That's a big fucking deal when you think about the fact that most studios rent out rooms at an 8-12 hour block, and you know if you don't get what you need to get done in that 8-12 hour block, the pressure gets on. The heat is on. And for me, it doesn't bother me because I'm quick at laying music, but some rappers, it can put a lot of pressure on them. Pac wouldn't have given a fuck anyway, I wouldn't have either. We were notorious for going into overtime, even when we used to go to Echo Sound, before he got to Death Row."

Considered their new thoroughbred, for Tupac and Jackson, time froze in place when they left the studio for the night, with everything precisely as they'd left it the next day upon returning to continue working on *All Eyez on Me*, it was an order that Johnny remembered had come from the top down:

> When we first got to Death Row, Suge put the word out immediately that when Pac was in the studio, it was off limits – even between our sessions. We kept the big room at Can Am, the big room was me and Tupac's room always. We'd bounce back and forth between studio A and studio B, but all my equipment stayed in Studio A at all times. It was very well protected. When my stuff was set up and ready to go, it was very respected and well protected. Like the

settings on the board, shit like that, no one touched anything. So once Pac and I were done for the night, that door was locked. Then the next morning, I'd walk back in and everything was exactly as we'd left it, still as is – including his Hennessey or whatever, everything was still the same. Then there were times when would *lock it down*. Lock-It-Down means we would make it where no one was to enter the studio unless it was of importance or you were to be on the record.

They ran a tight ship at Death Row. They kept the studio functioning and clean. It was a beautiful flow. There were rules there governing too, like, 'No one is to touch the equipment or put their hands on anything Tupac and I had going on. If the two-inch machine was still in the position it was in, it was not to be touched or tampered with. That was not to be tolerated. As relaxed as a recording studio is for the artist, you have to have rules and regulations for everyone else. I also personally loved the fact that when Tupac was on Death Row, it was a beautiful outlet because the records were instantly put out on the street, with no hesitation. When we recorded a record, in no more than a week's time frame - the record, as a single, was out, on sale at the record store. That was refreshing with the way major labels were doing things. Putting out a record can be so time consuming- with release dates. The corporate industry being so slow, they need to wake up and learn how to put records out. Death Row definitely held up their end of the bargain on the release tip. One thing that was definitely open there, constantly flowing was studio time at Death Row. And I'm not honestly sure another label could have offered Tupac that kind of freedom to record around the clock the way we were able to. It was never-ending, like the studio that never slowed down.

Protective of his label's biggest star not only because he'd made such a large investment in Shakur, but equally because Knight knew by blocking out any noise other than the sound of the hits the rapper and producer were churning out together in the studio, it would pay multi-Platinum returns. Once they got down to work banging out tracks, Suge's instinct proved correct as both Pac and Johnny had their finger on the pulse of precisely what the world wanted to hear from the rapper as he prepared to become hip hop's first true superstar. Seizing that moment with a piece of Radio perfection on *How Do You Want It* The crossover smash took the team to #1 on the Billboard Hot 100 Singles Chart for the second time in six months in June, 1996. Following on the heels of the Dr. Dre-produced *California Love*, the instrumental for *How Do You Want It* was one Johnny "J" had been working on in anticipation of Pac's release from prison and return to the studio and radio, nurturing the track through several stages of development:

> I test-drove it with four or five rappers before I got to Tupac with it. The original vocal hook was done differently before you heard it with KC and JoJo. The beat was done four years

before it touched down and got to Pac. When I showed it to Tupac, and he goes, "It's gonna be called *How Do You Want It*." So then next thing you know, right there in the studio, he's writing the verses, and he comes up with this melody and these words, and starts singing, *How do you want it? How do you feel? Comin' up as a nigga in the cash game, I'm livin' in the fast lane, I'm for real...*' So he goes in the booth and sings it himself, with no back-up singers there. This was before KC and JoJo were even thought about!

Honestly, I liked it the way it was originally done with Tupac as the singer. He sang the hook, and the whole song lyrically and melody wise, was written by him. He probably couldn't sing the notes in key, but I knew exactly what notes he was trying to reach. He had it. He had that gift, where he knew the melody, where it needed to go. I tripped off that, he was more than just a rapper. So then we tried out some girls singing the background, which didn't work out too well because the key was totally off. The females didn't come to the level we needed it to be at. Pac and I even had a discussion, and were like, "Naw, that ain't gonna work. We don't like them, we have to take the girls off." We tried another girl thing, with the same identical wording, same melodic pattern, everything you're hearing in the record was the same. It just didn't have the right feel with the females. So then Pac said, "Johnny, what do you think about

Jodeci?" and I said, "Not a bad idea." At that time, everybody was around, it was a big family vibe at Death Row. And so when KC and JoJo showed up, we laid them down. It was the last thing to go on the track, and it was like icing on the cake. It made my day to the fullest.

I truthfully did NOT know that was going to become the record it became. It was a three million selling single. A hell of a chart topper, and went #1 on the charts. That was the most unbelievable feeling you will ever have as a producer. And with Pac, there were certain songs where, after we'd finished recording, he would call it and go, "This is it. This is going to be the one!" And with *How Do You Want It* I didn't call it. Don't get me wrong, I didn't doubt the song, I knew it was a club banger, and an energetic record. But I remember my wife hearing it and going, "That's gonna be a hit." And then look at it, #1 on the Pop Charts. I remember that *How Do You Want It* was definitely Suge's number one favorite on *All Eyez on Me*. I remember as soon as the album went #1, I got a call from Pac. He said, "Johnny, do you know we are number 1 baby?" To see your album at number one, it was a high, it was unbelievable. We both just knew that it was a song that was meant to happen, and that it was gonna be a winner.

It was funny too, because after *How Do You Want It* went number one, I got what seemed to me like millions of calls on that, tons of them. I remember looking at some of the magazines, some of the ads, and my name was big as day, *PRODUCED BY JOHNNY "J"*. Real nice and huge, and I knew that was Pac. It was funny too, because after the success of that single, I started getting calls from everybody in the business, which really just worked to reinforce how special what Pac and I had.

That chemistry would set the formula for the entire album as the pair had their sound down to such a science that Johnny "J" shook his head in reflection, reveling at the fact that "with me and Pac, it was almost like the more we worked, we could do this shit blind-folded. It was just amazing that the more you locked up and knocked songs out, it was just a natural chemistry that flowed out with no hesitation, such that Pac and I rarely ever left the studio. We'd stay in there till the break of dawn, all my wife and I would see was a recording studio and a bed at the Marriot Hotel." Unlike many sound engineers and producers who stay slaves to the console by necessity at the expense of time missed with the family their supporting back home, for Johnny, because Shakur wanted him on creative call 24-7, he was afforded the rare luxury:

I kept my family with me in the studio because I was there so much. Maybe about thirty minutes at the mall to change into a fresh outfit, 'cause we had no time to go home, no time to do any outside activities. Because it was a consistent cycle - it was like this round-the-clock music factory that we kept going. We just kept going in this one mode, and me and Pac would work until I couldn't push buttons and he couldn't look at the microphone. We'd go fifteen, eighteen hours straight in a day. There was an energy there, a feeling of this consistent creativity that just didn't want to stop.

Pac also raised my bar as a producer tenfold. Because when I'm producing, I always try to put myself in different shoes, and become the listener, and then the consumer. I think of myself as the regular, simple, typical street kid on a skate board or in my low rider, and just put myself in that position. And really think of myself on that level, of how these songs really put in effect on me. *What vibe do they give me? What do they make me feel? What are they gonna make me do? What are the motivational aspect of things? Where are these songs gonna take me to?* Because I knew Pac's shit affected people like that. So it was a responsibility of mine. So I would put myself in those shoes. So I knew when he got out of jail, with the intensity and pace we were working at, we had a lot of hungry motherfuckers listening for that next Tupac classic, so we just went in the studio and started banging them out.

Over the course of the eight months and 150 songs he and Shakur produced together, to keep that energy infectious in the room, Johnny employed an age-old producer's trick of giving Tupac an audience to perform before in the vocal booth. Giving him a live backdrop that the rapper fed off of as he channeled that electricity into each of his vocal performances on tape, Johnny "J" is still grateful to have had the best seat in the house behind the console, confirming his memory:

> When we were recording, Pac loved the spectators. Honestly, it kept an energy in the room. But at the same time, we would block it out, any noise or any talking or any distraction was going on, he would block shit out so that you would look at him and think 'He's not paying any attention...' Even if there were so-called *groupies* around, you could tell his mindset was like, 'I'm not even thinking about that right now, I'm focused on the shit I gotta do behind this microphone, because what I just wrote and created, I gotta make this happen.' And me musically, I was on the same page. And I'd say the majority of his and my sessions had a crowd in them.

> We had all kind of inside jokes, but we always kept a crowd, it was our way of saying, 'Shit, that's our audience dude.' We had some ground rules - I remember there were times where it would get a little too overcrowded with people who just wanted to come in there, hang out for no fucking reason. 'Oh, let's go in and drink up Tupac and Johnny's Hennessey, and leach on 'em, and keep pouring Crystal,' without ever

having the decency to contribute to what we bought. And Pac and I noticed it together, because we were always the ones paying for the shit. Whenever we bought champagne, we always paid for it together, and we noticed together we had people coming in the studio trying to take advantage, trying to get a free ride. And we didn't really appreciate it.

Pac was sponsored by weed, and was sponsored by Hennessey too. Both of those things were mandatory at any given Tupac recording session - you had to have a cup of Hennessey and coke, and some Crystal mixed in at times. I didn't smoke blunts, it just wasn't me. That high wasn't a good high for me, the one time he finally convinced me to try it, I hit Pac's blunt, and my console - the SL9000, the board itself - that turned into the Startrek Enterprise. And I remember Pac saying, "Don't ever let Johnny smoke weed again!" I haven't touched it ever since that evening. As far as drinking, to be honest with you, we stayed tipsy through every record I recorded with him. We were under the influence, I'll put it that way to you. Pac, for his part, could do his thing - smoke whatever he wanted to smoke and drink whatever he wanted to drink - and still step into the booth and handle a song like he didn't have one drink at all.

We knew on certain songs that he recorded when he'd had one drink too many, and I think the songs speak for themselves, such as *Thug Passion*, we were all pretty drunk right there. It was just beautiful that I could lay my music without having to be drunk or whatever, lay it down on the two-inch tape, and get tipsy afterward. I didn't need it for creative chemistry, like 'I need to have this cocktail or this drink to create this vibe.' I could tell you that me and Pac didn't need it, 'cause if we'd been in there completely sober – which at times we were- we'd still have created the most beautiful music ever. I looked at it as an atmosphere thing, enjoying the moment, getting the shit out naturally and letting it flow. And I loved it because our chemistry flowed naturally.

Inviting fans inside the studio for a front-row look at his own record-making process as he produced many of the tracks that wound up composing the bulk of the legendary Makavelli bootleg series and official post-humous albums released in the years following Tupac's passing – including highlights like *Until the End of Time, Still Ballin', Lil Homies, Breathin', Happy Home, Thug n U, Thug n Me, Everything They Owe, World Wide Mob Figures, My Closest Roaddogz, Ballad of a Dead Soulja, When Thugz Cry, Letter 2 My Unborn, That Ain't Livin', Why U Turn Me On, LastOnesLeft, When I Get Free, Still I Rise, Thug 4 Life, Secretz of War, We Ride On Our Enemies, Changed Man, Fuck Em All, Never B Peace, Mama's Just a Little Girl, Whatcha Gonna Do, Fair Xchange, Thugz Mansion, Better Dayz, U Can Call, There U Go, This Life I Lead, Who Do U Believe In, They Don't Give a Fuck About Us, Fake Ass Bitches, and Ready 4 Whatever.* Along with the eleven tracks he produced on *All Eyez on Me,* Johnny deconstructs that catalog from the ground up, breaking his signature production process down to a foundational starting point:

> When I'm building a track, from the time I first started producing to this day, the SB1200 is always going to be a part of my musical chemistry, until the day I leave this earth, because if it ain't broke, don't fix it. Every drum track known to man on every song I've done since the day I started producing records has always been that drum machine. I'm a drummer, I was originally on the drums, and can play the hell out of the drums. Keyboards, you name it, I can play it all, have dealt with it all, I was a serious rhythm guy, serious percussionist, very into the marching band thing during junior high and high school. Then when the SB1200 entered the game around 1990, I knew that was my calling. That was all she wrote, and *Knockin'* *Boots* came out of that drum machine.

> My process for building a track was always this: my chemistry always began with sitting there and figuring out how the drums should go. I would always start with the drum track, I never sang a melody to myself yet, never thought about where I wanted to take a bass line, or any chords, nothing like that. I had to make sure that the foundation started with the drum track. Mandatory for me, to make sure the kick, the snare, the high hat was on point, the actual

pattern, where every simple element was going to go, then I'd just layer it up. Go into the bassline mode, go into the chords, which I would always foundation off the Fender Rhodes, and just do my thing. Just build and build till I couldn't build anymore. I love the Fender, I'm a mini-Moog guy, I love the Minimoogs, I love the old school instruments. For bass, I was always using the Kurzweil, which is still a part of my musical chemistry to this day. I don't ever plan to change that. Everybody's always...as soon as one keyboard's been popular, it's like 'Okay, that's a wrap for that one, there's a new introduction, another one out.' I never liked to jump on the bandwagon, and follow the trend of what everybody does. It's like jumping onto a new pair of shoes, sometimes you need to know how to keep the same shit on, just keep it clean, and know what you're doing. Some people think, *Yo, if I buy this new keyboard, it's going to make a hit record.* No, it's called, 'Motherfucker, if you know you have a musical ability, and how to create melody and concepts that are going to ring in people's ears, that's where it starts my friend.' It doesn't come out of some new keyboard you bought, it comes out of your heart, and your musical background. And my musical background includes every Soul record you could possibly think of, even Mariachi music, Latin music – you name it – it was in my upbringing. You hear jazz in my background. In some situations, I'll use sampling.

A good example would be a song called '*Ballad of a Dead Soldier.*' That was one I did based off of a Curtis Mayfield sample. So I would vibe off the way it was structured, and most of us at the time who would sample would listen to an 8-bar intro of an old record, or an old classic 70's song. And that song by Curtis Mayfield actually was from the beginning of the record, but what I would usually do that set me apart is: I would take the middle of the song, or wherever, and dissect it just out of some weird place. But once I take a sample, whether it be from the beginning, middle or end of a song, I would structure it out, dump it into my sampler, and loop it for a good four to eight bars. I was always good at sampling four to eight bars, some producers would do a 2-bar loop. It was rare that I would do a 2-bar loop, but I was good at looping a 4-8 bar sample. So once I had sampled, I'd start knocking drums out right away. I'd go right into my kick. My kick drum would go right into it immediately. And I was always known to keep an 808 Kick Drum in all my records. I don't know if you know this, but all of the records I produce consist of an 808 kick drum blended into the mix. That's mine as a trademark. You always put your little boom on, and mine was the 808. It just always kept a good frequency, a good theme in all the records I've produced. And I don't know what it is about me, but I just have to have that in all of my songs. Every record, every single song. I'm good at blending it, because you might not always hear it as loud as in other cuts, but it would always put a nice tone. A nice texture to the majority of my tracks.

Jackson's chameleon ability to travel back and forth between his own original instrumental composition and samples that were flipped so cleverly in their creative application within a track that they might as well have been his own. Whether Quincy Jones' *Body Heat* showing up in *How Do You Want It*, *Winter Sadness* by Kool and the Gang making its way into *Picture Me Rolling*, the title track's interpolation of *Never Gonna Stop* by Linda Clifford, or *Life Goes On* making use of *Brandy (You're a Fine Girl)* by the O'Jays, Johnny wove the roots of his own childhood record collection into rich musical tapestries that he recalled:

> I would often start building off the samples, and then just layer it and layer it and layer it. We kept the musical elements in the studio at all times- such as the guitar player, and the keyboardist - I don't care if we had to have horns in there, or a violinist or string section. Whatever it took, we always had the musicians in the studio with us at the time we were recording. I would have to guide them through what I wanted them to play, because most of them are musicians, not producers – so they would follow my lead, and play whatever I told them to play. Or even Tupac, he might sing a little melody or two, or hum a few lines, and the guitar player would go off that, and take it into another fade. Then I might say, "Naw Pac, watch

this- let me take it to another level." Then I'd guide the guitar player to another fade, and that's another layer of the track that would go on top of the sample. Then I'd look at the keyboard player, like, "Now, this is what I want you to do on the chords. I want you to structure the chords this way. I want you to use these sounds for the chords..." Whether it be a Rhodes, or whether it be a straight sound, or some weird Clavonette type of sound. Then I'd go into the mini-mood, and I'd say, "Let me get this high-pitched UFO sound, and do something real weird with it." It wouldn't always have to be Parliament Funkadelic style, I would just do something real spacy and shit, something psychedelic about it. I would just do shit like that, hit the weirdest note that would be in key on the mini-mood, and the shit just worked. And I'd keep it. And just build layer upon layer upon layer.

So by the time we got to his vocals, we'd musically have staked up – from the kick to the snare to the high hat, all the percussion to the guitar, keyboards, bass, and what- and those were on separate tracks. I'd say there were a good sixteen tracks, and we'd work on a forty-eight tracks, because we had two two-inch machines linked together. This was before Pro Tools, so we were working on the dinosaur of the time. We were just dumping the shit on forty-eight tracks. So I'd say about a good sixteen tracks before we got to vocals, but if I needed a seventeeth or an eighteenth track, musically they were open for me to use. Because I wasn't the type of producer that- just because you got forty-eight tracks in front of you, it doesn't mean you have to fill every fucking track. You got to be a fucking idiot to produce records that way. Just know when to call it. By the thirtieth track or whatever, most times it's a done-deal, a wrap. My advice on that point is you gotta keep it simple, simplicity is the key. Everyone has said that expression I'm sure throughout the music industry, but truthfully it's always been the key for me. You have to know when not to overproduce records. You need to know when to say 'Let me lay out a basic structure of where I want to go with my music,' and get some vocals done, and let the vocalist get their thing done, whatever they feel they needed to get off their chest. Then get a working vocal mix and build around that, then you can make the musical concept happen even better.

Say, for instance, I've laid the drum track, I laid the bass line, the chords are laid out, and maybe just a simple melody line. And a lot of times, I wouldn't have a melody line yet at that point because my melody line might clash with what the artist is trying to write. They may sing something totally different that may go against what I'm trying to create for a melody, so I don't like to put melody lines on records too much till vocals are done. I'm good at knowing how to work around the vocals, you gotta know how to respect the vocalist too. You can't be like 'I'm the producer, I'm the music guy, so I have to shine.' You have to know how to say, 'Fuck that, it has to be a 50/50 thing, right down the middle.' Sometimes you gotta know when to back off- as a musician and as a producer- and say 'You know what, I kinda overproduced it, I put a little too much on it. I'm getting a little too musically keyboard happy on my fucking song.' And so I would take some of the excess elements off to show a little more respect for the vocals that were on the song, and make it sound a little more like a properly-arranged record. As a producer, another very important thing is to know how to arrange your elements. Know when to bring in your elements, know when to take them out. It's having a musical gift and a musical knowledge to know how to create original music also, because I don't sample anymore. You can be inspired by an old record. But still – as a new or established producer – think to yourself, *Let me originate something that's going to be classic, and a memory until the end of time.*

By the time Jackson was ready for Tupac to step inside the booth to begin layering his unique multi-tracked vocal wall, *Rolling Stone Magazine* would highlight the rapper's success in making, "The most of this foundation." When making sonic decisions where space was concerned ahead of time, Johnny took care to construct each instrumental track designed specifically around how they best supported what he felt was a signature vocal delivery:

> He really invented that style too. And would lay a good five or six vocal tracks per song. Sometimes more than six. I had to how to criticize myself at times and say, "I overproduced the record, I got a little too much going on, let me eliminate some shit, mute some things out, and open it up for Pac, so he could do what he needs to do." His was a method of recording where he was thickening up the vocal quality, and also do subliminal stuff he could lay in the back of the song. Pac was known to do a main vocal, a double, then a triple that we'd call 'accenting' of certain things, where he would accent certain words. Then the fourth track we'd call the 'lollygaggin' vocal track, the 'fuck-around' track, things he wanted to say in the back, to talk a little shit while his vocal tracks were going. So I called the fourth track the 'talkin' shit' track, and when you hit that track, that was him laughing, giggling, responding to what he was saying.
>
> So that was pretty much our chemistry, and if you notice in the majority of every record I've done with him, the chemistry was always pretty much the same- vocally it was always structured pretty much the same: different topics, different melodies and formats, but structured out pretty much the same. Pac's thing when he was

recording was always, "Give me a little reverb." All he needed was a little reverb, always at all times. He didn't need delays. He'd say, "I need a gated reverb, I need this weird effect." He loved the harmonizing effect too when he recorded, and loved to go through a harmonizer. That was his favorite thing when I first met him. I loved that shit about him, he wasn't afraid to touch or try anything, and to take it to levels like that. He was creatively fearless, and I was too. So on all our collaborative levels, you could just hear that the chemistry was a locked-in deal, it was a marriage man. It was something that no one could break.

Pac, as a recording artist, I would definitely consider musical outside of rhyming. I loved the fact that I didn't have to sit there and get frustrated on the fact that he didn't know how to come into the song, or couldn't understand what sixteen bars were. He knew all that. But I would still actually sit there and count as he would recite the vocals in the booth, to let him know that's sixteen bars and that's enough. So he would look at me with my cues, and I'd count him down, "That's sixteen, stop there, it's time for hook." There were times when Pac was so good, when his rhythm was so together, that it was an automatic program. The majority of his records were always sixteen bar verses then hooks, and it just came together. And I loved it because he just knew how to form a different

type of rhythm on top of my beat, that you
wouldn't think would work, but it worked. It
was like this off-beat style he would do in his
doubles or triples in his vocals, and it would just
come in out of nowhere, and you'd be like "Wait
a minute, what the fuck was that?" Then you'd
listen back like "Oh shit, it does work!"

By spending such a concentrated amount of time together
working side by side in the studio, after a while, their process
became very much an intuitive one as artist and producer. Still,
for as much as he had to say on the mic, Jackson marveled at the
sponge Tupac still found room to become whenever he could
soak up something new about the recording process itself as they
worked. Careful to never step on Johnny's toes or turf as they
collaborated, the producer remembered Shakur nonetheless was
appreciative of every lesson he could absorb, proudly pointing to
his favorite moment as a teacher:

This is one I will never forget: when I taught him
was how to mute out elements. It's called how to
arrange a record. He'd never worked a board,
never used the cut button, or the mute button.
But I was always using them, and when he'd be
partying to it after the song was lyrically
completed, I would be sitting there playing with
the mute buttons, giving it kind of a live, on the
spot, spontaneous arrangement. And he would
look over at me, and go 'Oh shit, teach me that
Johnny.' And I showed him, and there were
times when I regretted showing him because he
got a little too happy with the shit. He was a

very quick learner, and he loved to mute out bass lines, and bring the Rhodes in, and bring the guitar in. Whatever the musical instrument was at the time, it was just a fun thing to do. And sometimes we would work the board together as a team, with him on the right and me on the left, and we're just looking at each other vibing, like 'Let's push a mute here, let's drop it all out, and bring it on back.' It was a real good party vibe.

It was open minded at all times when we were producing, and in general when I was producing Pac. Say, for instance, I made up with a nice keyboard or mood line, a real beautiful mood line, or something real catchy on a rugged, street level, he'd follow my lead. He'd go off of me, and go 'Oh, okay, J put down that nice keyboard line down, let me vibe with him.' Then it would work sometimes vice versa, where I would vibe with him, I would listen to actual way he would form the melody or structure out a different melodic pattern in his vocals, so when he would leave and I would go into a mix mode. I would think to myself, 'Let me do a little keyboard line under the melody he just created, and structure it a little differently, put a little different layer on it.' It was like making a cake, with the cherry at the top. It was just beautiful man. Pac and I definitely learned from each other all the time.

As *All Eyez on Me* took shape, Johnny remembered some of his favorite highlights coinciding with the real life Tupac's songs reflected like a musical movie reel, whether talking about the fast lane on the aforementioned *How Do U Want It* or the exhilaration and celebration of freedom captured in *Picture Me Rolling*. Or the tragic but resilient tone of arguably the album's most moving ballad, *Life Goes On*, where the visionary rapper even eerily foreshadowed his own coming death complete with instructions on how he wanted his funeral to go down. A song so real it even moved big, bad Suge Knight to tears when he heard it for the first time, Jackson still beams as he points to the track as:

> My favorite song I did with Tupac. That song had us in tears, we literally cried. There were times when we would hit those records, where we would hit home so much or touch down on a serious subject like *Life Goes On* or *Better Days* where it would literally make guys walk out of the studio watered up and crying. We actually made hard core guys, from the street, walk out of the studio in tears. Suge loved them, I could see that he definitely loved emotional records. I do recall that *Life Goes On* was definitely one of his favorites. We had people in that session that you'd call street guys or hardcore, they were deep into their thing and they broke down in tears. I can't believe I saw that. That record just had so many people emotional.

> At the time, I had the beat created way before I ever met Pac. There were beats that I had for four or five years inside my vault, and I kept all these beats on standby, because in the time

leading up to my collaboration with Pac, I never had artists who could meet the caliber of my music. So I felt like "I don't want to give this to just any rap artist or singer who was going to fuck my shit off.' It's just gonna be a nice track, but the listener's not gonna like the lyrics or singer. And there was just something about that song when I laid it down, I loved Gamble and Huff, the Sounds of Philadelphia, I loved all the old O'Jays stuff. So I started *Life Goes On* with the drum track, working my way into the bass synth, kind of tampering with the sample a little bit, so I kind of freaked it to add my flavor to it. Then layered those backgrounds on it, and that background vocal melody was in my head probably three to four years before I made it with Tupac, so I always had those backgrounds in my mind. I would actually sing that melody when me and my wife would listen to the instrumental in the car, house or whatever. And when the track finally got to Pac, I actually had 2 different singers sing two different sets of backgrounds.

Usually, you don't combine two female vocalists- the way I did it- without an egotistical little vibe or something, where one is like, "What the hell is that? I'm supposed to be the only female on this record." But I was like, "No, you sound beautiful, and you sound beautiful, so I'm gonna blend both of your chemistries into this song, so get up in the booth, and let's make it happen." So in terms of my favorite Tupac records, I'll always go to *Life Goes On*, which puts me in a very emotional state. I don't break down in tears, but there's been times throughout the years, and anniversary of his death where I'll put that song on and it kind of breaks you down a little bit. But that song is very therapeutic for me, because it makes me think about how he was so excited about how the song turned out at the end- and how he was just very happy with the philosophy and overall concept of *Life Goes On*. That whole memory of that evening will never leave my mind, it will be with me till the day I die. Pac's not here with me physically, but he is here, so I feel like he's with me whereever I go. I learned so much from him- that sometimes with things around you, you just gotta kind of go with the flow, and just gotta kind of accept it. I saw that in play from just being around him constantly, and we just kind of dealt with it together.

The mood in the studio was an altogether different one the day Pac blew up on tape on East Coast nemesis Biggie Smalls with the equivalent force of a bomb, laying what many have argued twenty years later is still the *#1 Diss* record of all time with *Hit 'Em Up*. *Newsweek* would even opine on the lasting power of the song's notoriety twenty years after its release, noting from the immediately, "That opening line—that egregious, confrontational, hate-filled opening line—was one of the most unforgettable utterances ever committed to wax by the late Tupac Shakur...(and) when the song was recorded it was

Tupac's venom that seemed the most pointed, his rage the most real...When the song dropped, it was too hot to touch. Fans eager for more East/West drama ate it up...Taken on it's own merit, it's one of the greatest diss records in hip hop history...(and) one of the most compelling rap records ever recorded." Such an effective one-punch knock-out that Johnny feels the world still hasn't quite gotten up off the canvas yet, the producer agrees in a moment of seriousness:

> That had to be the most hard core record I've ever done in my career, I haven't topped that shit yet. I don't even plan on doing any more records like that. I've made this deal- based on the impact of that song- that I don't want to do records going against any coast, or based on gang members going against each other, Bloods or Crips. I just don't want anything like that recorded again. I mean, we made history, I love the record, don't get me wrong, I'm very happy with the work I put in on it. The lyrics are a mother fucker though! It was a very angry rapper in the studio that night, Pac was upset. One of the angriest vocals I've ever done with him.

Boi-1da: That was a fucking crazy song! That's probably the most disrespectful diss song of all time.
Johnny "J:" When Pac is angry like that naturally, like before he step in the booth, you better leave him that way going into the session. Because one thing about Pac was that when he

would get upset on that level – and there are other records I did with him where he would get this anger in him, where it would just pour out on the vocals, even on like *Little Homies*. But you gotta just let him go, it's like a boxer in the ring. Don't fuck with him, just let him flow. He may have been an actor, and people might have thought he was acting out an angry part or whatever on some of his shit- not on that song, *Hit 'Em Up*. That shit was true feelings, true attitude- everything in the record that you hear vocally was from the fucking heart. You can't get any more authentic than that, because the man didn't have to front and lie.

It was funny on *Hit 'Em Up* too because, with the way Pac recorded his vocal tracks, he would get angrier and angrier with every vocal track he laid. He took that shit to another level of anger. Because when you got to the double, after he'd already completed the first lead vocal track, when he got to the double, and triple, and fourth tracks, he had gotten angrier and angrier. So that process actually amplified the intensity of Pac's vocal to the next highest level you can think of, to where his fucking voice was going out. He would do that shit so much at times that he would literally throw his vocals out, where his voice would completely go out. He'd usually be out a day, or a blunt and some Hennessey would bring it back. And it was good for him to have the day's break after we recorded *Hit 'Em Up* because his voice actually went out at the end. And especially after completing a record like that, he needed a breather, probably a day or a day and a half. So it was therapeutic at times when his voice would blow. Because of the venting, the shit he had to get off his chest in the studio.

As the album started shaping up, thanks in part to what *XXL Magazine* would later credit the achievement of Johnny "J" in being, "Able to give Pac a much more musically dynamic sound – something more free flowing and improvisational – and it allowed for a string of undeniable hits." As Knight joined the pair one night in the control room to listen in on their progress, he was so blown away by the rounded quality of the sum and substance of what he was hearing that Jackson remembered:

> Suge came into the studio one night, and me and Pac were in there having a good time working, and one thing I'll say for Suge and Pac and I, with *All Eyez on Me*, we were dumping out so many songs at a rapid pace that it ended up becoming a double-CD by default almost, because the next thing I know, Suge just made this announcement that it was going to be a Double CD! In fact, it became the first Double Album in rap history. He just said it right there on the spot.

His baby from pre-production through the final stages of the recording process, Johnny remembered keeping control of the sonic throttle throughout mixing and mastering, so much so that, "I made sure I was at mastering for *All Eyez on Me*. So I was right there looking at everything from song 1 all the way to the last record." Because of the conflicting demands of his career, once Shakur and Jackson had finished one of their studio marathons and the rapper ran off to shoot a music video or movie, Johnny took advantage of the down time to mix whatever batch of songs the team had just finished recording. Giving him a head start to keeping up with the rapid pace at which new material was amassed whenever their next session started, the producer gratefully confesses:

> In the mix process, Pac could not hang around for mixing, he would always leave, and I used to *LOVE* it when he would leave, I would celebrate. And I'm gonna tell you why: we would track our asses off. Say we'd tracked three songs in a day- which was usually our average – I've done the tracks, music's done, lyrics are done, the hook is done. So we'd get all that over with, and it would usually be a good three to four cuts, and I'd look at him and go, "Please leave so I can start mixing." Because if I was mixing, he would actually walk back into the studio, while I was working, and go, "J, I know you're mixing, but I want to cut another song. I got a vibe. I got another title for you. I got a concept." And it used to piss me off because I'd go, "I'm trying to mix man." And literally I'd have to stop what I was doing and address it. And it wouldn't mean a damn thing, because if Pac wanted to record, we were recording. And if he was there, he'd always go, "I know you're trying to mix Johnny, but we

gotta do another song." And I'd be like..."You dickhead." And he'd just look at me like, "Yep, let's do another one."

We had a lot of jokes like that between us, but he was always serious about interrupting me to record a new song. My approach to mixing was structured pretty much the same for all my artists, I didn't treat anyone very differently. It just happened that I did a lot more specific work with Pac, so we had our formula down. I have the easiest mixes you could ever imagine because they didn't take eight to nine hours, really because they couldn't with the number of songs we was pumping out of each session. I mean, some time-bandit producers that you have out there in the game take two to three days to mix one song. You got to be out your fucking mind to take that kind of time to mix one song. Usually, my rough mixes are pretty close to what you hear on the actual album, so when I transitioned from tracking to mixing, there really wasn't that much to change. In fact, some of the final mixes you hear are really rough mixes. I didn't even do a final mix, because they were so beautifully leveled, had the roughness I needed, I didn't need to EQ too much shit but here and there, didn't need to polish up too much stuff, because when you did it took the grittiness away. So I kept it gritty, by leaving the mix in the moment of the way we were tracking-whether everyone was tipsy, or partying, or

whatever – that was pretty much the mix. We
would do our little fine tuning, adjust the vocals,
put whatever effects we had to put on them to
enhance them or bring them out, but that was
actually how I would mix. I would mix a song in
a good three to four hours, maximum five hours
per track.

Reminiscing on the night he sat back listening to the results
of his and Tupac's tireless creative output, which – as BET
would later note had led to, "Johnny "J" producing the bulk of
Tupac's crowning musical achievement...lacing the influential
double album with lush, melodic West Coast funk" – Jackson
remembered knowing instinctively they were about to change
the game forever. With history-making ambitions on the
collective minds of all players involved in championing the
album to the finish line, from Johnny and Shakur to Suge
Knight, distributor Interscope, the media waiting to cover his
return, and most importantly, the fans clamoring for new music
from hip hop's first true Elvis Presley, the producer felt a
momentum as they crossed the finish line with recording and
handed the album:

With the whole level of *All Eyez on Me* was
going, from song one to where we finished what
we had to do, I knew *history was in the making*. I
felt the energy because I felt like, "Oh, now
here's my chance, here's my opportunity to let
the world know musically who I am." And now
lyrically, Pac can let it be known where he's at,
where his mind was at. And I loved that, and I

did deeply feel that history was being made, I
knew that it was going to be a huge album.

A studio junkie throughout the eight months and 150 songs
they produced together as much because Tupac was addicted to
his love of the recording process itself. Jackson proudly beams
back on the mountain of material they created together, offering
his informed opinion regarding the sheer amount of tracks that
Pac produced during his time at Death Row:

> My whole vibe on the whole situation was that
> he was on such a good, consistent flow that that
> explains the proficiency. I felt it was simply that
> the man had so much to say – especially coming
> off nine months in prison of not being able to
> record anything, and that's like a lifetime for Pac
> creatively – that he had to do it in such a fast
> time frame because it was as though it just
> couldn't stop, his creative vibe. It was like this
> never-ending, ongoing creative mindstate he was
> in. He couldn't take a two-week break, we
> couldn't even get a week off from doing an
> album, because he couldn't just sit down and sit
> there and play a video game, and not get a song
> done. It was just something in him that kept him
> riding, and he'd say to me, "Johnny, I can't stay
> on this break period, I don't need a break." I
> even remember him calling, and saying, "Johnny,
> we just finished *All Eyez On Me*, let's take a
> couple of weeks off."

So I was under this impression we were gonna take a nice little breather, but in all actuality, that probably lasted a day. We went right into the next song, and next song, and next song and carried on as though he could not stop. The spirits, and the creativity and the flow would not end. Where his mind state was just on this vibe where he would say, "Johnny, I gotta keep going, something's telling me to keep going." And when I look back at it now, that's the way I perceived it. You could just feel it in his attitude. It was as though, "Man, we gotta keep going till we can't do no more, till there's no more to come out of my brain." Like we were gonna drain the hell out of our brains till we couldn't create." It was so advanced, and so ahead of our time and the game.

Destroyed by the same news that rocked the rest of the hip hop universe on September 7, 1996 when his self-fulfilling prophecy came true, when life in the fast lane found him – undisputedly rap's heavyweight king after a #1 hit, *How Do You Want It*, and the 10 million albums he and Johnny had sold together in under a year – leaving another heavyweight champ after watching Mike Tyson at the MGM regain his second WBA Heavyweight title from Bruce Seldon. He was riding shotgun in Suge Knight's black BMW, when a gang-related drive-by shooting riddled his body for the second time in just two years. Johnny remembered feeling stunned along with the rest of the world, in a state where he found himself personally and artistically devastated:

It was like my other half was gone again. It was like being hit with the impact of when he went to jail. I was like, 'Oh no, not again man.' Creatively, I still had the most creative shit musically on my mind. It's just that when he left, I just wasn't motivated to create at the time. At that time, I wasn't happy with the artists I was hearing and trying to work with, because it was just unacceptable. Not up to my level. I felt like I was forcing the issue, so I decided to put the producing on hold. Not to say I retired, or wanted to stop producing records – I just wanted to kind of hold up a minute to evaluate everything, and see where things were going. It didn't affect my creativity in the long run, but Pac's passing was just a drastic hit...a real deep critical situation. I had a real serious break-down. I had arrived in Vegas like fifteen minutes before he actually died, and was on the way to meet him.

Me, my wife, Big Skye, and quite a few other friends got to Las Vegas, and all got the news together. It was like losing a big part of me, because I felt like I was left alone in the music industry. I felt like it was all me again, because he's not here. He was there in spirit, and our music is here to live and stay and go on forever. But personally, it was like I was back to the instrumentals, so it took me a while to bounce back. I felt really obligated to him. I was always open to working with other artists, but most of what came my way after he died was shit that didn't make any sense for me to record. I feel like there were so many more levels that I wanted to take it to with Pac, and when he passed, it was like I had to start over. I'm not saying in career-aspects, but I just felt like I was starting over.

Leaving a huge blank space in pop and hip hop that could not be replaced given how big a shadow and influence as a cultural icon Tupac casted. He represented rebellion like no one ever has before or since. An Army of fans marched to the beats of Johnny "J" underneath Pac's lyrics – as they still are today, generations later. Feeling the reverberations of he and Shakur's influence at play in every sub-genre of hip hop today, as it is with fans, Johnny proudly reflects in closing on the strength of their timeless ties:

Pac's always gonna be a part of me - no matter who I produce, no matter what I work on, no matter where I go in life. He's always there with me in spirit. He's part of my foundation for everything – part of my everyday routine. Me and my wife and kids – his spirit is even here with my family. But artistically – and personally – after that day, a part of me died with him I think. Today, I use that emptiness to motivate myself creatively, because I know there is more that's written for me, before I close the chapters. That's what Pac would have wanted. I just wanna keep going.

Footnote: Johnny Lee Jackson passed away on October 3, 2008 at age 39. He is survived by his wife, Capucine Cantrel, and their three children. This was the one and only interview he ever gave in a book about his creative process with Tupac Shakur in the studio. This chapter is a celebration and tribute to his timeless talent as one of hip hop's most prolific producers to ever lend his ear to changing the game with the sound he invented. **R.I.P.**

"Producing to me has always been about making the best beats I could make and finding the hottest voice that would complement the music..." – Pete Rock

CHAPTER NINE

NY's Finest – Pete Rock

Pete Rock has always been one of hip hop's great Kung-Fu Masters when it comes to the art of chopping up samples, an artistry that *Rolling Stone Magazine* reported, "Made him an icon among beat-heads." Over the past twenty years, in the prestigious estimation of PBS, Rock has been, "Recognized as one of hip hop's legendary producers." Fusing uncommon Soul and horn-driven jazz samples into a new production mold grounded in raw, sonically-barren beats – specifically hollow-sounding snares that cracked like they'd been recorded in a New York basement – that were then treated with Pete's signature DJ cuts and scratches, the result was timeless East Coast hip hop classics like *They Reminice Over You (Troy)*, *Soul Brother #1*, *Escape*, *Straighten It Out*, *Take You There*, *Searching*, *I Got a Love*, and *All the Places* by Pete Rock and CL Smooth, *The World is Yours* by Nas, Rakim's *The Saga Begins*, AZ's *Gimme Yours*, Raekwon's *Sneakers*, *Down with the King* by Run-D.M.C., Heavy D's *Big Tyme*, *Black Coffee*, *Blue Funk*, *Got Me Waiting*, and *A-Yo* by Method Man & Red Man among countless classics.

Rock would become equally celebrated for his fresh, re-inventive re-mixes, including such entertaining, out-of-the-box highlights as Johnny Cash's *Folsom Prison Blues*, which has received almost 4 million views to date and underscores Rock's talent for tackling anything with his own original spin. Rock's historically celebrated hip hop proper remixes include Public Enemy's *Shut 'em Down*, EPMD's *Rampage*, Gang Starr's *Militia*, House of Pain's *Jump Around*, Jeru the Damaja's *You Can't Stop the Prophet*, and Naughty By Nature's *Hip Hop Hooray*, *Light It Up* by Cypress Hill, Black Star's *Respiration*, Brand Nubian's *Slow Down*, Notorious B.I.G. *Juicy*, and *What They Call Me* by Rah Digga. Knowing he wanted to grow up to be a record producer from an age when most kids were still playing cops and robbers, Rock found himself playing with his records instead. He also played with the radio dial honing in on one of his earliest and most indelible influences when he first discovered the Godfather of Soul:

> My ambition to be a producer started from a young, young age when I was three, four years old listening to James Brown's music, he was one

of the inspirations probably in everybody's life in hip hop, and one of my biggest. My dad collected so many records, he had a huge collection, so from that I always had music around me ever since I was a baby. Then – being from the Bronx myself – I took that into learning about Afrika Bambaattaa and Islam, Cool Herk, and all the cool groups that were coming out in the parks and doing this as an activity before they started making records, that's the school I'm from. Then once I fell in love with that, that's what made me want to be into hip hop. There was just something about music that I loved, and learning what vinyl and a forty-five was.

An early talent scout who spotted Pete's natural ear for honing in on the micro-side of music listening and helped nurture it along in fundamental ways was his cousin Dwight Errington, better known in time as *Heavy D*, whose encouragement Rock credited with helping him discover his producer *training wheels* of sorts when D soon thereafter introduced Rock to the wheels of steel. Recognizing once his young cousin began playing around on the turntables that Pete had found his home base, a prodigal DJ was born, marking a pivotal point in his musical development:

My father always had turn-tables and equipment, but I never knew how to DJ back then. When I was a young, young kid, he had a big stack of 45s in the living room and used to play a bunch of records on this one turntable, and I seen him expand it and make it into two turn-tables. I never knew how to work that anyway until I learned that from my cousin Floyd, who was Heavy D's brother and taught me how to DJ.

At that point, it went from James Brown to Bambata to learning under the wing of my cousin Heavy D and my other cousin Floyd how to DJ, which I started learning at a young age when I was seven, eight years old, and by 8 I had it and was probably one of the youngest DJs around. The first time I ever saw any hip hop groups live was when all these clubs like The Roof Top and The Fever in Harlem were hosting shows. Where at a young age I would go and peep out artists like Kool Moe Dee and Doug E. Fresh. Guys like that.

Learning by watching and listening to early mentors like Heavy and his DJ Eddy F – the latter of whom would play another important part in Rock's development behind the turntables both creatively and commercially – collectively they introduced Pete around town to the hottest rising stars in New York's still very-much underground hip hop scene. The aspiring producer soon found himself part of an extended family that looked out for him whenever wisdom or opportunity arose:

Once you start to learn DJ skills, it just makes you want to get into producing, like you start cutting records back and forth in like a beat form, you can do all kinds of things DJing. That's where the producing came from, along with the inspiration of all those producers I grew up listening to. I got to learn about how to format songs under the wing of Heavy D, going with him to producers houses like Marley Marl and Teddy Riley, I was only fourteen, fifteen years old, and was seeing all this and how it would go down in the studio. Then Eddy F, who was Heavy D's DJ, I really learned a lot from him, and would take that and put it in the back of my file cabinet, and use it when I needed to learn more about how to make music.

I started out on B-1s, those are the old-school turntables from '79, '80, '81, and they made different kinds of Tecnics. I always DJ on Tecnics, and then when they came out with the 1200, it was like heaven came down to earth. Those turntables could not go wrong, you could do absolutely anything and everything on the 1200 Tecnic, and those have been a way of life for me for a long time. If I can't find some in the store, because they don't make them anymore, I'll go on eBay and buy them brand new.

That moment when arguably Rock's most prominent mentor to come along at the time, DJ Marley Marl, first became aware of the young diamond in the rough at that storied recording session would soon prove to be fated when Marl walked away impressed enough to take Pete under his wing. Already a local celebrity with his own radio program – the wildly popular *In Control Radio* show on WBLS – Marley would give Rock his first true big break in the way of commercial exposure and a platform on which to build a professional name and reputation for himself as a DJ on the rise:

> My first big break came from me DJing on the radio, as far as getting my name out there for anyone to know who I was. I was young, probably the youngest DJ on the radio at that time, fifteen years old on WBLS, with Marley Marl. I couldn't ask for anything better than that, thank you Lord. It not only taught me about music and about the business, and about how it really works behind the scenes, but it showed me that you could be successful in this if you just have passion in your heart, and me, I was always a passionate kid about anything because I'm a Gemini. Geminis are a little bit crazy, and I took that and just instilled it in my passion for music, and that's why I was so successful.

> I listened to the producers in the 80's. Marley Marl is one of my favorite producers and Howie Tee, who produced Special Ed and Real Rock Fan and UTFO. I paid attention to Larry Smith, and Russell Simmons, and Rick Rubin, and kind of said, "How can I differ from those guys and do something that they're not really doing?" So I just stayed in my room and kind of figured out, "How am I going to master this drum machine? How am I going listen to these records and make them the way I want to make them in the hip hop form?"

Rock's weapon of choice in that quest for mastery would be his still-beloved E-MU SP-1200, a drum machine/sampler combo that itself would become as much a signature of his sound as the deep-in-the-crates samples he mined to run through it as he worked away night after night teaching himself the ins and outs of the rhythmic arcadia. Giving Rock the freedom after studying genres like jazz, soul, and funk for years to finally take a part of any instrumental performance that caught his ear as a potential hook – *often for the first time anyone else had singled it out before* – and make it a song's centerpiece. He did the same with the beats he crafted underneath as he started to develop his own sound and style as a producer:

> My first real drum machine that I owned that was a hammy down was an E-MU SP-12, and then I got the SP-1200, which I've used my whole career basically. I think it was the way the thickness of it sounded, it made the kicks I sampled sounds thicker and bigger and better, and the snares and hi-hats as well, it made everything sound so full. I don't know what kind of chip they put in that machine to make it do that, but it's something that I'll never shy away from when it comes to drum programming. I have a lot of drum skeletons that I have – kicks and snares- that come from the drums off an SP-1200 to make a song.
>
> Building a song always basically comes from me listening to so many dope songs growing up, and learning the format by ear, but not knowing what the word bass meant. But as I grew older,

the way I would listen to music was weird, because I was like "Wow, why am I listening to it this way? Why do I hear this and this? Why do I love this part of the record only?" It was one of those things I just adapted myself to thinking about in that way when I listened to records.

I listened to records and I sampled stuff, then listened to samples creatively and tried to find a good, original sample and make something dope with it, and add stuff to it, keep adding to it and adding to it. That's one of the things that once I turned sixteen, seventeen, I started getting the hang of. Then, when I got to be eighteen, nineteen, I *really* got the hang of it. And that's when I got my break and signed to Untouchables with Eddie F and started doing remixes with him and a team of producers. We used to do R&B remixes back in the early 1990s, 1990/1991, we all kind of grew into it together, and once Eddie seen that I was passionate about the music and the DJing, I was someone just like him, so we were always at it and I learned a lot from Eddie. We were the ones who were experimenting with music, playing with different drum machines, and I started off on several behind him. He was the one who gave me the hammy-down 1200.

While Marley Marl helped him gain the exposure on radio to build a name with New York hip hop fans, and Eddie F helped him land his record deal, Pete again reserves his greatest credit for cousin Heavy D where teaching him how to write songs came into play. Reflecting fondly on the memory of the how now-passed mentor was among his biggest cheer leaders, Heavy gave Rock his first real production credits on the 1989 Heavy D & The Boyz album *Big Tyme*, co-producing the tracks *Mood for Love*, *A Better Land*, *Let It Flow*, and the *title track*, which became a hit on the Billboard US Rap Chart:

> Getting signed became a heavy ambition for me after seeing my cousin Heavy was successful. He used to push me to do it, and that was another thing that made me excited about doing music. I had a support system. Our families were all pulling for us, especially when I met CL Smooth and we got our deal. They knew that I had something special going on, and Heavy D was the actual person that really seen it in me. And that's basically how I was successful with working alone.
>
> With *Big Tyme*, that beat actually came from a pause button, I was pausing records, a Cameo record with some drums, and just kept pausing the parts I liked, and kept pausing it over and over and over again in rhythm on time, and Heav liked it, so we made it, and Eddie F helped me put it together, and that's how I got co-production credit on the record. When we started making music was where we would just suggest things, and it was funny because we were family, so we would argue sometimes and fight and not speak to one another for a day, then

make up and do it some more, that's how we did it as family. And once he was successful, he felt I had the hang of making beats, so he gave me a shot. He liked that I had my own style, he loved that, and said he learned a lot from me, just watching me make beats. He used to come down in the basement and watch me make beats. I used to have so many people that was around, like people I grew up with, while I was making beats. I had a big pool table downstairs, so I would have a bunch of guys come over and play pool and hang out, drink beer, and watch me make beats all night.

Following his work on Heavy D's *Big Tyme* album, Rock sourced those same basement sessions for tracks that would wind up on the first studio release from the dynamic duo of Pete Rock & CL Smooth on the well-received *All Souled Out* EP *Billboard Magazine*'s review of the album put a spotlight front and center on the producer's standout talent, noting that, "Pete Rock's unmatched production sound is already in place, fully-formed, drenched in obscure soul music samples and rumbling, cavernous bass. Characterized by his trademark sonic signature, muted and phased trumpet, and flute loops, the songs sound regal with endless depth...it is hard to imagine a stronger or more confident introduction."

The critical acclaim would continue, growing into a chorus when the duo released their proper debut album a year later, *Mecca and the Soul Brother*, where Rock would demonstrate with his singular ear for recognizing instantly memorable samples and flipping them into his own design with his production on the group's first breakout – and still biggest – hit, *They Reminisce*

Over You (Troy), Rock recalled being moved to produce the Tribute after "he passed away, he was young, and it was a freak accident. When you have someone like that in your life, it's very therapeutic when you lose them, you go back to the music and listen to it and it's therapeutic because it gives you feelings, emotions and shit like that, and that's what *Reminisce* does for me."

As his profile as both a producer and re-mixer continued to catapult into one of New York's most cutting edge and in demand as the early 1990s unfolded, though just in his early 20's, Pete would continue racking up studio credits with the biggest names in the game, from Run-D.M.C. to Doug E. Fresh, Public Enemy to Redman, EPMD to DJ Jazzy Jeff and the Fresh Prince and Naughty by Nature. In 1994, Rock landed a coveted spot on the debut album of the hottest rapper to come out of the Queensbridge scene yet, NAS on the instant classic, *Illmatic.* Producing what turned out to be one of the album – and artist's – most celebrated and important hits to date with *The World Is Yours,* driven by a jazz-piano infused instrumental that *The Source* correctly observed years later, "Would help change the course of hip hop forever," once it dropped. Rock remembered being drawn to work with the young wordsmith first and foremost for the fact that, as a producer:

> I felt like he was the new messiah on the block, he was very distinctive artist and had his own style, so basically that's what drew me to him and him to me, because how he is to rhymes I am to music, so that's how that came together. With Nas, it was always more than one take. He was the type of person that was always ready, he always had rhymes, and I had this one beat that

he loved and we made it happen. As far as the samples we used, *I Love Music* and *It's Yours*, I'm a jazz fan and used to listen to certain artists and my dad had me inspired by jazz as well, he had a lot of jazz records, like Amad Jamal, Myles, Thelonious Monk, Coltrain, you name it.

The same year, as Rock was busy laying tracks in the studio, in the esteemed opinion of *LA Weekly*, he was simultaneously laying, "The groundwork for much of alternative hip hop for the next twenty years," he dropped efforts in that direction including his follow-up with CL Smooth, *The Main Ingredient*, and one of Heavy D's biggest cross-over hits, *Black Coffee*, which for the producer was like a family reunion in the truest sense of the word. Now with both Heavy and Pete's careers in full swing and their respective schedules too full to allow the kind of constant creative hanging-out they used to do back in the day making records in Pete's basement, when they did enter the studio to work, the producer remembered it still felt like no time had passed:

> It was beautiful because he was so talented. He believed in me from Day one and kind of brought it out of me, the talent, because he also had talent, not only as an Emcee but as a musician. He loved making beats and having fun behind the scenes, and we thought it was fun. Every day we would wake up with each other and make a beat or play around and do something, it was something personal man.

That's how it used to happen back in the day, just to get a vibe on an artist I was working with, basically a read, and you get a read on a person by hanging out with them for a day, and seeing what the person's like even off the scene of music, and what he likes, what he dislikes, what goes on, and then I used to take that and apply it to the music. As a producer, I used to do that just walking along the street or being in my hood, just getting inspired by seeing things and having a story about it and trying to make a beat for it. Sometimes I would do that in my head, and then other times an artist would come to me with an idea in the same way from something they've seen.

Pete's re-mixes were spinning just as regularly as the records he produced by the mid-1990s. An art form unto itself where, remixes were done for dozens of artists. MTV would later note of one of its primary inventors that during these fertile years, "Rock solidified his reputation as one of the most crucial figures in hip hop." Breaking down the secrets to his science for hip hop fans and aspiring re-mix producers alike, the producer begins with the most basic concept behind stripping an instrumental away and rebuilding a new one in his own musical vision around the artist's acapella vocal track, reasoning:

The remixes were all about changing the beat totally from the original version and making something of your own, and I was fortunate enough for people to like what I was doing, because I was just doing it for me at first, being selfish, "I like this," but I wouldn't say it to anyone, I would fight within myself, and I always used to say, "I'm my own worst enemy because I'm my own worst critic." There's beats that I did where I said, "Mmm, I could have did it better than that."

It's what you use and how you use it. I make sure that it's a sample that no one's ever heard ever, and if it's something I can manipulate that I love and it sounds good, then I'm on it, like catch-up on a hotdog, I'm on it, and I just start to manipulate and do things and make it sound like something. That was the main thing, was finding that original sample or something that people never heard ort used before, and records that they *have* heard and used before, but just taking the ones they've heard, the familiar records, and doing them in a way where they're like, "Wow, you really flipped that around." I always used to want to challenge myself with getting jobs to do a remix, listen to the original, and say, "Okay, how can I top that? Because that's hot, I have to make something hotter." At first, I would take them to make a name for myself, and I wanted to let people know that I was a force to be reckoned with, that I wasn't on some half-ass shit.

Taking yet another creative leap forward in a move that symbolized just how much marquee value his name held among fans at the time he decided to step out with his first solo LP in 1998 with *Soul Survivor*, hailed as, "Flawlessly assembled," by the *LA Times*, while *Ebony* praised it as, "A true gem." A Top 10 hit on the Billboard Top R&B/Hip Hop Albums Chart, following it up in 2001 with *PeteStrumentals*, where his jazz and soul influences came into full instrumental bloom. Demonstrating the true reaches of Rock's ear as a tastemaster, the album was a mainstream critical hit, with the *Washington Times* hailing the collection as, "A benchmark of instrumental hip hop." *PopMatters.com* meanwhile praised Rock as, "An ambitious DJ as Instrumentalist," throughout the album that *XXL* spotlighted in an article as, "One of the first beat tapes of it's kind." A trend he would continue on his second solo outing, *Soul Survivor II* where MOJO concluded Rock was thriving creatively, "At the peak of his powers."

Soul Train would revisit Rock's dedication to keeping the genre alive within hip hop instrumentals in 2013 when felt Pete was worthy of the #1 spot on their Top 40 Most Soulful Hip Hop Artists rankings amid the iconic television show's, "Celebrating the 40th anniversary of the poetic urban music genre." *Soul Train* elaborated, explaining that, "The ranking was also a showing of gratitude to artists who've proudly and skillfully represented soul music while preserving its cultural and artistic relevance...considered the best among them was iconic producer, DJ and recording artist Pete Rock, having the esteemed honor of topping the list." Bestowed with his first Grammy win in recent years for Best Rap Album honoring his production work on Kanye West's *My Beautiful Dark Twisted Fantasy* record, Rock still feels the secret to his success has remained the same throughout the past twenty-five years:

> I just pick the right records. When you're doing
> it for so long, sometimes it just comes to you.
> When you dig and find certain jazz and soul

records, you're like, "Oh shit, never heard this." It's not always hearing it off the bat when you put the needle down on the groove. And that's how I used to approach certain records that I heard that I liked. It challenged me.

Entering his third decade with the status of "legend" now attached to his name like a Ph.D, Rock would prove he was a true Professor of his craft when he released his next studio project, *PeteStrumentals 2* in 2015, which proved his staying power as "the audible architect who has helped to build some of hip hop's most appreciated tracks," in the opinion of *AllHipHop.com*. The esteemed HipHop news site added of his latest offering in that tradition that the, "20-track creative kaleidoscope is just shy of an hour long, and it's intriguing tracks repping different hues of the hip hop spectrum are sure to captivate the listener from start to finish." No matter how busy or stacked with tracks his instrumentals might be, Pete practices the art of simplicity within his mixing process, explaining:

It's a comfortability that we have as producers that we get into, we're so deep into our funk, we just feel like this is enough for us, eight channels is enough for me too. I used to just stack sounds upon sounds and then take what I liked and kept that, and that was always important, it's called developing your own sound and standing in your own light.

I strive to be in my own light, and just do stuff that people weren't doing at the time, and taking what I knew and making it my own in a way

where I just took the style of music I was making
– the elements of jazz and soul and hip hop and
rock – and incorporating it in my music. It was
very, very important that I could have my own
sound.

These days, when he's not in the studio, Pete flies around the
world DJing for his international base of hip hop fans. With
such recent highlight globe-hopping stops including DJ Festivals
like Razzmatazz in Barcelona, Spain, Blackalicious in Berlin,
Germany, the Outlook Festival 2015 in Croatia, Electrosanne
2015 in Switzerland, So Miles Party in Paris, France, multiple
dates around the United Kingdom, Australia, and a battle
between Rock versus DJ Premier in Tokyo, Japan. Proud of the
signature sound he's sewn into multiple generations of hip hop
since he started making records over a quarter-century ago. For
Pete, his longevity has and continues to be centered in a
philosophy he first perfected as a teenage DJ of always grabbing
his listener's ear with something they haven't heard before he
put it in one of his songs:

It's the ethics of music that I came up under that
keeps the curiosity of my audience, or the
audience in the hip hop community. And giving
them what they want to hear, even if it's the new
stuff today – just giving it to them in a way
where it's *Pete Rockish*.
www.peterock.com

"The way I produce, I don't like people around me, because my mind is working a thousand miles an hour..." – N.O. Joe

CHAPTER TEN
Cinematic Soul:
Gumbo Funk and The Birth of Southern Hip Hop
– N.O. JOE

Southern rap – arguably today's biggest selling sub-genre within broader hip hop – has seen many influential producers help guide it's sound over the years, but only claims a handful of true pioneers, visionaries who first built the foundations of the sound out of their musical imaginations when no blueprint yet existed. Before trap music or Outkast and Organized Noize or Cash Money or No Limit, before Lil Jon and Krunk, before Miami and Maybach Music, there was Rap-A-Lot. And more importantly, there was Scarface, the true godfather of southern rap. It's first true superstar and first southern rap artist to ever crossover and hit #1 on the Billboard Top 200 Album Chart, like every trailblazing emcee, Scarface found a secret weapon in the form of a producer behind the curtain working the console dials like Oz in 18-year-old prodigy Joseph Johnson. A true scientist with designs on a sound that would change southern rap forever – including being widely credited as the first to introduce the Hammond B-3 organs into the subgenre's popular sound – BET gave Joe his due with their estimation that "when Scarface released his third studio album, *The Diary*, few could have predicted the extent to which it would reshape the sonic landscape of the south."

Long before Atlanta became the Motown of southern rap, the man responsible for shaping that sonic landscape in the first place was a young, unknown self-taught producer from New Orleans who went by the name of N.O. Joe. The ingredients of his signature Gumbo Funk sound is one he describes as, "A collage of great ingredients that go together to make one. And that's what I did. Basically, when you cook a pot of Gumbo, you may have sausages, shrimp, crab, chicken, okra, and a whole bunch of other ingredients, but it comes together and tastes good. With Gumbo Funk, it's nothing that's in a box. It's a collage of soul music, funk, pop, hip hop, EDM, garage house music that all mix well and sound good. So it's just a perfect blend of a lot of different genres of music. I was from the south and loved the soul of the south, so when southern fans heard those Otis Redding and Donnie Hathaway organs. It caught their ear. Then at the same time, I think it caught New York's attention with the 808-less beats, and then the guitars and the funk elements to my sound appealed to the California fans. Once I married everything together and blended it perfectly where you couldn't say, 'Oh, this is West Coast, this is East Coast...,' it was just music that everybody loved. I strategically put that together way back at the dawn of the 1990s."

A blend that no producer had tried to layer into one mix before. The tapestry of Joe's sound was truly the first of its kind, which in the esteemed opinion of *AllHipHop.com*, "Allowed him to develop rich soundscapes which (didn't)...just transcend southern rap, but all of hip hop. His gumbo funk sound allowed him to be one of music's best chameleons and artists and fans have been reaping the rewards of his talents for decades." Starting out as a student of the shelves of vinyl that lined the aisles and walls of his family's small New Orleans record store, Joe shares his fond childhood memories of growing up at the feet of:

> My mom, who ran a record store in New Orleans, did promotions, fixed hair and sold clothes. So all of those Otis Redding, James Brown, The Jackson 5...we had records everywhere! My mom basically did promotions, so when the artists came in town, she would take them around to the radio stations, they came and signed autographs at her record store, etc, so that's kind of how I grew up around the music business. My dad played a lot of jazz music around the house as well, so I grew up in a musical household. And my mom sung gospel music. I started out as a child actually singing, and got into the music at an early age.

Able to feel the music he was absorbing as a listener tangibly, Joe found his true calling within the music business when he got his hands on his first drum machine and home recording equipment in the early 80's. Setting up a bedroom studio where he immediately discovered he had a natural aptitude for navigating his way around the equipment from both a musical and technical side, the producer shared that he got his hands on this gateway gear courtesy not of his parents, but actually:

> From a police officer ironically enough in New Orleans. At the time, he had some equipment he loaned to me and a friend of mine. He gave us a Roland TR-606 drum machine and a 4-track, and I had a little Casio SK-1 keyboard. So that's kind of how I started off recording. Just kind of mimicking the old Stevie Wonder and stuff like that, and then hip hop like Big Daddy Kane(s) and the Dr. Dre(s). And when I first started making beats, I would listen to the old Run-D.M.C. and LL Cool J and count the bars, "Okay, 16 bars." That's how I knew how to format the beats and everything.

Turning his creativity into commerce in an early sign of the entrepreneurial instincts necessary to hustle one's way through the record industry in the unique niche of record producer whose job is essentially selling beats, Joe started doing just that in his early teens in the heart of New Orleans' legendary French Quarter. Making his music part of the soundtrack to the circus backdrop of street performances by break-dancers and constant built-in audiences to use as a sounding board for his newest beat instrumentals, even turning his DJ booth into a live on-the-spot recording studio, proudly recalling:

> With that 4-track, there was a place called Jackson Square. What I would do is go there, plug in my equipment at these little poles at the time they had there with electrical outlets on them. I would sell like beats and demos right in Jackson Square for like twenty-five dollars a song. Sometimes, I would just do the beat right there. And they would rap, because I had the microphone and everything right there. You had four takes (laughs), and that was it. A lot of guys came in with four or eight bar raps, and I'd have to tell them, "No, no, you gotta structure it like this here, just write the rest of it here. It's going to sound crazy if it's now sixteen bars." So I was actually coaching them along in the actual square during that time.

> That cop eventually came and took back his equipment. So next I met with another friend of mine who was in school named Cokie who called himself Coke the Crowd Knocker. He had a Yamaha RX-7, and they had the jazz bass drum. At that time, I was really looking for an 808, but I grew up in the poor neighborhoods, so those things were unattainable to get an 808 and stuff like that. But we would use the RX-7 and synch it with the 909, which was the drum machine I could afford at the time. To be honest with you, the only thing I liked about it was it

had the punch of the kick of the 808, but it didn't have the ring. I did not like the snares in it at all and wanted those 808 snares, so the 606 had pretty much the 808 snare. The only thing again I would really use the 909 for was the attack or punch on the kick, and I would take that and mix it with the jazz bass drum out of the RX-7 to get the thick sound of the 808.

Already in touch with the fundamentals that boomed most naturally out of the speakers in his head in the beats he was starting to produce, Joe's experimentations and manipulations of other drum machines to replicate the desired 808 sound and further discover new dimensions to his abilities within building rhythm tracks soon enough branched out into other instruments. Applying the same D.I.Y. spirit to his ever-expanding repertoire of skills in record making as he continued to prove his knack for pulling full songs out of very limited instrumental means – especially in comparison to today's digital universe of recording – N.O. Joe shakes his head looking back on how he pulled it off convincingly given:

> Back then, there were no keyboards really involved yet. They had little bass sounds and orchestra hits and all of that stuff. So in the drum machine, I had to make it sound like a record. I was programming bass lines and all of that stuff in there with Midi and the two machines up, and that's really where I kind of got into doing the music aspect of it. And making the best of what I had at that time. So whether it was a bass line or an orchestral hit, making it sound like a record.

That was my thing. And at that time, that's what really intrigued me into that RX-7 because it had some small keyboard sounds in it.

Then after that, I graduated into the SP-12. I got into the SP-12 because I had met Mannie Fresh at the time, which was the late 80's. Back then he was in a group called Gregory D and Mannie Fresh, where Gregory was the emcee and Mannie was the producer. They were actually signed to RCA Records at the time, so they had records out there already and were a big deal, in New Orleans at least. He was the one who turned me onto the SP-12, and I would go over to his house and use his SP-12. Then, he graduated to the SP-1200, which now had the floppy disc, and they had drum sounds in there. So that's where I kind of got introduced to everything in one without synching another drum machine up, because you could sample now.

Mannie Fresh: We grew up together, we went to school together, and all of that. That was my homeboy, and it's crazy to see him come from borrowing a drum machine to the greatness that he's done. It's incredible when you see cats like that.

N.O. Joe: So if I heard an 808 from the Beastie Boys that's just wide open or whatever, or Madtronics, whatever it was, I would sample it so I could have that 808 sound. So when I would go over to Mannie Fresh's house – and we laugh about this still today – I only had a certain amount of time, so I would go in there with all my records and cassettes cued up to where I needed it to be cued up at the sample, the sounds, and knew I had maybe only thirty or forty-five minutes to pump out some songs before he had to leave. So I would crank out five and six songs, and he'd be like, "Man, you did that many songs in that time?", and I was like, "Yeah!" From there, that's when I got into sampling before the MPC-60.

As his recording knowledge continued to broaden, whether he knew he wanted to sample studios beyond the Bayou or not, fate would intervene and make the move for him one serendipitous afternoon when he hustled his way into an industry convention to pass out demo tapes and a magic door of opportunity opened:

There was a convention that came to New Orleans called the BRE Convention, and man, I used to sneak in there, and I always kept a travel-bag of cassettes with me, and would pass my cassettes of beats around. Eventually one of my cassettes got into the hands of a Universal exec who, after hearing my tape, asked me to come out to New York, and even though I was still in my teens at that time, I'd learned enough to say to him, "We need to get the business straight first buddy." I remember I kept telling my parents I

was going to NYC, and they didn't believe me
until the day I had my bags packed and said,
"Hey, I'm leaving," so we had the talk: "Is this
what you wanna do?" And I promised I'd come
back and go to school. All of that.

So New York was an adventure for me, I got out
there and met a lot of people out there – Puffy
when he was still at Uptown, and Run and
Russell Simmons – and they booked me into
Chung King, where the Beastie Boys had
recorded *License to Ill*. While I was working at
Chung King, there were a couple of rappers from
Brooklyn who came in there who passed by the
room I was working in, heard whatever beat I
was working on, and stuck their heads in there
like, "I like that beat son! How much you charge
for beats?" So I told them, and then these guys
came back later on and checked out some beats.
This was the Boom-Boom-Bap era, and my beats
back then were like that. But they had kind of a
swing to them, and I had organs and all of these
other things going on.

So as they were listening, they told me, "Take
those few instruments out of there man, because
I want to be able to just feel it." So I took the
instruments out, and they bought a bunch of
beats like that, all stripped down, and I thought
This is easy! So I had guys from the Bronx,
Brooklyn, and Queens coming through the
studio just getting mad beats from me. And I was

just doing them right on the spot. I really kind of got a name out there before I got a name in New Orleans. They would go tell their friends, "Hey, they got this guy, Joe Cool, he's got some hot stuff." And I got a lot of work from those guys, along with working with some unknown artists on Universal that I was working with at the time named Brian McKnight on *Goodbye My Love,* and Jodeci's *Forever My Lady* record.

Though he could have stayed in the Big Apple working steadily on the studio circuit after the success of the Jodeci project, he was beckoned home by destiny's calling after a friend first hipped Joe to the rapper his sound had always been searching for, the one and only Mr. Scarface. A match that would turn out to be made in hip hop heaven and put southern rap on the national map for the first time ever in their collaborations to come, Joe remembers first being hipped to Brad Jordan, aka Scarface, on a trip back home to visit his family:

I went back to New York for a while, and wound up working with some more R&B acts like Joe and even D'Angelo before I moved back to New Orleans and got into working with Scarface. Before I'd moved to New York, a friend of mine had told me about The Geto Boys, and he'd let me hear *Mr. Scarface is Back,* and as I was listening to this record, my reaction was, "Damn, this dude's hard!" So when I heard that, I just started doing music for Scarface, not even knowing I was ever going to meet him or work with him. One thing that caught me straight off about Face was the thickness of his voice. Then, the way that he presented his lyrics and told stories, from a certain perspective. I'd never heard anything like that before *on a record*. I'd always heard it in my neighborhood, but I'd never heard it on records like that. I really appreciated that, and was like, "Man, I can come harder than those tracks he was on!" I loved the tracks, but I was like, *I can take it to the next level. I know I can.* These are things I was saying internally, not to anybody else. So I started planning for it before I ever met Face for the first time.

Finding himself creatively energized by the challenge, his next moment of producer providence would reveal itself when a chance encounter in a record store put him face-to-face with the intended target for his new Gumbo Funk sound, recalling that the karmic encounter played out "when I'd first gotten back to New Orleans from New York, I used to go to this record store called Blockbuster Music, and one day I happened to walk in there to get a record, and it just so happened that I laid eyes on this guy, and was like 'Dude looks like Scarface!' Then I was like, 'Naw, this can't be, this is crazy,' but I saw this guy who was with him walk into a different aisle, so I walked over and asked him, 'Hey man, is that Scarface?', and he actually said "Yeah..." I was shocked, and it felt just then like fate, so I just rolled the dice and said, 'Listen man, my car is parked right out front. I'd like you to hear a couple tracks, just maybe a few seconds, and if you don't like it, you don't have to go in and get him,' so he was like, 'Alright, let me hear what you got.'"

Knowing this was his make-or-break opportunity, Joe thankfully had the new sound that Scarface it turns out had been looking for ready and waiting to unleash as he remembered surreally floating out to his car:

> I couldn't believe this was actually happening, so we went out to my car and I played him a little bit of the *Lettin' Em Know* track, and when the beat first came in, he was like, "Woah! Wait, stop, stop, stop." Then he ran back into the record store and got Face out of there. So next thing I know, I'm staring directly across into the passenger's window and there's Scarface in the flesh, and now he's like "Let me hear what you got!"

> So I played him track after track, and he was like "Dude, what's up?!", and I told him straight out: "Man, you know, I've always wanted to work with you. Look, I've got some more tracks," because I didn't stay too far away from the record store, so we actually went back to my house and I started pulling floppy discs all out of my closet, and played him a few full songs and he was like "Who is that rapping?", because I was actually rapping on a few at the time. Then he says, "That n#gga's dope..." And I told him that was me, but kept playing him more tracks and they had that edge to them because after a few more he said, "Dude, I want you to produce my next album!"

Scarface: Joe had a song called "Nova" and as long as my shit sounded like that Nova record sounded, I didn't give a fuck. Whoever that was rapping on that motherfucker, I didn't want to see him at all! That sound like a villain, and when Joe told me that was him, I was done, I was fucking done.

An offer that would change the face of southern rap forever, raising it from an underground to national level based on the wings of the momentum Joe and Face were both brining in raising their own games to meet the moment. Feeling fortunate to this day for the favor chance paid him by putting him in the position any producer would have dreamed to be in, the lucky hand he was dealt is one:

> I still trip myself out thinking back on to this day: the fact that if I hadn't stopped at that record store that day, I wouldn't have met him and we wouldn't have made music together over the next twenty years, so I guess it was just meant to happen. It was like God just said, "Look, he's in there, here's your future." From there, took a little trip out to Houston for a couple days, and now had to meet up with James Prince to work out the business. I never wound up meeting him on that trip, but had brought my MP-60 with me, and had everything programmed in there. So when I brought it out to Houston, I remember there were 15-20 guys in this little 10x9 room and they had these speakers and this little amp. Face had brought all his homies out there, so when I walked in there with my drum machine, they all looked at me like, "What the hell is that?" Because in New

Orleans, we were working with Ensoniq EPS 16+, which was a sampler workstation that was totally foreign to them, they didn't know what the hell that was.

Unaware when he first walked in the studio that he was in the presence of the Geto Boys, nor that by the end of the serendipitous session he would be producing their album as his first official collaboration with Scarface and Rap-A-Lot, Joe tripped himself out watching the whole room do the same once his music first came over the speakers. Hitting everyone with the same stunned look Scarface had reacted with, the still-in-his-teens producer remembered the moment as a call-back audition of sorts where:

> They're watching me plugging that and my MPC-60 in, and I could feel people literally breathing down my neck it was so crowded in there. So I plugged everything up, pressed play, and everybody was like, "Woah!" So as I started playing beats, everybody started rapping, and this was at like 10 AM till like 1-2 in the morning, and I was *still* playing fresh beats! I had a whole bunch of beats, so from there, Face got me back in touch with James Prince and we had to work the business out, because the first record they wanted me to work on was the Geto Boys record *Till Death Do Us Part*.

Though he'd already gone through the watered-down version of what would have been his first thrills at seeing records he'd worked on chart on the Billboard Charts with Jodeci, with his first run out of the gate with Rap-A-Lot, N.O. Joe would land at #1 on the Billboard R&B/Hip Hop Albums Chart with *Till Death Do Us Part*. *The Source* and *Rolling Stone Magazine* – the latter highlighting Joe's push toward "live instrumentation and bluesy, soulful samples" – both awarded the album 3.5 out of 5 star reviews, giving the producer a trial run to use studio as a laboratory of sorts to further refine the sonic of his Gumbo Funk production sound. Along with the album's success in "helping to spread the sound of H-Town gangsterism to hoods nationwide," as the group's hometown Houston Press would later note, the record's successful competition as a Chart Topper would rack up an additional win on the singles chart where *Six Feet Deep* cracked the Top 40 on the Hot 100 Singles Chart, and rocketed all the way to #2 on the Hot R&B/Hip Hop Singles Chart, all in the same month of his nineteenth birthday! For Joe looking back, the craziest part of his success wasn't that him finding it at an age when most kids are just starting to find themselves as college freshman. For the producer, the amusing irony that he'd created the sound not in a fancy studio with all the technological trimmings at his finger tips, but instead:

> On the Washing Machine in my mother's house
> back when I making beats dreaming of working
> with Scarface! A lot of those early records, and
> *Six Feet Deep* was one of them, went down that
> way. That track in particular was a real heartfelt-
> type of song where I remember I was going for a
> Marvin Gaye or Lionel Ritchie *Easy Like Sunday
> Morning* type of vibe. I always liked the feel of
> that type of song, and the Geto Boys put the
> perfect type of story over it about their homies
> passing on, and that worked out to be the right

musical backdrop for it too because it became a #2 hit on the Hot Rap Singles chart.

On that album, there were songs that were hits in the street too, like *It Ain't Shit* and *No Nuts, No Glory.* Cats even told me, "Yo man, your music is street, but it's uplifting as well and can get you in that mode where you wanna go do what you gotta do to it. We rode to motherfuckers on those records, and it was those same records we had a truce on as well!" So it brought out all those emotions, because it was street but it had that southern down-home organs and swampy guitars and different musical elements like that.

A blueprint he was just beginning to unveil for the world, hip hop's true introduction to N.O. Joe's gumbo funk sound would make it's mainstream musical debut on his next collaboration with Scarface, a tour-de-force whose impact was still reverberating years later when iTunes complimented Face on, "The decision to bring aboard N.O. Joe, the producer who would go on to guide the sound of Texas hip hop in the 90's, and whose partnership with Face continues to the present. *The World Is Yours* is the rapper's first attempt to formulate his own funk sound. N.O. Joe makes the beats slower and thicker, and the pace here is less frenetic than on the first album, reflecting the growth in Face's stature. The tone is still furious, and you'd be hard-pressed to find a rap song from 1992 that packs a punch as forceful as *Lettin' Em Know, The Wall,* or *You Don't Hear Me Doe.* Knowing he had the science down within his own sound, as he began to blend it with Scarface's vision for the record. Joe detailed the distinction he was seeking to draw from the legendary rapper's first album, revealing of his sonic ambitions:

> Just say from the *Mr. Scarface is Back* album, what I wanted to do was not have it be so sample-based and within the "southern rap" genre we were pioneering back then, I wanted to create a sound that was pretty much a mixture of everything, and when Face and I first met and he heard my beats, he had the vision to see this was a new and innovative sound.

> If you look at the chord progressions, I think I was one of the first hip hop producers to introduce the "gumbo," if you will, in my instrumentals of soul, delta blues. That "gut bucket" soul. Those were new influences in hip hop as far as both the streets and radio was concerned at that time. And nobody was doing that before me. I had those types of tracks before anyone ever had heard of it. I used to always think to myself, "Man, if I could find the right artist's voice to lay overtop some of these tracks, I think I could change some things." Then, Scarface came into my world and we did that.

> **Scarface:** In all honesty, I think Joe and I were a match made in musical heaven. He's got music and I've got words. Words and music, and I think that's what makes us a perfect match.

A sound he'd largely conceptualized in his home studio converted from his mother's laundry room well before his beats found their way to Scarface, to this day, when N.O. Joe pops in *The World is Yours*, he's taken back on an especially personal ride down memory lane. A musical time capsule that truly measures just how far ahead of his era the producer was as a visionary considering the blank canvas he was working with as far as outside "*southern rap*" reference points. As he translated the new sound was hearing in his head out into his trusty MPC-60, Joe confirms:

> A lot of the music I made with Scarface on our first album together, *The World is Yours*, was pretty much started and constructed years prior to that. Back then, I had played the keyboards when I was out in New York and sampled everything that I played inside of my MPC. I used to do music in the back of my parents' house. I grew up in what they called a Shotgun double house, and my bedroom and the laundry room were in the back on the left side of the house, but on the right side of the house, the kitchen was in the back. There was no central air or anything like that. The A/C only went on at like 9 p.m. or 10 p.m., so in the summer time, it would get super hot. Like 98 degrees outside, and at least 100, 110 degrees inside that house. So I'd be in the back in the laundry room there with my drum machine sitting on top of the washer along with this big old 22-inch amp plugged in. I used that room because it was the only one in the house with a lot of outlets for as many plugs as I needed.

Man, I remember so many days being in the back with a wife-beater on, just sweating like crazy pumping out beats on that MPC once my parents would leave for work in the morning. I used to BLAST that thing, just making beats all day. While I'm proud to say my parents were supportive of what I was doing, *once they came home*, I had to take that equipment and move to the other side of the house to the kitchen once they would tell me to turn it down! As a matter of fact, even though I would work with headphones on once they came home. Whenever I would finish a track and want to listen to the mix through that big wolfer, one of them would routinely come running in and say, "Hey, you're going to wake up the neighbors!"

Rattling his neighbors' walls hard enough with the way his beats hit to not only shake the windows just short of breaking but "as a matter of fact, one time, I remember some guy came around the front of our house banging on the door, saying 'Hey Joe, you literally knocked a couple pictures off the wall!' That's what I was after though man, and I just worked every day honing my craft, where I would come home every day after school and make music, and eventually got so addicted to it that I really didn't want to go anywhere. My friends would come over at night at 8, 9 o'clock and say 'Hey man, you wanna go out to this party?', and I'd be like 'Naaah, I'm kinda in the middle of something,' and would just keep on making music all night long. Part of my strategy with putting in that kind of grind, beyond just the love of making beats, was that if I ever ran into a new artist, I always wanted to be ready with a bunch of new music that was ready to go, and that's exactly what wound up happening with Scarface."

As they got down to work in the studio on an album that *Vibe Magazine* would later celebrate for its importance in helping to, "Establish the multitude of musical styles in the developing Houston sound. It could be hard boiled trunk funk, it could be solemn piano melody that was more reminiscent of the blues." *Spin Magazine* would add of the impact that, "With his second album, Scarface pushed himself further towards the mainstream with the help of producer and eventual UGK collaborator N.O. Joe. *The World is Yours* is steeped in the G-funk of *The Chronic*, but with a distinct slow swirl that could only have come from slow-rolling Houston." Viewing Dr. Dre's latter masterpiece as a sign that rap was ready for something new across the country, he tapped into the opening as an opportunity to push the sound boundaries even farther, moving the bar in the process:

> On that record, because after *The Chronic* came out with the live playing, it kind of gave me the green light to fully go ahead and do that, even more full-on than we had on The Geto Boys record. So I incorporated more live playing on that album, along with sonically going in a direction that on the final mixes of *Till Death Do Us Part*, they'd told us to remix because they thought it was too wide (laughs). So on *The World is Yours*, the mixes were better because I had a chance now to go in and expand it and make it more dimensional, wider and fatter-sounding snares and stacking certain things together and bringing things one time inside the song and that was it. I had a lot of the stuff pre-

done already and what wasn't done was already in my head, so I added a lot in the studio because now I was really able to spread my wings and really venture out in doing that record, and Face would come in and he played some bass lines and I usually had the production already going, and he might play a little guitar line, and I'd say, "Oh, that's dope, let's add that in there." So we would collaborate on stuff like that, and that record was his baby, coming off the success of his first solo album.

Deconstructing one of the new elements Joe introduced to hip hop within his gumbo funk sound on *The World is Yours* were the sunken sonics of his clap sound heavily treated with effects and buried in his mixes versus their traditional placement. More prominently in the front without losing any of their power. It was an example of the cinematic dynamics the producer introduced into Scarface and southern rap's sound for the first time the world had ever heard it. Instantly mimicked at such a widespread rate that it would quickly seem like the trend had been around forever. Joe as its originator breaks down the original science behind discovering this element of his sound, describing an experimental creative backdrop where:

During that time, I was always perfecting kind of the clap sounds. So I had a lot of different claps that I would use, and would have them playing in reverse mode. Kind of way in the background. I would just reverse them in the drum machine, and get the attack just right on it to where right before the snare comes in, the reverse clap would hit as well. I did everything manually back then, so the effects were done inside the MPC and ASR-10 as well, so we used some of the effects in there as well.

On that record, it was also all about the hand claps and that poppy snare. The snare that I introduced on the Geto Boys record also came in on *The World is Yours* album. And that was actually sampled from the group The Meters. They always had a certain drum sound, and that drum sound we used on the Scarface record actually came from The Meters. Not from the record, but from the actual drum. A friend of mine uncle played in a band with them, and he actually left that snare drum over at his house. And we sampled it all types of different ways. We hit it with sticks and belt buckles and pennies and quarters to get all kinds of different sounds on it. We actually used a little cheap Shure SM57 mic to record all of those sounds. Those expensive mics like the U-87 weren't available to us yet. So we'd just take that cheap mic, and put it at the right angle and make sure it doesn't distort. Even if it distorts, that was still another sound we had that we could stack. For certain songs I would use the sleigh bell in the background, and like a ride cymbal. I would use those on certain songs because I liked the high-end sound of it. It always had that tingling top-end to it.

One of hip hop's first producers ever to break away from sampling to introduce live instrumentation as a fundamental within his production amalgam, Joe had the opportunity to mentor another aspiring genius in Mike Dean, a mellow multi-instrumentalist who would go on to become Kanye West's right-hand man in the studio, but got his start working under N.O. Joe's tutelage. Seeking to take advantage of Dean's talent for interpreting Joe's musical ideas on instruments like the guitar, which added new instrumental dynamics to his Gumbo Funk sound in the process. As they experimented, the producer remembered calling on his early days as an assistant engineer working in the R&B world in New York for reference, reflecting how much he picked up on the art of record production during the experience:

> When I was recording live instruments, like Mike Dean's guitar for instance, that is a technique I'd learned after talking to Allan Toussaint and asking him, "How do they process the guitar sounds? What did they use? How did they get this, etc?" Because a lot of different musicians had recorded at the studio we were working out of, which is where he recorded like The Meters, and all of those bands. So I just spent time being nosy and seeing what was used in the process so that I could achieve those sounds in some kind of way, instead of just having a raw guitar. So I was researching those old records, asking a lot of different, older guitar players that played on a lot of those records what different sounds were called, etc, that way I could better explain what I wanted Mike to play

in the studio. Then, approaching the live mix of it and actually playing the things I heard in my head and getting a tone. That was challenging at first, but was so exciting to me as well.

For that album, I went out and bought my first Minimoog and a Moog Prodigy synthesizer. So a lot of those sounds were a combination of some of the real instruments, like the Roland JV1080, and the stuff that was in the keyboard. In doing the music, whatever keyboard it was, you could never really just go there and say, "Oh, this is what he used in here," because it was always mixed with something, and was always tweaked.

Once they were ready for Scarface to lay down his vocals, he stepped up to the plate to answer Joe's hard-smacking beats with an equally-powerful vocal punch that hit the ball out of the park with what Billboard correctly argued was, "A huge leap forward from his debut, both in terms of production and rhetoric. He works here mostly with producer N.O. Joe, who crafts a...distinctly modeled style" that inspired Face to grow as a lyricist, delivering, "Personally introspective rhymes rather than his heedful narratives of the past." Seeking to draw the deepest possible response lyrically out of Brad Jordan as a rapper knowing the full range of his exploratory genius as a street poet, Joe's soundtrack was the musical paper Face was laying his words down on, a responsibility he never took lightly given the bravery he was asking for from his collaborator:

Face didn't have too many outside people around him in the studio. He was usually real private about his music when he was making it. So he may have his brother Warren or a close friend in there while he's recording. But for the most part, it was me, him, the engineer, and maybe one or two other people who were close to him.

Most times, he would take the track home, then come back in the studio the next day and lay the vocal down, and it was usually one or two takes and he was done.

Scarface: I write the first verse right there on the spot, then come back and write the second and third verse the next day. On *The World is Yours*, my favorite cuts were that motherfuckin' *Lettin' Em Know* and *The Wall*. God damn, that mother fucker was on! I think that was the start of my career. That record right there started my career, because honestly, *The Wall* tapped me into me. That was the record that did it. That record let me know that I was a bad motherfucker! That's when I first started smoking weed and working in the studio...

N.O. Joe: Back then, we used the U-87, which I ran through a Summit mic-pre and a Summit compressor, which I liked because it was a real warm sound. Scarface has probably one of the most powerful voices in the business man, so much so that he actually blew a U-87 out one time. But I liked the Summit mic-pre back then.

On later albums, I actually like the LA-2A better and a Poltec on his voice, but on that record, we went with the Summit mic-pre and compressor. When he was tracking vocals, he liked to have a little reverb on his voice, I used the Lexicon, and then a little delay, but nothing too crazy. I always wanted that edge in my beats because his voice was just so edgy, so I wanted to make the snares and kicks and everything like it was coming at you full-flair as well.

Many of the album's most dazzling sonic dimensions would find reach their desired depths and heights during the mixing process. Rather than being a winding down part of the record-making cycle as most artists view it – it was in fact showtime for Joe as the album's producer, representing the zone where all his creative decisions along the way needed to add up as part of the album's final formula sonically. Not so much a puzzle as a Matrix from the way Joe viewed the grid pre-Pro Tools as he fit the various pieces of their vision together into the new sound that *The World is Yours* introduced to hip hop. Joe viewed the recording console as his millennium falcon cockpit, allowing him to jump into hyper-space as he raced toward the finish line for the highly-anticipated album:

On *The World is Yours*, coming out of the drum machine, that was the mix I wanted, but I got a chance to spread it out on the board. So I wanted to start from that mix, and getting the spread-out version of it, I was able to widen certain things and the main thing was the drums, just to make sure they were just like not polished drums, but that they always had an edge on them. I never cared about the red, like when you're sampling stuff, "Oh, don't let it go in the red!" I don't care about the red, if it sounds good there, then red is good. So those sounds that I had, a lot of them were sampled super-hot, one of the reasons being because I liked the sound, and the other reason being when I played it out of the drum machine, I wanted it to sound like a record. So I had to sample those snares high so when I'm playing a beat for someone, it's like a record, so transferring that onto the SSL, the process was just to make it a bigger sound.

But it was mainly about the drums and basslines, and with the bass, what I learned early on is if wanted to have that super low-end bass, I wanted to make sure that we took some of the low-end out of the bass line and kind of mashed it with the 808, which had to be in tune with the song. With the bass line and everything punching on it, the bassline had to punch and be in your face, and the 808 had to be right there under it to give you that rumble, and the snare had to knock you across the head, and if there was a kick on top of that 808, it had to punch you in the chest. That's how I describe mixes.

Demonstrative of the enormous trust Scarface placed in the producer's hands where the fate of his commercial breakthrough was concerned, Joe was grateful for the fact that "he trusted my ear at that time because of the Geto Boys record, so I pretty much mixed a lot of the stuff and then Face would come in and give his final approval. I always mixed 90% of my records I would say, unless I was out of town, and in those cases I was probably pissed because it didn't come out the way I wanted it to." That trust paid off handsomely for Face as he was embraced by the rap mainstream like they'd been waiting in 1993 when *The World is Yours* took the charts and world of hip hop by storm, laying a path forward the dynamic duo's next trail would blaze for southern rap as a genre with *The Diary*.

Truly Joe's baby from the moment the spark of genius first struck his creative mind as an impetus, in the breakthrough that followed the producer deserves credit to date for first hearing before anyone else in his position had caught on, "Rooted in Joe's own idea of mixing church with Scarface's rhymes as a menacing orator," as *Vibe* pointed out. A merger that would storm southern hip hop with the hostility of a corporate takeover, placing a strangle-hold on the charts altogether as, "One of the greatest solo discs ever to leave the beltway...firmly established Scarface as a solo mainstay." The esteemed hip hop critic continued – would further celebrate the album musically as, "The sonic equivalent of a fists-in-the-air, blood-on-the-wall, helicopter-detonating, action-adventure flick."

Exactly the elements southern hip hop needed to resonate as a competitive, credible sub-genre as Joe and Scarface locked themselves away in the lab to begin work on what BET would later deem as a, "Thirteen-track Opus...regarded by most critics and fans as the perfect album," this was Joe's first Spielberg moment as a producer, where he introduced the birth of cinematic Soul. Born out by hip hop historians as a moment for southern rap's evolution as a commercial genre that, "Cannot be understated" in the opinion of National Public Radio, NPR's inability to ignore the impact of the album helped legitimize Joe's foresight, singled out *The Diary*'s producer for utilizing,

"Live instrumentation, the emotive influence of southern blues and the steady, relaxed pace of California g-funk. The lackadaisical tempos and southern-fried instrumentation, replete with simmering organs and twanging guitar, soon became a Rap-A-Lot trademark. Challenging Scarface to succeed in, "Elevating his career to the level of the legends in the game." In the estimation of *XXL Mag*, the pair fed off each other's creativity with a natural chemistry that Joe likened to:

> Martin Scorsese and Robert DeNiro, that's how Face and I were like in the studio back then, because he loved my music and I loved his vocals, so we just married that together, and I always knew what he wanted musically. We never had a battle in the studio, and if he said something to me like, "Hey, I don't like the bass line," or whatever, I'd just hit the mute button and we'd come up with another one. We worked really well together because pretty much everything I brought in, he liked, and we pretty much shaped it up from there, whether he wanted to change a couple little things or whatever. I was always open during our productions like that, there were never any boundaries with us. So we always worked great together.

Scarface: On *The Diary*, Joe and I, we just vibe bro, like I said, it was a match made in heaven. Nobody can beat that vibe man, like that's a Dr. Dre-Ice Cube-N.W.A. vibe, nobody can beat that N.W.A. vibe. Nobody can come back and produce N.W.A., you might be able to produce Cube or Ren or Eazy - rest his soul, but you will not be able to re-produce that N.W.A. chemistry without Dre. If you look at everything Dre was a part of building, and then you take Dre out of the equation, it's just not that good anymore. If you take N.O. Joe out of my equation, I'm not that good anymore.

Coming out the box "with beats that are slick, simple, and to the point," Entertainment Weekly was impressed with the fact that "this album's understated production oozes streetwise certainty." With the platinum success of *The World is Yours*, Joe had earned the freedom for the first time in his career to stretch out in the studio uninhibited by time limitations of fighting the clock while they found the record's true voice. Sensing and seizing on the opportunity he had in front of him, the producer remembered:

> At the outset of making *The Diary*, when they signed that new deal with Virgin, I said, "Wow, okay, now I can expand the music to whereas I can touch the suburban kids and everybody," just knowing that that record was going to be well-promoted across the world. That's what made me step my game up, and just really go all out, and Scarface, he gave me a lot of creative control, and said, "Joe, just do what you feel." So I always did the music first and the music pretty much told him what to say. At that point, I was looking for growth, and wanted to give him a bigger sound, and we'd actually discussed that, so approaching the music from a pre-

production standpoint, a lot of that was done at my studio, 104, and in the big studio B at Digital Services on a 48-track digital console. They were the state-of-the-art studio in Houston at that time. I believe the only studio in the country back then to have forty-eight tracks digitally, which was great, because normally we always went beyond twenty-four tracks.

So on *The World is Yours* for example, we had to pull two machines together and it was a pain in the ass, to the extreme that I'd ask "Is this really worth it?" Because there were so many other things we could be doing with that studio time, and it kind of took a little bit of the creativity out of the recording process, so to be able to upgrade to digital on a 48-track console was a major step up for us.

Now afforded the room as a platinum producer he deserved to spread out across a panorama of tracks in a lock-out environment that bred a spirit of exploration that paced the album lyrically and musically, Joe and Face were both clearly looking to dig deeper and pool their respective wells of inspiration. In the creative process, they would unearth what AllHipHop.com would later deem, "The greatest southern solo offering in rap history." For N.O. Joe, building the perfect beast began with the foundational focus of the album's rhythm tracks, taking advantage of the time and freedom to perfect each element of every song's individual drum kit. This began with the relational proximity of hip hop's most fundamental instrumental basics of drum and voice, which – in a moment of production instruction – for Joe centered around his focus on:

> Each song on that record, where the snare had to be tuned just right for it, which also related to the depth of his voice. Because once he'd laid his vocals down for a song, I liked to come back in and tweak the snare. It's a little crazy how I approached it in my head once I heard the vocal on it, because I tuned the snare and the kick a certain way to kind of marry the vocal. A lot of the drum sounds were done again using the MPC-60, and some sounds from the EMU Classic Keys and the Roland JD800, and those were sounds that were designed inside of the JD800 that weren't stock sounds.
>
> Coupled with that, during the making of *The Diary*, I would take a lot of my sampled drum sounds from *The World is Yours* era and because we were working in a better studio now, those sounds were EQ'd and compressed through Neves and SSLs and LA2As, and I would re-sample them over and over again until I got the sound I really, really wanted.

As they d off that foundation, the moods created by live instrumentation was another key emotive element within the album's soundscapes Joe was determined to unlock in the blend of programmed drums and instrumental performances that he and Mike Dean's laid down throughout the record. Reasoning that by abandoning the traditional territory of samples in place of recording real musical tracks, the listener would feel the lyrical and musical results on that much more real a level, the visionary soundman explained:

> The idea was really to keep it authentic, because you can have live playing but if it doesn't have the right compressor or the right EQ or the right tone to it, it's just played. So I always wanted, when you a guitar sound or something like that on one of my records, it's almost like I pulled it off of the record and sampled it with the same tone or whatever, but I had it played my way by Mike Dean or whoever was working with me in the studio.

As Joe kept the bar raised high, Scarface met expectations by exceeding them when he showed up to record vocal tracks, with Joe recounting a laser-sharp focus throughout where, "He always came in super-focused and ready to go." Throwing touchdown verses on tape like Peyton Manning in what were truly Superbowl-level performances throughout, the team would score a key touchdown with *Never Seen a Man Cry* on the Top 40 of the Billboard Hot 100 Singles Chart while reaching #2 on the Hot Rap Singles Chart in the same time with a grand-slam hit that the LA Times hailed as, "The best song on his album." A new perspective for rap fans to consider introspectively as the song was designed to naturally inspire such reaction, the hypnotic soundscape that floated beneath Face's mesmeric vocal was one for all it's resulting complexities that in it's creation, Joe revealed was:

Pretty simple musically, but it had a deep tone to it. I did the beat for that on the MPC-60 II, which had just come out. When we mixed the song, of course you heard those sleigh-bells and another ride cymbal. That was a blended sound of a ride cymbal where the bass was taken all out of it. And the old EMU toy cymbal, so there were like three things that made that high jingle sound in the background. The beat had a swing to it, and I always had this back-beat to the song that went, "Boom boom boom – tic – boom bom boom." And none of that stuff was quantized. I didn't quantize any of that stuff, that's why it felt like that. I just played it live in an 8-bar sequence, but it was all free-hand. So you could never say, "Let me get these sixteenth triplets," or blah blah blah. It was never that, it was like a real drummer. Of course I wanted to make sure you had that thick kick under it, and the bass line was right there in the middle. The snare was basically a combination of that Meters snare I sampled. But I actually cut it short, and stacked two more snares on it.

We didn't have a chorus to the song, so what I did was I hummed kind of a church melody to Mike Dean, and I'd found this organ sound I used to use a lot back then that was a mixture of a Hammond with a Leslie mixed with an organ out of Vintage Keys, and then we added some effects on it. That was pretty much the catchy part of the song, and I told Mike "We gotta have a melody in that chorus that touch your heart," and when I hummed that melody to him and he played it on tape, it just stuck. Then when Face is rapping about outer space, I thought we should get a Sitar sound, and we put a spacey-sounding reverb on it. So it just gave it that eerie but honed spiritual-gospel movement.

As he stepped in the booth to lay the trance-inducing vocal, versus some sessions where he took more of a hands-off approach when Face showed up with a clear idea of both what he wanted to spit and how he wanted the character of the vocal performance to play out, Joe proudly remembered *Never Seen a Man Cry* remaining a little bit more his baby. Nurturing the song at every stage of it's production in part because he knew what how special a song he had on his hands, Joe confessed years later that, "I think that was the first record that was being put out and promoted on a major level, and in the studio, that *Never Seen a Man Cry* would be that song, so I knew it had that feel to it, and it was different enough where people felt it, but I have to admit even I didn't know it would hit like that." To make sure Face was portraying precisely on tape what he intended to based on how they'd blueprinted the masterpiece, Joe had to apply a little Scorsese as he helped direct the rapper toward the right headspace within his performance:

When he first did that *Never Seen a Man Cry* song, it was just more of a calm, mellow vocal delivery, and I remember I was like "You know what, you should go in almost like a preacher on this one, with the organs and all of that stuff..." And he was like, "You go in show me how it should sound." And he was laughing at me dude. Because I was in the vocal booth rapping in this imitation-low tone. "Greeted his father with his hand out, rehabilitated slightly, but glad to be the man's child" Like that. As soon as he heard that, he went in the vocal booth and followed that tone. Once we developed that, then from there, he had a whole new style. The way Scarface tells a story on that song, the words he put together and his tone and delivery of that story. I think that's what gave him the ability not to be heard as hardcore, because it was controlled and was more musical in the delivery. He had his ups and downs, and really became a story teller on that record I felt.

Scarface: The way Joe's drums play puts me in my comfort zone, the way those drums move gives me a pocket. I'm a pocket rapper, okay, I find that pocket and I annihilate that motherfucker. I give a lot of rappers a lot of credit, but I give myself the most for being the most versatile, I feel like nobody's better than me at using my instrument , which is my voice. I can sound one way on one track and another way on another track. Every song is taken into another level.

Every emcee has a song about getting it on with another dude's chick, it's almost a required rapping to keep in the spirit of the braggadocio that has long ruled rap as one if it's chief requisites. With *Goin' Down*, not only did Scarface and N.O.

Joe do so with a melodic seduction that made the song a celebration almost in spite of itself, but logged one of the greatest *Banging Your Baby's Mama* anthems of all time. Always a master of originally flipping the samples he picked to interpolate as part of his instrumental DNA, the brazen and blazin' sexuality of the song's instrumental informed and pushed the point of Scarface's lyrical horseplay to heights as the track still ranks among Face's fan favorites twenty-five years later. It was irresistible ear candy that Joe sweetened by adding:

> A sample from the *99 Luftballons* by Nena, and that was an idea Face had, he actually came up with that vocal melody on the chorus, and his uncle Eddie – who was a beast on the bass – was actually the driving force on that song because he really put the emphasis on that bass. So it sprung from his idea, and I added the beat, and then shaped it into a track where it still had that 80's feel to it but it was still hard and edgy at the same time.

> **Scarface:** My uncle Eddie Wilson plays the bass on *Goin' Down*, and I put the melody, "Wah, wah, wah, wah, wah, wah, wah." I got that from a Candyland commercial. That's where that came from, from a commercial on TV. And the little piano knocks, that was me and Joe.

In spite of the latter chart successes to come, Joe remembered staying in a headspace that was the equivalent of an actor staying in character throughout a movie shoot, never losing sight of his great ambition, "In crafting *The Diary* record where we never thought about singles or anything, we just did great music. We were pretty much in our own world, and I would fall asleep at three, four in the morning in Studio B at Digital Services. It was like a dream for any record producer!" Subbing as his hotel along with work and head space, Joe as head producer felt lucky to have a loyal side-kick in protégé and prodigy Mike Dean, who dutifully committed to Joe's vision for the project's determined scope. Spending his days and nights in the studio in a deliberate blur of a backdrop where Joe appropriately defined dedication in the form of:

> Me sleeping on one sofa in the studio and Mike Dean would be asleep on the other, and would sometimes wake up in the middle of the night and say, "Hey, I hear a bass line!", and Mike would be right there, "What is it?" Mike Dean was there the whole time, and really helped me flesh those ideas out, and whenever I would tell Mike about them, he was always open to it and wouldn't stop till he had the part I heard in my head. We were both very dedicated to that record.

Like any brilliance that required explosions to arrive at its apex, without the fires blazing on full flame among all parties involved, there wouldn't have been the same infernal honesty that produced such results. For all the fawning they received later, in the studio, Joe admitted moments when he and his creative partners as a consequence of their friendly fire produced along with the music:

> Times when things got tense, like someone would punch in on the wrong line during vocal

tracking, or two creative personalities might butt heads over something we were doing within a song, but we use to have this expression we'd say, like if Face was in the studio and things weren't going his way, I'd say, "Oh, relax snapperhead." We'd just start joking around and I'd try to break ice, because if you don't, everything at that point is going to become where he can never do anything right. So we'll take a break, or even have him come out of the vocal booth and play him a track he hasn't heard before that I know he will like, and have him to in the other room and write to it. Just to kind of ease the tension, that worked well.

Staying in charge of the console from creation through completion, including the all-important mixing stage, Joe sought to bring out the best sonic weapons he had at his disposal. Indicative of a curve he's always strived to stay working on the cutting edge. The producer explains that's where it's related to the sound he wound up with for the final product that legendary hip hop periodical *The Source* ranked among its Top 10 Best Albums of 1994. Concluding that the producer and rapper had, "Tapped into something new," Joe raised his bar for excellence starting with the state-of-the-art:

I like to be ahead of technology all the time, and we already had analog sounds, and we did the final mix through a half-inch analog tape machine, a Studer, and to me, that kept it clean and the drums were already warm. Me personally, I thought taking the analog and putting it on [CD] and then running the [CD] through the Studer and then bringing it back to a digital format, which was DAT at the time. I think some of the DAT machines like the Tascam and the Sony, man, I don't know if it was the converters in there or what, but the stuff from the DAT, even though it was digital, it still gave a certain sound that I liked.

Once, "The man who played a pivotal role in lacing *The Diary* with a ground breaking sound." As BET properly celebrated the producer's achievement, handed the album in to Rap-A-Lot/Virgin, the reaction from label on down to critic and consumer was equally as enthralled, intoxicated really. From the south to the midwest, the east coast to west coast, the *LA Weekly* crowned it an "absolute masterpiece, outstanding at face value and finer with each listen." Still appreciative years later that he'd had the opportunity to take the time to reach that level of perfection, N.O. Joe takes out moment to, "Really thank Face and James Prince for letting me open up my musical pallet to present something to the world that was different from what everybody else was doing at the time."

A gamble that paid off handsomely for all parties involved, Billboard – another instant addict –complimented the record for being one "where you rarely, if ever, feel inclined to skip a song. And that's something you can't say about the work of most rappers, particularly ones as creative as Scarface." Representing Joe's first multi-platinum victory, and an even bigger one for putting southern rap on the mainstream map, the producer proudly mused:

That record was important commercially too because it was really the first big release that Rap-A-Lot had on Virgin, and sure enough, when *The Diary* record came out, it really put the south across the board, and people were feeling that music on the West Coast and the East Coast, it caught everybody's ear and it was a sigh of relief to me. I even met Trent Reznor from Nine Inch Nails in New Orleans around that time, and he was like, "Man, I *love* Scarface, I love the music!" And I was like, "Wow. Really?" And he was just humming melodies and stuff like that from the record. That's when I knew like, "Man, everybody's listening to this." We couldn't be put in a box anymore at that point because everybody loved it.

Making clear he was here to stay, Joe was busier than ever in the studio, starting by playing catch-up with his promise to a young hard, hustling emcee in the vocal tone and delivery of Scarface who'd been sweating the producer to take a shot on him. Given the producer's oversubscribed schedule, that meant knocking one of the mid-1990s great underground classics out in record time, delivering under pressure an album that despite almost no radio play, bubbled up from the underground hot enough to stay on the Billboard Top R&B/Hip Hop Albums Chart for twenty weeks! One of Joe's favorites to this day, he celebrates *Rigormortiz* – still considered a cult classic to this day – as an expansion of the sound he and Scarface had first discovered together over their previous two outings, recalling:

DMG, man, that was my boy right there! He was from Minnesota, and was actually already there when I first came into Houston, and he would NOT let anybody else touch his record. I told him at the time, "D, it's going to be a minute man, I'm working on all these other projects," and he said, "I'll wait Joe, I'll wait." And he waited and waited and waited till I finally got around to doing the record after about a year. Ironically, we then turned around and actually recorded that record in a very short amount of time.

Joe's talent for banging out instrumentals that commanded a vocal response of equal intensity, whether on the laid back or hard charging front, dictated that DMG bring his A-Game each and every time he stepped to the mic throughout the recording of *Rigormortiz*. The melodic energy bouncing around within the sonic walls of the album's finest cut, *Pure Dope, No Cut* demonstrated just how potent the producer and DMG's creative chemistry could be in the studio, with Joe raising the bar once again from the point of view that, "I really got a chance to expand musically with DMG man, and to experiment and so I was able to give him some up-tempo stuff on that song, I had a great time working on that song."

Knowing their latest discovery had the potential to follow in the model that Scarface had first become a star introducing to hip hop as a new style, Joe knew he had to bring the same kind of strength to the instrumental tracks as Face rapped over for DMG to credibly hold up on the corners his music would be product-tested on. Steadily building a reputation of his own as the producer of an Urban Soundtrack for millions of hoods around the country as blocks hustled and bustled in all of life's everyday ways to the rhythm of the beats he was making, N.O. Joe remembered being driven creatively to deliver by the reality that, "Those instrumentals had to be believable given the type of lyrics rappers like DMG and Scarface and DMG were rapping over top of them, they had to be authentic instrumentally in the moods they set, both for the artist and for his audience."

In the height of an era of hip hop where a new breed of emcees were desperate to step to the mic to prove how seriously the world should take them – in the mold of Heavyweights like Scarface and Ice Cube – Big Mike entered the ring for his shot at the title on 1995s *Something Serious*. From the moment the opening bell rang, Big Mike answered Joe's call to bring it, coming out swinging like a journeyman prize fighter finally getting their title shot. As Mike's head trainer, N.O. Joe remembered he and fellow corner man Mike Dean paid the project special attention for its potential, seeing the emcee was hungry and ready to rise to the occasion:

> That record was pretty much my baby, because I got to do a lot of things that had been inside my head musically. And both Mike Dean and I were growing musically, and he understood what I was trying to convey to him. He understood what I was hearing in my head. I think that's why the record came out so great.
>
> I even got behind the mic on that record I believed in it so much: that's actually me singing on the hook of *Player, Player*. That hook melody just came to me with the music, "*I'm just a playa, playa...*" I always was imitating Al Green's voice,

and on that one, Mike had said before I started producing the track, "Joe, I want a player type of song," so we kind of went in the direction of Al Green, and when he heard me singing that hook, he knocked his lyrics out right there and we wound up recording and mixing that song in the same day. All the instruments were played live in the studio on that track by Mike Dean.

As his infectious influence had continued to reverberate further and farther and deeper into the urban culture across the south, Joe soon got a call from fellow Texan Pimp C, another pioneer who helped steer southern rap toward the dominant sales end of the genre it's today become. Hustling in the studio as he had on the streets, Pimp C was eager to tap into what Joe had his finger on the pulse of so precisely among their generation of hip hop fans. Though he and Pimp C would go on to co-produce the legendary UGK's breakthrough LP *Ridin' Dirty* together, Big Mike's album would provide the first glimpse at the promise their collaboration had to offer after:

> Pimp C co-produced *Havin' Thangs* with me. He that track in, and then he sang the hook on it as well. That song was kind of derived from like a Bill Withers track, and Pimp C, his voice was like a Curtis Mayfield, soulful-like, *"Just another young ni$$a havin' thangs man..."* When I would hear him sing, he wouldn't be confident about his singing, and I would tell him in the booth when he would suggest we get someone else to do the hook, "Dude naw, you need to sing, you got a voice."

The ground wouldn't just rattle but would break once again for the southern rap genre when Joe – coming off his collaboration with Pimp C on Big Mike's LP – teamed up with his bandmate Bun B to head into the studio with UGK (Underground Kingz). Emerging with another masterpiece that iTunes even years later would acknowledge of it's import in hip hop history that, "It has been said that *Ridin' Dirty* is to the south what Public Enemy's *It Takes a Nation of Millions to Hold Us Back* is to New York; namely, a work of such immense and enduring power that no one making hip hop after it's release can completely escape it's influence. Easily one of the most unified rap albums ever released, *Ridin' Dirty* wastes no space, every song contributing to a cohesive whole. Far from the patchwork assemblages of so many hip hop efforts, the album follows a single sonic personality — a dark, rich tone with the warmth of soul music — from the first song to the last. Every song is a mini-masterpiece, finely detailing a specific theme or scene...The reputation of *Ridin' Dirty* will only grow with time; hip hop has rarely been rendered with so much gravity."

Putting together two of the most progressive ears pushing the south towards its new zenith on the same team, their sense of friendly competition elevated the bar as ambitiously as Joe and Face heading into *The Diary*. With *Ridin' Dirty*, the producer fondly recalled the same sense of creative comradery at play in the studio:

> Pimp C man, we were partners, bless his soul. We did the whole *Dirty* album together, and putting that record together, it felt so good because it was like it was meant to be. When I first met Pimp C, we kind of bumped heads a little bit because he's a producer, I'm a producer, and I was cool first with Bun B, his partner in

UGK, who'd initially asked me if I'd do just a couple tracks on the record. When I told him I was in, he said, "We don't have a big budget," and I'd told them, "Listen man, I just love doing music so your budget is your budget." I saw the potential in UGK, and I was honored that they brought me in on it, and vice versa, they were like, "Man, we're honored you're coming aboard." So I wound up overseeing that whole album, and doing a bunch of tracks, and me and Pimp C were a team, so in constructing that record, we wanted to make sure the whole thing was solid.

Basically how we worked was: Pimp C may have a record and not know quite what to do to improve it. So he'd give me the tracks and I'd finish it, or I may bring a record to the table, and he'd come up with a chorus right there in the studio. It was like back-to-back. He'd bring something in and I would bring something in, and we'd marry them together. We never really butted heads in the studio because we respected each other's craft and gave each other room. For instance, he knew when I was working in the studio on a track, I don't like people around me, so he'd go chill out somewhere give me room, then when he was doing certain things, he'd want to be by himself so then I'd give him his room and then we'd come together, and he may say, "Joe, that guitar part in that little last piece of the song, I don't like that." So I'd say, "Okay, that's cool, let's either change it or take it out altogether." And vice versa, I might say, "I'm not sure I'm real comfortable with that bass line." And he'd say, "You come up with something else?" And boom, I'd give him something and he'd say, "Oh, that's dope. Let's lay that Joe." We never settled for anything less than the best, so whether it was him re-writing a verse over or re-singing a couple things in the hook, we always respected each other from that sense. There were no boundaries.

One of southern rap's first true dynamic duos, combining their rhyming and melodic sensibilities into a sound that vocally validated the group's legitimacy. And was on par with a rare club of hip hop teams capable of covering both ends of the stylistic pool credibly. With Joe's background producing both R&B and rap, it was a perfect combination for him to be producing, especially when it came time for co-producer Pimp C to lay down his lead chorus hooks. Taking more of the lead from behind the boards in helping Pimp C decide find his voice behind the mic in the vocal booth, N.O. Joe remembered of his dearly-departed collaborator:

At first, as he was still developing that confidence in his voice, before he was going to go in the booth and sing something, we'd sit in the studio and we'd practice over and over again, and next thing you know, he was on a song singing the whole thing, versus just the hook. As a matter of fact, at that time, I was getting ready to do some R&B stuff and told him, "Dude, we should write some R&B songs together." He laughed it off at the time, but he was a very talented artist. And always wanted to learn."

We had so much fun doing that record, and that was when I had Pimp C singing on more songs, he'd joke with me, "You got me in here singing...", and I'd say, "Dude, you got that old-school voice, we gotta lay that down." So he would be in there recording the vocals and I'd say, "Watch your pitch, watch your pitch," and he'd say, "Joe, I ain't no singer!" And I'd respond, "Yes you are," because he had that voice. We actually honed in on that on that album.

Following another trend Joe had become used to where despite almost no label or radio support, the album still became a mainstream hit upon release, cracking the Top 20 on the Billboard Top 200 Albums Chart. Word on the street simultaneously catapulted the record all the way to #2 on the Top R&B/Hip Hop Albums Chart. N.O. Joe was frequenting the Top of the Billboard Hot R&B/Hip Hop Chart with such prevalence by now that hip hop fans soon came to call him a regular, hitting #1 again with A.Z.'s debut LP *Doe or Die*, producing the title track and earning praise from *Spin Magazine* for giving AZ, "A powerful platform, with his southern-style funk."

In 1998, N.O. Joe would reach the mainstream summit once again when he took Ice Cube to #1 on the Hot Rap Singles Chart with *Pushin' Weight*, where Billboard further congratulated Cube for, "How ambitious the album was...Designed as a hard-hitting record." That music's most famous mainstream critic concluded, "Certainly takes no prisoners." Coming as hard as he ever had when he got the call to hook up with Cube in the studio, Joe took the opportunity to push himself into yet another new musical mesa, revealing that conceptually, "My thing with that collaboration with Cube was to say to hip hop fans, 'Hey, listen, this is a whole new sound from me,' and sonically, if you listen to it, the single *Pushin' Weight* for instance has a different twist to it. So working with Ice Cube really gave me a chance to really expand musically what was hidden in the back closet, and say to the listening world, 'Hey, these are the new sounds I'm crafting,' and he heard that and said, 'This is the sound I want.'"

Entering the new millennium as one of southern rap's hottest producers having consistent cross-over success in the mainstream, his signature sound was about to find a whole new generation of fans when it was catapulted up onto the silver screen in the timeless cult classic movie *Office Space*. Chosen by writer/director Mike Judge to serenade key visual scenes within the movie where the music needed to pace the action and emotional moods of the characters to a perfect "T," N.O. Joe would find himself crying laughing along with the rest of America's workforce watching Samir and Michael Bolton famously and furiously destroy a faulty fax machine in a field – first with a baseball bat and then manically with his bare hands. All the while, Joe's drums kept movie viewers' heads bumping and fists pumping with an equally glorious sense competing intensity throughout.

Twenty years later, the scene has sustained a second wave of popularity as a fan favorite among yet another new generation of hip hop fans/movie watchers on YouTube, where the clip has received millions of views over the years as a streaming, social media and smartphone favorite. A phenomenon that blows Joe away years later in reflecting on how it truly became part of the movie's voice even though, "It's crazy because when I saw that movie for the first time, I didn't know they were using any of our songs in it. And then when I saw the scene where they were destroying that laser printer in the field with our music in the background, I was like, 'Wait a minute, that's our music!'" Ironically, despite the huge opportunity for a whole other world of exposure his music would be given in the film, Joe revealed that versus a fancy studio, "That song was one I actually produced at my house. And originally it was meant for this female rapper Boss that was signed to Rap-A-Lot. I forget what happened where we didn't work together, but *I almost forgot about it.* When they got the Geto Boys back together, I went to play them some songs and remembered, 'Wait a minute, I forgot about this one track. And when they heard it, they flipped and wanted it."

A good turn of luck for all parties involved – producer, artists, filmmakers and public alike as the movie would have been inarguably incomplete without it – the ominous tone of the instrumental became a signature of Joe's throughout the 1990s. It was one he'd first designed as a musical personality he described as "this thing back then I called a '*Scary Bus Ride,*' where it had kind of a hard type of feel to it but it was still gangster, the whole sound. I would make these weird filters on the guitars I would have inside of the keyboard, because I had some live sample of guitars in the keyboard, the ASR-10, that I would just kind of filter out and make them sound real weird. All the synths you hear in the background of that song are the ARP Axxe and I had the Oberheim and the Minimoog and Moog Prodigy. So putting that together, I also put a filter on a piano sound I had in there coming from the ASR 10 that I had looping through a Lexicon reverb. I had other sounds going through a foot pedal and then sampling it back into the drum machine, so in creating that track, I just wanted it to be angry." Making it a point as he usually did to manage the song's musical moods from recording all the way through mixing, the producer – employing his usual mix-as-he-produced approach both to protect the integrity of his original vision for the song as well as a matter of efficiency – Joe revealed:

> When I'd mixed *Still*, the song that wound up on Office Space, at my house. It's actually a two-track mix because I misplaced the floppy with the multi-tracks on it. It was still all good because ninety, ninety-five percent of my songs I mix myself, so you could actually take my tracks, and I could send them to you spread. You could have great engineers and mixers, but it's not going to come out the same because as I'm producing, I'm mixing as well. They don't know my vision of where I want to go with the track, and it's no insult to these guys, but I just never trust somebody else with that: for instance, if I have 3 snares layered with each other, the worst thing sometimes you can do is bring them in the studio and spread them back out again because you might not get the same blend. You have EQ on each one of the tracks and whatever else, whereas in the drum machine, when you layer them, it's like they've already EQ'd themselves. Most of my drums were EQ'd already that were sampled back in, so the only thing I had to was layer it and tune them to where it sounds like one. I'll

put it like this: the snares are like harmonies blended perfectly.

N.O. Joe would continue his winning streak into the early 2000's, hooking back up with co-producer Pimp C to knock out the majority of the track listing to 2001's *Dirty Money*, proud that even though he now had what most identified as a signature sound, he successfully kept it different for "everybody: UGK, Scarface, The Geto Boys, Devin even, if you go back to those records, there were all songs I produced but UGK didn't sound like Scarface, Face didn't sound like Big Mike, Ice Cube didn't sound like anyone else. I never did that, because I always honed in on the artist and giving my style to them so it sounds like I tailored that sound to that artist. I always did that, and it was no different on the *Dirty Money* record."

Joe's plan to continue collaborating with Pimp C in the studio was put on ice when C wound up catching a five-year prison bid in 2002. Coincidentally right as Joe got a call to fly back to New York to work with vet L.L. Cool J on 2004's *The DEFinition*, where the dynamo producer was pumped up to show off, "The club side of me that really never came out before that because Scarface and the Geto Boys weren't 'club' artists, but I remember meeting with Kevin Lyles at Def Jam, and next thing I knew L.L. people's were calling to tell me, 'L.L. has recorded to this track that you sent,' and my reaction was 'Wow, L.L. Cool J? Cool!'"

By the time Joe hooked back up with Pimp C for a third time in 2007 following his release from prison, critics like the New York Times were finally acknowledging that, "It's now clear that Bun B and Pimp C were ahead of their time" with *Ridin' Dirty*. Ten years later, the impact of that influence had come full circle on their self-titled *Underground Kingz* Double-

LP. Both the emcee and producers alike lined up to share track time with the legendary duo, including fellow heavy hitters behind the boards like Marley Marl, Juicy J and DJ Paul, Jazze Pha, and Lil Jon and of course N.O. Joe, and in front of the mic with appearances by Big Daddy Kane, Rick Ross, Talib Kweli, Kool G Rap, Scarface, Charlie Wilson, Outkast, Too Short, Slim Thug and Geto Boy Willie D. A family reunion in every sense of the world, Joe proudly counts the record to date as:

> Definitely in my Top 5 of all time. Because with that record, Pimp C had just got out of jail and he called me, and said, "Listen man, we're working on this UGK record, and you know that I can't and will not do it without you. Do you have time?" And I was like, "Shit yeah!" On that record, they had a larger budget, and one thing I really respected about Pimp C this time around was he said to me, "Last time, we didn't really have money in the budget to really pay you, but we're in a much better position now, so however you need to do it, I'm down with it. Because you was with us when we really didn't have anything." And Jive was really behind the project this time. But Pimp C showed me so much love on this project, and we worked so good together man. It was like no time had passed between us, but we still knew as co-producers the change in times and knew where to go musically. We still wanted to keep it classic, but knew at the same time how to keep it current.

On that record, it was like we never missed a beat, and in putting together that record, we had so much fun. Just looking through the eyes of Pimp C, he really was getting a chance to work with everyone he wanted to work with, there were no limitations, and to me, that was just the world to me to see him happy and in that mode, especially coming out of being locked up.

Sending UGK, N.O. Joe and Co. back to #1 on the Billboard Top 200 and Top R&B/Hip Hop Albums Charts in the same week, the fan-and-critical feeding frenzy reflected just how strong the staying power of the group's influence had remained in their absence. Strongest as a sum of their parts, *XXL Mag* would importantly note that, "While they each have their individual strengths, the heart of the UGK appeal lies in the richness of their chemistry, as heard on the N.O. Joe–produced *Living This Life*. Demonstrating just how far technology had traveled in real time with Joe's ever-evolving talent as a producer from analog to digital, N.O. Joe and other hip hop pioneers like him were arguably the first to work, "In the box" considering the entire tracks they created within samplers and drum machines.

By 2014, when the producer linked back up with his longtime wingman Scarface to begin working on what would become the legendary emcee's most celebrated new studio album in years, he had become so comfortable working in digital that while some fads were trending back towards vintage equipment, "As far as going too much out of the box, I didn't want to experiment too much, but by the time I started working with Face on *Deeply Rooted*, I'd managed to import a lot of my signature sounds I had in the 90's, into Logic and Contact. Just like I started to do when I was making that last UGK album in 2007. Now, eight years later, I've advanced that with Native Instruments package as well. So when I'm making tracks now, I use those sample folders in Logic, along with whatever plug-ins sound cool as well. Like the Moog synth or Arturia Lab, which actually has something like 5,000 different classic synthesizer sounds to choose from, and I tweak the sounds."

Celebrated across the board by mainstay critics like *Vibe* as, "His best body of work" since his still-iconic early records like *Mr. Scarface is Back* and *The Diary*. As a full-circle affair, Joe sought to make *Deeply Rooted* as authentically layered with both the past and present as possible in context of its production reference points. Thankfully, along with the conveniences of digital technology to import a 1993 snare sound into a 2015 Logic session with the simple slide and click of a mouse, Joe had a photographic musical memory bank to raid when required as he began building his latest masterpiece:

> I have a crazy type of memory, because I can actually go in and listen back to any record or song from my catalog and tell you exactly what instrument was used and how it was used, so I'm able to draw derivatively from our classic sounds at any moment we're feeling inspired to draw from that well creatively. That was important because there's a few sounds that are signature to Face that I used on this album, for instance, the sample from the Hammond B3 organ is still the same sound I used back on *The World is Yours* and *The Diary* albums. They're the same exact

sounds only now, I might process them differently.

> Or for instance, with the drums, man, back then, I thought I had too many, but now, you can near go crazy, because I could spend 3-4 hours looking for the right snare. I might start off foundationally with something I used back in the 90's. And then there may be another snare that I found in those three hours that really compliments the snare I'm layering over. I built a lot of beats like that.

Bombarded with compliments where his rejuvenated vocal performances were highlighted throughout, AllHipHop.com noted that, "Lyrically, the album is on point and, as far as the beats, N.O. Joe (who handles the bulk of the production) knows how to compliment Face's delivery better than anyone," resulting in, "One of dopest hip hop albums in recent years." Bringing the best out of Scarface simply by giving him his best musically as a producer, Joe remembered that his lyrical counterpart was aided by the fact:

> He'd been working out and had lost a lot of weight, so he felt good and his energy in the studio was great. I felt like he stepped his game up on the lyrics with this album over some of the other recent records we've made together, so he stepped a couple notches up on this one. He was like a totally different person, so it was like we were back working together again in the 1990s, everything felt fresh and he always nailed

it on every vocal take. There's a track off the album called *Do What I Do* that's going to be another stand-out song that features Nas and Rick Ross, everybody just brought their A-game on this album vocally, there's no filler. It's like Face to the next level, because individually as a lyricist, I can say he covered a lot of areas topically on this album, everything from Ferguson on.

One of my favorites vocals on this album called *Dope Man Pushin'* that could definitely go in the club. It's still Scarface, it's still a hard song, he's just straight-street on it, just super-raw. His voice is like probably the raspiest I've heard it in a long time, he sounds like a monster on there actually, because when he comes in at the top of the song, you're like "Oh my God!" He sounds like Godzilla on this one.

Scarface: I think it was Joe, Poke, Irv and myself that really salvaged that record. That's the greatest record that almost didn't come out. I didn't want to release it, but Joe and Spoof thought it was brilliant. I love putting fuel to the fire, that's been my game plan from day one: I'll come in with the start of the project, and Joe will always finish that motherfucker.

Turning the spotlight to longevity from a business point of view – arguably the trickiest profession within the music industry given artists can generate money from live shows while producers have both the overhead associated with running a studio to think about plus chasing down labels for overdue royalties. In the producer's experienced opinion, this juggling act necessitates a trust-but-verify mentality and approach where Joe bluntly shares his opinion with the millennial generation:

> Business-wise, nowadays, records don't sell, so the one thing I can say to that young bedroom producer coming up making beats for everybody and their brother is get yourself some kind of a standard paperwork that you sign with everybody where back-end when you're doing music, because an Attorney these days is pretty much the same price as he was in the 90's. That might cost you $1,500, $2,000, and that might be the max that you're getting to make the record.

> You might consider instead of selling tracks outright for seventy-five dollars, one hundred dollars like a lot of producers do of leasing tracks instead for like twenty-five dollars with an option to buy that has a back-end built in. It becomes very basic when it's all laid out in writing, and most rappers – if they're eager to have your beat – will sign on to whatever arrangement you lay out for them. But as a bottom line, if you can get some kind of standard paperwork that can reassure you that you'll get some type of royalty, that's always worth it, and have some kind of a standardized contract that can be modified depending on the artist/project. That's my advice.

While he has recommended that up and comers avoid a "Signature Sound" like the plague. N.O. Joe has been rightly labeled as, "Legendary," by *The Source* for precisely those stylistic elements of hip hop fans know him best for helping invent and introduce that have now become mainstays. Forcing the Grammy-nominated producer to acknowledge that, "At some point, some of my sound was mimicked," he takes the longview perspective that, "I applauded that. It was like, 'Hey, you guys recognize me, that's good.' My big focus starting early on in my career was,I didn't want to stick to, 'Every song you hear, that's N.O. Joe. Yeah, I know he used this here...' I never wanted to have just one certain sound to where you knew me right off the bat. So for instance, DMG had similarities of Scarface, but Scarface still had a different tone to his record than DMG. And when I did Big Mike's record, that had a different tone than anything else, along with the UGK record. So I tried to give everybody their own signature sound from me, so it's not all the same. But it definitely still had my stamps on it."

Always a near-impossible task for an artist to pick their favorites following the adage that, "They're all your babies," for a record producer, it's especially difficult. Considering he manually put his records together from scratch based on what he heard in his head, putting a best of list together may sound like torture. But Joe prefers to pride himself on the diversity among them versus putting his greatest hits in any order of priority:

> I can say each one of them has a different feeling. I would call them all my babies, because I got a chance to do what I couldn't do with Scarface with UGK. And I did with Big Mike what I couldn't do with the Geto Boys, and with Ice Cube and AZ, I got a chance to branch out. I have a bunch of favorites on those Scarface records, I could say, of course, *Never Seen a Man*

Cry, Jesse James, Still from the Geto Boys album,
those would be some of the ones you would best
know me for. As far as production moments, *The
Diary* was the record where I was given a lot of
freedom, and Face was willing to push the
envelope as an artist. That's why I would say
that record is special to me. As far as underdogs,
the two records I would probably highlight are
Big Mike's *Somethin' Serious* and UGK's *Ridin'
Dirty*, because nothing serious was really put
behind those records, those were word-of-mouth
records that went gold with no airplay or label
support.

Back then, I don't think I thought of what we
were doing as pioneering a sound. But absolutely
when I look back now, that was the start of
southern hip hop music. The Geto Boys,
Scarface, UGK, those were the first southern rap
artists to chart at #1 on the Billboard Top 200
Album Chart for instance. And of course what
Scarface's *The World is Yours* and *The Diary*
albums did, both debuting at the top of the
charts, that was ground-breaking for the south. It
put us on the map. Then, of course, you had
Outkast, 8Ball & MJG, and Suave House
movements. But it all started with what we were
doing back then. If you really look at it, like
even with the samples that were chosen for my
records, whether it was James Brown or Aretha
Franklin or Otis Redding, they were from down
south. But it wasn't considered "southern"

music, they touched the hearts of everybody.
And that's what we did!
https://twitter.com/N_O_Joe

"I don't even call myself a producer. Me, I call myself a therapist. So I've already acknowledged that artist's career and studied their shit." – Drumma Boy

CHAPTER ELEVEN
The Architect of TRAP – Drumma Boy

Southern rap has three central hubs: Atlanta, New Orleans and Memphis. In the ATL, the millennial generation has had few hip hop producers whose beats have hit as architecturally in designing a sub-genre as Drumma Boy's have had on building the trap genre. Authenticating his influence, *DJBooth.com* has singled Christopher Ghoulson, aka Drumma, out as, "One of the early pioneers of trap." DJ Mag argued that, "Thanks to visionary producers like Drumma Boy, Mannie Fresh, Shawty Redd, and Mike WiLL Made-It. Trap brought rap music to a new sonic dimension: with dark energy, a gothic feel, street culture (guns, drug houses, strippers) and an allover gigantic sound. Trap records dominated mixtapes and local radio, and blew up in nightclubs and strip clubs across the south."

One of Drumma Boy's signature distinctions from among the competition was his introduction of Classical music elements into beats made for the street. Indicative of the rich stylistic pallet he painted with as a produced, it was also reflective of the stratum of musical influences that shaped him growing up. Feeling fortunate to come not only from a musical family who supported his development, but one where his parents, both accomplished musicians, recognized his prodigy early on. As Drumma recalls, his father – James Gholson, is principal clarinetist for the Memphis Symphony Orchestra and teaches at the University of Memphis – instituted a rigorous regimen of training and practice to make sure he was in touch with his full potential as early on as possible:

> My father was more my mentor as far as the technical side of music, the theory and the educational standpoint. My dad would have me up an hour and a half, two hours before school, and he would start doing speed-reading tutors, rhythm-ace tutors programs to help you count notes: sixteenth notes, eighteenth notes, thirds and triplets. It was just like sickening almost, but I look back at it now like, "Man, what would I do without it?" It was crazy! It was like training for the Army before being in the Army.

It's like having a newborn where you put a basketball in that baby's hands the first day, and all of his toys are basketball-related. By the time he's two or three, you have him dribbling, and by the time he's four or five, you've got him shooting, and by the time he's six or seven, he's doing tricks with the ball between the legs and around the back. By the time he's ten or eleven, you got him dunking on a certain size goal, working on his jumping. So every year for me growing up, it was a new aspect of music, like when I was two, I have a picture of me right next to my father playing the baby bottle. I'm holding it up next to my father's clarinet trying to imitate him. As a little boy, you want to be what your daddy is, or whatever man that's around you that you look up to the most. And at three, I was playing the recorder. Then it went from there.

With my appreciation of Classical music specifically, my dad was from the orchestra, and it was just the respect level of what people were thinking about in the time period they were thinking about it, first of all, and second of all, in a sense, especially like Beethoven who lost hearing and was still hearing music. Like, you lose your hearing but you're still hearing shit, it was just the weirdest thing to me because I swear I used to be like "Damn, I used to think I was weird because I was hearing stuff but nobody else could hear it." So I hear a full beat going on in my head right now, but you can't hear it, nobody would be able to hear it but I'm able to transfer what's in my head to notes. So I can actually write the notes out on a music sheet, which first of all is the difference between me and most producers, second of all, I can play the notes. That's the thing my dad taught me to do: "Okay, you can play it by ear, alright, now you need to be doing it by rhythm, now you gotta do it by notation."

Where his dad guided him on the music side, his mother was his mentor on the business side of the schooling, teaching him the invaluable art of networking from an equally-young age. Growing up a member of Memphis's extended musical family, Ghoulson remembered the lessons Billie Baker Gholson started imparting to him via introductions with members of Rock, R&B, Soul and Gospel's royal family. Exposing her son early on to etiquette on how to handle being behind the scenes like it was where he always belonged, Drumma shares his memory:

My mom came up in the opera, but she was also in the church choir. She was a business woman and an entrepreneur at the same time. So I got a lot of hustle ingredients and a lot of knowledge about the music business growing up, and was introduced to a lot of people: "Boy, come on in here and speak to Isaac Hayes. You don't know Isaac Hayes?" So I was exposed to the shit as a kid. We grew up cool with the Presley family, all of the stars in Memphis: Marvin Gaye, Curtis Mayfield, all these cats were friends of the family. Side by side with that, as a kid, I grew up with Funk, Marvin Gaye, Smokey Robinson, and Curtis Mayfield. I got all that, and putting me in touch with just a vibe, so I didn't know who these guys where at first when I was hearing it. And of course, then I was hearing re-runs and still being caught up to certain times I missed.

So my mom would tell me about certain Michael Jackson concerts, or Marvin Gaye or Curtis Mayfield concerts, just bringing me up to time periods that she knew that I missed. But she would tell me about it, or play the album and tell me, "Ah man, I remember my first time going to the first concert." And then playing it and introducing it to where I'd be able to remember the names and songs by artists. So just coming from parents who appreciated a certain time-period or certain music is like priceless because without that exposure, I wouldn't have that knowledge and that feel. That's mom again right there, so she was my mentor as far as like awareness.

Drumma's destiny would become even more clear to him when his early exposures to the music business were expanded to include his first introduction to a real recording studio. Describing the moment with the same vivid sense of childlike wonderment that first gripped him when he walked into the new world of discovery, the producer reveals that the visit killed two birds with one stone when it helped give him a professional name that has stuck since walking into the studio for the first time as a kid with my older brother Insane Wayne, who was friends with Jazzy C who plays keys for Three 6 Mafia. I remember walking into the studio and see all of these lights: red, green, blue, orange, all of this equipment, and I said, "Daaammmnnnnn!" that was all I said. And they all busted out laughing, because I had to be ten or eleven. They were like, "Look at him, look at him!" You know how it is when you see a kid get overwhelmed with joy. As far as curiosity, that probably killed it for me. I was like extra curious now, like, "Making beats?" Because I already had music in my blood, so putting a beat with it became a natural fit for me. By that age, they already called me 'Drumma Boy.' That was actually my ornament on the Christmas tree, so it was just meant to be. I remember my first piece of equipment was a Roland XP50 Workstation. My first keyboard ever.

As Christopher graduated into his teens growing up against the backdrop of the late 1990s pre-trap southern rap scene that at the time was dominated by early pioneers like Mannie Fresh's Cash Money bounce and Outkast among others, he was already at work planting the early seeds of his own original sound. Testing his experimentations out on the millennial generation, he would find himself able to produce music for as a target audience with laser-sharp instincts because he was one of them. Getting early practice producing beats not only for urban but for the equally-important suburban hip hop fan after his parents divorced and he moved from the city there to live with his mother. He remembers that his creative mind opening for the first time:

> Getting into the beats was crazy. I started off making bass tapes and was really getting in trouble in South Memphis, the hood I was living in, the school I was going to. My mom wanted me to move to Cordova in the suburbs of Memphis, predominantly all white, which I did, and it really changed my life. It introduced me to a different crowd, a different style, it was like night and day, because before that, the neighborhood I was living in was predominantly black, so moving changed my outlook, my humor, just being able to entertain and make both crowds laugh, being able to perform in front of each crowd, and being birthed into a whole new culture. That really opened my eyes and changed my life. One of my best friends I made at that new school, he had the alpine system and the new Mustang and the eighteens in the car, because most of the kids from that area were rich, and I said, "Man, I'm gonna make this dude a mix-tape," gave it to him for free, and he came back and paid me $100 for it anyway.
>
> After that, he would come to school late after that on purpose, playing my tape in his system all loud so everybody knew he was pulling up. We'd be like, "Here come White Boy Jimmy," which is what everybody called him, and he was like the homie of everybody's, just a good dude.

So he was, "Yo, Drumma Boy made me a little bass tape for $100," and next thing you know, a couple other kids would come and be like, "I want a bass tape, $100," and I started making like $300, $400 a week, and that turned into $600, $700. Then, I remember one week I made like $1,500, $1,600, so the name was buzzing. I was actually playing Varsity Basketball in ninth grade, and the coach was like, "Yo, we want to start warming up to your beats," and I was like "Cool, lets do it!"

So we started warming up for our basketball games to my beats, and all the folks from different schools, other basketball players and the people who would be coming to our school to watch the games would be saying, "Man, ain't you heard about this dude named Drumma Boy, they warm up to his beats," so it was just word of mouth. A lot of the kids in area thought it was cool because nobody had ever done nothing like that, and we was winning so it was just a good movement, we went to State in my twelfth grade year, and it was something that we had started as a tradition every year of the team warming up to my beats, and it's something that they still do now in fact. It's crazy, because now I have hits to go with the practices, and when I go to games, I get people who stop me and say, "Hey, I remember when they used to play your beats before games, now they play Put On and Lose My Mind." They joke with me about it, because

I used to tell them then, "Yeah, I'm gonna have some songs on these beats one day," that was back when I was just hobby talking. I was just making beats for fun... I'm still making beats for fun!

Christopher's proverbial foot in the door moment would arrive while he was still a teenager when he produced his first major label cut for Tela's *Double Dose* album, released on pioneering southern rap label *Rap-A-Lot Records*. Cracking the Top 20 on the Billboard Top R&B/Hip Hop Albums chart and appearing on the Billboard Top 200 Album Chart, where Drumma would find his position ranks improving rapidly in the years to come, the song featured guest performances from Nashville-based hick hop star Haystak, Gangster Boo – the sole female rapper in Memphis-based rap group Three 6 Mafia, and Yo Gotti. The latter artist's appearance would provide an introduction that would prove Drumma's next "big break" in a rhythm that would shape his philosophy about how to navigate the doors that opened for him as his career continued to move forward:

People ask that all the time, and I always say, "It's a continuous process of *feet* in the door," because with each door you open, you have another one to go through, and understanding that life in the music business is one big-ass maze. Definitely there are levels, and one big foot in the door for me was Tela's *Tennessee Titans*. That was my first song on the radio. Not only did I produce the song, but I was an artist singing on the song. So it got me a whole bunch of publicity in the city, popularity, and I was in high school still. And I was only sixteen. I got a $7,500 check, and I was still doing it for fun then. So that was a big deal for me, just to make that happen at the period of time I made it happen.

Finding himself in the unique position of being on the ground floor during the early millennium of a new sub-genre of hip hop as one of its inventors, Gholson would soon be producing key career-kick off hits for a new generation of stars who would rise to the ranks of trap's biggest stars overnight marching to the beats Drumma Boy was laying down for them. Featured among these pivotal early bangers for the producer as his career began its launch came with 2005s Yo Gotti's *That's What's Up*, a song that was a hit in the best possible place Christopher could have been looking to build a buzz:

When I did *That's What's Up*, that was huge in the street, and got me a lot of work as far as inner-city cats and dudes who was keeping their ear to the street. Because when I first got with Jeezy, Yo Gotti was one of his most respected artists, that's one of the first things he told me was, "Man, I love that stuff you did with Gotti." And that's how Jeezy and I got cool, because of my relationship with Gotti. He respected Gotti because of everything he talked about on his own records, he knew Gotti did that for real. He knew Gotti was authentic and wasn't a replication like a lot of these guys who act like they been here and done that but really not.

After the boom of trap music caused enough buzz to rattle the ear of the New York Times, in cover story profiling the fact that, "In the last decade Atlanta has moved from the margins to becoming hip hop's center of gravity, part of a larger shift in hip hop innovation to the south." The Times, after studying the scene, gave their esteemed opinion that, "Of the four producers driving the city, Drumma Boy's tracks rumble the hardest. Two of his finest recent songs, Gorilla Zoe's *Lost* and Young Jeezy's *Put On*, are languorous, almost frightening in their stomp." Taking fans back to the moment when he first pitched Jeezy the track, Drumma deployed a bold sneak attack tactic where:

> I pulled up on Jeezy at a McDonald's parking lot, and gave him a CD. Then he went one way, I went the other way. He called me back two months later and said, "I got a secret for ya, listen to the radio tomorrow." The next day, when I put on the radio, the first thing I heard was, "I put on for my city, put on for my city." And I was like what the fuck?!

> It's difficult to pick a favorite for Jeezy man because I'm still stuck between *Standing Ovation* and *Put On for my City*, those were two huge hits, with two different meanings. *Put On for my City* was our first Grammy nomination, *Lose My Mind* was our first platinum plaque together, and *Standing Ovation* is what first solidified me and Jeezy's relationship. We've made at least three to four million dollars together between me and him.

In 2005, When Young Jeezy's *Standing Ovation* hit the streets, clubs and soon the charts off of the two million selling *Let's Get It: Thug Motivation 101*, the album's title spoke volumes for the headspace of both the artist and producer. Drumma Boy was in a creative headspace that he likened to the zone of an NBA player driving toward the net. Catching cross-over praise from legitimizing mainstream critics like Entertainment Weekly and *Rolling Stone Magazine*, who celebrated the way tracks including the one Ghoulson produced, "Grab you by the ears the way they should." A craft the twenty-two-year-old already had the equivalent of a Master's Degree in by the time his name was starting to ring out, he confirmed of the consequence of his collaboration with Jeezy:

> Producing *Standing Ovation* really was the biggest foot in the door for me, because it was my first multi-platinum plaque. That success put me in a different arena because now people were starting to call me 'multi-platinum producer' and it made me a lot of money. We did over a million ringtones, which was great as far as publishing, and the album did over three million copies, and I had fifty percent of the publishing.

A success that would solidify his inextricable link among fans with Jeezy's sound and that of trap itself, fast bubbling up from the underground as the hottest style in the south, it was a teaming that almost didn't happen. Revealing for the first time the true saga behind the make-or-break beat finding its rightful voice, Drumma explained that while:

Standing Ovation really triggered and confirmed our relationship, the original beat was sold! So I ended up having to go back and re-do the track, and originally when Jeezy was saying, "Yo, yo, I need this beat, I need this beat," and had played me the original version. My stomach sunk because I was thinking, *Fuck, what am I gonna tell this dude, what am I gonna do?* because the original was sold. So I told him, "You're not gonna believe this man, but the beat is sold, so I'm going to have to re-do the beat. The guy already paid me for the track, he's already released it, there's nothing we can do. I can't go back, that's bad business Jeezy."

At first, he was really mad at me and didn't talk to me for a couple days, but then he called me back and was like, "Man, look, I'm going to give you the acapellas, you come through for me on this shit, I got you." And it was funny because I had been telling him prior to the situation, "Give me some acapellas, give me some acapellas." Because that was one way I learned how to make beats. I would take the acapella from a song on the radio and then put my version to it to see if it would compare to the original. And then get opinions from other people: "What you think? You think it's harder than the real version," just joking around. But now it comes to a situation with Jeezy where he *has* to give me acapellas, which he does, I go back home – and mind you I live fifty minutes outside of Atlanta at this particular time in Stone Mountain. So I did the first version, took it to him all the way down at Patchwork, which is this studio he likes to work out of in downtown Atlanta, played it for him, and he was like, "Man, what the fuck is that shit? That shit ain't harder like the last version. Man, hell naw!" So I was like fuck, because that shit hurt. But I was like, "Fuck, I gotta get on this dude's album." Because at the time, he had the biggest mix tape out ever in the history of Atlanta, and the buzz on this dude was crazy. And this was near when he needed to hand in the album. So I go home that same night and make another beat, turn around and take it back to Patchwork. Mind you, by now, it's 2:30 a.m. I play it for him, and his reaction was "Ehhh, not quite..."

So I was like, 'Oh My God!' Go all the way back home, get home about 3:15, do my third version, and am talking to myself all kinds of ways while I'm making it, like, "Man, you gotta do this shit Drum, you gotta do this shit Drum, it's the fourth quarter," talking to myself, hyping myself up. Took the shit back to him the next day, and the third version became *Standing Ovation*. Just to see him smile when I pushed play, and then he comes to me with that hand open, "You did it nigga, this is more than Trap, this is more than Word, I am the Trap." And for dude to say that, I was like, "Wooooh," so the third time was a charm.

Then when I was mixing the track, I remember shaking my head thinking to myself, "I'm on this nigga's album, I gave him the album opener," because it was track #2 after the intro, so that shit was HUGE for me. Then I'm fittin' to get my platinum plaque, then all these publishing companies started calling me, "Yo, we want to do a pub deal," and that shit changed my life because I was able to get my Pro Tools rig, I was able to get my microphone, get the car I needed, and that's all I needed to take myself to the next level as far as production. After that came Shawty, after that came *Gimmie That* by Paul Wall, after that came Lost Gorillas, then DJ Drama, and then everything I wanted to come because I was in a situation to handle it.

Dealing now with major labels like Def Jam and Atlantic, who handled one of the millennium's true kings of the south, T.I., Drumma would first link up with Tip in 2008 after his release from prison, producing singles including *What's Up, What's Haapnin'* and *Ready for Whatever* on the two million seller that debuted atop the Billboard Top 200 Album Chart. He still holds a fond place in his heart years later for the hit because *Ready for Whatever* was the first song we did together. Ever! And he had to change the lyrics on that shit twenty, thirty times because it was so fuckin' crazy the way he was telling the story. He basically told you exactly what happened with why he went to prison, and his lawyers were very, very leery on the way he wanted to release it. So they had to edit it and edit it and edit it until they felt like it was cool. Then we went on to do *My Life,*

Your Entertainment, which featured Usher, and then *What's Up, What's Haapnin'* and then we did *You Ain't Missin' Nothin.'*

With his street cred on high alert around the south, in part because of his collaboration with Gucci Mane, who'd already popped up on Drumma Boy's radar via their work together on 2008's wildly popular mixtape *The Movie*, which he produced in its entirety. Drumma was the maestro behind 2009's Gold-selling *The State Versus Radric Davis*, as well as a prolific factory of mixtapes including *The Movie: Part 2 (Sequel), Burrrprint: 3D (The Movie: Part 3), The Cold War Pt. 1 (Guccimerica)*, and *Wasted (The Prequel)*. Smart enough to spread his sound out across every format he could to continue collaborating with Gucci outside of strictly the major label framework. By 2010, as a result, *XXL Mag* donned Drumma, "The producer behind Jeezy's rise to fame, most of Gucci's highly acclaimed projects and one of the most influential engineers out of the south period...(he's a) gifted the culture with some of it's greatest works." Ghoulson had a déjà vu when he linked up with Gucci again in 2010 on the heels of his release from prison, remembering when he first walked into the studio, he found himself working in the midst of:

A celebration of his release from incarceration! There was a big celebration at the studio, and when he came in, there was a thousand people asking him for something, waiting on him to do this, and you could tell there was a lot of stuff annoying him, and he was still smiling, like me. I know there's many times when I'm irritated but I don't let the world know that, he's one of those people, where he'll have a bunch of stuff going on mentally, but he's still able to deliver.

That's the key ingredient in this industry man, because when he got out, we went in the studio, I gave him a beat CD, because he said, "Man, I'm so ready to rap Drumma, I ain't got time for you to make no beats from scratch, give me something right now. What'cha already got made for me?" And I had twenty, thirty beats already in his folder, because we knew he was locked up for a year, and I'd told him, "When you get out boy, I got a whole folder for ya!"

So the first song he goes in the booth to do was *Abnormal*. He's like that. Sometimes he comes in just freestyling, where he'll go right in the booth and come up with something in twenty minutes and get a whole song done. I've seen Gucci do a whole song in fifteen minutes, and I think one of them was *Beat it Up*. We did that shit extra quick. Trey Songz came in and dropped the hook right quick, put his verse on it, "You can lay it down, and I'ma beat it up!" That shit was done quick as fuck.

I play the keyboard all the time and don't look at it. And having all those people in there was crazy. But it was weird because it felt like a club. That's the energy that made me make that song *No Hands*. Everybody was talking and I couldn't hear what I was doing, I couldn't hear the claps or none of that shit, but once the beat started coming together, that's when everybody shut the fuck up. I made the beat in like five or seven minutes. The footage of that is actually online somewhere. In Gucci's case that day, it was like, "I just got out of jail and been locked up a fucking year: I want everybody I can see around me, I want pussy, niggas, weed, liquor...all that shit." All his friends were around, so it was like a family reunion. *I Think I Love Her* – that's one of my favorites I would have to say because that shit bangs like fuck every time it comes on in the club. That's one of my favorites.

In terms of my own preference for whose in the studio when I'm making beats, it always varies: one day I might want just me and the artist here, another day I might want all women here, another day I just might want my girl here, another day I might want all my boys here. Gucci's a dude who has heart and doesn't care what people think. For me, honestly, it's hard for me to work with people who do too much thinking, because it always kills them. Gucci is probably my favorite dude to work with because he's so fun and easy to work with, so it's never a problem.

By 2012, Drumma Boy had become a household name among hip hop fans, and whether you knew his sound by name or not, rest assured, you'd heard it regularly on your radio.As legendary *Vibe Magazine* affirmed, "From the clubs to the radio to the house parties, his music can be heard literally everywhere...If you don't know by now, then you should probably get familiar...(with) the flag bearer of southern hip hop." For Christopher, who'd won Indie Producer of the Year for the three previous years in a row at the sSouthern Entertainment Awards, he took his success in stride, keeping his head down in a nod to, "My mom and my dad and the way they brought me up. They brought me up to always keep my nose at the same level as everybody else, and not to walk around like I'm bigger than anybody else because I have a platinum plaque. Some of these motherfuckers out here astonish me by their attitudes. It's like, 'man, you got one platinum album and you're walking around here like you done some shit.'"

Working harder than ever in that spirit to permanently imprint his "Drumma Boy Fresh" brand on the hip hop culture at large, his sound foundationally fundamental enough to trap to have earned his own distinct following over the past 10+ years. Drumma – staying in the tradition of pioneers like Jay Z and Sean Combs – invested in himself, launching a solo brand of Mixtapes and albums on his own label, Drum Squad Records. His early catalog included 2009's *Welcome II My City*, 2011's *The Birth Of D-Boy Fresh*, 2012: *Welcome To My City 2*, where MTV in it's review noted that "Drumma Boy aims to inspire those in his town to be the best they can be," and 2014's *Welcome To My City 3*. Framed around a celebration of Memphis's rich and often under-recognized pool of considerable rap talent, Drumma's collaborators reflected his elite status as a producer, scoring appearances from OG's like 8Ball & MJG, Three 6 Mafia, Juicy J, Lil Scrappy, Gucci Mane, Pastor Troy, Yo Gotti, 2 Chainz, Bun B, Young Buck, Gangsta Boo, Reggae star Junior Reid, Young Turk, and shining a spotlight on up and coming emcees from his hometown.

Made possible by the fact that, "If you got a certain fan base of people who respect your mind. If I got two, three million people who respect my mind, that means they gonna let me do what the fuck I wanna do and appreciate me for that." Whether Drumma has a name or an unknown in the vocal booth when he's producing a track:

> That shit has absolutely has nothing to do with anything. Stardom and celebrity status, in the studio, if I tell somebody, "This is what I need you to do." It's about me and him, it ain't about how big of a star he is. I've told Jeezy plenty of shit, or he'll call me like, "Man, what you think I should do?" At the same time, you can put your foot down to a certain point with an artist. But the sad part is, they're the one cutting a check, so ultimately it's their product: they're the ones who are going to go out market and promote the record. At the end of the day, their name is on it. So you can come to a rock and a hard point because your name is on it too as producer. But if they're a new artist, you have a little bit more room to move because in that situation, you're the one whose got a whole bunch of songs in the Top 100.

The future looks as bright as ever for Drumma Boy, who in addition to his Drum Squad Record label, has branded out even farther entrepreneurially with his own film production house, which produced the critically-acclaimed *Know your History* chronicling the history of the Memphis music scene. His branding endeavors also boasts a clothing line Fresh Family, and even his own signature sparkling wine as brand ambassador for Moreno BHLV. Hooking back up with longtime collaborator Gucci Mane in 2016 following the rapper's release from Federal prison, during his 3-year stint, Drumma kept Gucci in the streets courtesy of a huge extension of their mixtape catalog, including 2010's *The Appeal: Georgia's Most Wanted*, *Burrrprint (2) HD*, *Mr. Zone 6*, *Jewelry Selection*, and *Ferrari Music*, 2011's *Gucci 2 Time*, *The Return of Mr. Zone 6*, *Bricksquad Mafia*, *Writings on the Wall 2*, and *Ferrari Boyz*, 2012's *Trap Back*, *I'm Up*, and *Trap God*, 2013's *Trap God 2*, *Trap House III*, *The State versus Radric Davis II: The Caged Bird Sings*, *Free Bricks 2*, and *Drumma Boy's 2K13 4th Of July Playlist*, 2014's *The Return of Mr. Perfect*, and 2015's *1017 Mafia: Incarcerated*, and *Mr. Clean The Middle Man*.

To no one's surprise, the team returned immediately to the studio in 2016 with Mane fresh out and free from incarceration to lay down tracks on Gucci's highly-anticipated comeback LPs, *Everybody's Looking*. Debuting at #2 on the Billboard Top 200 Album Chart and generated the single *All My Children*, which iconic hip hop periodical *The Source* noted for fans was, "Produced by Drumma Boy. The track is straight to the point in true Gucci fashion as the hook." Staying as prolific as ever, the Mane would release two other new studio albums in 2016, including *Woptober*, whose highlight tracks MTV singled out to include "the Drumma Boy–produced *Out the Zoo*, Billboard, for its part, noted among other distinctions that, "Gucci Mane...working with Cool & Dre and Drumma Boy...becomes the second artist to reach the Billboard 200 with a streaming-exclusive album," and the fourth quarter effort, *The Return of East Atlanta Santa*. Closing with the advice that producers seeking to follow in his footsteps, even at the height of their success, to never get comfortable. Drumma Boy advises staying loyal and the same philosophy he has since the start of his career to A.B.H. (Always Be Hustling), one that allows him to show no sign of his role slowing, musing:

People underestimate producers so much because there's a lot of regular producers in the game, and they lead by example. So you'll see them just doing what the A&R say and kissing the record executive's ass. But a producer like me would rather have a legacy. I know I'm going to get paid, so the money aspect of the shit has never been an issue. If you focus on that, you're going to hamper the creative aspect thinking about when you gonna get paid and all that bullshit as opposed to making a hit record. If you make hits and make everybody else want to work with you, it's contagious, so you just got to be contagious in a positive way. That's what I focus on.

https://twitter.com/DrummaBoyFRESH

CHAPTER TWELVE
Lose Yourself - Jeff Bass

Imagine winning an Oscar against the backdrop of gritty urban Detroit...It sounds almost cinematic, and that's precisely how Grammy-winning producer Jeff Bass - half of the multi-platinum, multi-instrumental production team The Bass Brothers who produced many of Eminem's greatest hits, including *Lose Yourself, '97 Bonnie & Clyde, Without Me, Sing for the Moment, White America, and Cleaning Out My Closet* to name just a few -

still views the moment looking back twenty years after an unknown Marshall Mathers first walked in he and his brother Mark's studio on 8 mile in 1995. Recognizing they had their hands on a gold mine of talent, the team mentored and developed EMINEM into the equivalent of the heavyweight contender they took all the way to the status of Rap God. Crediting brother Mark with bringing rap's biggest-selling artist of all time to his attention, Jeff remembered:

> The initial meeting with Eminem took place after he went on the radio on an open-mic night, and my brother heard him, made the call to the radio station to get his phone number, and he'd come in and my brother Mark heard him first. So the same night, he called me up and said, "I just met with this kid, this white rapper," and at that time, I didn't like rap music at all, but Mark was like, "You gotta hear this kid." So I made plans the next day to come over, meet Marshall and hear him rap first-hand, and so the next day he came over and rapped for me and I didn't understand one word he said. He was doing that whole thing like he does in *Rap God*, and afterward I said to my brother, "I don't know what that is," and Mark insisted, "He's amazing!" So I was like, "Okay," and my first impression was: I wasn't feeling him so much, but only because I didn't understand it. Then, once I opened up my mind musically and started listening to what he was really saying by reading some of the lyrics he'd brought with him, it

suddenly dawned on me, "Wow, that kid's a story teller."

Recounting the shot the brothers gave him first-hand in a conversation with *Mix Magazine* back in 2000, Eminem recalled the kindred moment born once Bass brother Mark had heard him rap on the radio that night: "Mark heard the shit on the air and called the studio on the spot. We met later that week...I started making a name for myself around Detroit and so I took my income tax check to make a single. Marky and Jeff liked that; they thought it was cool. 'What about a production deal?' they asked. I said, 'Yeah.' I started winning rap battles around Detroit...By this time my voice had matured, my raps were better." As they set about molding Mathers in the studio, Jeff remembered finding he had his own learning curve to conquer stylistically as:

> I started putting my producer head in use as far as thinking, *How can I make him slow down and enunciate and just tell us a story about whatever the subject is, and where I can understand what he's saying?* That's how it all began, when we got him to do that, and he was absolutely open to being coached back then. He was just grateful that: here's these two guys from his area who are taking enough interest to take care of him. Bring him in the studio with his boys, and he did whatever he had to do, which back then was just record, record, record, and work on who Eminem was as an artist, he was grateful for that.

Turning the page back to his own beginnings growing up in the 1970s in Detroit, Bass was the product of a naturally musical household where both he and his younger brother Mark discovered at a young age their mutual musical synergy. For older brother Jeff, he remembered a stylistic sensibility shaped by cross-section of radio stations he was constantly surfing between back when:

> Detroit back then was a mecca for everything. I was intrigued by Led Zeppelin as far as rock, Zeppelin and Jimi Hendrix, that got me going, and then I was really influenced by all of Motown's music, heavy R&B, funk, and I just gravitated to it all. So I would listen for hours to these records, from the artists above to Earth, Wind & Fire, Toto, and jazz like '75, '76 George Benson. I really gravitated to the R&B feel, blues, soul – I just loved it and it definitely moved me.

Serving as his brother's first musical mentor of any kind, as Jeff graduated into his teenage years in the late 1970s, he stepped onto the musical stage for the first time as part of what was essentially a local teenage R&B sensation, Bass recalled that his younger brother was never far behind, even though the pair, "Are four years apart, and he's younger than me. We both were just surrounded by music all the time, and even at a young age, he had picked up the drums at seven or eight years old. That was his first instrument, and he remained a drummer-percussionist throughout his career, where I handled all of the music end: guitars, keyboards, bass, piano. My father played drums and piano, and my mother played piano. So at a young age I was bouncing around on both of them at like seven, eight years old. I didn't get my first guitar till I as eleven, which was a nineteen dollar guitar. It was the best investment my family ever made actually. So I started off back then jus messing around, and then about twelve, thirteen years old, took like six months worth of lessons on the guitar, and it just came natural to me. This was 1973, 1974, so I was listening to all kinds of music back then." Taking the songs they were hearing on the radio and turning them into garage band cover songs, the Bass brothers began to hone their chops, with Jeff unable to remember a time as children when they:

> Always played in little groups together, including one where I was in high school and he was in middle school at the time. We would play in little bands throughout high school, then I graduated high school in 1979, and in 1980 I got my first record deal with this little R&B group named Dream Boy I was playing guitar in. I was in the group with four other fellas I grew up with and we actually landed a record deal with Quincy Jones' label Qwest Records when I was at eighteen years old, and we were on Qwest from 1980 to 1985. We put out a couple of albums, had a couple R&B hits, I don't think anything got over seventeen, but at least we had radio record and I was able to tour off it.

Though Dreamboy never became a mainstream act, the experience would prove to be the equivalent of going to college for Jeff and Mark Bass as the brothers soaked up life on the road. Taking in a million lessons about everyday life in the music business from countless tours opening for veteran acts, the Bass Brothers did it with the complete support of their parents:

> Since Mark was four years younger, fifteen years old at this time, he actually dropped out of high school – my mother and father gave him permission to take the G.E.D. – and he went out on the road and toured with us, setting up drums and making sure things were kosher for the shows. Then he would also played percussion in the band a lot of the time too, that was kind of fun. We were young, so he was fifteen, sixteen and I'm nineteen/twenty, and we're traveling around the country playing the music!

> We had hit the jackpot, even though there was no money, you got paid garbage, but it never was about the money. It was always about, "We're getting to play music? This is frickin' awesome!" During these years on the road, Mark was also starting to gravitate more toward the technical side of things, and after a while, I even went to recording/engineering school in Ohio, because I thought at the time, "If I don't ever make it as an artist, I'll need something to fall back on." I didn't go to college because we were on the road so much.

A few short years later, that back-up plan would ironically wind up being the thing that spring-boarded Jeff and Mark Bass into mainstream stardom as Eminem's primary producers alongside Dr. Dre. Drawn to the recording studio years before they ever aspired to produce other artists in pursuit of cutting their own band's demos, Jeff shared his memory that he and Mark were already writing songs together at that point:

> Back in high school - now this was obviously when we had no money - what we would do was scrounge up as much as we could and go into a recording studio for as many hours as we could afford, and we'd just cut songs. We didn't know what we were doing really, and then in late 1980, right before the Quincy Jones deal, a couple of managers picked up on us and kind of backed us financially. It was not a lot of money, but they put us in the studio, and were trying to teach us how the process of writing and recording worked. I think I was nineteen at the time.
>
> So we cut a few demos, and one of the reps from Warner Bros. was in town and got wind of us because one of the radio stations in town, WJLB – and specifically a disc jockey named Mojo – every day would play our music. The support in Detroit back then was unbelievable, and through that we got the deal with Quincy and while we were in the studio all the time, I was gravitating towards the production side of things: the songwriting and production side. I was just honing those skills day to day, which was nice.

Taking on more and more production work as the 80's came to a close, Jeff and Mark landed their first major production gig with Tycie and Woody through Elektra Records, working under the moniker Funky Bass Brothers in the early 1990s. In 1995, the team took another step up when they appeared on George Clinton and the P-Funk All-Stars' *Dope Dogs* LP, with Jeff playing what became his signature instrumental combo on many of Eminem's earliest hits: guitar, organ and synthesizer, while his brother Mark was a programmer on the record.

As the Bass Brothers continued to hone their respective skill sets, they made the collective decision heading into the mid-1990s to strike out on their own after "my brother actually had his teeth knocked out in a fight and there was a lawsuit, he won the suit, and with the money he got, instead of putting it in the band and being smart about it, he bought some recording equipment and then we set up a little recording studio in my mother's basement, so that's how we started our first studio." Soon the duo were bringing in enough business independently to allow an expansion into what became The BASS Mint Studios, a building on 8 Mile in Detroit that Jeff remembered:

> We bought and turned it into a studio for like no money, but we were able to scrounge up twenty grand. In that studio, there was no live room to speak of, there were two little, small vocal booths that were each probably the size of a closet, and we would do drums in there, and would mic the guitars and basses in those rooms. Then attached to that was a two bedroom apartment upstairs, and we would actually throw some drums upstairs and record drums in that big living room. When I say big, it was actually about the size of a small garage, so it was small.

Then all the walls, since we didn't know anything about building a recording studio, so all the walls were made out of what they call T1-11, and it had the craziest sound for any instrument that you put in there, basically that gave it its own special little reverb. It sounded kind of like a room reverb with a lot of decay, and we didn't know how to soften things up, and we couldn't afford any outboard gear, so we had one compressor and one gate, that's all we had, so when we recorded, we would play – let's say my brother's playing the drums and I'm playing the guitar – for five minutes straight, using the same compressor and same gate, whatever it was set at. Then we'd add this Roland keyboard that had a sampler, and we would take samples of us playing, and put it into that keyboard.

Back then, we were using Shure SM 57's and 58's, we used those, and then we also had a couple of AKG's we used, and we probably used mics in the wrong way back then, but we just used what we had, and however it came out, that was the sound. We didn't have the luxury of having an engineer at that time and had to do it ourselves, so even though I went to Engineering school for a couple of months, I didn't know what we were doing. So whatever we could afford, if someone said, "I've got an old AKG," our response was always, "Hey, yeah, I'll take it!" Or we'd use a kick drum mic for the bass amp, so we didn't have much gear – that's where we did our earliest work with Eminem.

Eminem's first album, *INFINITE*, according to the New York Times, accurately represented the aspiring rapper's, "Pilot episode...Here we see Eminem less angry and more ambitious. He is twenty-one and living in his mother's mobile home, on the verge of being a father. In the songs he dreams of being a star, with concert tours and albums in stores." The Bass Brothers believed in this same vision for the rapper, and launched his career commercially with *INFINITE* as the first release under their WEB Entertainment banner in November, 1996.

During these early days learning the ins and outs of running their own label and studio on a shoe-string budget, the brothers had discovered what would become something of a uniquely signature sound for the Bass Brothers – to save money – as they began sampling *themselves*. A departure from what was the standard sampling operating procedure that dominated hip hop at that time on radio, Jeff reasoned that the move made one hundred percent sense for all parties involved, citing their first collaborations during 1997s *Slim Shady EP* recording sessions, where the elder Bass brother chuckled back at his memory of a conversation that turned into a challenge of sorts from:

> His manager, Paul Rosenberg, who said to me at the time, "You're not going to be able to produce a hip hop album without any samples," and I was like, "Watch me!" Because I could play all of the instruments, and when it came to anything like horn-wise, I could write the horn lines, and then bring someone in to play it. The same thing goes for break-beats, my brother

Mark – a lot of those drums that you would hear on the *Slim Shady LP* and earlier records – that's him actually playing the drums. We rented a studio called The White Room in Detroit, and recorded drums and percussion for that reason, so we made our own break-beat, as opposed to taking drums off a break-beat album. So a lot of the sounds came from just ourselves, making it sound like we took it off of somebody's record.

I remember an important decision I made as a producer when Eminem first came into our studio as an unknown artist, I said to my brother at the time, "I'm not sampling," and at the time he said "What are you talking about, hip hop is built on sampling?" And I said, "I get that, but I'm not doing it. If you want me to be a part of this project, I'm not doing that. I'll make my own samples: I'll play the Rhodes myself, and I'll sample myself." So it was still a sample, but it was a sample of me." And I obviously had to prove that to Eminem because sampling is how he'd come up learning rap, where his DJ would just take samples of other people's music and he'd rapped on top of it. So I had to prove to him that we could do this, and in a business sense, it makes more sense because we didn't have to pay clearance on anything, so we'd own one hundred percent of that song.

Once the brothers had signed Eminem and begun working with him day in and out on the recording of his *EP*, the rapper found in Jeff as a producer, "Almost like a Big Brother figure, that's what I was to Marshall back then, because I was much older than him – ten, twelve years older – and he used to look at me like 'Is this good, is this not good?', and he would absolutely take all the criticism and all the compliments from me." A common hat for a producer to wear among the many others that often define the full range of roles they play in the studio – from psychologist to coach to critic to cheerleader and on and on – Jeff and his brother Mark found in their young artist an eager team player:

> During recording sessions he would ask me, for instance, "How was that?" after a vocal take. And I would tell him at times, "Honestly, I think you could do that one better, that line could be better, etc." So he was WAY open-minded for that type of work ethic in the studio with me and my brother. Another example of that came when we were songwriting with Eminem back then it was a team effort, because a lot of times we would actually do it right on the spot, so I would come up with a musical idea and then Mark and I would be recording it, and Em would be sitting in another room listening, writing the concept for what it was. So he didn't know musically anything - like theoretically, he knew nothing.
>
> All he knew – and I had to figure it out from the psychology – is "How am I going to explain to him what we need to write and record?" So I figured the simplest way with Marshall was to

say, "Explain things like this: a sad feeling, an angry feeling, a happy feeling, a confused feeling," and then I would play him pieces of music that would emotional take you to those places. So it became the norm for him and I, if he would come in the studio and if he was pissed off at his ex-wife, he would say, "I'm fucking angry, I need something," and I would be able to tap into what he was feeling. If he was funny, I would be able to tap in. I knew exactly what motivated him to come up with these songs.

As Mathers' now-legendary Slim Shady persona was born in the studio during these sessions, and Eminem's vivid talent for painting dark lyrical canvases began to come to life, he challenged the brothers to tap deep into their own creative wells to draw whatever musical moods the rappers' lyrics called for. Arguably no more provocative and brilliant an example of this synergy can be found on the album than the wildly controversial '97 Bonnie & Clyde. A brilliant parody of the family-man-themed Will Smith hit that had come out the same year, instead of singing to his child about G-rated fatherhood themes. Almost as ominous as the lyrical content is the haunting instrumental that Jeff and Mark composed underneath, an accomplishment the elder Bass Brother still remains proud of to this day:

That song right there, originally, Denaun Porter came in with the idea of using Paul Simon's track, 50 Ways to Leave Your Lover, and I couldn't use that because I wasn't going to pay the clearance to use that. So I kind of stuck in the same mode, and changed it up for what fans now know as *Bonnie and Clyde 97*, and I remember when I played it for Marshall, he LOVED it! He loved the chord progression we used, and it put him in that mode, that feeling where it's kind of sweet sounding, but then again it's dark and haunting.

I think that that particular song started with the drums, and as soon as I heard Mark's beat, I figured out which key I wanted to do it in, and it just flowed. It was just like, that chord progression had something R&B like to it too, so if you break down that track instrumentally, you can interpret it a couple different ways. It's dark, but it's also kind of funky and has this cool little groove to it, and then on top of that, Marshall – his lyrics obviously took it to a whole other level. I remember when Tori Amos recorded her version of the song, it was amazing, because she felt that too as an artist, she felt exactly what I had been feeling, and then she just took it in a whole other direction and made it her own.

The instrumental attributes of *97 Bonnie & Clyde* were reflective of the broader soundscapes that rolled throughout the album's recording, and out of their small Bass Mint building, a signature sound for the Bass Brothers was born. Taking fans beyond the compositional side of the that sound into some of the "out of the box" tricks and techniques the brothers were applying to traditional recording concepts as they tracked. One that would prove key among them in opening new sonic doors came when Jeff began applying an insider Motown-era recording trick that he'd picked up while working with George Clinton, explaining:

> I'd learned a tip back when we used to record with George over at United Sound. I had run into an old Motown musician, and I was curious how they got their sound with their instruments. And a couple of them said to me, "Listen, don't change your strings, and don't exactly tune it perfectly, just kind of do it by ear." So I ran with that little tidbit of information, and part of the sound came from things not always being in tune, and old dirty strings, and the next thing you knew, we had a specific sound that Eminem was tied to, and that's where that sound came from.

Along with old strings, the brothers were working on vintage equipment that helped flesh out both *The Slim Shady EP* and *LP*'s sonic character throughout Bass brother productions that *Billboard Magazine* argued, "Mirrors his rhymes, with their spare, intricately layered arrangements enhancing his narratives, which are always at the forefront." MTV would observe twelve years after the album's release that, "The production...by the Bass brothers...has held up incredibly well. The beats are full of bass-heavy hallucinations and create huge, scary sandboxes that allow Em to play." Such compliments regarding the music's durability still make Jeff shake his head thinking back about the realities of how limited a list of equipment was, and in reality what the team was working with leading up to Eminem's signing with Dr. Dre and Interscope. Following in the classic indie tradition of doing more with less, Jeff quips that at the time of the signing, their recording gear was so antiquated by comparison to the type of competitor high-line studios like 54 Sound:

> At that time, we were working on an old 16-channel Tascam console recording into two Tascam 24-track machines, and tape at that time was I think one hundred and fifty dollars a reel. And you got sixteen minutes of recording time. We couldn't afford that, so what we did to economize was – like for Eminem – to use the first eight tracks for one song; and then the next eight tracks as song two; that's how we recorded him to conserve on tape. We had to keep one SMPTE track free of the twenty-four, and then we would hopefully have a good sound of the first eight tracks that was the first song. We would bounce that track down to two channels, and then Em would go do his vocals. We did that for every song, and the whole *Slim Shady EP*. And the album was done like that.

The Slim Shady EP would have implications for the careers of all involved, the most important being – as *Rolling Stone Magazine* reported in 1999 – that, "The eight-son EP...(landed Eminem) his deal with Interscope." A reality that hit the Bass Brothers with the same impact from the production side that it had for Eminem as an artist. Legitimizing the brothers overnight as one of the hottest production teams in the industry, they now had the backing of Dr. Dre and when they discovered that the legendary producer wanted to use the bulk of their productions from the EP on what would become Mathers' major label debut,

The Slim Shady LP – along with a few new tracks they'd be producing as well. Jeff remembered feeling like a kid in a candy store upon hearing this news, beginning with:

> On the *Slip Shady LP*, we were able to expand the equipment. So we had better keyboards to play with, and this was in 1998. Whatever the latest Kurzweil K2K model was I was using, and the Korg Triton. I would use those two as my main synthesizers, and then I had several different basses: a Fender P-bass, a fretless 4-string bass, and then for guitars. I had a Fender Stratocaster, and a cheap acoustic Yamaha guitar. We also switched over to a good Sony mic in the middle of *The Slim Shady LP*, because Dr. Dre had a Sony mic and Marshall wanted that same mic so we bought one. That was pretty much it as far the instruments I would use.

With the Bass Brothers responsible for laying much of the rhythmic foundation of Eminem's major label debut - eleven out of fourteen tracks – on *The Slim Shady LP*, they charted a sonic course that would help them sail into the digital age as a studio as well, with Jeff adding that among other studio improvements and upgrades, "We were still recording on a Mackie board, but at that time, we switched over to Pro Tools." Allowing them more creative breathing room to spread out among the virtual tracks, Jeff also decided to expand geographically as well, heading out with Marshall and Mark in 1998 following the record deal signing "to L.A., where I leased a little room at the Mix Room for like three years, and the three of us moved out there for a while to work and finish the album up. A lot of material was written out of that place for *The Slim Shady LP* and *The Marshall Mathers LP* too." Building on work on bed tracks they'd already completed back in Detroit – including much of the albums' drum recording – Jeff revealed of that hybrid process that for the bulk of the album, Eminem was flowing over:

> A combination on *the Slim Shady LP* where a lot of the drum tracks are live, and then what we would do is, besides the live drumming, I think it was the Triton that had drum loops in it, so what we'd do is lock the loop up with the live drums, so it was a combination of the two. It would be like a two-bar loop off of the Triton, and then my brother Mark playing live on the 2/4 bars.

> During the recording of that album, we'd rented a live drum room called The White Room in Detroit that was a pretty large room back then, maybe 30 x 30. It was in a loft kind of setting so it had really tall ceilings, which sonically allowed us to get really big, banging drum sounds, almost like John Bonham, or we would close-mic the drums, depending on what the specific track called for. We also definitely used compressors as much as we could, and we used to do a lot of triggering with the electric bass, triggered by the kick drum. So every time the kick drum would come in, it would trigger the bass note that I played. So *Bonnie & Clyde 97* for instance, was done that way, and *"Just Don't Give a Fuck"* was

done that way. So we used triggering in a lot of the kick drum and bass.

Bouncing back and forth off the walls of Eminem's imagination were a full range of lyrical emotions requiring musical serenades that spanned the dial equally stylistically, with more distressed and depressed anthems of struggle like fan-favorite *Rock Bottom* and *If I Had a Million Dollars* to full-fledged dance floor bangers like, *Come On Everybody*. Mathers would hallenge the Bass Brothers' throughout to authentically deliver with matching musical cinema instrumentally. One particular point of pride within the reactions he fielded to the material they were producing came when Jeff remembered picking up the phone one day to the sound of:

> Dr. Dre on the other line, and says, "Dude, we're in a little friendly competition now." And I remember I replied, "What are you talking about?" And he goes, "That track is sick! It's the simplest track I've ever heard, and now I've got to get back in the studio and try to come up with something that's gonna..." I remember telling him at the end of that call, "Hey, we're all in this together, I'm not in any competition with you," but I took it as quite a compliment.

> With something on the darker side like, *Rock Bottom*, in the studio, that was still a fun song to make, because it's just so sparse and airy sounding because of what he was talking about, I think the instrumental went so perfectly with what he was saying, and we knew it had to be

just like that. It got him in the minor mode, thinking that he was at the end of everything. That was one of the better productions on the album, I thought, in terms of the sounds I chose to use with the keyboard and real guitar and bass. I thought those particular patches, like there was a choir patch I remember using that went really well in the song. I even added this chorus patch on one of the keyboards after he put his vocals on it, which ended up being a big part of that song. *If I Had a Million Dollars* was another one I had fun producing because it was so simple and dark.

Singing was one thing that fans began to hear Eminem do first-hand on *The Slim Shady LP* in what would become an instrument in and of itself, and in time one that led the chorus of the 2010 anthem *Not Afraid* to #1 in the U.S. and Top 5 in fifteen countries, and on memorable hooks throughout his major label debut including *My Fault* and *97 Bonnie and Clyde*. A craft that he learned first-hand under the tutelage of the Bass Brothers – who had first identified the unique tone of Mathers' voice and encouraged him to utilize it versus bringing in outside chorus hook singers – Jeff described an organic collaborative writing process:

From early on, how we would do it was: once the track was in place and he was getting ready to write his raps, and it came to the hooks of the song, what I would ninety percent of the time do is, either on the guitar or on a string patch on the keyboard, would play a melody to go along with the song. And he would pick up on that melody and then use it and just replace the melody words, so I would actually have something in there – like the chorus melody for, "Just the two of us, just the two of us" in *Bonnie & Clyde 97* or *My Fault* and he would replace the melody with a lyric. So a lot of times, the hook melodies that he sang came out of something I gave him musically as a suggestion.

My Fault was a true story actually. What happened with was I had a studio on 8 Mile Road, and back then, little groupies used to come in, and there was this one girl who was a heroin addict, and Marshall basically wrote that lyric about her, because she was *fucking* crazy! So there's actually a little bit of truth in that song, and then I just came up with that melody because I came up with the bass line first, that he winds up singing on the choruses. He just loved it, and it was a funny, funky kind of a groove.

Handed in in late 1998, expectations were high for the best-kept secret in underground hip hop that was about to explode upon pop culture in what would be a much-needed shot in the arm for Eminem, Dr. Dre, and the Bass Brothers after investing so much money, studio and creative time in the development of a rare level of talent that *Spin Magazine* argued made Mathers the "most promising new rapper" of the dawning millennium. Fans thankfully reacted with the equal fervor as critics after *The Slim Shady LP* debuted out of nowhere at #2 on the Billboard Top 200 Album Chart in February, 1999, selling almost 500,000 copies in it's first two weeks of release alone, and 5,000,000 copies in total. Nominated for and awarded Best Rap Album Grammy Award, when Jeff first received the news of the nod, it came out of the blue courtesy of the U.S. Postal Service after:

> I got a letter in the mail notifying me I'd been nominated for producer of that particular album, and I didn't really understand what the hell that meant, to be honest with you, because we never went into it thinking about Grammys and record sales, nothing, just creating a brand, so initially winning a Grammy was never a goal of mine. But when I heard that I was nominated, along with my brother and Dr. Dre, it really was quite an honor, because it kind of showed us the masses were accepting what we were doing.

Without much time to stop and celebrate, Interscope immediately wanted another album to follow up the overnight success of now four million selling *The Slim Shady LP* In a heavy nod of loyalty. When he could have succumb to pressure to go fully with Dr. Dre and had the star power by then to have his pick of any of the biggest-name producers working in the business, Eminem chose instead to stay close to home. Opting to pick up right where he'd left off with the balance of Dr. Dre and the Bass Brothers, heading back into the studio to make their second major label album with Mathers, Jeff remembered while the chemistry was still very much the same between he and Em, their formula's ingredients had shifted slightly.

First and arguably most importantly, Jeff's longtime studio sidekick Mark had taken what his brother described diplomatically as "some time away" from the business. Leaving

Jeff in the Captain's chair with a new co-pilot, Eminem himself took much of the rhythmic lead throughout the seven tracks he and Jeff co-produced side-by-side for the new album, with the rest of the record being handled by Dre's camp. Elaborating more fully on the new creative landscape he and Mathers were now navigating, Jeff began with his recollection that the rapper was eager to expand an experiment with beat-making he'd begun:

> Toward the end of *The Slim Shady LP*, when he was starting to program drum machines himself. He was working on this one drum machine, this big box, that had all these sounds in it, and we taught him how to program it at the start of the album, and he wound up doing a lot of the drum programming himself on *The Marshall Mathers LP*. He started growing, and he learned the word "percussion," so whenever he said something technical, it was always, "Yeah, I'm going to add a little compression on it..." or "Yeah, when I add a little compression on it, it'll sound better," he used that word all the time. I think he learned it from Dre, because he would always be watching when Dre was sitting behind the mixing board, asking him "What are you doing?" and Dre would say, "Adding some compression." So he picked up the term, and he could hear the difference when you slapped on a compressor on a kick drum. For instance, you can hear it punchy, and he liked that.

So once he began programming his own beats, I said as the producer, "Go for it, I don't have a problem with you coming up with drum lines, I'll play to anything," so that's how he started being a producer. That's also where heading into the making of *The Marshall Mathers LP*, my brother Mark was no longer involved in the recording process, so Marshall enjoyed putting together the drum beats in his place, and we just went with it. It was cool for me because it was less stress, all he had to do was program something and then I just had to do my thing on top of it.

Thankfully, the caliber of beats Mathers was quickly showing an accelerated artistic aptitude for programming was up to par with what Bass's peers would have submitted for consideration, and fit perfectly into a new sound the producer was in the midst of creating around the turn of the millennium. Termed "CLAP MUSIC," a cross-bred sound that blended hip hop beats and key elements of classical music, Jeff found himself freer to pursue this vision because:

> I took more of the lead in production on *The Marshall Mathers LP* because my brother wasn't as involved in the making of that album, in the sense of hands-on musically in the productions. So I was pretty much on my own in the day-to-day writing and recording process. At that point, Marshall always had first dibs on everything I would be doing musically, and ninety percent of

the time, he would actually sit in there with me while I was doing it.

What happened was, on that album, everything was raw. So I would record songs from beginning to end with the hopes of going back to those songs and cleaning it up, fixing notes and whatnot. Instead of cleaning it up, Marshall and I decided, "We're just going to keep it raw! Let it go, I want you to hear all my mistakes on the bass, and guitar and keyboard. I want you to hear it like that." But what we did continue is what I called "CLAP Music," which was to me classical music with rap, and a lot of the tracks on *The Marshall Mathers LP* had a classical vibe to it. So I would take the chord progressions of a classical piece, mix it with hip hop drums, and some dirtier sounding patches on the keyboard, and that came up with another level of what we were developing with Marshall.

Eminem concurred, confirming to *Mix Magazine* in 2000 that in the studio, the atmosphere was one of creative tunnel vision where, "Were pounding out the hours...makin' an album. I knew what I was doin' more on this album, was more experienced at it; so (was)...Jeff. Every album is a learning experience." Working out of Detroit and L.A., Bass remembered that "all the tracks we produced were recorded at our studio at The Mix Room, and then we went to The Record Plant in L.A., and songs like *Drug Ballad* and *Amityville* were done there, and then we went back to Detroit and finished the rest of the record up at 54 Sound." A historic studio locally to Detroit, it was immortalized in reference in Eminem's *8 Mile* film, and at the peak of recording, Bass experienced what would be any producer's dream of having the entire studio on lock-out while he juggled production on:

> *The Marshall Mathers LP and* D-12's *Devils Night* at the same time, so I would go from room to room with different songs from different artists- at 54 Sound, there are three rooms, and I had them all going at the same time. That studio is owned by my business manager Joel Martin, and because by then he was my full-time manager as well, and I didn't really have to worry about the hourly rate anymore. That was our home studio, so anytime I wanted to record – no matter what time of the day or night it was – I could go in there and record all day long or all night long. At that time, I was working with Steve King – who recently passed away – and another engineer Tony Cabana, and we worked our asses off because all we were doing was cutting records left and right.

Deconstructing the intuitive process that can develop between producer and artist where Bass had come to know what the rapper wanted to hear musically even before Eminem had presented him with a song's lyrical concept. Jeff highlights the story behind the creation of *Criminal*, a live fan favorite, as an ideal illustration of their recording routine throughout the album:

I'd be creating the track having no idea what Em wanted to talk about lyrically, as far as the concept of the title and lyrics, a lot of times it would just be completing the track itself. So let's say I do a piano riff, which in that particular song, the whole track was based on a piano riff, and I would actually add all the elements that we ended up hearing on the final record, so I would have almost a finished track of the song, and then he would be inspired by that track and start writing what he felt. So when I say finished, I did the track at the Record Plant in L.A., and then we would bring the record back home and he would record his vocals here in Detroit, and then any tweaks on the track I'd have to do - like adding one more element to the music - I would also finish that up here in Detroit. When that particular song was mixed, and Dr. Dre actually mixed that record with Richard 'Segal' Huredia, they added that intro from the bank robbery, which completed the song.

But what would fans make commercially of the months the team had spent slaving away in the studio? A brief highlight reel: a record-smashing 1.7 million copies sold in its first week, 25 million in total worldwide, and according to *Time Magazine* – who declared the album in 2006 one of the 100 Greatest Albums of all time – the third best-selling album of all time; #1 in twelve countries; and three Grammy wins including a second Best Rap Album award. The *L.A. Times* argued the album, "Solidified Eminem's reputation as a superstar and a serious artist." Salon added that the MM LP's success, "Made him a sensation."

Rolling Stone Magazine felt the results Mathers had achieved with Dre and Bass had elevated him to the status of being, "Simply better than any other MC in hip hop." Billboard had praise for both Mathers, calling the album, "A hyper-surreal, wittily disturbing thrill ride," while finding that, "The production is nearly as evocative as the raps, with liquid basslines, stuttering rhythms, slight sound effects, and spacious soundscapes...always drawing the listener in."

For as successful as *The Marshall Mathers LP* had been, it made Bass and Mathers that much more ambitious heading into recording on the rap phenomenon's third album in as many years, *The Eminem Show*, a true trifecta that solidified any doubts – in the esteemed opinion of *Rolling Stone Magazine* - that Eminem had graduated to "the top of his game," adding the high compliment that, "He's quickly becoming an expert beatmaker. Every track has some sort of melodic edge...He's learned so much so well as a producer that Dr. Dre's three contributions are hard to pick out without production credits." As Bass had watched the emcee mature both as an artist and producer over the seven preious years, he'd blended into the fabric of Mathers' sound in such an inextricable way as both a composer/producer that he felt totally comfortable handing more of the lead reigns over behind the console because:

> Marshall was definitely stepping up as a producer himself on *The Eminem Show*, because by then he'd learned what the actual role of a producer was. I was definitely a write and producer on that album, but Marshall knew what he wanted and had learned how to say "I want a guitar right here," even though he couldn't play a guitar, he

could tell me what he wanted. That's where I kind of took a step back on that record from having total control of arrangement and where we put things in a song, and let him tell me what he wanted, and *it worked*. He learned through making that album that, "Wow, I have the potential to produce records." He could actually just sit in a room with musicians if he had to and hum to them melodies he heard. They could in turn pick it up and play those parts. Then, have the engineer take a piece of that performance and put it where he wanted it in a song.

As in any recording scenario, sometimes happy accidents make for the greatest inspirations, and nowhere on the album is this more true than with its first single, *Without Me*, a Grammy nominee for Record of the Year. The song began very much as a joke, as Bass remembers, after Mathers and his co-producer were kidding back and forth in their very own brand of studio speak that Jeff describes as:

A fake language that Marshall and I used to use that was like a cross between Arabic and Jewish, and I'm Jewish and was singing Jewish songs to him, and one day after the bass line was laid down, I came up with this cheesy-sounding saxophone that came from the stock sounds in the Triton. I remember I was sitting in 54 Sound, and had just grabbed it and pulled up that sax part and started playing that (begins humming out the lead melody line to *Without Me*) – that's actually a derivative of the Israeli National

Anthem actually, Hatikfa. That song has a melody that's similar feeling-wise, and I was like, "To me, that' funny as hell." Well, when Em heard that, he loved it and instantly went in the vocal booth and began singing along in that language of ours following that saxophone melody line, and it was really started out as a joke, but it only took us about a half hour to make that track!

I had done a song earlier called *Purple Pills* for D-12, and there was a crazy sax part that I had done for them, and then the bass line in that song was some crazy low bass sound, and I said, "I would love to emulate that for another song," except I couldn't do it as shitty as that. So I remember I just kind of started playing the bass line to like a Michael Jackson-sounding drum loop that they had programmed, and became the one you hear in *Without Me*.

On the other end of the spectrum, Mathers and Bass would achieve one of their greatest studio moments together on what *Rolling Stone Magazine* declared, "The record's most powerful moment," the smash hit single *Cleanin' Out My Closet*. Driven by a distinctive snare rim-shot that the rapper even references at the top of the song's vocal, letting Bass know, "I have no snare in my headphones." *Entertainment Weekly* would further underscore the correct choice Eminem had made in emphasizing the drum as a centerpiece of the song's instrumental arrangement. Noting that, "The song is both fragile and furious, and the syncopated music-box arrangement matches it in tension." A musical feature that Jeff remembered Mathers was almost obsessed with from the first time he heard it, the producer confessed to feeling:

> Early on like, "Where the hell's he going with that?" But there's a method to his madness. If you listen to the way he raps now, it's clear that he finds his own rhythm within that beat, and then works off of that. That's why his rhythms are so amazing, and he just fills those rhythms with lyrics. That song started out as one that was going to be called *Skeletons*, and I just came up with lead guitar line (hums melody), and I recorded that guitar line just to a straight drum click. Then when Marshall heard that, he programmed a crazy thing with the rim shot going on and on like he was doing it, and then I got so caught up in what he was doing. He raps off of different instruments, so in *Cleaning Out My Closet*, that rim-shot is a crazy pattern that he came up with, and that's how he uses his rhythms. I was thinking about that so much – the drum track – because I'm driven by rhythm, so when I hear a rhythm on the drums, that inspired me to what I do on the guitar and keyboards.
>
> When I finished the whole song instrumentally, and I realized afterward I'd never laid a bass line for the song, so there's absolutely zero bass line for that song! I didn't realize that until there was a lawsuit with an artist in Belgium, I think, who

sued saying we stole the song from him, where he claimed I'd stolen the bassline from him, so I actually had to do a video affidavit and I remember I was sitting in the studio with lawyers and a camera and the whole thing, and I remember my engineer Steve King brought up the original track, and there *wasn't even a bass* in there! When Steve King mixed the song, he took my Fender Rhodes, and he tweaked the bottom end of it to sound like a bass! But it wasn't a bass, it was my left hand playing bass notes, so that was a funny story within that song.

Marking the first hit single Marshall had sung the chorus on, Bass felt that the song reflected the full maturation of the rapper's voice into an authentic instrument he'd mentored from Eminem's inception as a recording artist. Complimenting the progress he'd made as a musician, CNN in the network's review of the album, praised Mathers' ability to deliver a, "Both fragile and furious" performance on *Cleaning Out My Closet*, one that from a tracking standpoint, the rapper considered very much a co-production, relying on Jeff to help craft the chorus hook:

> It was definitely a collaboration. In fact, in the mix you can hear the string line that's in that chorus, and he just followed that string line vocally. It's a violin-sounding patch, and for that song, I'd gone back to using the trusty old Korg Triton, and by that point, I'd also bought a Kurzweil keyboard that got a lot of play on that album. With the Triton, I was always a fan of the

variety of patches, and I was able to go inside and tweak them a certain way that wasn't exactly what was standard in the box itself. So I would tweak it inside the keyboard, just to make the sounds either shittier - *most the time shittier* - because it was just part of the system of trying to make something sound like you took it off of an album.

Sing for the Moment would represent another musical touchstone for the album, one of those anthems that an artist can grab the hand of every fan with, and keep them waving long, "After we're gone, while our spirits live on through the lyrics that you hear in our songs," as Eminem rapped in the song's final poignant lines. The track's production was demonstrative of the kind of elite creative freedom Mathers had earned by that point, and of just how far his reach went in flexing that freedom: all the way into the sacred realm of Aerosmith's most timeless ballad *Dream On*. The fact that the rapper had not only received permission to use Steven Tyler's original chorus, but equally with the recruitment of Aerosmith lead guitarist Joe Perry to contribute an exclusive solo to the song, was equally reflective of just how much many of the biggest artists in the music business wanted to work with Mathers. A demand created no doubt in part by the wildly successfully duet between Elton John and Eminem at the Grammys the previous year performing *Stan*, with *Sing for the Moment*, Jeff remembered being impressed with Mathers' concept - and ambition - when he'd first approached the producer with:

The idea Marshall for the song, which was *totally* his idea, so he came to me with just that set chorus, just Steven Tyler singing, and he said, "I want to use this in a song, can you do something with that?" And I was like, "YEAH I can, but are we going to get permission?", and he replied, "I don't know," so he put his manager Paul on that. In the meanwhile, we started building the track, and I tried to emulate a track that would go along with *Dream On*, and came up with actually playing the opposite way that Joe Perry did, and it played off the originally really well, and Marshall programmed the drum beat on that song, but I played the toms with my fingers, just the turn-arounds in that song, I used the toms from one of my keyboards, I remember just because it was convenient for that moment. Then later we were going to add real toms, and I was like, "Naw, we can make those sound good," because the timing was not quite on, which was kind of cool, and it worked so well for that song.

Then when the hook would pop in, it was like, "Wow, that was meant to be." Originally, I actually wanted Steven Tyler to come in and sing it, and he wanted that too at the time, but ultimately Marshall was like, "No, I want it off of the original record, just like this." But at the end of the song, I'd done a guitar solo and then Steven Tyler heard the mix and said, "I love the track, I love everything, but you gotta get rid of the solo at the end and bring Joe Perry in," and I remember initially Marshall's reaction was, "No Way! Jeff's solo is badass, it's gotta stay in."

Well, Steven Tyler then came back and said something to the effect of, "Well, I'm not gonna do it then. If Joe Perry's not on it, I'm not on it," so they won and we relented. Joe Perry put his solo on the end and we took my solo off, which I didn't really care about, because I thought it was fucking cool that Joe Perry was on my song!

The Eminem Show would wind up being so highly anticipated that Interscope – in an effort to fight the album's early leak online – took the rarely-before-risked step of moving up the release date to a Friday, meaning that Soundscan would only record two days of sales versus the traditional seven. Not surprisingly, it wound up being a gamble that paid off after *XXL Magazine* reported at the time that, "The album secured the top ranking by moving 285,000 copies in just one weekend. The album was originally supposed to come out on June 4, but thanks to people pirating and illegally downloading the album on peer-to-peer networks, the labels released it early. With the help of strong singles like *Cleanin' Out My Closet* and *Without Me*, *The Eminem Show* sold 1,322,000 copies it's first full week of release." It would go on to move over 10 million copies, grab the Best Rap Album Grammy Award for the third year in a row, and according to Billboard, make Eminem "the gold standard in pop music."

"And the Oscar goes to..."

The Academy Awards' Best Song Oscar category is arguably among it's purest in terms of the typical behind-the-scenes lobbying that usually goes on among movie studios where Best Picture and Best Actor campaigns are concerned. The award goes quite simply to the best song in its category, without the same consideration for critical reaction or commercial implication, one poignant example being Memphis rap group Three 6 Mafia's surprise win in 2006 for Hustle & Flow's anthem, *It's Hard Out Here for a Pimp*. The cutting edge is walked in this category by composers, artists and producers who capture moments of musical magic that help define a two hour film's spirit in four to five short minutes. *Lose Yourself*, 2003's winner for the Best Song at the Academy Awards was one such moment, and for its primary composers, Marshall Mathers and Jeff Bass, the journey to that triumph was truly epic as throughout much of its development. Bass confessed that while they knew the song had something special to keep them working at it:

> That track was not written in conjunction with the 8 Mile movie, and though it felt so good every time we pulled it out to work on it, we didn't know what it was yet - I remember something about that track felt amazing, to Marshall and myself, and we kept pulling it out every time I would go over to the studio. It didn't matter what studio we were working out of or what else we were working on that day, we would always have access to that track, but for a while, we never knew what to do with it. Then once Marshall got ahold of that script for the film, he applied the lyrics to the instrumental track, because I recall my manager calling me up on the phone to say, "Hey, you got the single for the movie," and I asked, "What single is it?", and he replied, *Lose Yourself*, and my reaction was What's *Lose Yourself?*" because I wasn't in the

studio when Marshall did the vocals and didn't even know the final title. So I went over, listened to the finished track, and at that time actually he was still filming the movie!

Taking fans deeper inside the musical studio story behind *Lose Yourself*, he begins with it's infectious, signature guitar riff that introduced the song to #1 in twenty-four countries around the world – and still launches basketball, hockey and football crowds into frenzied applause more than a decade after it initially took the world by storm. Bass remains proud to date that he kicked off the song's opening moments, though he admits there's been times over the years where he's grown understandably weary of the fact:

> I've been asked a *million times* what made me come up with that guitar line, but I understand why because it's the driving force of that song. At that time, I had done a song for Royce Da 5'9 and Eminem called *Rock City*, it was in that era, and something that I heard in that song made me go back to the studio, and I came up with this guitar line. It was recorded on a 98 Fender Stratocaster – the Jeff Beck model – with a little bit of chorus on it, playing through a Rocktron – a little guitar processor- and then from the Rocktron right into an SSL. Then the bass I played was just this piece of shit old P-Bass running D.I. into the SSL. Eminem's DJ, DJ Head, had programmed that drum track on an MPC, so I played the guitar to the drum machine, and then there were no keyboard parts

at the time, it was just one hundred percent guitar, bass and drums. Eventually we decided to take off my guitars, except that one guitar you hear throughout the song. And Louie Rusto came in and played some keyboards on top of the guitars I was doing, and that's how that song came to life.

An instant smash from the first spin the song had on radio, and still in rotation around the world years later, for Bass, every time he hears the opening strum of his guitar, the producer-composer-multi-instrumentalist confesses to feeling the same butterflies he did as a kid when he'd laid eyes and ambitions on:

My first nineteen dollar guitar from Sears. I can reflect on that and go, "Thank God my father bought me that guitar!" You can go to any sporting event of any kind today, all these years later, for instance, at a Michigan Football game where there's 100,000 fans in the stands, and if you hear that song pop in, you hear the guitar first and 100,000 people are screaming and doing air guitar! I still get friends of mine who call me from events like that and say, "Dude, listen to this, this is crazy, this is you!" So it becomes surrealistic really. Because what can you say? You just have to be humble, and thank God taking that riff out of my heart for me and me being able to share that with the world. To read *Billboard* or *Rolling Stone* and it's ranked as one of the most classic songs of all time, it's kind of incredible!

These days, Bass stays as busy as ever running F.B.T. Studio, which the Detroit Free Press in January, 2014 highlighted as one of a handful that make up, "The bustling epicenter of Detroit's music recording scene." Located ironically just down the road from Eminem's own Effigy Studio complex, the DFP reported that after finding themselves, "Flush from their success as producers for Eminem at 54 Sound, brothers Mark and Jeff Bass decided in 2004 to invest 2.2 million dollars in their own custom studio up the street. At the center of it all is a massive SSL 8088 mixing board, capable of taking 176 separate feeds of sound. Bass says it's the biggest console in Detroit." Truly a family affair, in addition to co-owning the F.B.T. with his brother, the elder Bass revealed:

> For me, the most exciting thing is waking up and meeting my son in the studio. Second generation is kicking ass right now. To me, he grew up in the studio with me from three years old on. And from him to go through college going into Film Composition, he came out, he works for the company. He's an amazing artist. So for me it's to wake up knowing that he's right there, and has picked up a lot of my tricks of the trade, and then he adds something new to it with his knowledge of theory. To me, the fact that my oldest daughter sings and my current wife is a lyricist, and she writes lyrics with me. It's fun, because this has become a family business. So bringing the family into what I love to do and them taking it on as theirs, it's just a wonderful accomplishment.
>
> *www.jeffbassmusic.com*

"His résumé is diverse and potent." – MTV

CHAPTER THIRTEEN
A Milli – **Bangladesh**

Hip hop has long had its share of colorful stage names, from DJs like Hurricane, Funkmaster Flex, and Jam Master Jay to producers looking to make an analogous statement between their name and sound: *Timba*land, The *Bomb* Squad, Pete *Rock* and *Bang*ladesh. Dropping bombs on our ears for over fifteen years in the game with Top 10 hits like Lil Wayne's *A Milli* and *6 Foot 7 Foot* – which have received over 58 and 53 million streams on

Spotify respectively; Ludacris's breakout hit *What's Your Fantasy*, and more recently, The Game's 2015 underground hit *El Chapo*. Announcing his presence with authority from the first track that jumped off on Ludacris's first major-label release, *Back for the First Time*, where *Rolling Stone Magazine* celebrated the collection – half of which Bang produced – as a, "Bounce-inducing, sweat-producing soundtrack," while Luda's break-out hit *What's Your Fantasy* would launch both *artist* and *producer* on their respective paths to stardom. Hailed by *The Village Voice* as a "Dirty south classic," the futuristic beatscape was one that Bangladesh revealed:

> I produced entirely on my MPC 2000 from sounds I had recorded into the MPC, and just formatted and sequenced and programmed into the machine. Back in the day, I would get sounds from anywhere, I would sample sounds from my cousin's Casio keyboard – probably something you could buy at Target – into the MPC. Inside the keyboard, there were loops of melodies and different music, and I would just play sounds note-for-note into the MP and when I came up with the melody for *What's Your Fantasy*, I just played it note-for-note into my pads and just did that. That song was on the re-release of an independent album he put out called *Incognegro*, and he took that and played it on the radio and it became a hit.

By the time Bang teamed back up a year later with Ludacris for his sophomore LP, *Word of Mouf* was out on both Luda and Bang as one of the hottest emcee-producer sounds coming out of the *new south*. Again given the opening ball on the album with its lead-off track, *Coming 2 America*, of the third of the album he produced, Bangladesh remembered feeling like a newly-drafted player in the pros trying to put as many points up on the board as he could score:

> I was in the zone, and even though it was new to me, I was getting really creative, just really getting anything: sampling anything, chopping anything, using sounds that were just against the grain. Back in the day when Ludacris and I were in the same studio together, I made beats right there and he'd record them right there. I have to be really hands on and doing it to hear it, I don't hear the beat before I program it. Now, lately, I just give him beats and he'll record them where he's at.
>
> The tracks I made for that album were ones that I was coming up with at the time we were recording the first album *Back for the First Time*, and then after that first album was recorded, I was still creating, so there was stuff that possibly could have went on that album that didn't make it. So he had already had in his mind that he wanted to use those tracks for his next album.

Amazingly, the producer had landed his first hit before he'd ever settled on his professional moniker, leaving him scrambling to come up with something as catchy as the hits he was starting to bang out. Remembering the all-important process of finding his way to a professional pseudonym as one where art-imitated-life in the symbolism that the moniker held for him personally, as well as musically:

> It kind of went with everything that I was going through as somebody creative that was finding their way and finding their sound in the game when it's kind of hard to bring something new inside something that's going a different direction. So it was kind of foreign, my sound was kind of foreign already, people didn't really understand it, and it just went along with the struggle. It had the word *bang* in it, and just sounded to me like Timabaland, Neptunes, and everyone else who had dope names.
>
> I had already made a hit before I really had a name that I wanted to go with that meant something. Basically, when we first started to move around and tour, that word kind of developed as something we would say. There were two or three of us in the clique that would use that word to describe something cool, so it would be like, "Man, that's Bangladesh right there." So it was just a cool word to use. After we were using it, I woke up thinking, *Damn, that would be a perfect name. Bangladesh!*

Already displaying a flair for the imaginative in the beatscapes he was putting together early on in his career, *Spin Magazine* would correctly observe as a signature of his style that, "Bangladesh doesn't have a sound exactly, though there is a kind of Timbaland weirdness-gone-weirder approach to beatmaking that's very much his own." Taking an endlessly open-minded, try-anything approach to his sampling methodology that travels well beyond the traditional rhythmic boundaries, Bang confirms:

> It could be anything. I started getting sounds from just random things like a children's story, anything random. I could be anywhere, hear something, and want to get it. It's just really normal for me to think against the grain, because I was really influenced by people who thought that way, and it just became where regular stuff just kind of got on my nerves. I think if you're in control of what you're making, where you can make anything, why make what everybody else is making?
>
> For instance, I was in my kid's school once, and my two year old daughter does tap and ballet. The ballet teacher was listening to something I'd never heard before, it was instructional for kids, and they was just doing what the lady said on there. But the little sounds they had in the background I was interested in, and I kept asking about them. I asked the teacher if I could burn it, but I didn't have any CDs on me. So she ended up giving it to me.

In 2008, a pivotal moment would arrive when his sound went mainstream and Bangladesh became known – as he would be so acknowledged by MTV – as, "The maestro behind Lil Wayne's *A Milli*. Donned as, "Perhaps the most influential beat of the 21st century" according to Billboard, where the track hit

#1 on both the Hot R&B/Hip Hop Songs and Hot Rap Songs Charts, *Vibe Magazine* celebrated the smash as, "One of Wayne's most revered records of all time. A single that earned him Best Rap Solo Performance at the 2009 Grammy's and gave *The Carter III* ammunition to sell a million records it's first week of release in June 2008, *A Milli* made it's game-changing impact." Taking fans back inside the studio to recount how he first put the signature hook that became the song's sample together, Bang revealed that before Wayne ever even heard it:

> I had that sample for *A Mili* and put it in there, that was part of the beat before Wayne's vocals were on it. That's actually from *I Left My Wallet in El Segundo* Remix by A Tribe Called Quest, it was kind of a Reggae version with Phife Dog saying *A Milli*, and I sampled it into my MPC, and slowed it down to make it sound like you hear in Wayne's song.

By the time *XXL Mag* declared him, "Rap's go-to beatmaker for his enormous drums and repetitive samples that stuck in your head for months." Following the world-wide phenomenon of *A Milli*, Bangladesh was getting calls from every big name star in the business. Named one of six top urban producers at the 2010 BMI Urban Music Awards, the *L.A. Times* wrote in a feature article that Bang, "Has been slowly rising to prominence over the last decade by being the sonic mastermind behind songs from such artists as Ludacris, Ciara, Kelis, Missy Elliott, Usher, R. Kelly and Beyoncé – he was responsible for the latter's most recent singles, *Diva* and *Video Phone*." Designing *Diva* as almost the sister track to *A Milli* in the similarity they shared with a pre-placed signature hook word already in the song before Beyoncé had ever laid ears or vocals on it. Bang remembered:

> I think that was the thing to do at the time, to sing on rap beats. So I would be making rap tracks I felt like could be sung on. If you're working with a singer who doesn't have too much swag like on *Diva*, you would put more of a musical element in there to give that artist room to swing a lot. Even without the music, Beyoncé would still be singing a lot. But she got so much swag, that she didn't need the musical element. When I did the track, the word Diva was already in there just like A Mili was. Then Sean Garrett finished it, took it to her, and she rocked with it. She sat down when she recorded, and killed it.

Squeezing a lesson out of Gucci Mane's hit *Lemonade* on how his beat-making process physically goes down, Bang began as he often does producing from concept down, confirming that "In that instance, I just wrote the sample into the MPC and put it in pattern. It was really a simple beat, and he had the *Lemonade* concept already – yellow everything – and the part where you hear the hook, there were two pieces to the sample, the verse area and then the hook. That was another sample I'd had in my computer for a while, it's from *Keep It Warm* by Flo and Eddie. The hook part I just had the raw sample, it was talking about money or something and he didn't really like it, so he wrote a whole other hook to the basic beat, and I just felt like this creation needed the whole sample, the song needed the change to happen. So I just produced it afterward, instead of creatively debating with that. I knew I had to change the words to the sample, and Gucci just do what he do. You have his vocals, so you can just take them and manipulate them." Remembering the collaboration as a happy accident that found them in the studio together after:

> I happened to be in Las Vegas for an MMA fight, and got a phone call to go to Vegas to work with Gucci while I was already there! So I thought, "Man, that's crazy," so we were working out of his studio in the Casino, and with Gucci, it's just real fun and easy, because all that really has to be happening is you have to just create in front of him. That's what inspires him, and he's so creative and does it so much where when he's gonna come up with a song, it's easier to do that than playing him beats, because he wants it to really belong to him. So it's really easy with Gucci, anytime he comes to the studio, all I gotta do is really just put a couple sounds on and he got the song, and I can finish producing it later.

Tha Carter IV was the kind of rare, highly-anticipated event that is in the modern era of record sales reserved only for the industry's biggest super-stars, and Lil Wayne – just off his release from a year in jail and attracting more mainstream media attention than ever, and his project was the hottest, most in-demand producer gig in the business in the moment of its making. Contributing what would become one of the biggest hit off of the album with *6 Foot 7 Foot*, one of three Top 10 hits and evidence, in the esteemed opinion of BET, that, "The two artists have the chemistry to make hit songs." With over 3 million digital downloads and 82,331,352 views of the music video to date, Bangladesh stormed into the second decade of the millennium with another colorful example of his flair for identifying unique hook sample perfect to fit a hit. Bang shares of his inspiration for this latest collaboration with Wayne:

> 6 Foot 7 Foot is a sample from Day-O (The Banana Boat Song) by Harry Belafonte. I'd heard that song so many times before then but had never thought about sampling it. I just chopped it up and did my thing to it. I was using a drum machine software by Native Instruments called The Machine, and had that beat for a while before I actually gave it to anybody.
>
> Somebody I was talking to at this publishing company, a good friend of mine at the time, he was trying to give it to Wayne's A&R, and the dude he sent it to hit me back and was excited about it being for Wayne. It was a no-brainer for his voice, and I've always liked that Wayne's not afraid of the beat, because a lot of rappers have a sound, there's not too many rappers who can adapt to all weathers, and can get on any track and do anything to it. A lot of people who have their audience who like them for a sound, they're timid to really get outside that comfort zone, so it could have been easy for Wayne to say, "Naw, I ain't feelin' that right there," because I've heard artists do that so many times: "I feel it, I just don't know what to do to it." or "I like it, I just don't know how to come on it."

> That's what real big, established people would say, but Wayne knew what to do with it. Something massive like that, that's always what you want. Those are the impactful joints that kind of shake up the game.

Now hooked back in with Wayne and his growing Young Money Records family, which featured two of hip hop's newest multi-platinum sensations, Drake and Nicki Minaj. The latter of whom had become the genre's biggest female rap star since Lil' Kim and Foxy Brown, and Missy Elliott. Fast racking up hits inside of her debut album *Pink Friday* including the #1 Hot Rap Songs and US Rhythmic Charts single *Did It On Em'*, which reached #2 on the Billboard Hot R&B/Hip Hop Songs Chart and #25 on *Rolling Stone Magazine*'s Best 50 Songs of 2010 List. The song's success for Bangladesh was a classic example of what he points the patience a producer must acquire throughout their career as they deal with the reality that songs bounce sometimes from one artist to another for years before finding a home. Shaking his head at the *epic* game of pass-the-song the track played before finally winding up in the hands of Nicki Minaj, the producer began by affirming:

> That beat was made a long time before anybody really did it. I made the beat, and this was probably after *Tha Carter III*. Wayne was working on *Carter IV* when I sent him some beats, including that one. So a couple months went by and I hadn't heard nothing from him, and I was in a session with Game. I played Game the beat, and Game did a song to it. It was really

dope, and one of the best Game songs I'd ever heard before. It was jamming like that.

So probably a week after I did that song with Game, I was really excited about it. Then, my people that gave Wayne the beats for me, they emailed me and asked me if I still had that beat, and I knew what that meant: that he'd either already recorded it or he wanted it. So I told them Game had already recorded it. They said, "Man, Wayne recorded it too." We were trying to figure out a way to let him know that Game had already worked on it because they said that Wayne was so into the song. He was playing it for people every day when they came into the studio. So shit hit the fan! He was mad about it – he was mad at them and he was mad at me. After that, I think he went to prison, and nothing actually ever happened with Game's version either.

So next, I gave the beat to P. Diddy when he was working on his album. He liked the beat, but didn't wind up liking it enough to do it. That's when he was also managing Nicki Minaj, and he played the beat for her. Ironically, she'd already heard the beat from Wayne! But because it came through Puff, it made her feel like it was free because Puff had it, versus hearing it from Wayne. So she calls me and asked me for the beat, and told me she'd asked Wayne for it for her album. So she told me, "Wayne said I could have it." So I was cool with it. When the album was done, I saw an interview with Wayne saying that he never said she could have the beat, and that was his beat! (laughs)

Never shy about pushing boundaries, Bangladesh finally took the proverbial leap into solo artistry in 2013, dropping his first solo release in the form of the Mix Tape so impressive to the hip hop and mainstream music media that *Spin Magazine* declared that, "In another era, *Ponzi Scheme* would be a notable producer album, like Pete Rock's *Soul Survivor* series or something. It's not so much of a reminder that Bangladesh has a strong rolodex. Though, as a showcase for the diversity of his talent: he sounds as comfy putting a trap beat beneath Rihanna (*Cockiness* from 2011's *Talk That Talk*), as a 30's vaudeville sample under Trinidad James (*My Girl Pu$$y*), like the wackiness of its motif. He further establishes himself as one of the most creative and playful producers of his generation...Bangladesh, like all visionary producers...is important." A prelude to his forthcoming full-length solo debut, *Flowers and Candy*, which he built musically and conceptually around the brave artistic notion that:

> To get people to know who you are, you have to give them who you are. It's real scenarios, real stories, in the club mode, in regular song mode, just real emotional-type songs that you can relate to and understand that it ain't just party songs and how much money you got. It's real situations where somebody's going to relate to different things, and you get to know who I am, and that's how you really become an artist. You

give people who you are. That's why I named it *Flowers and Candy* because a lot of people have a misconception of how I am and who I am. So they're going to understand who I am once they hear the project.

A Grammy-winner who at this point in his career has amassed virtually every award and accolade a producer can aspire to in a career, Bang has always kept his eye on what he sees as the greatest prize: the opportunity to wake up every day and go into work doing what he loves for a living, confessing that, "I don't even think about the awards. I've been blessed to get some awards, but I was getting them unexpectedly, like, 'Damn, I got a Grammy, oh, I got another one.' It wasn't like something that was supposed to be happening, so I never really thought about it. It's cool. Not too many people got Grammys." Turning to what gets him most excited about making records once he is in the studio after so many years behind the boards, versus making a hit with yet another hip hop veteran; the producer prefers working with:

The new artists, they are fun because it's dope to break an artist, where you can say, "Man, I helped make this artist." It's kind of an accolade to have, and it's more impactful than an established artist. With an established artist, it's like, "Damn, that's dope you did that." But when you produce a hit where an artist wasn't established before, that's a whole other level. If it gets my interest, then that's what I wanna do. No matter if you're established or new, because they both help each other. You gotta stay relevant with the established artists because it gives you room to create the new.

Closing with advice for new producers themselves just starting out working with unsigned artists in bedroom, basement and garage studios. Bangladesh believes that keeping a balanced eye on the past, present, and future all at once is required to compete and succeed in the digital age of recording making:

> It's hard work that leads to other work and other opportunities. Just know your history, study the people that came before, and really know the difference between now and then. I think the respect level for it would be different, and the quality would definitely show. Just really stand out, and do something else. Don't do what everybody else's doing. You wanna be making that shit where you're standing out. And you never want to get comfortable. You always want to focus on the next thing or what the new sound is...the hottest tracks.

After recently launching his own label, Bangladesh Records, the producer has been focused on expanding his brand into new territory after he signed the Atlanta-based group Famous 2 Most. He's still saying busy with high-profile collaborations with rap legends like Ice Cube and Eminem, and maintaining an ambitious collaborations wish list including Pink, Andre 3000, Prince, Big Sean, and Kanye. His career confirmation was one of a premonition Bang had long before he first *made it*. After sustaining a longevity that is rare within his chosen profession, though the producer remains confident, it is not without the occasional reflection on just how far he's truly traveled in living that dream:

> It trips me out to know where I came from and to know that just the dream I had before was made a reality. That's the only way it trips me out. For me, I think I was so knowing where I was gonna be already, so it was kinda not a big deal when it happened. I was happy, and very into it, like, "Damn, it's happening!" But it wasn't like it was unbelievable. I feel like I'm talented enough to be on these projects, and even more to come. I definitely look forward to the opportunity and will take it all.
>
> *https://twitter.com/mrbangladesh*

CHAPTER FOURTEEN
Building the Perfect Beast – Frequency

If building the perfect beast was what producer Frequency set out to do with the making of *The Monster*, then this #1 hit in twenty countries worldwide smash would prove to be the true studio *Frankenstein*. Though the song would ultimately become the 2015 Grammy winner for Best Rap/Sung Collaboration, Frequency reveals that its journey actually began where, "The original production of the track was way, way different than what you end up hearing on the Eminem song." A wonderful demonstration of the metamorphosis a song can grow through that represents what the art of record producing is all about at heart. The hitmaker recalled of its inception:

> Basically, the original version of the track was just piano, kick drum, and a couple other little percussion sounds. When I approached that track, I was like, "Okay, this is a hip hop track, so I have to make sure that the drums hit hard and that Em can rap over it. But at the end of the day, it's a pop song, so I need to make sure it translates on radio."

Possessing precisely that kind of, "Great staying power in the mainstream music landscape," according to *The Source*, this chart Godzilla reflected a blend of musical melting pot of influences that, stripped down – *Vibe Magazine* reported – were rooted in those of the song's producer, Bryan "Frequency" Fryzel, a, "New York native...(who) perfected his craft by digging through his parent's immense collection of records. The song structures he learned from those early R&B musicians from the 1960s and 70's helped to dispel his method of 'just creating a beat' and shaped the sounds into something that'll stand the test of time. His passion for constructing those sounds can be felt on Eminem's *Monster* hit." Deconstructing *those sounds* back down into their crates from his days spinning records at college house parties, Frequency credits the platform for allowing him to begin honing his instinct for what sounded good to him versus what sounded good to the crowd. A key connection he remembers first making it:

As a DJ: it's just great to see how people react to different types of music, and when you're DJing and you're mixing different songs together. It's also interesting to kind of see the common threads between different songs and different genres that work. So whether you're playing a hip hop song and you go into a Michael Jackson song, or even something from the 70's, you can kind of see the common elements of different types of songs. Even though they're from different eras and different genres you can see what is infectious about that.

I started out in 1997 using a PC, and I had Kool Ade - that was the sampling program I used, which was pretty rudimentary - and I was just bringing samples in. I didn't have a sequencer or anything, so I was basically just pasting sounds on top of each other and consolidating them, and pasting a snare on top of what I'd consolidated. So it was a very early in my learning process. I was really into computers at a young age, so I kind of had fun with that, and then around my junior year of high school, graduated into a MPC2000 and started with that.

Learning the art of layering from the ground up, he began by building his own beats once, "I started DJing parties and high school dances, and would do remixes and stuff, find an acapella of whatever - Jay-Z or a Ludacris song that was out at the time - and do my own little remix of it and every once in a while would play it. I remember I did a couple Missy Elliott remixes just for fun. This was before Serato DJ. I'd have the Missy Elliott twelve-inch, and then I'd have my Discman hooked up to the alt of my mixer. I could basically play a CD of whatever I'd burned on my CD-R. So it was kind of hard to mix them in because I didn't have it on the record. But I would always try to throw it in a little bit just because it was cool to hear your music on a bigger stage."

Feeling bold enough to enter the famed KING OF THE BEATS competition, 2006 would prove to be the break-out year for the producer after he blew away the best the underground had to offer. Winning the competition in a moment of glory that he still marvels at as, "Definitely awesome. I think Pete Rock was one of the judges. And I met Dante Ross through that and I'm still cool with him." His phone blew up even hotter in 2008 when Snoop Dogg came calling, inviting Frequency to work on the *Blue Carpet Treatment* album. The volume got even louder on his buzz when the multi-platinum Trackmasters production team of Tone and Poke came knocking the next year, pointing to, "Probably the biggest thing that I picked up from working with them was actually making a record or song versus just making a beat. Because with Tone and Poke, we were really creating stuff from scratch with singers and songwriters in the room."

Smartly, as his name began to ring out and the phone started ringing with more opportunities to get his production style before new sets of ears across the stylistic spectrum. Frequency began branching out into collaborations with pop songwriters like local New York solo artist Bebe Rexha, who'd first emerged on the scene after winning the Best Teen Songwriter at the National Academy of Recording Arts & Sciences annual Grammy Day event, beating out 700 other contestants. Taking a chance on Rexha at a time when he was ironically starting to move away from a focus on hip hop production in favor of pop. Frequency's gamble would eventually pay off for both he and Bebe when the song became the biggest rap crossover hit on the Hot 100 pop charts of the year once Eminem got his hands on it:

> Really the way that song worked was we were working with this artist, BeBe Rexha, whose a pop artist. We were working on stuff for her. She wasn't signed at the time. She was just an artist I thought was really talented. And we had done a couple dance records and had done a ballad, but not hip hop at all. We were working on a song for her, and basically the way I work now is I'm not working with a lot of rappers as much. I've been really doing more pop stuff, where usually the most important elements are the melody and the song, like the track is kind of secondary.

> So when I'm working on a track like that, everything I'm doing is in consideration of the chorus, so it's not like, "Here's a track with a vocal on top of it," it's more like, "Okay, this is an amazing chorus. How can I best support it with the track, and not get in the way of it?" So we'd done the song, and I knew Regan Mouralis at Shady Records for about ten years. He was one of the first people I met when I used to try and shop beats in New York. We had a party at the studio - it might have been a holiday or something. We were having a couple of beers, hanging out, and I said, "Oh, let me play you

this song I'm working on," and played him the original full song with verses and bridge, etc. But it was all sung, it wasn't a rap song. His reaction was, "This is great man. If you wanted to make it a hip hop track, I think it would work great for Eminem. He's working on a new project..." So I went back to everyone I'd collaborated with on the song, and said, "This is an amazing opportunity. Are you all down for it?" Because it was originally a song for Bebe, and I wanted to make sure everyone was cool with me trying to take it in another direction.

Not surprisingly, everyone involved in the song's writing voted to green light the song's reinvention, and it was a challenge Frequency had been training for years as he constructed an amalgamation of instrumentation that would dazzle critics from front to back and coast to coast and put the producer's name on the international map. ABC News hailed the song as a, "Career highlight" while *The Source* – long regarded as among the most coveted endorsements an aspiring producer can hope to be blessed with – trumpeted the, "Pop-oriented, upbeat track as possessing all the production ingredients required for great staying power in the mainstream music landscape." It was a prediction that would prove true for both the hit and its creator. Knowing this was his shot at the big time, Bryan rolled up his sleeves and quickly got down to work after I got the nod from the team. The only things from the original version I left on that was her chorus vocals and the piano, and I just kind of built the track from there. I haven't been on an MPC in about six or seven years, so everything for that song was entirely done in Pro Tools. I basically use Battery as my MPC for drums, it's kind of laid out the same way. I use Pro Tools because now when I'm making tracks, I'm making tracks at the same time. I'm recording vocals at the same time while I'm mixing. So I need to have everything in the same place:

> The piano is from Alicia Keys, a Kontakt piano library that she sponsored. A lot of the other instrumentation you hear I'm running through different plug-ins to get different sounds. So like a guitar-amp simulator or distortion, and I'm using a lot of filters, so there's a lot of filtering that goes in there with a lot of different sounds running and out. Then the guitars were all recorded live. Basically, I had the track done with the piano, a bunch of synths – including a pitched 808 on the chorus and I would have used Battery for that. Some strings using L8 scoring strings, which is a string library for Kontakt, and a Trilion for the bass – the drums, and then laid the guitars live on top of it, which were done D.I.

Perhaps most impressive from an instrumental study is the blueprint for the track's rhythmic foundation that Frequency designed, solid enough to keep the song sitting atop the Billboard Hot 100 Singles chart for four straight weeks. Built upon personalized patterns of beatwork designed around a wall of sound concept where, "That drum track is really lots of layers of different sounds, so there's one snare that start's a verse. And then half-way through the verse, there's another snare that comes in underneath it. You don't really hear it but you feel it. There's probably four kicks on the main part of the song, and I usually have one kick that's going to give me the tone of what the kick should be. Basically, the main kick sound, and then I'll have another kick underneath that that's going to give me more of a sub-punch to it. It doesn't really have a tone or note to it, but is just kind of for the sub. Then on the chorus, I'll usually have a couple more kicks where I take all the lows out. I am using that for more of an attack. So when you listen to the song, the drums are punchy in the verse, but they hit a lot more in the chorus. That's because I'm adding another layer of kicks." Along the way to finding the perfect blend within his beatscape, the producer put his ears to work:

> Playing with the frequencies, so some of them have all the lows out so it's just the high part of the kick you're hearing, and vice versa, some have all the highs out so it's just the low part of the kick, so ultimately I'm trying to make it sound like one kick, but I'm using different kicks to make that sound.

> Then when you get to the chorus, there's maybe three or four other snares and then a clap. Then another clap with a really long reverb, and then a clap with a really short reverb. It's really just layering sounds in a way where you're not really hearing that there's a new snare there. But there is, and it's just kind of moving along. That's one of the things I learned from pop records is that every two or three bars, we have something new happening. Even if you're not really paying attention to it, there's a little hi-hat coming in or a new kick sound.

It's kind of like subliminal thing to keep your attention, so it was really about adding all these little elements as the song goes. There's really no part of the instrumental that repeats, so basically during every of loop of something there's something new that's happening even if you're not really hearing it. Then near the end of the song when it goes into the little dub-step breakdown, that's a completely different drum kit, completely different snares and kicks.

Happy to hand the song's mixing off to the studio shaman who'd first framed the sonics of Eminem's sound, the legendary Dr. Dre, who Frequency revealed he technically had the opportunity to share mixing duties after. "They called me and said, 'Dre's mixing the song in a couple of days, and he mixes on an SSL board so they have a limited number of tracks because they're using hardware.' So basically, what they said was, 'Instead of us trying to figure out what should be louder and what should be softer,' because they were going to have to bounce things down to stems. I had like eighty-five tracks and they had to go down to forty. So basically what I did was I pre-mixed some of the parts. Some of the guitars were blended the way I wanted them to be, and some of the snares – if I had five or six snares – I was blending them down to two snares, and some of the hi-hats and sweeps and other effect sounds and my plug-ins to send to them. So I condensed my mix of the track down to foty stereo tracks, sent that to them, and then Dre did the final mix of the song, probably two weeks before it was released!" Not daring to vocalize any private nit-picking he naturally was prone to after putting such concentrated layers of time into the song's production, Frequency confessed:

> The first time I heard the finished mix, it was kind of overwhelming in so many respects because being a perfectionist, all I was hearing was "Aw, I wish this was louder, or I wish this was that," so I wasn't really focused on the fact that, "Okay, Eminem and Rhianna, these are pretty much two of the biggest artists ever in our generation, and they're on my song." That's just kind of my nature. But after that, it was just an amazing experience to hear something that I worked on in my little cave be on the radio.

> To me, the success of that record, along obviously with Eminem rapping the verses, is really the melody on the chorus, that's kind of what carries a pop song to the top of the charts is the melody. I saw YouTube videos of little 5-year-old kids singing the chorus who don't know about anything other than the melody. So it really attests to how important melody is. You can really put it in any box you want, whether it's a hip hop song or a pop song, or a dance song, and at the end of the day, it's really that melody that puts it over the top, in my opinion.

With the success of *The Monster*, while Frequency had the option to focus his creative currency on scoring more work with hip hop's biggest acts of the day. He instead poured his passions into expanding his production pallet into the rock arena with

The MisterWives, a NYC-based rock band whose *Frequency* produced debut Billboard would excitedly conclude, "Matches big ambition with an even bigger sound," with a sonic spectrum that is, "Bursting with rock'em, sock'em action!" Cracking the Top 40 on the Top 200 Album Chart and Top 10 on the U.S. Alternative Albums chart, Bryan recalled that in switching hats from hip hop to pop rock, "The way I produced most of their full-length debut, it's something I hadn't done previously because everything is for the most part live. There's some programming, but we're recording live drums, live guitar, live bass, live horns, and we're recording snaps and claps in my bathroom because there's that cool reverb on it. On their first album too, so we were all experimenting together. And it was really nice to not really have any rules to work within."

MTV would rank their *Reflections* single one of their Best Pop Songs of 2015 and a "favorite summer anthem." The risk paid off. It has been not only the trend, but the bedrock. Equally a launching pad for *Frequency's* success as a producer. It's a foundation he proudly stands behind in dispensing advice to the newest generation of hip hop producers who hit him up for advice on Twitter or in person: *NETWORK, NETWORK, NETWORK.* Reasoning that while, "Obviously, talent is important, you have to have talent." The ability to match the upbeat mood of your music with an equally buoyant, team-player-esque personal impression is, "Probably applicable to any business or industry, is that it's really about people and how you interact with them. In this business, reputations spread really quickly. So for me, it's really about building relationships – especially being a producer. You kind of are a therapist in some sense trying to coach a performance out of an artist or get them to step outside their comfort zone, or get someone to feel comfortable to make a mistake. Because that's when you can come up with some of your best stuff in my opinion: when you're not thinking and are just kind of fucking around and a happy accident hits you. In order to get someone to feel that relaxed, you have to be personable as a producer. I really think it comes down to people skills and how you interact and collaborate with people. It goes beyond just relationships with artists and other collaborators, and kind of goes to the business too. Because you have A&R and music executives who if you're friendly with and they like you, goes a long way toward getting you production work. For instance, with Shady Records, so you never know how a relationship when you meet somebody is going to pay off down the road. So you need to treat every relationship you make in the industry like, 'This could be the one that's going to change my life.'"

Another clue to cracking the code for the kind of repeat success Frequency has achieved throughout his career thus far comes with his commitment to thinking outside the box with the chances he takes as a producer. Treating every new studio sojourn as an opening to take his ears somewhere new musically and sonically versus finding a comfortable corner, the leaps of faith he's taken so far have paid off handsomely in affording him the freedom to repeat the ride over again in a business that gives many producers only one such victory lap. As this one continues to rack up hits across the stylistic landscape, his ambition remains as pure as the day he first took the chance on the career with the same probability of success as making it into the NBA, but a shot Frequency has always been willing to chase no matter the risks for the love of:

> Being able to do different things in the studio. I really like going outside of my comfort zone, in a sense, and just doing things that I don't think I

can do or wouldn't have normally done a couple of years ago. So I'm really always looking for something different. Whenever it's something where, "I don't think I can do that," I wanna try it.

https://twitter.com/freqshowmusic

"I love challenges in the studio!" – Sir Mix-a-Lot, 2017

CHAPTER FIFTEEN
The King of *BOOM* – Sir Mix-a-Lot

Long before the millennial laptop generation, hip hop fathered the original bedroom record producers. Absent the digital technology that does ninety percent of the physical work these days, the process back in 1987 was a literal laboratory of experimentation and imagination that came off of the streets and spilled out in the beats. That widened the eyes of visionaries like Sir Mix-a-Lot who assembled through a D.I.Y. process of trial and error. Finding organic creative connections with technology that had revolutionary sonic implications as a new sound was first shaped on tape., Mix-a-Lot recalls a chaotic creative bedroom backdrop where:

> It was a sonic freakshow! Take *Swass* that was pretty interesting in that you could tell I was learning as I was doing it. The record sounds so sparse, I didn't even know what a compressor was, and I didn't use any compressors on the record anywhere! So it sounds really kind of thin and doesn't smack and hit radio like most records of that era. That being said, it made the record unique in some kind of twisted way, kind of like the three-headed guy at the circus or something.

Reminiscent of a sci-fi movie backdrop where a new robot is assembled out of old parts, Mix produced a new sound that blended New Wave influences like wildly influential genre godfathers Kraftwerk. The legendary German Electronic synth-pop band would have a massive influence on producers like Mix-a-Lot who credits the group with being the primary reason, "That I decided I could do music, that's where it came from literally, because I saw they didn't have a band, they had these little pencils hitting these things that looked like oil cans and boxes and sound was coming out. I was like, 'Wait a minute, these guys don't have a band,' and I fell in love with it. I mean, if you listen to all that early Afrika Bambaataa and all that Scorpio stuff, Grand Master Flash, that's all influenced by Kraftwerk. Nobody wants to give them credit, but that's bullshit man, because those guys – to me – they were the ones that let me know that I could do music. James Brown was a big influence, and obviously Bootsy Collins was the *main* influence behind Mix-a-Lot *the character*, because I grew up around pimps. That's what I grew up around and I heard a lot of game. And Bootsy Collins had game, so he was my influence on the character, but Kraftwerk was the one: when I saw that technology, I've always been a technology guy, always. I've been building amplifiers and power supplies since I was fifteen years old from scratch. So what happened was, when Kraftwerk let me know things were accessible. Now, I was trying to figure out how do I do this." Starting at the foundation, Mix-a-Lot remembered before any other musical element, his ear was not surprisingly drawn first-and-foremost to:

> Dabbling around with drum machines, and I remember I couldn't afford back then a two-track cassette recorder, that was still $1,000. So I started to figure out, "How can I make songs when I can't afford a multi-track machine, which I don't even know how to use..." So the very first Dr. Rhythm drum machine that Roland made was called a DR-55. I bought one of those, and I bought two cassette decks and a mixer from Radio shack – long before the Flashformer I had already made a Transformer. So what I started to do was I took the DR-55 and a raggedy synthesizer I still own called a 'Moog Prodigy.' I would do passes through the mixer and take the cassette deck and record a pass. Then, I'd take my other cassette deck and play that last pass and dump in another pass. I would do it live, and it sound like shit obviously because after you copy

something five, six times, it sounds like snow.
But necessity also bred creativity, so I learned the
high-end pieces I recorded first. And the bass
pieces I'd record last because it was hip hop and I
wanted thunder. You start understanding
frequencies when you didn't even know they
were called frequencies yet. And that's how it
started for me.

Laughing looking back at the fact that he did so much with
so little, Mix-a-Lot reveals that, "Half the record I recorded on
four-track cassette. Then half-way through, I made enough
money doing live performances and stuff like, that the other half
of the record was recorded on a Fostex quarter-inch eight-track!"
Free to wheel in whatever direction his muse pulled him back in
hip hop's open range days when innovations were made with
next to nothing by comparison to today's digital world of
endless virtual plug-ins, as he bumped toward the thumping
BOOM that drove the classic *Posse on Broadway*, Mix had to first
speed past the limitation that came with reality:

I didn't have access to any good equipment, but
necessity breeds creativity, so when I was making
that track, I remember had an 808 by then, and
the 808 was a very expensive machine at that
time, but were kind of archaic: what was in by
then was the Linn drum and the DMX, so what I
did was had an 808, an Oberheim DMX, I had
the Fostex eight-track, I had a Jupiter 6 and a
Juno 6. I didn't have Midi then, so we were
using what they called Synch, which wasn't very
nice. Synch and the SMPTE, you had so much

bleed in a quarter-inch reel to reel, and when you use a SMPTE track, it just bled all over the track, so you couldn't do that either. So I wanted to use an 808, but the 808 drum machine I had was one where sometimes, the tempo map would fuck up and then it started to wander, so you'd be in the middle of the song and the damn thing would go from 90 bpm down to 85, and it kind of screwed up your track.

So what I did is, I found – again in a second-hand store – a chips-burner. You could burn stuff onto microchips, and in the back of it, it had a sound input! I remember, I was like, "What the hell is this?" So anyway, I took my microchips out of my Oberheim DMX, found out what chips they were and went out, and bought empty chips. And I thought I would have to format them, but I didn't. I ended up putting the 808 sounds in my DMX. *Nobody had ever done that* before me, and that's where the sound came from. I took the 808, put it in the DMX, and programmed *Posse on Broadway*.

Back then too, I programmed all my own songs, I didn't – and don't – believe in playing the same loop over and over and over. All of my parts were programmed and laid out. And I did a lot of things that came from my DJ roots. For instance, I would often like to improvise words by programming punches wherever the words were. So you hear all of that stuff with it. All of

that was programmed via DMX *without a click*
and tracked directly to the Fostex. I wrapped
everything from there. It was literally two-
tracks. I didn't have enough tracks to spread
them out obviously, so I just recorded the two
tracks right off of the DMX. Then, I recorded
my vocals, and that was it.

An enormously influential single and album for hip hop,
Mix-a-Lot correctly crowned himself the, "King of the Beat in
the great Northwest" on the title track *Swass*. Another of his
signature hits that *Sound Magazine* noted, "Successfully sets the
immature tone of the album –exploding through your speakers –
as Mix-a-Lot's sonic alter ego arrives, rapping with a mechanized
helium effect confessing his adoration for buttermilk biscuits.
The shenanigans by no means stop there. Throughout the
album, Mix impersonates a sci-fi, intercom robot, his own posse
of women and a Middle Eastern gold jeweler all before his
insightful piece, *Square Dance Rap*." In creating this wildly-
inventive cast of characters to populate the albums' songs, the
producer revealed a unique method by which he first demoed a
potential voice before laying it to tape, uniquely keeping in mind
how it would sound as an end-product in the same time:

I listen to songs all of the time. I think the best
way to listen to a song if you want to get an
influence and not steal it, is drive by a person in
a car whose playing music with the doors closed.
There's something about the way you hear the
song, it's not the same, because you don't hear
the high end. As an example, *Swass* directly came
from Prince's *Kiss*. How did I hear *Kiss*? I heard

it on the street in a guy's car, a Cadillac Eldorado – I remember it like it was yesterday. It was turned up really loud and all you could hear through the doors was that hypnotic bass and rhythm track. That's what it sounded like. And I was like, "What is that?" I didn't know it was *Kiss* until he rolled the windows down. What I did was took my little walkman out and mumbled just that into the little recorder it had on it, went home, and obviously I couldn't use the gallop that Prince used. So basically I just literally kept that part I'd mumbled onto the walkman radio and put it on the song. So when you listen to *Swass*, you hear this horrible beat box of me mumbling the rhythm of *Kiss*. That's all I was doing. And I took my Prodigy and played that little signature keyboard part and that was it. But it all came from Prince's *Kiss*. When I tell people that, they say it doesn't sound anywhere near the same. But if you mix them on two turntables at the same time, they mix perfectly! (laughs)

What's also funny is that, when you produce yourself, you're almost never happy. Specifically, I remember how frustrated I was doing that album because I couldn't figure out what delivery was right. So on the song *Swass* for instance, I'm mimicking Sgt. Slaughter or somebody, and I'd listen to that and go, "No, I don't really like that." Then I was listening to the Beastie Boys and obviously *Paul Revere* and

Slow and Low was a heavy influence on *Posse on Broadway*," that's where I felt I could do that clear, kind of nasally delivery that Ad-Rock had, and that influenced me. That *One lonely Beastie I be*. I could do that *perfectly*, like real clear. I started copying him initially. When I did *Posse on Broadway* the second time, I got rid of the kind of Ad-Rock inflections, the nasally kind of sound, and came up with my own thing. I kind of settled on that as a vocal style until *I Got Game*, which is where Rick Rubin really brought out a better delivery in me...much better. I can't even remember if I did many backing vocals on *Posse on Broadway*, I think I only did one back-up vocal track. On the chorus track, what I did was I ping-ponged a bunch of stuff in the eight-track, so you hear just a bunch of me (laughs).

As part of the original bedroom studio generation, Mix-a-Lot literally turned his into one, tracking the actual vocals that wound up on GOLD-selling singles like *Posse on Broadway*, *Swass*, and *Square Dance Rap*. By building his own make-shift vocal booth, chuckling at his inventive improvisation where, "What I did was, my mom had a lot of wool blankets and stuff. I was trying to figure out how to record my vocals where I wouldn't get this slapping noise off the walls. I couldn't afford the little Styrofoam eggshells, so I took those big old wool blankets and I would hang them. One side would be my head and one side would be the mic stand. And I dropped the mic down so that you couldn't hear the blanket rubbing against the bed. I would literally record the lyric living in the projects under a blanket. That's exactly how I did it!" Already wearing the kinds of multiple hats at once that all innovative producers do, Mix acted not only as an artist and a producer, but engineer synchronously recounting a master class in multi-tasking where:

> I recorded all of my own vocal tracks on that album. It's interesting because, back then I didn't have a lot of money, so I had a couple SM-58s, a couple of SM-57s, and then I had this weird little Senheisser mic – it had a gold face on one side and a black one on the other – and I used that. The reverb I used was just a RadioShack Realistic Reverb. It wasn't the spring reverb, it was kind of a goofy, hybrid digital spring thing in a little black box. That's what I used.

> From there I came up with creative ways of making an SM-58 kind of sound like it was recorded professionally, with A LOT of EQ. I had a 31-band EQ that I'd gotten from a second-hand store, an old Peavey – I had two of them, and still have them actually – one for each side, because they were mono. So I had thirty-one bands of EQ, but I didn't have anything to excite the vocal. No compression, so I really started to learn a lot about when EQ is necessary. It's more of a subtractive method that works as opposed to adding it. Everybody that buys an EQ for the first time, it's always there just adding frequency. Before you know it, you just turn everything up 3DB. That's all you do.

Much like fellow West Coast pioneering rap producer Dr. Dre, who has for years admitted hating the sound of his own voice on tape, Sir Mix-a-Lot divulges the truth that he, "Actually started producing other acts because I didn't want to rap. Most producers don't want to, because I had more fun as a DJ because that's what I did. I used to rock turntables and all of that stuff, so I didn't really want to rap. So I did *Square Dance Rap* because I didn't want to use my voice. What I did was took my Polaris four-track cassette deck, turned the speed all the way up. It had three recording speeds and I turned it wide open, and recorded all the music at high speed. It sounded normal. Then, I turned everything all of the way down to low speed. I delivered my vocals, so it sounded like a Smurf. And I used this country accent because I didn't want anybody to know it was me. So I created this little Smurfy character and it was this stupid ass song. But I had my friend Nester Rodriguez, who was also a DJ up at K-PAC. He put it on the radio and it hit! So now I was like, 'Oh my God! How am I going to perform this shit live?' Because it was kind of a joke after I'd gotten the idea of doing a live square dance record. Obviously, I couldn't start a career doing Smurf voices, that wouldn't last very long." Knowing he had his own unique tone, Mix set out on a search that would ironically improve his skills as a producer. In the same time agreeing:

> I was still trying to find myself. I started to experiment with different deliveries, and of course I was copying people – copying Run-D.M.C., copying the Beastie Boys – just looking for something... Some kind of a cadence or style, and to be honest with you – and I'm jumping ahead a bit – but I really didn't find that style until after *"Posse on Broadway," "My Hooptie,"*

and a song I did Rick Rubin noticed called *I Got Game*. He called me, and said, "That song, there's a very unique delivery, that's clear. It's clean. You're not trying to sound New York. You're not trying to sound L.A. You use slang and it's very creative in the way you use it. It doesn't sound like anybody else." So that's who really dialed me in as far as what I wanted to do vocally from that point on – but that's where it came from.

Crowds seemed to be reacting with more favorable reviews of Mix-a-Lot's animated vocal entertainment on the mic, still getting the shivers today when he share the still-amazing memory of the first time he confirmed he had chemistry with the crowd, a connection that began not at his first show, but rather out on the tour where he'd been product-testing his sound around the West Coast. A rush artists describe like no other to watch fans embracing their sound for the first time, for Mix, the experience was no less adrenaline-filled:

I never will forget it. Fresno, California, 1987, I remember it like it was yesterday: we were playing a place called the Wilson Theatre, and *Square Dance Rap* was the song I thought everybody liked. Which, let's be honest, I was a little bit ashamed of, because it was a gimmick. I was like, "Ah man, I don't want to be known for a gimmick!" So we went through our set, and *Posse on Broadway* was the second to last song. Once they heard the cowbells, I could hear people clapping. When that Godzilla noise that I did with my mouth through an old shitty harmonizer, that wasn't good for anything. But I would literally mimic Godzilla and lower the pitch on the harmonizer. The little thing that introduces each bar, that's where that came from. So when I did that, the crowd went NUTS! And I'm thinking somebody else is in the building, like, *Did Prince just walk in? What the fuck just happened?!* It really threw me off and I messed up all of the words because I was so blown away because now the crowd was singing the lyrics. I never will forget it.

The song became a ganger's favorite. Gang members were driving down the street playing *Posse on Broadway* LOUD. It was really cool. At the same time, it was interesting, because it was also blowing up with what we used to call, "The desired demographic," aka the white suburban teenager. I remember being in my studio, thinking, *Okay, this Square Dance Rap, this'll get the white kids.* And boy was I wrong! *Posse on Broadway* and another song I remember going to the suburbs to perform that they loved was *Rippn.* They would go crazy man! Then, I learned that an artist should never try to predict what the crowd is gonna like, because you're never gonna be right. You'll be full of shit every time!

Mix-a-Lot had actually began performing years earlier not behind the mic, but rather behind the turntables as a DJ, a common lineage of so many peer producers of his generation who got a priceless education on every fundamental tenant of record production. From developing an ear for what beats, grooves and hooks got the crowd going before their eyes all dependent on what records they spun and mixed, to the physical side of putting on a show performance entertaining a crowd, to the technical side of working a mixer and the turntables themselves, and developing a reference sample library to draw creativity from in the studio, Mix also credits DJing with giving him his professional stage name, an obvious reference to his royalty behind the wheels of steel:

> *Sir Mix-a-Lot* was kind of a DJ thing. I always thought Lancelot the character was just the ultimate pimp. That was an easy one there, so I kind of hung on to it. I got my first turntable back in 1981, and it was a belt-driven turntable. Obviously scratching was kind of harder, so what did was I took wax paper and put it under the belt. Well, initially the wax paper had too much spin where I couldn't release the rivet properly when I was trying to cut stuff in. So what I did is, I cut another piece of wax paper out and I intentionally put holes in it, so the felt could grab at various points. It would slip, but grab also when I had to tweak a cut forward. So that's what I had: two belt-driven turn tables and a Realistic mixer with this transformer button I put on it.

> There were no high school dances back then. Because remember, hip hop was so new then

that nobody over twenty-five wanted to touch it. So I did the Rotary Boys Club, which I grew up right up the street from. I grew up on 19th and right in the middle of the hood. I made my own speakers – I bought subwoofers and mid-ranges, a saw and made speakers. And I would take them up to the Boys Club at night and we'd do these parties. All of the money would go to the kids to play basketball and all of that. I didn't care about money. I just wanted to DJ. That's where I first learned to understand crowds and being a DJ really helps with music. It helps you to understand crowds and what moves them and what doesn't.

Many scratches on the turntable later, after *Posse on Broadway* cruised to #70 on the Billboard Hot 100 Singles Chart, a respectable debut given how new hip hop itself was to mainstream chart success at the time. Mix-a-Lot was now officially on the map. Shifting into high gear to keep refining his production craft as he invested like any hungry producer not in *bling*. "GEAR! I remember how thirsty I was for more gear. And I was hoping I could make money, so I could have a real studio. If you see my studio now, it looks like a five million dollar studio. I got so much shit in there I don't even know half of it. But back in that era, I was limited, but quite anal actually about how I recorded. The process was one where I just kept coming up with stuff until something worked. I just didn't have the right gear. So I'm actually ashamed sonically of that record. But I'm proud of it because I look at it like, 'God damn, I was just a kid man!'" Just twenty-three years old and already Seattle's head hip hop standard bearer, Mix-a-Lot was out to prove his sound was one that would reverberate for years to come out of hip hop's speakers, confirming:

> I come from Seattle, so everybody has always thought, "He's a flash in the pan, the guy got lucky. Blah blah blah." But I was always about making business decisions that moved me forward. For instance, rather than a fancy car, the first thing I bought when I got a check was my studio: I bought a MCI two-inch sixteen track because it sounded better than the two-inch twenty-four track by far. It got more room on the head. So I bought two of those and I synched them together, bought a big old Soundcraft mixing board, and all of that stuff back in the day. I knew my true love was making music. I couldn't keep paying one hundred and fifty dollars per tape and two hundred dollars an hour to do something that is really a hobby you happen to make money at. So I said, "Okay, I'm gonna buy that first," and I've always re-invested in myself.

Someone else who was invested in Mix-a-Lot's potential was visionary record man Rick Rubin, who Mix credits with, "Playing a HUGE part in my career. There was something he saw in me I didn't see, and Rick Rubin, for me, taught me the difference between making mediocre songs and huge fucking hits." Knowing Mix was on to one when he listened to some of the producer's early demos for what would become his first #1 hit, *Baby Got Back*. A song whose production and vocal performance simultaneously made Mix a Grammy winner for

Best Solo Rap Performance. Long before the awards and platinum plaques, Mix revealed that versus the booty-shaking club banger that wound up taking radio and dance floors by storm:

> This is gonna crack you up, but initially, *"Baby Got Back"* was a slow song. I'm talking about *Posse on Broadway* slow! Because keep in mind, other than *Rippin,* "Before *Baby Got Back* I was known for songs like *My Hooptie* and *Beepers.* Slow, heavy tracks. So that was where I was going with the original version of *Baby Got Back,* and then Rick Rubin – in the midst of the album – took up-tempo, and had actually said that very thing: "We need something up-tempo." Initially, he kept pointing to *I Got Game,* which remember, he had signed me for. And also referenced another song I did previously called *Attack on the Stars.* That was the dumbest song I did in my life, and a desperate attempt at attention. But I knew we needed to hit it out of the park on this album, and I was more open to his input. So next he said, "Give me something fast." That's when I went back to my Kraftwerk roots and started coming up with some different stuff.

His studio was even more sweet by then as he'd kept investing the majority of the money he made from live gigs and royalties into upgrading his equipment from *Seminar,* which was recorded on two sixteen-track two-inch tape decks that were synched together – talk about a headache – and after that album,

I'd taken the few bucks I had and bought a digital recording system called 'The Atom' made by Akai. It used those Sony Hi8 video tapes. So it was twelve tracks per Atom. I had two of those machines synched together to create twenty-four tracks, and I was using a big old Peavey board. I compared it to my Soundcraft and it actually sounded better. So with the Atoms it was early digital recording, but not as refined obviously as it is today." One fundamental element of Mix-a-Lot's production style that he remained loyal to throughout his beat-making career was his beloved:

> AKAI sampler, which I stayed with for years. By then, I had also gotten my hands on an MPC-2000 and an MPC-60. In building the beat for *Baby Got Back*, what I did was to start out was obviously with just the regular 808. It sounded so much like *Rippin* that it was kind of boring. I remember thinking, "I've got to do something different here." So what I started to do then was layer snares together. First, I took the body of an 808 snare, kind of toned down, and then sampled a second 808 snare that was kind of toned high. Then I rode the competing frequency off of the high one. So in other words, if there was something resonant in the low one that I really liked, say at around the 400 mark, I would do a hard 24db slope right at the 400 mark on the *higher* snare. So really, it made the 808 snare sound like two times bigger. But not louder, just wider.

Then I took my mouse, and literally mimicked a crash on an open hi-hat, and put that over top of the snare. It had this really sloppy effect going where every snare sounded like a weird kind of a crash. That really gave the song a lot more energy. But it was still just, "Boom, splash, boom, splash!" That's all it was. So then I started to dabble around listening to a few Kraftwerk songs for influence. There were a couple in particular that just grabbed me. So from there, I started to do something that I've been doing for years, which was to program these weird, syncopated pieces. Instead of doing them in eights, I did them in sixteenths. Then ran that through the whole damn song man. Then, I started picking up little horn stabs, because I wanted something to kind of break it up so it didn't sound Techno-y. Then I added a little bass line, and oddly enough, the idea for the bass line came from that same Kraftwerk song. So that's where *Baby Got Back* came from. It was a hodge-podge where I introduced these new musical elements along with using a lot of my sounds from the past, including the 808 cowbell. And keep in mind, the 808 cowbell was *not* very popular in 1992. Then I added a little bit of 808 rim-shot, and used all of the 808 cymbals, and hi-hats. Really a traditionally 808 kit.

A song that got the bass in the boom box, bedroom stereo or car wolfers shaking as much as the ladies backsides on dance floors all over the world, Mix-a-Lot, long a scientist of BOOM, spills the studio secret that to ensure maximum speaker rattle resonation. "Another thing I did do was brought in kind of a regular kind of gated kick drum, and what I would use that for was, by then, a lot of people were listening to music on different things in that era, and I noticed that in a small speaker, an S-10 or something like that, all you could hear from the 808 was just a hum, but there was no impact. So I took a gated kick drum, and rolled it off at about fifty hertz so it didn't compete with the 808 hum, and I kind of brightened it. I had the old Aural Exciter Type Cs back in the day, and I would run that kick out and go through those Type Cs, and then come back in to brighten the kick up. So every time you heard the 808 kick go 'BOOOMMM,' you also had a little short gated, powerful kick. And I turned it way down to like half-volume, which also gave the kick a little bit of impact when you were listening through small speakers or a stock car radio of that era, etc."

Looking back at his years signed to Rick Rubin's Def American Records as almost a University-level education in both the record business itself and most importantly for Mix-a-Lot personally, where Rubin's tutelage was concerned, record production. Pointing to the most important sonic lessons he took away from working with one of hip hop production's true pioneering godfathers as beginning with, "Frequency, for Rick, it was very important because he hears differently. I think he hears in chunks, based on how he used to articulate what he wanted me to try. Like, 'If you do this here,' or 'I think it's a great song, however, I'd try something different on this. Maybe this, move this over here, take that out,' and you think he's butchering your song! I'll give you an example, a lot of the punchlines in *Baby Got Back*, he called me on the phone and said, 'I want you to accentuate the punchlines,' and I was like, 'What the hell does that mean? What do you mean accentuate? Say them louder?' I didn't know what he meant, so I started yelling the punchlines, and he called me back and said, 'You didn't do anything to the song,' and I said, 'You said accentuate.' But what he meant was 'drop outs.' So if you listen to *Baby Got Back*, you'll hear the punchlines of the song – which when I think back now, this might have made that song a hit – because every time there was a poignant line, a line that everybody's gonna remember, I dropped the music out. That was all Rick Rubin, and he'd said, 'Any time you have a punch line, I want you to smack all the music out' and at first I said, 'A little bit?', and he said, 'No, all of it.' At the time, I remember I was just blown away, like, 'Dude, you're gonna fuck up my song!' But boy oh boy was I wrong. That guy is a genius."

Always a brilliant director of the characters he co-starred on his records, whether they were Mix-a-Lot playing multiple personalities on one album or guest-stars like the white girls whose forever funny parody opened the song, the producer discloses that versus being plotted out from the start, the hit was in fact a surprise last minute addition, so much so that *Baby Got Back* was done. It did not have that intro in it, and I'd taken it down to Rick. He liked the song as it was, and so did my manager Ricardo. But I had this idea of something I still wanted to add as a finishing touch, because at that time, *Valley Girls* were really popular. I mean, they were everywhere, you saw Valley Girls all over the place saying, 'Like Oh my God!' So I came up with this idea because I wanted to make a serious point without *scaring* people, and my thinking at the time was, 'How do I let people know this is not just a song about butts, that this is a song about America's perception of the African-American physique?' So ultimately I thought, 'How better to lay that out than to take the absolute, most comical version of America at that time, which was the Valley Girl, and super-impose that over this song that describes my love of for African-American female posterior?!'"

Mix's hometown paper, *The Seattle Times*, saluted the wildly entertaining sketch for its success in, "A serious message despite its playful tone," and as he pulls the curtain back on his memory of coaching the two girls heard talking in his own studio as he produced their performance. He knew to be truly poignant that it had to be perfect:

> So when you hear the white female voice sarcastically come in at the top of the song with that, "Oh, my, God Becky, look at her butt, it is so big...rap guys' girlfriends." All of that came from me. Now I had to put that on the track in a way that made everybody feel good and the song needed a story. At the time, the girl that actually did the part, I was dating. She had that physique, so talk about a narrative (laughs)! But everything came together perfectly and that's how that part was born. I just got her in the studio, and coached her on what to say, "Okay, we're going to try this, this and this. I need it to sound like this, say this and that." I'm a controlling cat in the studio because I like shit just right.
>
> I recorded the vocal for *Baby Got Back* on an AKG 414 microphone. I didn't want to use the old vintage U 87, because I don't like microphones that color my voice. Some people love that. They love the warm or smooth

sound, but I don't. I just want an honest delivery. The 414 at *that time* was the best microphone for my voice because it had this inherent flaw, which was this little natural DPS at around 800 hertz to 2K because my voice has a nasally twang to it. So obviously it was just a natural roll-off. That's why I started using that microphone.

Celebrated years later by Billboard as a, "Pop culture touchstone," for the fearless subject matter mix so stylishly tackled within the lyrical landscape. The song has stayed relevant as arguably the boldest statement on the subject through the years. Even as recently as 2016, major news outlets like CBS News, *Vanity Fair*, *Cosmopolitan*, and *The Hollywood Reporter*. They threw the song back into the headlines widely running a story where *HR* highlighted the fact that, "Sir Mix-a-Lot's Grammy winning hit *Baby Got Back* may be twenty-four years old — but the song is still as relevant as ever. With the ongoing conversation about beauty and body-type ideals, specific lyrics, as well as the general sentiment of the song (that some men like big butts and cannot lie), continually resurface in pop culture. Both Katy Perry and Khloe Kardashian, two women known for celebrating their curves, were praised when they cheekily referenced the line, 'L.A. face with an Oakland booty' on social media (Perry in 2012, Kardashian in 2015)." Stepping back into the headspace he was in while working on the song's lyric, Mix-a-Lot opens up, explaining:

I work alone because I'm kind of a recluse like that. So on the lyrics, and this is kind of the spooky part, I – prior to having pop success –

had no idea that the majority of America didn't like girls with curves. When I found that out, I was *shocked*, like, "REALLY?!" Because I'd seen Dolly Parton, and thought, "Oh, the white guys agree with us." But it suddenly became obvious that wasn't the case when I started casting girls for my music videos and we were using Hollywood directors, because the Hollywood directors would always screen out the girls *with the curves*. We're talking the late 80's, early 90's now pre *Baby Got Back*. I kept noticing it and seeing it happen to where it actually started to offend me, to be honest with you. I even had one director tell me after I asked him during a video shoot casting, "Why didn't we pick this girl, this girl, and this girl?" – and I'm quoting directly – "Well, I thought you said you wanted beautiful?" And I told him, "They are beautiful," and he said, "When you say 'curves' to me, I think *whore*, not beautiful woman." And my reaction was like, "WOW, you've got to be kidding?!?!" I remember my manager Ricardo was sitting right there with me when this guy said that, and that's where the inspiration came from. I knew right then and there that the song was going to write itself.

The kind of lightning in a bottle creative moment all songwriters grab instantly when they strike, Mix remembered that as his muse took over and he strapped in for the rush of the write, shaking his head at the marvel of the mystery of inspiration that, a serendipity that, "Happens to me when I'm writing, all the time, all the time. But you know what's funny about the writing process? Some songs are forced, where you push it and lie to yourself and go, 'That's pretty good!' But you know in your heart that it didn't happen the way great songs happen. And *Baby Got Back* was something I believed in. I've always been extremely proud of my culture, and you gotta remember, I grew up on Parliament Funkadelic. Parliament had an album titled *Motor Booty Affair*, and if you look at the inside of that album, they showed you pictures of sisters with curves because that's what the African-American male has always liked! So it's not like I created this. Also, at the time I was writing that song, I was heavily influenced by Luke Skywalker and 2 Live Crew. Not necessarily musically so much as what he was doing on stage. Starting in the late 80's, I'd been out on tour opening for Luke, and that's part of where the *Baby Got Back* sound comes from. It's based on Miami bass music. Magic Mike was and remains to this day a good friend of mine. Back in the day, he taught me how to program Miami music. Then at those live shows, seeing Luke bringing girls on stage who actually had those bodies with no shame. Unapologetically, I loved it! I loved it because he was kind of bucking the system. Now it's normal to see that, but it was new then. I thought it was beautiful to see him praising sisters and going against the grain of what the 'record industry system' was trying to tell them to do at the time."

Looking back at the song's phenomenon a quarter-century later, Mix feels, "Was like the perfect storm honestly, and when I started writing *Baby Got Back*, I felt that it needed to be said a little differently. I felt like it was easy for us to say, 'Oh girl got a nice ass and I want to screw her. But I think it was sending the *wrong message*, in that we were telling America, "Hey, these curvy women, we want to screw them, but we don't want to marry them. I wanted to correct that. So as a songwriter, the question then became, 'How do I do that but still have a tongue-in-cheek kind of sense of humor?' That was probably the hardest thing of all in writing that song. When I put out *Baby Got Back*, it wasn't to make money, and it wasn't me trying to figure out the demographics. It was actually what I felt. (laughs) What a concept?! It just turned out that a lot of people agreed with me."

Twenty-five years later, Jimmy Fallon invited then *NBC Nightly News* Anchor Brian Williams onto the *Tonight Show* to rap *Baby Got Back*. *Rolling Stone* amusingly reported that in his performance of the, "Timeless rump-shaking anthem, B-Will delivers the track with an unflappable, avuncular aplomb that would make Walter Cronkite cower. Though as always serious props to whoever compiled this at the *Tonight Show*. Using the last syllable of Kim Jong-Un's name to recreate Sir Mix-a-Lot's 'Uh, double up, uh uh,' was an excellent touch. Though nothing tops Kathie Lee Gifford's brief, but unforgettable guest spot on the 'make me so horny' line." A dizzying thing to remember even two decades later. The whirlwind that followed as *Baby Got Back* reigned supreme on the Billboard Hot 100 Singles Chart for a record five weeks, knocking Whitney Houston's *I Will Always Love You* out of the top spot was a rise Mix still gets a rush recalling because:

> It was so meteoric and so fast that I remember sitting in the hotel after that show, which was a great show. But I remember sitting in the hotel actually nervous, because keep in mind, I'd never had pop success. I'd had success, but I could stay off of the radar which made it easy for me to do what I wanna do and walk around, and go to the movies. But there was nowhere to

go but down. So I started to prepare myself to fall off. I really did. I was like, "Oh shit, this is it. I'm done!" (laughs) "Once you go #1, they turn on you..." BUT, the next day, we were coming out of a show and Heidi called and said, "Arsenio wants you on his show!" I was like "Arsenio?" And that day, we went off and went to L.A. As I'm meeting before the show with my publishing company at the time, Polygram, someone from the company looks at Ricardo and I and asks, "How does it feel to be banned?" I was like, "I got banned? What the hell are you talking about?" And they were like, "Yes, MTV banned your record, blah blah blah."

Now I'm *really* thinking it's over, right. And I'm upset, like, "Wow. Are you serious?" Heidi's loving this, and she said something to me that I never will forget: "When you go #1, it's a bad thing. But when you get banned *when* you're #1...you're Elvis Presley!" From that point forward, I really started to understand the enormity of this track. It was bigger than the system because it had actually turned everything on its head. It was really interesting to watch, and I credit Heidi because she was a genius. Everything she did was just so perfectly timed that when we did Arsenio. Instead of me doing an interview about blunts and having a good time, the interview turned serious. That was the best thing that could have happened to me. On that day, on that show, that's when I knew,

"Woah, this song became a phenomenon!" But before that, it was just a song. I had a good feeling about it and *Baby Got Back* stood the test of time!

Long a master of making songs people moved to – whether dancing or driving down the boulevard cruising with his music bumping loud out their sound system – on *Mack Daddy*, along with a lesson in the beauty of big butts, the producer/rapper would give listeners a crash course in both BOOM and the cars to zoom around in while doing it. Arguably the FIRST rapper to put luxury sports cars front and center as a fixture in his music. Not only in raps, but also in high performance engine sound effects from Lamborghinis and Ferraris! With his image, Mix-a-Lot would flash these rides in his videos. One of the very first rappers to showcase a sportscar as part of a legitimate hustler image at the height of gangsta rap:

> I did it on purpose too. Because keep in mind, in that era, everyone was pushing an Impala or they were riding around in videos in the souped-up trucks and stuff. If I did that, I would have just been mimicking Compton or mimicking the Bronx. It wasn't me. I was into exotic, and was the first rapper to really associate myself with luxury items. But in a way that wasn't sell-out. In other words, I didn't buy a luxury item and then assimilate myself to something else. I was still me. I would still go out and shoot guns in my back yard and make these obnoxious videos talking shit because it's what I did. But I also prided myself in not being

a drug dealer. Also, I was never ashamed of my
intelligence or my wit because it seemed like a
lot of rap and sports stars acted stupid when
they were really smart. I always used to say to
myself, "God, what must his mom think?"

A reflection of Mix-a-Lot's explosive success that followed
with the album selling over two million copies and making the
producer a millionaire, a result of the momentum that came
when, "The single went triple platinum pretty quick, scary quick
actually. And we started to do bigger venues, but keep in mind,
this was happening simultaneously with gangster rap. So we
ended up on bills with hardcore cats – and I love hardcore
gangster rap. I listen to it to this day. But, in that era, you
couldn't insure a building. And it was too hard to do shows, so
we didn't get a lot of those big, giant shows. If *Baby Got Back*
had hit in this era, I'd be parking $100,000 a night easy. But it
just never did really pan out. Thank God I started to really
understanding publishing and licensing and synch deals and all
that stuff because that's really where my money was made. It
then forced me to become a more efficient business man."
Instead of moving into a highline apartment in downtown
Seattle, Mix-a-Lot retreated for the sanctuary of the woods
building his dream house and state-of-the-art recording studio.
That was in and itself a separate dream come true as it would be
for any producer to have their own 24-7 lockout playground to
create in:

My studio was in my house, and I wanted to
live way out because I make a lot of noise. I
build a lot of shit and I have a lot of company.
A lot of guys coming around making noise,

hollerin' and screaming. I wanted privacy. It took me a while to get used to it, because I'm still a city boy to a T. I mean, I'm not a country guy that goes hunting and fishing and all that shit. But I wanted space. It was very important to me, because when I moved into my new home, it was all about my studio. The previous owner had a 53-foot swimming pool. He got mad at me because it was his masterpiece, and I gutted it and took all that shit out. When I bought the house, I said, "I want a studio right here." Sonically, where I grew up, I had a police siren in the back of a vocal track, so it was quiet out there, private, and again, I could make the noise I wanted to make. More importantly though, and this was really key: I had *room* to do what I wanted to do. I could expand, I could do anything I felt like doing in that space, which is what helped me, because sonically I could design my room any way I wanted to.

Right after I did *Baby Got Back*, I bought my first digital studio. Way before Pro Tools, it was called Sound Tools. Which was still Digidesign and was two tracks, not really a mastering suite, but more an editing suite. So I would edit all of my masters on Sound Tools. Then what I started to do was, as I got more adept at dabbling with digital audio, by the time *Return of the Bumpasaurus* came out, I was using Pro Tools. I was recording things within Pro Tools, but I was coming from outside of the box. Pro

Tools really hadn't mastered their in-the-box techniques yet, so I was running Pro Tools II. I had three of those 888 interfaces, which had eight outputs each. But because they didn't have the in-the-box mixing thing down pat, I would literally run Pro Tools. And then mix out on my mixer and dump it to DAT. So you still had that big, thick sound because the mixer is what was giving it to me.

Widely unrecognized for the true measure of his influence on hip hop through present day throughout contemporary pop and after being recognized by the L.A. Times when they suggested the key to Mix-a-Lot's longevity could be thanks to their hypothesis that, "Biggest strength may be that he's a master of hooks." As the 1990s bumped on, the producer's boom remained among the loudest as he dropped *Chief Booty Knocker* in 1994, earning him a return to the Grammy's with a nomination for Best Solo Rap Performance. In 1997, *Return of the Bumpasaurus* shot him back up the charts with another monster club and radio hit with *Jump On It*, which the producer brilliantly designed as a call-and-response banger that could be customized to whatever city listeners happened to be partying in. First coming up with the idea after he sampled some promos of the single to radio, MTV reported from Mix's marketing move caught fire after he raced back to the studio after, "The single came out in July. Radio stations across the country have been whipping up their own private remixes, inserting their city's name into the, 'What's up _____? What's up?' shout-out portion of the song. Mix, never one to miss a publicity boat, quickly scurried into his Seattle studio and whipped off personalized versions of the song for fifteen cities. Word is Mix

is busy working on at least fifteen more personalized mixes."
Flipping a b-boy classic for a new generation, the producer knew
he had stumbled onto a hot concept when:

> I heard *Apache (Jump On It)* by Sugar Hill Gang.
> I always thought the best thing about the Sugar
> Hill Gang. They had the coolest hooks, so you
> look at some songs like that. So *Jump On It* was
> really me saying, 'thank you' to a lot of the cities
> that I had frequented on the road. That's really
> all the song was for, it was to say thanks. You
> may not know this, but I actually did about
> eighty versions of that song just for cities. In
> other words, if I said L.A., in that version, I
> would shout out all of the surrounding areas. So
> I'd do San Bernadino, Orange County – "What's
> up OC?!" I'd do all of the radio stations, which
> was probably the biggest mistake I ever made
> because that shit took a lot of time! Literally
> days, almost two weeks, in the studio recording
> all of those different versions for different cities
> and their surrounding geographical areas. But I
> think it was worth it. I really do.

That tradition of sampling iconic hooks would continue in
the millennium with Mix-a-Lot himself getting the treatment,
returning to the top of the charts when CeeLo Green flipped the
classic *Swass* chorus and turned it into a world-wide #1 for girl-
group sensation The Pussycat Dolls with *Don't Cha*. Hitting #2
on the Billboard Hot 100 Singles Chart 2005 and reigning atop
the charts around the world in the United Kingdom, Australia,
Canada, Switzerland, Ireland, the Netherlands, Denmark,

Austria, Belgium, Norway, New Zealand, and the European Hot 100 Singles Chart. The smash hit sold over three million copies. Mix couldn't help but find flattery in the fact that the new generation is doing the job for him of introducing his sound to millions of millennial listeners as it racked up an astounding 124 MILLION YouTube views:

> You know what's funny? I absolutely love it! When I heard The Pussycat Dolls' version, I said, "Woah! That's pretty good. I kinda like that." And it was actually kind of out before it was cleared, which was fine by me. We worked it out. CeeLo Green – who produced the track – and I. What I ended up doing was entering into a deal just for *Swass* with Nottingham Entertainment, because Nottingham was administering the publishing on that song. I knew if I used Universal or Polygram at that time, it would have actually created a big problem because two companies trying to clear a song would have taken too long to get on movies and stuff like that. So I did that in the interest of keeping it productive.

Lightning would strike twice when in 2013, Nicki Minaj reinvented Mix-a-Lot's signature song with the chart-topping tribute *Anaconda*. It snaked its way to #2 on the Hot 100 Singles Chart, and broke social media records when it stole the twenty-four hour streaming record after racking up almost twenty million views in one day. Happy his music's reverberation is keeping booties shaking twenty-five years after it first took the world by storm, Mix closes with advice for the millennial generation. Reasoning first and foremost that there's no downside to branding:

> If a star of Nicki Minaj's stature calls and you talk to her...say, "Hey, you're welcome to do what you wanna do. Have fun with it!" That's important for artists to think about at any point in their career. Because it's such a hard business to make money in it right now. I really think the kids need to dial this in. That although yeah, a lot of music is stolen and a lot of people take your stuff for free, the revenue streams have broadened such that you really don't need a record label anymore to make a name and a dollar in this business. Find a good publicist, and find companies that you can hire third party to do the work. But own your brand, because you are now a walking, talking brand, versus being *branded* by your managers at the record label. *www.sirmixalot.com*

CHAPTER SIXTEEN

Kicking It in Tennessee – Jon Connor

What if MUD had a sound? What if "MUD" was in fact a metaphor for a musical mix that blended country and hip hop and had been rumbling up from the underground atop 16-inch truck tires, blasting out of sound-systems where previously the only competition was crickets? Places smart-ass city slickers dismiss as spots, "Where nothing's ever going on." When in fact, TENS of thousands of people have routinely showed up over the past ten years each weekend to help launch an underground movement today known within the genre most generally as COUNTRY RAP, or in its most popular mainstream tag, as HICK HOP.

Two events put the sound on the national map in recent years: first, a high-profile, front-page cover story about the sound that caught the esteemed Wall Street Journal's ear in 2013 after making millions of dollars independent of any radio rotation or major label support, it was reported, by, "Blending *country* hooks with *rap* phrasing and a healthy dose of mud – plus some help from Wal-Mart– an enterprising group of southern artists have created a fast-growing new musical genre." The second event came the next year in 2014 and was truly the commercial Big Bang of country rap when the world was introduced to the phenomenon of BIG SMO. Spotlighted appropriately by *Rolling Stone Magazine* for having the "Best Cult Fan Base" at the CMA Music Fest that year, Smo's ascension to the Boss of the Stix came thanks to a D.I.Y. ethos that has long driven Country Rap's underground rise.

The name behind the production of many of country rap's biggest signature hits – totaling over 43,000,000 views in sum in an industry which regards YouTube as the unofficial metric for radio play since terrestrial radio gives it none – is Jon Conner. HickHopMusic.com hailed the producer as, "The total package: he can produce as well as anyone in the business in any genre, and he's bad as hell on the mic. He's got a more traditional hip hop sound when he's delivering his vocals, but his production could be classified as a genre unto itself."

Growing up in Newark, Delaware in the 80's a hip hop baby as part the genre's first generation, Jon's gateway into rap came like so many of his peers, came in 1986 when the Beastie Boys dropped the BOMB with *License to Ill*, the Def Jam/Rick Rubin-produced masterpiece that captured Conner's imagination from the first time he popped the tape in: "I started rapping when the Beastie Boys came out in fifth grade, and I joined my first little rap group. A buddy of mine, Mike Higgins – who was in the group and is someone I still talk to to this day – me and him hit it off. He actually helped me write a couple of my first raps. I remember a couple weeks later, we were in the cafeteria rapping and when I kicked my rap, the positive response I got from my friends who heard it. Just that feeling, I wanted more of it, and wanted more people to go crazy when I kicked a rap." Raised alongside the Beasties on a healthy diet of Run-D.M.C., Eric B. & Rakim, Wu-Tang Clan and Guru and Premier; Conner was sharpening his rap tongue into a word-wielding weapon:

> By the time I got to high school, there was a DJ who had a little set-up at his house that was capable of recording. A couple of my other friends had a little situation with a guy named Bill Moore, who had his own recording studio. That wound up being the first one I ever went to, and that in itself blew me away.

After hustling his way into an internship with Ruffhouse Records at twenty and getting his hands on his first drum machine, an Alesis SR-10, introducing him to the world of sampling. An art form he would master through HOURS digging through the dollar bins at his local area record stores – of which thankfully there were HUNDREDS back in the early 1990s to mine for musical gold – along with an equal number of hours Jon then spent back home in his basement studio experimenting with the great wide open frontier. Soon, his pioneering paid off after his demo made it up to NYC and into the ear of DMX *What's My Name* producer Self Service, who Conner recalls, "Heard my group The Unit's demo and said, 'The raps are okay, but whose making the beats?'. He wanted to meet me. When I got up to New York and he saw I was white, he was like, 'This is crazy!' Then told me, 'Your ear for samples is amazing.' Then took me under his wing."

Seeing his first big payday, $10,000 out of his collaboration with Self Service, the producer is still proud of the day, "I took that check home and showed my wife, and she was like, 'I can't believe you made that kind of money doing music!' My mom has been my biggest fan since I started. She's the one person who I can say knows every song, every lyric, and always told me things like, 'Don't work with your back, work with your mind.' And really pushed me. So when I showed her that check, it was awesome." After working with Self Service for a couple years, Conner took up another studio apprenticeship under the coaching of the now-legendary D-Moet, producer of early New York hip hop classics like, King Sun's *Hey Love/Mythological Rapper*. Taking an opposite approach from his previous position behind the boards where now he was in the vocal booth as a rapper after, "Moet believed enough in me that he signed me as an artist to his label, EMF Recordings. Which in and of itself was a dream come true for me to sign my first legitimate record deal as a rapper. It was a great time because I was learning how to produce by him producing me."

Conner eventually ventured home to Delaware and returned to producing, opening his own studio after, "I almost had a deal with so many record companies it would make your head spin. I lived and died with every meeting, because you'd go in excited. Thinking, *We got a meeting with such and such, and everything seems cool in the meeting.* And then you're waiting weeks to hear anything. It seemed like an endless carousel. It's not like being a white rapper now. Back then there was such scrutiny. After enough meetings where nothing panned out, it really took its toll on me, and I took a break from rapping."

After spending years on the New York scene trying to break into the big time as both a rapper and producer, Connor's *big break* would ironically come not in the bricks, but down in the sticks. "After a friend of mine Steve C, who owned Hellaware Records asked me if I'd produce a song for Stak for a mix tape he was putting out." Admitting that initially he was reluctant for the simple fact that, "I was an east coast hip hop head with a heavy bias to anything other than east coast hip hop. But I ultimately agreed." Introducing Conner's sound for the first time into a hybrid where Billboard found Stak, "Conveying tales of rural life over the slick beats of urban hip hop," the east coast infusion, "Refines the Tennessee native's earnest brand of southern rap." The industry's leading music magazine would observe as the producer himself was beginning to see - and hear - that he just might be on to something:

> We flew down to Tennessee, and got in the studio with Stak. Like any good producer, I had a [CD] with fifteen, twenty beats on it. When I got back to Delaware, I got a call from Stak telling me, "You're undefeated on the first five. You're my new producer." And we began crafting some songs for a Def Jam South album that would eventually be part of the WHITE BOY trilogy. Some of those tracks included *Roll With Me, Bonnie and Clyde, White Boy*, which was actually the song where Stak said, "Damn Jon Conner, this beat is the shit!" And people came up to me for years after that saying that

line and that put me on the MAP in Nashville because he was one of the biggest rappers in town at the time, and really helped to start branding my name as a producer.

Released in August, 2004, arguably the most popular of the album's 16 cuts were the Conner production features, racking up over FIVE million YouTube views between them - 2,804,141 for *Bonnie and Clyde*, 1,994,161 for *White Boy*, and 216,993 for *Rollin' With Me*. This marked the first time Conner could measure his music reaching listeners with real time data, and by far, *Bonnie and Clyde* was the fan favorite, and a song that opened the producer's ears to a key discovery that he credits with ultimately evolving his production style, remembering that *Bonnie & Clyde* was one of those records I produced for Stak that was supposed to be on the Def Jam South album, and though I did the beat on my MPC and ASR-10, Tim Hill played piano on that record, and it was originally a sample, but when he re-did it, it came out so much better because it wasn't just this piano loop playing over and over again. Then when the strings got in there, it was like 'Oh wow, this is amazing, it came out so much better.' Also, when you can talk to the player and produce him on what to play and how to play it, it's like talking to the record player. So I started to throw myself more into learning the southern sound because I now had a client in Stak that was using my beats who was outside of the box of my normal East Coast sound." Seeking to take his foot in the door an important step further, Conner jumped at the invitation from Stak's record label to become one of his official in-house producers, confirming:

When I really started diving in, I ended up moving down to Nashville after the *Start to Finish* record to work at Street Flavor on a more full-time basis. When I got down there, he had Dave Davidson – who was the band leader for Led Zeppelin – playing a violin and he brought in a guitar player to re-cut the guitar sample I'd used off the acoustic guitar CD, and I was like "WOW! We don't need samples!" A light bulb went off and I never sampled again.

Conner would experience an equally-as-momentous revelation that ultimately held even greater implications for his career personally and the evolution of Country Rap as a sound more broadly one fateful day when, "During my time working at Street Flavor Records, on a break in one of the studio sessions, I went to the corner store and when I got there, there was a guy who jumped out of a BIG muddy truck sitting up on jacked-up tires, and he himself was covered in mud, and had the boots, the cowboy hat, the whole nine, but Lil Wayne's bumping through the speakers, and it hit me like a ton of bricks and I said, 'There's a whole segment of people probably in his shoes that love hip hop for the beats but probably can't identify with the lyrical content.'" Knowing he was on to something big, Conner brought his vision back with him into the studio where he initially thought the timing was perfect for Haystak:

> During that period, we were creating *Crackavelli*, where I produced *Make Ya Fly*, *Baked*, *Freak Show*, *Kindness for Weakness*, and *Sail On*. I was now focusing on making tracks with country-driven toppings with a hip hop

bottom, and was pushing Stak to go in that direction. But he was more of a southern rapper than a country rapper.

Racking up another hit video on YouTube with over 1.6 million views of *Sail On*, the combination of Stak's flow and Conner's beats by 2009 caught the attention of *Spin Magazine*, who celebrated the rapper as a, "Southern white outsider icon." It was evidence the musical mainstream was starting to take a peripheral notice of a sound the producer was helping to pioneer, as he found himself drawn deeper and deeper into the grass roots of country rap as it began to bubble up from the underground and onto the Billboard charts. His next studio collaboration with Stak –*Hard 2 Love* – would score Jon his first rankings on the Hot R&B/Hip Hop Albums Chart when the album reached #28, while climbing all the way to #13 on the Heatseeker Albums chart. Conner's personal highlight would arrive when the album did on the Billboard Hot Rap Albums Chart, peaking at #15, while his YouTube winning streak continued in the same time as the video for the title cut racked up an astounding-by-most-indie-standards 3.5+ million views, with *Let Me Hold You Down* a close runner-up with over two million.

Came a Long Way would prove a fitting title for the journey Conner had already made in his five year collaboration with Haystak. With their final studio collaboration, the champagne cracked once again after the album entered the Top 40 of the Billboard Top R&B/Hip Hop Albums chart for a second time. While luck struck twice in the Top 20 of the Top Rap Albums Chart, he couldn't have predicted it at the time. Jon was preparing to head even higher up the charts and YouTube count when fate intervened and introduced his beats to then-unknown

Big Smo, who by happy accident had discovered Conner's increasingly country rap beatscapes as:

> I was sending down tracks to Stak, and in all, I produced a total of forty-two tracks for Haystak over a period of years when we were working on the *Hard 2 Love* record. At this point, Big Smo had started working for Stak, traveling with him on the road acting as his hype man on stage, and then shooting his music videos. Well, unbeknownst to me, as I was sending beats to his Gmail account, it was Smo who was actually downloading them for Stak. And as Stak heard them, he told me, "I'm southern, that's country. But I got a guy named Smo and he's kind of doing that."

An introduction that could be likened to Dre finding Snoop from Conner's perspective in how naturally his beats sounded like they were tailor-made for Smo's voice before the producer had ever even heard him flowing over top. The ramifications for Jon's career would prove as major as the label Smo eventually signed to. And based off the strength of the first track of Jon's he ever recorded over. Which is the now signature *Kickin' It in Tennessee*. A song with not just legs, but wings. The organic story of the way it first took flight is as inspiring and classic as any HIT story in the business. One Conner never tires of telling to this day:

> At the time I was working with Haystak, Smo was working as his engineer/hype man/videographer, and cutting his teeth. When I

would send beats to Haystak, Smo would be the one to physically download and import them into the sessions. On some of the tracks I was sending down, I was using slide guitars and dobros and things of that nature. Stak had passed on those, but little did I know Smo was moving them over into a folder for himself.

One of those songs became *Kickin' It in Tennessee,* which now has fourteen, fifteen million YouTube views, and was the song that really set Smo ablaze in the country rap genre. He to me became everything I envisioned seeing that day when the guy jumped out of the truck covered in mud listening to Lil Wayne. It was the perfect embodiment of what I saw. Whereas, Stak wasn't willing to jump all the way into the country rap, Smo embraced it and said, "This is my sound."

The journey from demo to YouTube sensation would be one of those beautiful slow burns in the business that eventually explodes. Conner remembered recognizing the song as something special the second he heard his guitar player first lay down the signature slide-acoustic guitar hook. Instantly catchy to the ear, when it caught Jon's sitting behind the console. Like so many of music's greatest moments, he remembered it as something as a happy accident where, "We were in the studio, and my guitar player Vinnie was strumming on the guitar, and I had mentioned to him, 'Hey, let's try and make some stuff along these lines.' So we didn't have a proper slide and I think he grabbed an empty beer bottle and used it as a slide, and played what became the sample riff for *Kickin' It in Tennessee*. As soon as I heard it, I knew there was something special about it. It was playing overtop of a simple beat, because it was really in effect a demo of the sound I was trying to get across to Haystak. So it only had the guitar, drums, and a bassline. A very simple, barebones, skeleton track. But again I just felt it had a vibe and a feel to it that I really liked." Knowing immediately he'd struck a chord that rung a little more harmoniously down south, the producer remembered:

> It didn't fit anybody I originally played it for up in Delaware. So I knew this was heading down to Stak in Tennessee. Smo loved the record when he heard it, so he recorded *Kickin' It in Tennessee* to the MP3 I had sent down. That's what you hear today. There was no post-production, or final tracked-out mix. What fifteen million people heard on YouTube was what I sent in that MP3 as a demo. He cut to it, shot a video to it, hit me up on Myspace and said, "Hey, I shot a video to this beat you did for Haystak, I want your blessing before I release the song." And I said, "Hey man, the music's already made, shoot me the song. I'd love to hear it." He shot me the video, took a listen, loved it...two thumbs up!

> **Big Smo:** Jon was one of Haystak's producers back when he had Big Boyz Beats. There was an opportunity that came up where I was given some of JC's tracks that he created. Stak's method of paying me for a bunch of videos I'd shot for him was to say, "Hey, I got some of

these beats that came from Jon Conner, I'll pay you in tracks because these are a little too Country for me. Not really my lane." And I was like, "Cool! I'll take whatever I can get!" See, he would have me go into his email and download these tracks from Big Boyz Beats, and I didn't even know who Jon was then. But as soon as I heard these tracks – especially *Kickin' It in Tennessee* – I was like, "FUCK! This is it right here!" It was only minutes later that I was sitting on a song.

I had a buddy of mine that was out at the house that day named Tommy Donegan, and he was like, "Man, how do you write these songs?" I told him, "It's fuckin' easy!" I had just kind of gotten to this point where I had taught myself like an easy way of writing, and I told him, "It's like you want to find the end and then build backwards." So we're just sitting out here blowin' pine, and that suddenly became the first chorus line: 'Rollin' on them back roads, blowin' pine.' Because that's what we were doing all the time. Then I sang to him, 'Sipping on that moonshine, all the time.' And the melody was just there. But I didn't know yet that I was writing the chorus to the song. I was just explaining to my homie, and told him, 'It's simple, you just kind of map it out: 'Rollin' on them back roads, blowin' pine.'" And suddenly, it hit me and I was like, "Shit! I got a chorus!"

For the now-household voice that brought the song fully to life, when Smo first heard the track as an unknown artist on the come-up, he exclusively continues, sharing his own memory of immediately gravitating toward the instrumentals because, "Prior to my Jon Conner experience, it had been all tracks that we'd made ourselves. So we didn't really have in-house guitar players and stuff like that. Until actually Charlie Bonnet III came along, he was the first guitar player I was really able to pull in and have play on top of tracks we were making. But Jon Conner had a way of really bringing that hip hop element. And like he says, 'The trimmings or toppings,' or what I would call, 'The Fixings.' Bringing those two together in a way that gave me the platform to really lyrically say the things that I was living. And to say the things that made me the person that I was. In doing so, made me the artist I truly was. Jon had tapped into the artist that had just been lying underneath inside of me, and it was because of those tracks that the real me was able to come out. Musically, with Jon's tracks, it was the first time I'd ever heard country and rap in kind of a raw form. Not as produced, but put together so naturally."

The east coast edge that Conner brought to the track married perfectly with the equally-as-rugged rural lyrical landscape Smo was rapping about overtop. It would soon catch the ear of an untapped sea of country music fans just like Smo looking for soundtrack to their *Kuntry Livin.* But six years before that iconic country rap staple dropped, Jon revealed that, "The funny thing is I gave him that beat in 2008. It wasn't until two years later that they called and said, 'Hey man, we want to get some more beats from you.' So *Kickin' It in Tennessee* had been released on an album in 2010 called *American Made.* It featured a few other tracks I'd produced for him that had also made their way into that folder, including what became *C.W.G,*

Old Dirt Road, and *Fly Away.* When *Kickin' It in Tennessee* hit around 500,000 YouTube views, Smo's manager Dan called me and said, 'Hey, were cutting another record.' And I was brought into the Smo camp by Dan." While Smo would prove to be the heavyweight champ of country rap, the fans cheering him on were where Conner's producer headspace was equally-focused; knowing he was sitting on an oil well about to blow:

> While Smo had been up working with me in Delaware, we'd really hit on some things. He'd told me about the mud culture and mud bogs and just how this music was taking off down south. I was just so happy to hear that this vision I'd had for this sound of mine had a home for it. That there was a culture already built around it. So when he got back, I called him and said, "Look, I am just really intrigued by this whole culture, and this is a sound I want to explore further. You're the perfect voice to this sound and I think I can be a big help to what you're doing. I'd like to move down because imagine what we could do if we were together in the studio every day." So he was like, "Man, come on down." So at the beginning of 2011, I jumped in the car with everything I could fit in it – including my wife – and we headed down to Shelbyville, Tennessee to start working with Smo where I was officially his producer.

His third and final trip to Tennessee would prove the charm. While driving down, the producer remembered keeping the foot to the floor as, "All I could think about driving to Nashville for now my third time was 'I feel like we have something.' I was excited to get down there and get to work on this sound. Nashville being the home of country music, I knew I'd be able to find the players that I needed to pull off the sound that I had heard in my head." Once he'd landed in Tennessee, as Smo began to lift off, ironically, Jon wound up taking on much the same role his artist first had for Haystak. Documenting the rise of the country rap's grass-roots come-up first-hand from both the stage and behind the scenes as Smo's videographer:

> I went out on the road with Smo as a videographer and hype man in the band. That allowed me to soak in this country rap culture that had been developing, and being out there, listening to the music they were listening to. In seeing how music I had made was resonating with the average country rap fan helped me even more in the studio and say, "Okay, this is what they like, let's give it to them on steroids!"

> They say it takes 10,000 hours to master something, and now, I'm about 40,000 hours in. But I put X amount of hours on emceeing, and X amount of hours on producing. When I was rapping heavy, I wasn't producing, and vice versa, because I totally jumped in to whatever space I was in. Then it finally got to where I had enough hours and it all merged, which was all around when I first met Smo.

The powers that be in the industry – desperate for any leads on new stars who would sell in an era where fewer and fewer major-label-backed artists were – took immediate notice of the independent noise Smo, Conner and company were making, so much so that Billboard soon reported of the camp's progress that, "After releasing two independent albums...Smo went back into the lab, the studio he'd built on the ranch with musical partner DJ Orig and industry vet Jon Conner to begin building his empire, developing new artists, honing his sound and working up several music videos and short films. That began developing a following on YouTube."

That empire rose on the weekend rides of the fans who blasted the music Smo and Conner were making out of their muddy trucks. As the crowds grew at mud bogs courtesy of an odd marriage that formed between artists who couldn't find any other venues to host their sound and fans who couldn't find anywhere conventional to go see the artists perform live who were the soundtrack to their rural lifestyle; a bond between artist and fan was struck. A once-in-a-musical-lifetime movement that formed before Conner's eyes and ears as he captured it first-hand visually and musically on film and record, he prided himself as the fans did on the fact:

> We were doing everything ourselves: from videos to social media content, running the website, to booking the live shows, everything was done by the five or six guys that were in the camp. I was privileged enough to hear the story from Warner Nashville president Chris Stacy myself, where he'd been on vacation on his boat surfing YouTube, and came across Smo's video for *Kickin' It in Tennessee*. Back then, it just had maybe 100,000 views, but they kept watching it grow.

We would go out during the weekend, and out on the road. We were able to hone in on a sound just being amongst the fans, hearing what they were riding around at the mud bogs listening to in their trucks. That helped me tap in directly with the consumer. I remember hearing stuff I'd produced for Smo and Moonshine Bandits coming out of the speakers, thinking, *Man, this is so awesome that these people are using my music as part of their culture!*

Big Smo: From the *America Made* project, whenever I was introduced to Jon Conner, we then did the *Grass Roots EP*, where I went to Delaware to Jon's studio and said, 'Look, I want you to produce this EP,' and this was pre-Warner, and he was all over it and had great ideas and perfect concepts for the sound that would match the artist I am, and we built these records out in Delaware, then came down to my studio in Tennessee and cut the vocals, all in-house, still D.I.Y., and that's when I introduced Jon and Orig, and I said, "Guys: you're a great producer, you're an excellent producer, together you're going to be unstoppable!" That's when they worked together on what became *Kuntry Livin* as a team.

Rolling Stone Magazine in a nod to Conner's east coast rap influence, would note that, "*Kuntry Livin'* sounds like Run-D.M.C.'s *Walk This Way* stomped out of Queens and ended up in the rural south." The genre was born that would change the trajectory of country rap forever. Taking fans inside the laboratory for a look at the science behind his sound at work, Conner reveals that while the scenery outside the studio may have differed, the vibe inside was an extension and the next dimension of a process he'd first cultivated years earlier in, "The way I approach my production of country rap is very similar to how I grew up making beats in the east coast fashion. I would put on a record listening for that sample, trying to find the piece or pieces I wanted to use out of a record. So when I would create a track for Smo, I'm listening the guitar player or the dobro player or the fiddle player like it's a record, listening for that four to eight bar measure of magic that I can build the beat around. I feel like even though it's live instruments, I'm capturing them and manipulating them in a way that's similar to a sample, so you still get a hip hop feel." Pointing to one of the MONSTER YouTube hits off of *Kuntry Livin'* as an example of that magic in action. Conner proudly turns the sound up on the 10.5 million ears who were addictively drawn to bump *Workin'* recalling that as he put the song together in the studio, not surprisingly:

> The first thing we had was the guitar. We identified a really cool guitar lick Travis was playing, captured that, and immediately what I do once I have my guitar going is to put my snare in there, because now you have a count. So once I have a good-sounding snare in there that's snapping, then I get my kick out and it's feeling good, then everything else pretty much writes itself for me. It's done in five, six minutes, and it literally takes me longer to settle on a

sound than to program it, and then I wrote the chorus to *Workin'* with Alex King.

With any of the songs like that or others I produced for Smo and even today with my own Dammit Boy artists, if you're around me in the studio and mixing a track, the kick drum and 808's, you have to feel it. So when you're sitting in your car or your truck, the door panel has to rattle. It has to thump punching you in your leg. That way you feel the record. So you combine that with these beautiful toppings – the banjos, the fiddles – and the combination of those two sounds to me. I really enjoy producing that kind of music.

Giving Smo's millions of fans a peek inside their creative process together with Smo in the booth, Connor likens their back-and-forth as artist and producer to a foreign tongue spoken only by musicians in the studio. One where, "We come up with a language – me and the artist – for their sound that allows us to communicate, and even though Smo and I had found a formula with *Kickin' It in Tennessee*. You can't keep doing the same song over and over, so we pushed the boundaries with *Kuntry Livin'* and said, 'How far country can we go?' If we thought there wasn't enough hip hop in it, we pushed that direction. And you find out where the boundaries of the sound are. Then as long as it has the happy medium, it can lean a little one way or the other way. So it's a feel for me. If I get that feeling, then I know we got something." Translating that 'something' specifically into how he and Smo worked building his signature vocal stacks on tracks like *Anything Goes,* which boasts 3,672,050 YouTube views to date. In the bonus of a rare appearance from Jon behind the mic boldly predicting that, "Fifty years from now, they'll still reflect on what we did today." In the moment, he favored:

> Smo using a U 87 to record the *Kuntry Livin'* record, because he's got such a rich voice. That really worked well with him. I'm a big fan of keeping vocals dry. When I mix a rap vocal, nine times out of ten, I keep it dry. When Smo's in the booth, I think what makes Smo is he's got a great voice. He's got this big, deep, baritone and he doesn't have to speak very loud into the mic to have a presence on tape. So with producing him, it was more or less just making sure he was in the right tone. If it was a happy song or a sad song, that I was feeling that from him - because it's more than just the writing obviously. It's how it's conveyed. It's the conviction within what you're speaking that allows somebody to connect with it. Because they *feel* what you're saying, not just hearing it.

With *Kickin' It in Tennessee* at just shy of fourteen MILLION views by 2014 as the *Kuntry Livin'* album dropped, and over thirty million total YouTube views with Big Smo for songs Conner had produced, he knew his own moment of truth had arrived for those closest to him. Where all the years of sacrifice that plagued not only a dedicated producer, but his equally-as-dedicated family. Mom and dad were the first to bounce cheering out of their seats after the album that took the Billboard Top 40 by storm, representing the FIRST break-through by a country rap artist in the genre's history when

Smo's major-label debut reached #31 on the Top 200 Album Chart. For Conner personally, this marked his first time in the Top 10 of his personally most-coveted chart, the Top Rap Albums Chart, this time coming TWO rankings shy of the #1 spot. Even giving a Johnny Cash-like middle finger to the deaf ear country music radio had turned to Smo's sound when the Billboard Top Country Albums chart proudly displayed Smo at #6 after a lifetime chasing a dream that was finally delivered to fruition.

A reward for any artist that spreads infectiously to that of their loved ones whose belief sustained them on the way to the big time. Jon beams with pride at a family who since his teens has without a flatline in heartbeat remained, "So supportive, and that gave them something that everybody knows, like, 'Oh my God, #3 on the Rap Albums chart!' Then staying in the Top 10 for twelve weeks was just confirmation that we were onto something." History would be made as Big Smo became the first country rap artist to sign a deal with a major label. Let alone Warner Bros., legitimizing a sound most labels had laughed at along the way as Conner and company built their very own sub-genre within broader hip hop:

> The *Kuntry Livin'* album went on to sell 250,000 copies, which in this day and age is A LOT of records believe it or not. It spent twelve weeks in the Top 10 on both the Billboard rap and country album charts, and it was just amazing: the realization of every dream you have as a kid, and so on the rap rhart you see Nicki Minaj, 50 Cent, Big Smo, just to realize, "I produced that record and people are buying it right there between the biggest names in music." It's just a

feeling of arrival. We'd made it, were amongst the big dogs, and it was something we produced in a little country store-turned-studio in Smo's back yard on little beat machines and the beat thing. And whatever we could get our hands on. I remember when Warner came out to the studio, they looked around and said, "You made all of that music out of here?" They couldn't believe it! So to know at the end of the day that we made a country rap classic, it was an amazing feeling.

In the four years since *Kuntry Livin'* launched and legitimized the Country Rap genre into its mainstream, Conner has stayed busy working with an all-star roster of artists who along with Smo helped create a legitimate genre for the sound Jon first heard almost a decade before. Like any smart producer, he's kept his sound spread smartly across the entire field of players. Tapping once again back into athletic pedigree he learned the hard way from hits he didn't want to take as a QB. Now as one for the genre, they're smashes he's happy to take, racking up more YouTube and Billboard Chart toppers. Highlights included new school country rap stars-on-the-rise like Alexander King. Who sings Conner's praises to date as a coach in the studio he can always trust as someone who, "I always know is going to be pushing the envelope of what's next. That's what I always look forward to when I'm getting in the studio with J.C."

Jon, now a MVP of his game, walks out into the stadium country rap has truly become as a genre these days with a Quarter Back's perspective. As he takes a 360 degree look at the greatest hits roster of artists that are now part of his production resume, he proudly points to his work with one of its true

Godfathers as a measure of how far he's come. Teaming up with Sparxxx on tracks from his *McCosh Mill Road* album and more recently when Bubba appeared on Conner's own Dammit Boy Entertainment release *Too Drive to Drunk* by Charlie Bonnett III and I4NI. Directing the single's video as well, which currently sits at under 100,000 YouTube views and climbing. And on Conner-produced tracks off the 2016 *Muscle Car* EP, the producer regards his work with Sparxxx as another full-circle moment in his career, musing that, "When I get to work with a Bubba Sparxxx, now you've got a guy who cut his teeth with Timbaland, so he's already a professional emcee. So I don't need to teach him anything, I just need to push him and inspire him and make sure his tones are right. Bubba's a consummate professional, and lights a fire under your ass to make sure you supply him with a perfect track." Returning the compliment in spades, for Sparxxx, after working with so many of hip hop's biggest producers, from Timbo to Organized Noise, clearly considers Conner right up there among the elite:

> **Bubba Sparxxx:** Jon as a producer really comes at it from three different angles: from the angle of being a top-notch beatmaker and track guy, the angle of being an elite-level producer in terms of understanding melody, understanding key, and having a real understanding of how you need to put songs together musically. And that's not an easy thing to do. Especially, when you're talking about putting whole albums together, whole projects, and shaping those types of things. Jon is comfortable with all those hats on. The third part of it that I think really takes it over the top is being an artist, and being a

rapper. So there's just no angle he can't come at it from that he's not comfortable in the studio making happen.

In 2017, Conner's beat-making operation is headquartered just outside Nashville, TN. At Dammit Boy Entertainment, the multi-media company he co-founded with longtime country rap staple David Ray back in 2014, together they develop the next generation of country rap artists like Mic Manic, Tinnman, Big Chuk, Forsaken, and former Smo co-producer/DJ Orig among other talent. Today in its renaissance, country rap has blown up into a legitimate sub-genre of hip hop and a multi-million dollar business with Conner sitting at the center as one of its top go-to producers, working with all its biggest stars, from The LACs and Lenny Cooper to I4NI (which features C.W.B. co-founders D-Ray and Stump) superstar Jelly Roll, who excitedly shares that, "I like working with Jon because I like working with people who are really hands-on, that I can really sit down and gel with, and he's definitely one of those guys."

West Coast country rap kings the Moonshine Bandit's, whose 2017 *Baptized in Bourbon* album (including highlight track *Red, White and Blue Collar*) debuted at #3 on the iTunes chart, are another of Conner's recent clients. It's the kind of chart ranking he's now used to, but doesn't take for granted for a moment because, "To become who I have as a producer, it took me twenty-something years because I had to learn, from making beats, producing, being produced as a rapper, and performing live – all these different aspects that gave me this tremendous perspective." Talking to aspiring country rap artists who found a home in Jon's sound, the producer in closing passes on the same sage wisdom that his own mentors did twenty years earlier to a new generation:

> What I tell artists now is, I always took it coming from a team background: you sit your time on the bench, work hard, and practice. And when you're ready and you've proven yourself, you'll get in the game. Then, when you get in the game, you've gotta show what you can do to stay.
>
> *www.dammitboyentertainment.com*

Producer extraordinaire." - *The Village Voice*

CHAPTER SEVENTEEN
Dean's List – Mike Dean

Mike Dean was born to be a record producer. From his ear as an engineer to his multi-instrumental musical ability, Dean has been banging out hip hop hits for decades, and still remains as relevant today as ever, thanks in part to his longtime creative association with Kanye West, with *Rolling Stone* donning them, "Faithful collaborators," in 2016. Alongside NPR's recent acknowledgement that, "In the early 1990s, he helped create the sound of Rap-A-Lot Records and the bones of dirty south rap." The span of the producer's influence over hip hop stretches generation and is still in play today.

Hailed as, "Maybe the most consistent behind-the-scenes hero in hip hop over the past two decades" by *Vice Magazine*. When Dean shares the secret of his success at the top of our conversation. He emphasizes the fact that regardless of what high profile project he's in the studio working on, and he treats it all like, "A normal day, you have to keep your feet on the ground. No one respects you if you're star struck." Born with music in his blood, Mike grew up against the backdrop of the Bayou in rural Texas outside Houston, revealing:

> My sister and brother both played music. They both played saxophone and my sister played piano. And my mother is an art teacher. I think I was eight or nine when I started playing piano and saxophone and things like that.

Like most children who discovered a talent for music early on in their adolescence, Dean was fortunate to find himself in the hands of a teacher –Jane Ambuhl – who nurtured his talent across a broad range of stylistic study. Forcing her student along the way to lean not on his gift for improvisation, but instead all of the unromantic "work" that came with sight reading. The rigorous regimen of playing a classical music catalog of all the greats including Beethoven, Chopin and Mozart. Dean remembers:

> I went into piano lessons with her where she didn't let me play by ear for years. (laughs) And she wanted me to read music. She pretty much

my whole technique of playing came from her. She taught me how to hold my hands right and I took lots of music theory classes. And she took me to the Music Teacher's Association competition each year, which I always won.

Though he would become famous for his work within hip hop and R&B when he grew up, as a teenager, Mike grew up primarily a rock & roll radio kid, "Listening to classic rock like Pink Floyd and Bad Company, Black Sabbath, but not really R&B so much. My first band was in the ninth grade, I was in a band called Freight, and we played classic rock and southern rock, like 38 Special and Lynyrd Skynyrd." Known more recognizably for his keyboard chops, Dean was already an accomplished guitar player by his teens as he discovered his multi-instrumental ability, "Playing grooves on the guitar. And to date, if you listen, all my bass parts are like old *Cream*, *Jack Bruce*." It was through this Rock Band Portal that Mike would synchronously encounter his talent for producing bands alongside playing in them, recalling of that fated introduction that, "When I was in my second or tird band, they had a Tascam four-track, a reel-to-reel, and that was my first experience recording, overdubbing and things like that."

Certain at a much earlier age than most of his peers what he wanted to "be" when he graduated, Dean had already accelerated enough in his development to be offered full-ride music scholarships to several of the best schools in the country. No doubt a thrill to his parents. Still, Mike turned down the opportunity to go to college when another came knocking he knew in his heart he couldn't refuse:

I graduated in 1983, and I'd known since I was a kid that I was going into music professionally. Once I started playing, that's pretty much all I wanted. When I graduated high school, I had a scholarship to Eastman School of Music in Rochester and Berkeley School of Music in Boston. But I had an offer at eighteen years old to go out on the road playing for Selena that was too hard to turn down.

Much like a high school NBA prospect thrown right into the pros, the education Dean would receive in real time with his ambition as a touring musician would serve him for a career to come. The gig would give him the kind of rare look behind the curtain at just how much of a "business" the music industry truly was. Especially playing for the team's notoriously tough coach, Latin teen sensation Selena's father, Abraham Quintanilla Jr. Eventually graduating to the prestigious position – especially for such a young age – as the band's musical director before he was even twenty-one, Mike considered his four year stint playing with Selena to be a college unto itself. It would prove to be one where as he cut his teeth on the road. He leaned on his extraordinary ear to learn a whole catalog of Latin music as he went along, becoming a permanent part of his pedigree as a player in the process:

> It was all new to me. I learned a lot of new chords, learned a lot of chord progressions, almost like jazz but it's a little different the way Mexicans interpret music. I played with her for three or four years, and was really into that Latin

music scene for a while, the Afro-Cuban stuff, and Cuban-style music.

By his early twenties, Dean had retired from the road in favor of setting up shop in Houston, where he kept up his live chops playing around town with his own band Mazz. He also worked with local underground hip hop groups as he started developing his own sound as a producer. Calling on what would prove to be one of the sharpest engineering ears in the business in years to come along with his multi-instrumental pallet as a player, Mike began working out of a home studio producing a local hip hop group, called The Death Squad:

> I was twenty-three, twenty-four at that point, and had a couple drum machines. My first was a Sequential Circuit's DrumTraks drum machine and the Alesis HR-16. My first recording machine was the Commodore 64. It kind of changed my life, because you could do eight tracks, which was a big deal back then.

Dean's life would change again after he linked up with another local engineer, Peter Reardon, in-house sound man behind the boards for the biggest hip hop label in Houston, Rap-A-Lot Records. An axis turning local talent from around town into a new generation of stars, one of whom would shine so brightly in the coming years – in part with Mike Dean's help – that he lifted southern rap all the way to the top of the Billboard Top 200 Albums Chart for the first time in its history. The aspiring producer recalls getting his start working with Scarface after he got his first foot in the door courtesy of:

> Peter Reardon was the Geto Boys and Rap-A-Lot's in-house engineer and I hired him to mix the Death Squad album. He told James Prince, Founder/C.E.O. of the label about me. He put me on a weekly salary and put me in the studio to learn how to mix and stuff.

Thrown into the lion's den recording every hungry emcee coming in off of the street looking for a shot to follow in Scarface and the Geto Boys' footsteps, as Mike worked his way up to recording that upper echelon of talent, he made his bones as an all-purpose engineer for the label. Recording everyone on the early 90's Houston rap scene from the 5th Ward Boyz to Too Much Trouble, Ganksta N-I-P, and 2 Low, he learned the brick and mortar interworkings of record producing in a proper studio. Dean first cracked the Geto Boys inner circle when he engineered Bushwick Bill's *Little Big Man* LP before finally landing a session working with Face engineering *The World is Yours*.

It was during these special sessions that a seed would be planted for the potent chemistry that opened up on the now-legendary *The Diary* between Face, Dean and another young producer, N.O. Joe. Recognizing Mike's multi-instrumental talents immediately as a musician as well as an engineer, Joe remembers happily taking advantage of the mercurial Dean as they sought to employ an at-the-time revolutionary in the samples-driven world of hip hop production strategy of making samples out of original performances versus the traditional path of pulling them off other artist's albums:

> **N.O. Joe:** The idea was really to keep it authentic, because you can have live playing, but

if it doesn't have the right compressor or the right EQ or the right tone to it, it's just played. So I always wanted, when you have a guitar sound or something like that on one of my records, it's almost like I pulled it off of the record and sampled it with the same tone or whatever. But I had it played my way by Mike Dean.

I remember me sleeping on one sofa in the studio and Mike Dean would be asleep on the other. Sometimes, I would wake up in the middle of the night and say, "Hey, I hear a bass line!" And Mike would be right there, "What is it?" Mike Dean was there the whole time, and really helped me flesh out those ideas. Whenever I would tell Mike about them, he was always open to it. And wouldn't stop till he had the part I heard in my head. We were both very dedicated to that record.

Dean tried during these formative years to pick up all of the business tips naturally woven within the production process itself. Whether associated with the overhead to operating the studio itself from the cost of tape in the analog era to electric bills and administrative costs where music publishing was concerned. At the same time, he began to rack up both player and producer credits, crediting Joe in part with helping him make the transition to player on the records he was recording. Mike counts this as an invaluable asset that would eventually land him working with Kanye West in the same capacity:

N.O. Joe came in about that same time, and he
was working with Scarface while I was working
with Bido more. In my sessions with Joe, I was
the engineer and he was the producer. He saw
that I played a few instruments and started
having me play on records, not as a producer,
just as a player. That sort of led up to me starting
producing. Joe was the first one to show me how
to play an MPC, which is a sampling drum
machine - all the drum machines before that had
pre-set sounds.

The masterpiece that the producer would help N.O. Joe and
Scarface craft would set new benchmarks commercially and
creatively for southern rap on a national level for the first time.
For Dean personally, it would provide another of those
invaluable lessons on how the business side of making a record
worked. Revealing that another motive for he and Joe's move to
perform the actual music they were sampling on the album came
when Rap-A-Lot C.E.O. James Prince's insisted. Mike chuckles
recalling:

There wasn't any sample clearance back then.
(laughs) and you could sample anything you
wanted. There were no rules. You could do
whatever you wanted and it would sound like a
rap tune still. You know? We would change stuff
up just enough to make it legal, so J. Prince
didn't have to pay the clearance fees.

Diving into his highlights from the creation of *The Diary*,
where twenty years later in assessing its legacy status popular

critics like *XXL Mag* were musing over, "What it meant for hip hop as a whole," and how it, "Elevated (Scarface's) career to the level of the legends in the game." By then, the publication had hoisted Dean to the same status among hip hop producers, donning him a, "Houston legend." Teleporting fans back inside the studio to a time where, as *Vibe* attested, "Gangsta rap had plateaued and Scarface was ahead of his time...(as he) assisted Mike Dean and N.O. Joe in crafting what sounded like the soundtrack to a hip hop street opera. From top to bottom, *The Diary* is what solidified Scarface as one of the greatest hip hop artists of all time." Dean remembered that as the trio rolled up their sleeves and got down to business:

> Face played a big role in developing the sound of the album. Back then, he dabbled in keyboards and guitar, because all his uncles played. He could DJ and scratch. All that shit. And he had a very credible musical sensibility. We were way different from one another in the way we played, and that helped us create some really unique stuff.
>
> **Scarface:** You put somebody like Mike and Joe and Tone and me and Bido, that's who was around making those records in the early part of that Scarface era twenty-five years ago. That was that shit like '93, '94, '97, and '99 records. And then you put those guys together and you have an awesome combination, no question.

Where Mike would truly make his mark upon the album would come as a performer, handling the bulk of the organ and electric guitar work. While kicking in as well on bass and engineering duties, and in opening his war-chest, he reviews an arsenal of go-to gear at play on the album where, "Back then, I used either an Ensoniq EPS keyboard or the Ensoniq ASR-10. We used that with the sampler and played through that with the guitar and used the effects on the guitars, like adding the echoes, and I used a Korg M3 Synth. That was my go-to electric piano. My keyboard playing style on that album came from jazz band in high school and playing a lot of Chick Corea stuff, and playing jazz stuff. Just kind of mixing it all up together with chords I learned from Selena's family and all of that meshed into that style." While they kept the core team to the three collaborators throughout the album's recording, one guest contributor they were happy to have was an Obi-Wan figure of sorts who influenced the album with his unofficial presence over a few days where Dean revealed that New York's most legendary producer, "Marley Marl was the one who taught me and Scarface tricks with sampling and stuff. And how to make 808s work right. He just showed up at the studio in Houston and stayed a few days, which was cool."

Mike would play key parts on Top 40 hits for Face that would be his breakout into the mainstream, including, *Never Seen a May Cry, I Feel Ya, Goin' Down* and *Hand of the Dead Body* off of *The Diary*. His follow-up collaboration with Scarface on 1996's *Untouchable* LP, again co-producing with N.O. Joe, also saw him stepping out into co-productions with other names blowing up in the game as Mike's own name began to ring out. Highlights included collaborating with Tone Capone on *Smile*, Scarface's duet with hip hop's biggest star, Tupac Shakur. The teaming came at a time when MTV importantly noted that, "Throughout the 90's, no one could question his clout throughout the south. He essentially defined what it meant to be a southern thug rapper years before anyone even coined the term 'dirty south.' This became glaringly evident in the late 90's when a massive wave of young MCs arose from Houston, New Orleans, and Memphis emulating his style of hard-boiled, ghetto-bred, straight-up hardcore rapping. Besides serving as the father of southern thug rap, it seemed as if every hardcore rapper wanted to align himself with Scarface during the 90's – everyone from Ice Cube and Dr. Dre to Tupac and Master P collaborated with the former Geto Boy – all in an attempt to foster credibility among the loyal southern rap audience."

Shaking his head looking back at the fact that he's a member of the small club of producers blessed with the opportunity to work with Tupac during the most prolific period of his career professionally in the eight months between his release from prison and before his death in September, 1996. Dean personally engineered the hip hop superstar's vocals for the album in those final months of his life. A surreal experience given who he was recording, revealing of the rarified opportunity to produce a vocal session with Tupac:

> We were in the studio with Pac the day they did that. They originally laid that song down to another beat, which was kind of wack. Then after he died, I got the acapella vocals back, re-did the music, and played all the keys on it. And Tone Capone did the drums.

> Musically, that track is all the Korg Trinity. That album is Korg Trinity heavy, but we had a lot of gear...ten, fifteen keyboards in the studio. ARP's, you name it. The Korg had just come out, as had Pro Tools, which I used when I recorded *Smile*

editing Pac's vocals, stuff like that. I like it because you can produce a lot faster. So I've always worked digitally. Even way back when we were recording all that Geto Boys stuff. It was all recorded digitally, reel to reel!

Scarface: I think Mike and Tone Capone were really the producers of that record. Tone Capone came up with that hook, Johnny P. sang it, and I think Tupac made that song good. The *Smile* record was a big record because Tupac was on it, and Tupac had lost his life. That's what made *Smile* a big record. Maybe the part where I say, "I'm a dreamer," that may be the best part of my rap.

By the late 1990s and into the early 2000s, Mike had developed a sub-specialty underneath the umbrella of the many hats he wore as a record producer, specifically as a mix engineer. Landing him in the unique role of having the final sonic say on how masterpieces like Scarface's 2002 classic *The Fix* and 2004s *College Dropout* by Kanye West. The latter rap star was so impressed with how Dean impacted his sound that he made him a permanent part of his production team going forward to present day. It was an evolution Mike recalled beginning twenty years ago back. "When I first started mixing at Rap-A-Lot, back in '92, and did early records for the label like the *Player's Choice* album by Too Much Trouble and the 5th Ward Boyz *Ghetto Dope* and *Gangsta Funk* records. By the mid-1990s, I mixed Scarface's *Untouchable* album and then the Geto Boys' *Da Good, Da Bad and Da Ugly* LP. Then I mixed *The Fix*." Giving fans a sneak peak inside his in-high-demand-around-the-clock mixing process, Dean divulges some basics for fans:

> When I'm mixing, I start out with drums. For me, it's all about kick, snare and vocals. Everything else is just extra bullshit. That used to be my philosophy. Still is I guess.

> **Scarface:** I think that Mike Dean is an exceptional musician. I think he's probably one of the best engineers in the business, and his mix game is impeccable. So when you put somebody like Mike and Joe in the same room together, it's getting ready to be some shit!

After returning in the same capacity to mix 2005s *Late Registration*, West expanded Dean's role by 2007s *Graduation*. He graduated to a full-fledged member of Kanye's production team and inner creative circle, helping West produce the ground-breaking, electro-extravaganza and Grammy winner for Best Rap Solo Performance, *Stronger*. Playing the guitar leads and synthesizer riffs that helped drive the song to #1 on the Billboard Hot 100 Singles Chart, as well as around the world in countries from Canada to the United Kingdom, all the way to New Zealand. Mike coyly revealed of the notoriously-secretive West's creative process in creating the song that, "It's the same stuff I use live." Although he would confirm that, "I played the synthesizers on that one."

Mike would show up as co-producer on the #7 hit *Good Life*, another Grammy winner - this time for Best Rap Song for both Dean and West in 2007. For the last decade, his involvement in West's creative core has become more and more intricate. To the point where Billboard in 2016 reported that, "He's now Kanye's right-hand in the VIP invite-only recording process." While he's sworn largely to secrecy when it comes to revealing much about what goes on behind the curtain, Dean did share what impressed him most about West's unique brand of musical genius as a record producer, band member and compositional collaborator:

> It's awesome! Especially with samples, because he takes stuff I would never think to sample. And chops it up like nobody would ever chop it up, which is really cool.

Dean's association with West has brought with it the added bonus of putting him in the room working with many of the best emcees in the game, including the Merlin of word wizards himself, Jay-Z, who he co-produced on the duets album *Watch the Throne*. Where he recalled the biggest thrill was having a ringside seat behind the boards, "Watching two of the best emcees in the world just going at it, and neither one of them were writing anything down!" With the mainstream media appreciation Dean has consistently received as a stabilizing musical anchor for Kanye West's eccentric muse throughout their multi-album collaboration together, which has included such mind-stretching, boundary-pushing, critically-acclaimed albums as 2009s *My Beautiful Dark Twisted Fantasy*, 2013's *Yeezus*, and 2016's controversial *The Life of Pablo*, making Dean a superstar producer to a whole new generation of hip hop fans.

When asked about his favorite words of wisdom to share with the droves of aspiring engineers, players and producers who he encounters in the studio, on the road, and online on his social media networks, including twitter.com/*therealmikedean* where he has 88,000 loyal followers, Dean points to the same fundamentals that made him so indispensible as a jack-of-all-trades in the studio who could switch hats as required, from engineer to composer to performer, offering the tip:

> You've got to understand the relationship between notes and frequencies, because every note is a frequency and every octave is double that frequency. And if you understand that, you can see that in music. Then when you're producing, you can make sure it's harmonically correct.

With *The Village Voice* correctly pointing out in 2016 that while, "The wizard-like multi-instrumentalist...has long been a respected," he has been "little-recognized" for the contributions he has made as "one of the main influences in shaping the underground southern rap sound." As BET added, that today dominates hip hop. Dean has successfully translated his talents for playing across the stylistic spectrum into additonal successes with pop legend Madonna on the recent global hit album, *Rebel Heart*, as well as global R&B sensation Beyoncé on the surprise 2016 hit LP *Lemonade* and Frank Ocean on his #1 *Blonde* album among other collaborators.

Now in his early 50's, when asked what still gets him most excited about making new music each new day in the studio, Dean reverts back to his *tech geek* side, confessing that, "It's new gear I think. New software, things like digging through new sounds and making new sounds." When pressed to reveal some of his go-to gear in the home studio where he both makes and mixes tracks that wind up routinely on radio these days, he breaks down and highlights:

Minimoog Voyagers, the Roland Juno-106, and the Triton. I use every piece of software I can get my hands on. I like to record with either a U-67s or Sony C800G vocal mic and I use an Ableton for making music.

Mike recently used that home studio to bang out his own humorous parody of President Donald Trump's campaign crisis with the leak of the Access Hollywood tape. One whose twist was original enough to catch coverage in mainstream media like *Entertainment Weekly* and *The Source*, who said of Mike's musical comedy: "Imagine a song with the hardcore beats of *Yeezus*, the commercial cheeriness of a political campaign ad, and the lyrics an even more unfiltered Donald Trump. Producer Mike Dean reacted to the leak of Trump's lewd comments in the most Mike Dean way possible — remixing Trump's words into a catchy jam."

With his calendar as booked as busy as ever these days working with A-list stars across the hip hop, R&B, and pop spectrums, the producer still has plans to make a detour down to a different part of the south where, "I'll probably go to Nashville pretty soon and do some country stuff." While he keeps his ear tuned in to the present most of the time given the constant demand on his talents, Dean closes with a final reminiscence on his favorite musical contributions to shaping southern hip hop's mainstream evolution, taking a proud papa point of view on picking between them:

> I'd probably choose all of them. I really like *Smile, Good Life, and Stronger.* I think that was the sound of an era.
> *You can hear more at www.Deanslist.net*

CHAPTER EIGHTEEN
B-boy for Life – Afrika Islam

"B-boy" is arguably the most common cult of personality bouncing around in east coast hip hop history. A movement that anyone was welcome to join so long as they could MOVE. One whose revolutions remain as relevant today as they were when head-spinning street soldiers first took to the concrete dance floors to set it spinning into motion. Short for "break boy," this army counted as many "break girls," or "b-girls" in its ranks as "b-boys," who collectively made up hundreds of break-dancing crews around New York City's five boroughs with a scene centered in mid-1970s in the Bronx. Propelled by originators of a signature DJ-ing style known as *breakbeat* that served as the soundtrack to the b-boy culture and break-dancing battles, laying the foundations in the same time for what would become one of hip hop's defining rhythmic principles a decade later.

Starring a visionary cast of turn-table trailblazers, this storied club featured A-Players like DJ Cool Herc, The Rock Steady Crew, Kool DJ Dee, Grandmaster Flash, The Zulu Kings, the New York City Breakers, SalSol, The Seven Deadly Sinners, Shanghai Brothers, The Bronx Boys, Rockwell Association, Starchild La Rock, Rock Steady Crew, the Crazy Commanders and of course, one of its most storied forefathers, Afrika Bambaataa, and his Universal Zulu Nation. Known in b-boy circles as the "Amun-Ra of hip hop culture," who as an inventor of break-dancing, had his own following of b-boys and b-girls who would follow in his footsteps once they stepped out from under his wing, including offspring Afrika Islam, who proudly:

> Being that I grew up in New York City, it was a Mecca of music, and multicultural. The South Bronx was definitely a place where it was post-gangs influence on Black, Puerto Rican, the influence of WBLS – which was a black-owned radio station in New York City and WLIB, which was a Caribbean radio station in New York City. Then of course all of the pop stations that existed that were playing Top 40. You still had the advent of *Soul Train* and *Midnight Special* on TV as far as music coming to you. And I still haven't even said dance yet. So take a

combination of all of that in a borough like the South Bronx. Being that the South Bronx itself was the home of hip hop, you could understand what my influences were: I was a b-boy, I was a Zulu King b-boy, and I was a Rock Steady Crew b-boy. So I came up in that melting pot.

So musically, you gotta go to James Brown, you gotta go to Sly Stone, Sam Cooke, Little Richard, Chuck Berry, Louis Armstrong, George Clinton, and Grand Central Station. Those were direct influences. But at the same time, you gotta go to everything that came out of Motown, Stax Records, *and* you have to go to the local groups that came out of New York City: which were anything that created Salsa. You make that combination with James Brown and Sly Stone, then you'll have your melting pot. Along with all the rock of course that was out there. I would specifically say from Grand Funk Railroad to Vanilla Fudge to Led Zeppelin and Hendrix. That's who influenced me coming up as a child. But they also influenced Afrika Bambaataa, Kool Herc, and Grandmaster Flash – that's where all hip hop was built. And I'm a pioneer in hip hop. That's who were my direct influences.

Prizing Afrika Bambaattaa's guiding influence as both a cultural and musical mentor that the producer both modeled and named himself after when he chose the professional moniker Afrika Islam, the producer's apprenticeship under Bambaataa's wing continued, "As a producer, where we have to look at my

work with Afrika Bambaattaa and the Zulu Kings, his influence
specifically on me was the fact that he was the master of records
and he played such a substantial amount of music, more so than
any of the other DJs at the time."

Jumping off the sidelines as soon as he could to get behind
the wheels of steel and put everything he'd been studying into
the full effect when – in 1977 at just ten years old – he joined the
Zulu Kings-inspired progeny and now legendary Rock Steady
Crew, who the New York Times years later would credit for
moving, "Break dancing off the curb and into the mainstream
when it was founded in 1977...They started out as street kids.
The dancing kept them mostly on the right side of the law.
They came from the Bronx...The expression – the style of it –
was a mix of rhythm and blues, Bruce Lee movies, poverty, and
summer heat. It was what you did because you could not afford
boxing lessons or Little League gear. You did it on the blacktop
near a fire hydrant with a crowd of street gangs and bikers
looking on. The dancing was a subculture...(and) Rock Steady
emerged from this cauldron to become the premier break dance
group in New York." Soon keeping the beat for his crew of still
world-famous breakdancers like Crazy Legs as he would in later
years with pioneering west coast emcee Ice-T, Afrika Islam – in a
fascinating history lesson for hip hop fans – traced his own
lineage within the group as the next natural extension of:

> The original Zulu Kings in the Zulu Nation.
> The Zulu Kings were the original group. Rock
> Steady branched off after the Zulu Kings, which
> would have been Johnny J or Charlie Rock or
> myself, when we went to the next level and
> became DJs or emcees like Pow Wow. Who was
> a Zulu Nation b-boy who became part of Soul

Sonic Force with Afrika Bambaataa and Jazzy J. So then the next level went to Crazy Legs and Doze and Buck Four and Frosty Freeze. That's the Rock Steady Crew. That was the next level and the next generation of b-boys as hip hop progressed and moved onward and expanded. That's what it was.

When you look at the original Rock Steady Crew DJs, the originals were Mike and DJ Q-Bert. I look at any DJ like Honda or Aladdin, or those that I was really close to that were the next generation from me that went all over the world and came under me and Jazzy in order to become that next battle DJ – because that's basically what it was. What I was doing was just trying to expand my horizon by not keeping it hip hop, but making everything I do hip hop. That expands the universe of hip hop in a culture. Because if it's dance music, twist it, and make it hip hop. Play it your way with their records. So in a sense, it's like, I'm not rocking the beats, I'm rocking the turntable: whatever you put on it, I'm gonna rock in my way, I'm gonna twist it. That's coming back from being a pioneer, an original, because that's what we were faced within. There were no hip hop records. There were only records that we made into hip hop classics. That's a difference.

Breaking down some of the recording-spinning rudiments he picked up as he began studying the science of DJing hands-on.

Afrika Islam recounts an education on the evolution of his learning to use the turntable itself as a rhythmic instrument where "you saw people put tape on the record in order to mark it or set up a certain part where the break started, well you already found the IQ and spin back and scratch. Well you learned one to ten of the fundamentals, so you start emulating what you might have seen as a complete package. But if you don't understand how to build the foundation, then there's a lost art. So I had a Ph.D in beats because of Afrika Bambaataa, so it would have been real simple to just sample record one to record million, but to try to actually break away from what I learned, you gotta void everything that you know and write."

Exercising the acrobatics of juggling the musical and performance perspectives of being a DJ with the masterful musical coordination as he did so while mixing four turntables simultaneously, Islam quickly stood out in the constantly-competitive crowd and b-boy culture as he continued honing his skills on the battle circuit. Squaring off against the hottest DJs from around the five boroughs and soon beyond. The producer proudly points to the history he feels lucky enough to be a part of when:

> I was with Jazzy J in the original battles for the world championship. Being a Zulu DJ and all my practices and being a student of Flash and Grand Wizard, I had to battle them. And to keep respect. You can't battle someone with his own technique, it's just sacrilegious. It's his thing, so you have to invent something else. If you want street cred and to test your skills against the best – which of course we both had to do, me and Jazzy J – so what me and J did is we became a

Tag Team, a real battle tag team. We played against Flash. We played against whoever. When we would come out, we'd lock arms and play four turntables. That's what we did to create that tag team and scratch at the same time.

So you learn to syncopate a record that you're not controlling, not just a continuous loop. It's just like juggling. So once you start learning, you can juggle one, you can juggle two, three. So that's what I did. I went to the lab – being my bedroom at home – and I just figured out *How would I do it if somebody else was playing with me?* So I kind of played just with myself. That's what I did. And I was smart enough to have a basic beat to follow, because the other three beats that followed it were being manipulated by me. So I was able to lock in one or two beats on top of it. And scratch or I'm able to scratch three records and have the basic beat play.

Taking his skills from the streets to the airwaves in the early 80's when he became the DJ for his very own radio Zulu Beats radio show on local New York station WHBI, providing him another invaluable education in honing his ear to precisely what an audience wanted to hear from him. This instinct would lend itself naturally to producing his own beats once he began working with Ice-T. And in recounting highlights from his training camp on the air, Islam proudly begins with his dubious distinction as:

The first hip hop DJ on the radio with the Zulu beats. And hell, we were playing drum machines from cassette tapes at live parties, and I always saw the beat, "Where's the beat?" I'm a b-boy first, "That's a dope beat," because I'm a dancer, and didn't really understand radio. When I did the Zulu Beats radio show in 1983 on WHBI, it wasn't really about that either. Zulu beats was about putting hip hop on the air, unlike Mr. Magic who put Rap on the air. But the Zulu Beats had put me on the air. I was interviewing Crazy Legs, I was interviewing Ghandi, and Fab 5 Freddy. And at the same time, I'm playing battles at Harlem World.

Just because he'd become a local star on the b-boy scene spinning records didn't mean Islam had lost any of his moves on the break-dancing circuit, proving so when he stepped out from behind the turntables after being cast to get down as a break-dancer on screen in the feature films *Flashdance* and 1984s *Breakin'* I, where ironically Ice-T was cast as well rapping while b-boys got down. The duo would wind up co-starring in the sequel, 1985s *Breakin' II: Electric Boogaloo*, collaborating for the first time on wax together at the same time on the film's soundtrack on the cut, *Party People (Go Off)*, which featured Islam on the cut behind the turntables, where Ice proclaimed, "He's the beast from the East and I'm the best from the West!"

Cementing their creative chemistry as they would embark the next year into the studio to make their first album – and hip hop history – together, the *LA Times* captured a sense of how close the two already were in a 1985 feature where they profiled a, "Master rapper is a young man who goes by the name of Ice-T, ice meaning cool and T being short for Tracy, which is his first name...Ice-T was wearing black leather shorts, sneakers and an Adidas baseball cap. With him, sitting frog-like on the floor, was a man identified as Afrika Islam who, I was told, is famous as president of a hip hop club in New York called the Zulu Nation."

A revolution on record that would mark West Coast rap's Big Bang, *Rhyme Pays* would mark the debut of Ice-T as an emcee and Africa Islam as a producer on wax as they invented the template for Gangster Rap together. Moving musically all over the map as acrobatically as a b-boy break-dancing, Islam put his DJ mentality to work keeping the crowd on their feet by constantly switching up records as he wove multiple rhythmic beds into the same song, transitioning with an imagination that *Rolling Stone* described as, "A backdrop (of)...rolling, spare beats and samples...for the rapper's charismatic rhymes." The first hip hop producer to successfully merge East Coast beats with West Coast gangster rhymes bouncing overtop. The producer remembered feeling like the record was a logical successor to the influence his mentor Afrika Bambaataa's had already had on the city of lights, with *Billboard* noting that, "Before Ice-T's ascension, L.A. rappers were known primarily for a synthesizer-dominated sound indebted to Kraftwerk's innovations as well as Afrika Bambaataa's 1982 hit, *Planet Rock*, while...hardcore rap was dominated by the East Coast. That began to change in 1987, when Ice-T's debut album, *Rhyme Pays*, was released."

As he raided his life-long record collection for inspiration, Islam remembered experiencing something of a full-circle moment in realizing just how far his b-boy Culture had traveled in its influence on a national level. Taking him from New York all the way to pioneer a new sound on a new frontier, he proudly carried the torch Bambaataa had passed him:

> Being that I had access to all the records Bambaataa had, I had an infinite number of beats. And that was evident in the work that me and Ice did. But Ice-T was more of a lyrical rapper that wasn't truly based in the beats. As in the sense that those who would have been around us like a Scott La Rock or Rakim or Doug E. Fresh or Kool Moe Dee or Big Daddy Kane or E.P.M.D. or even Biz Markie.

> Ice is telling a story, so his delivery is based on Iceberg Slim. And being that I'm a fan of Iceberg Slim, I automatically knew where it was coming from. So dropping into a beat, that wasn't hard at all. But it was taking the emphasis out of the music when he was trying to keep his point. That was the key to it.

The first b-boy to light up the West like Bugsy Siegel when he first lit up Las Vegas, Islam was about to turn L.A. into a literal BOOM town as he dropped what iTunes years later donned, "The immortal single '6 'N the Mornin' which helped to define gangsta rap." Proving that genius sometimes is as simple as it sounds in hip hop. Every punch of every beat, break and sample he programmed was deliberately designed by Islam like a painter making careful strokes onto a canvas. As he blended SP1200 with the Roland 808 that would become the bedrock of West Coast rap production, Islam revealed:

That big boom popped out just from me turning up the 808 in the studio and blowing the speakers out. And the engineer came running in saying, "Yo man, what are you doing?!" That's "*6 'n the Morning.*" That song boomed and they tried to cut it back because we were blowing up speakers. Somehow we got to a point where we didn't put a real big gate on it and let the delay play and it was just kick and snare. That's where you got that massive boom on that song. We recorded that song on an SP-12 and an 808 and the original 12-inch version we did on an Oberheim DMX.

Ice's style was based upon creating imagery and explaining the gangs of L.A. and explaining pimp life and the hustler life. So I was just trying to build the right soundtrack around him that would deliver what he wanted without making people go nuts on the dance floor. It was more so to keep that groove going where they would get a chance to listen to what the hell he was saying like *You Played Yourself*. *6 'n the Mornin'* dropped because it was simply what it was supposed to be, telling a story about when the cops raid. So that beat was the right beat.

The first street anthem of its time, the legendary blueprint he laid with *6 'n the Mornin'* would become a popularly-mimicked beatscape as the new genre found its legs. Inspiring the likes of the genre's future, Dr. Dre, to pay homage of the sort Islam paid to Bambaataa with *Planet Rock* when Dr. Young programmed beats for two of N.W.A.'s biggest hits that sampled Islam in the same tradition:

> In Ice's situation, if it wasn't for my friendship with Eazy E and Dr. Dre as a DJ, they would have never been able to do *Gangsta Gangsta* and *Dope Man* if it wasn't for *6 'n the Mornin'*. You gotta give it to Ice for dropping that tempo to *6 'n the Mornin'* because the whole West Coast followed that. Then, eventually all of the south, even though it was a New York thing. Of course me being from New York and being with Ice made ours an East-West Coast collaboration in the true sense. And without us dropping that tempo down, there never would have been a *Dope Man* or *Gangsta Gangsta* because it's the same beat. That dropped the West Coast down to then do g-funk music. Because if you listen to World Class Wrecking Crew, the original DJ group where Dre's from, they were up tempo. So I see where the root of the branches are because I was there.

The instant their sound hit the streets, it became the official soundtrack of the hoods in Ice-T's home turf of South Central Los Angeles. And as his boom was heard from farther and farther out into the White America, it revealed an untapped market that would commercially fuel much of the legitimacy hip hop would take on as an art form as it gained mainstream credibility. Afrika Islam would be the first producer to pierce the ears of the suburban teenager, and as a consequence of he and Ice's provocative breakthrough, *Billboard* would later confirm that, "With the release of *Rhyme Pays*, the West Coast was well on its way to becoming a crucial part of hip hop." *Rolling Stone Magazine* would authenticate Marrow as, "The first West Coast rap star to get those themes over to the massive record-buying public of Middle America."

Ice-T's position as West Coast rap's head shot caller would solidify itself nationally when he returned to the silver screen the next year. This time stealing the scene with his voice alone as he narrated what the *New York Times* in 1988 deemed, "Perhaps the most eloquent depiction of the rapper as gangster, an image that is catching on among a new generation of hip hoppers, particularly on the West Coast...over a slow, nightmarish electronic rhythm, Ice-T delivered an apology for the 'gang-bangers,' the violent gang members." Another key elevation for both the rapper and his producer arrived when *Colors* became Ice's debut on the Billboard Hot 100. Islam remembered when the opportunity first came knocking with the film as one he knew they needed to answer with as dope a beat as he'd ever laid down for Ice to menace overtop. Starting with the eerie opening notes, which he created:

> We played the melody through the drum machine. *Colors* was an 808, an SB-12 and a 303. That little sound effect thing you hear at the beginning and throughout the choruses was a mistake! It happened with the engineer. He was using an echo and the echo kept going. So when he tried to stop it, the last one made that sound you hear on the record. And I said, "Hold that. What's that?" And then we used it in the song. It was a weird, mechanical, chilling sound that fit what we were doing.

Scaring the shit out of mainstream music critics fascinated by and yet in the same time nearly afraid of the dark realities Ice-T was exposing for the first time on tape, *Spin Magazine* would credit an important part of that shiver effect to the fact that, "It's relentless downbeat gives the backbone to the bleak vision of dead-end violence *Colors* depicts." As he programmed the song's ominous pattern, Islam remembers basing the beat around following Ice's lyrical cadence:

> When we did *Colors,* he based his lyric off of *King* Sun-D Moet's *Mythological Rapper.* So I just followed the same pattern but added in the mood that would let you imagine, *What would you listen to if you were going to do a drive-by? What state of mind should you be in?* And being that we'd both been part of the game, we just put it together. I think that has a lot to do with the difference between me and any other producer: I'm from the floor up. Ice is from the floor up. So we did understand the fundamentals of what we listened to pre-studio. What we listened to ourselves. West Coast was on the low and New York the up-tempo. But when we came together, it was a meeting of the minds in picking out what we did to get the message across. That was my job.

Inventing a production style that established the sonic dimensions whose space he filled with new sounds and possibilities that a new generation of up and coming producers would soon start imitating and re-creating in their own interpretations. It was all based on the blueprint Islam designed as a re-invention of his b-boy record making roots where, "Since we were kind of the first to flip what an SB-12 should be. Because the SB-12 and Linn drum machine were basically made to be a substitute drummer, with a small sample space and I guess they weren't thinking of somebody who was going to loop a song into it. Then once you broke the first rule of not putting the kick and snare and looping an entire song and then putting the kick and snare into it, the possibilities were infinite as well as limited only to the point of how far your technology could go. But if you just take this back very simply to the 808, the 808 was not made to be successful. It was basically a toy for those at Roland that made it. The fact is that it galvanized and flipped and that the big decay became the big boom that revolutionized music and busted so many monitors and speakers in studios. That in itself revolutionized music." A master of manipulating the new wave of cutting edge drum machines and samplers hitting the market just as they were hitting the studio to deliver Ice-T's next West Coast hip hop innovation. Islam's own as a producer was centered in a philosophy:

> That's where the real talent was: what you did with the limited machine. You made it limitless in everything that we were doing because we broke the hand-cuffs. And I think that was from thinking outside the box. This goes across the board –909, 808, 303, the LinnDrum, DMX, SB-12 – we just changed the game. And if you were a b-boy and a DJ, that also goes down to the 1200 turntables. Nobody was supposed to take the matte off, put a slip-matte on, spin records back, and scratch on things.

With the video in heavy rotation, MTV would later argue that Ice and Islam's artistic growth between *6 'n the Mornin'* and *Colors* made him sound, "Stronger, both lyrically and musically, with more incisive lyrics, than anything he had previously released." The same could be said for the sophistication of the soundscapes Afrika was crafting for his one and only studio sidekick. And with this sonically cinematic instrumental, the producer remembered feeling drawing muse from the movie's dailies:

> When we were working on it for the film, in my head, I'm thinking, *This is about a drive-by, turn the lights out, car's moving slow, and you're on one mission.* That's what the story was about. Or like the scene in the movie when the two gangs are walking toward each other getting ready to riot in the L.A. county jail, that was the idea. And when the producers heard it, they were like, "Oh shit! That's it!" They'd never heard anybody talk about gangs like that, and with that backdrop, sure, it made it official. It made the movie look like it was really portraying reality. It really did. And when *Colors* came on the radio that was that national break-out!

By far the biggest star of the West Coast's burgeoning hip hop scene. By 1988, Ice-T truly had the *power* to keep pushing the envelope as his sound evolved into what Afrika Islam's hometown *The Village Voice* contended just two short years into their career was already, "His own sound: flat, clipped, quick-lipped, and when he sticks to his subject, his narrative style is as gripping and understated as Islam's sample." The eclectic patchwork of samples that the producer and emcee constructed for each of the album's musical chapters told stories of life in the hood so profound and provocative that *AllHipHop.com* would later decree *Power* to be, "Groundbreaking to say the least. Joints like the *I'm Your Pusher* and *High Rollers* depicted the ups and downs of getting fast money; sounding like nothing else on the radio at the time." Starring samples overtop his rhythm tracks that radio had indeed never spun before. Afrika Islam brought gangster rap to the airwaves in true pimp style with when he cleverly colored the classic 1972 hustler anthem *Pusherman* by Curtis Mayfield from the *Superfly* soundtrack into the song's melodic personality, even bringing a real pimp in to resing the chorus:

> We didn't sample anything and got somebody to come in and sing, a brother by the name of Pimpin' Rex who was a real pimp to sing that hook. And the vocals were recorded in the closet at Evil E's house! We took it from Curtis Mayfield and flipped it. It was his record but we were just trying to say we were selling records as dope. It's the new hustle. That's what Ice was trying to say. What I wrote that beat on was a LinnDrum. Everything was programmed on a Linn 9000 with an 808 synched together. Then, the bass line was written on an SH-101. And that I just wrote in to mimic Curtis Mayfield's *Pusherman*.

> With *High Rollers* too. Basically because of the theme of the song, I had to go back to something that was blaxploitation. And *Paying the Cost to*

Be the Boss was the right song to do it. So I made that with a 909 and a Linn 9000 together.

Recorded at Syndicate Studios West, aka DJ Evil E's house, while the trio was working on a tight budget, they had the freedom of a lock-out clock to work around. Taking as much time as they needed to create what MTV would compliment as a, "More assured and impressive record," while *Spin* went a step further, hailing it as a, "Near-masterpiece." Tackling the title track on his trusty SP-1200, Islam once again brought his breakdance roots to bear in harnessing the raw *Power* of what he heard the instant Ice first dropped the concept on him:

That was a straight b-boy record. It didn't have a lot in it. It was a straight b-boy record because that's what he's saying, "Power!" I gave him the most powerful b-boy record I could. And the minute one heard that, he would automatically salute. And if you can catch his lyrics, shit, *Power* is being used at the b-boy battles still today! They sped it up a little. But when that shit comes on, it does the same effect: it makes motherfuckers throw down and hit the floor. That's what I wanted to achieve, not to make heads swing, I wanted to make m'fuckers get down on the floor. Basically, move out of the way! That's the truism of it. When you put it on, I'm throwing my skills down, I'm doing headspins, I'm trying to bust your ass! It's an aggressive record, and b-boy records are all break-beats, so they're aggressive. And Ice is talking about power. The strange thing was, everything Ice talked about, he was living or had lived: the power of money, power of bitches, and the shit is all true.

Ice-T specialized in sex rhymes as much as he did gangster tales. Often within the same song space, and always with the sort of inviting suave reserved only for a true pimp's way with words. With *Girls L.G.B.N.A.F.*, he would talk ladies right into the mood and out of their panties overtop a true party romp of a beat where Islam broke more new ground with:

> What I did with that was a double drum machine, two together – one at a faster speed, one at a lower speed – and I locked them. That's why you got this weird, syncopated beat. Two drum machines at two different speeds. Nobody was fucking around like that then, but that's what it was.

Precisely the type of gag order radio was trying to keep on hip hop by keeping it off the airwaves. Ice and Islam would respond even more aggressively with his third studio album, *The Iceberg/Freedom of Speech... Just Watch What You Say!*, which put the first amendment front and center in a brilliant counter-attack on censorship. Knowing he needed to deliver his own knock-out punch with the beat he made for *Lethal Weapon*, the album's flagship single and statement, Islam entered the ring ready to swing because:

> Like I said, "Nobody was fucking around like that back then." I wrote it on the SP-1200. It's all samples of different things. I had written the

drum beat first and the bassline first. When he heard it, he came back to me and said, "I got this idea," and then I dropped all that back in and just kind of fine-tuned it. And the horn section, that's from a classic b-boy break called *Razor Blade.* Which you only knew that record if you were in Zulu. So we just pulled the horn from *Razor Blade* and it was scratched in the way it's supposed to be. And the rest of it was what I wrote.

By the late 1980s, James Brown had become as much a standard element of hip hop sampling as b-boy breaks, and Islam called on the Godfather of Soul when putting together the musical elements of the album's other hit single, *You Played Yourself.* With Ice dropping science overtop an infectious horn hook from Maceo Parker and Fred Wesley on *The Boss,* the producer played along once again with a SP1200:

I wrote the beat on it. Evil E was part of the equation because he came in the studio and looped the sample over my beat. He was talking about a pimp thing, a player thing. "You played yourself," so you had to have that, "I'm sitting at the Apollo, I'm sitting at the nightclub listening to the Last Poets." You had to have that in order to understand what he was saying. It was supposed to make you bounce for a minute.

In the four short years between the time *Rhyme Pays* and the appropriately-titled *OG Original Gangster* dropped, West Coast rap had gone mainstream courtesy of both the trail Ice-T had blazed, and the fire that followed when N.W.A. rocketed to #4 on the Billboard Top 200 Album Chart with *Straight Outta Compton* and protest anthem *Fuck the Police*. Demonstrating he remained as relevant as ever in his ability to impact the direction of hip hop culture as it continued its shopping mall invasion, *The Source* would years later credit Ice with introducing, "The first time the term 'OG' was heard by the masses, thus given birth to a commonly used term in society today within its creation." Giving him license to take it once again back to the old school even as the production team kept his sound as cutting-edge as ever, Afrika remembered feeling that because:

> We were moving up in technology, that's what the songs needed. Once Ice named the project *Original Gangster*, that's what the record was. It was Ice rapping about that hustler life, that's what it was to him. OG was a collaboration between me, DJ Aladdin and SLJ. Basically, they were following like The Bomb Squad ideology. It was my ideology for arrangement but it was their ideology for how they wanted to put down their samples. The way they put down their samples was a more structured composite of song form, because that's what the record needed. It needed song forms because of the way Ice was dropping the hooks.

Arguably the biggest and ballsiest move Ice and Islam busted on the record was an experiment that worked so well *Rolling Stone* would later credit the band for, "The countless rap/metal acts they spawned," and with *Body Count*, the speed metal rap group of the same name was born. Marking the next studio project he would embark on with the rapper-turned-singer. Afrika was excited by the challenges involved in producing an entirely different style of music, basing his production on a philosophy where, "Ice had the ability to cut the album at Warner Bros., and they said yes. So the songs that came out were based upon the two schools of thought: 'Let's do the rock and twist it and do it our way. That's what you got, our version of rock. And put the same topic that we would have put into a Ice-T record on a rock format record.'"

The *L.A. Times* described *Body Count*'s sound as a, "Balanced blend of black, white and Latino, rockers and rappers, grungies and yuppies, was as mixed as *Body Count*'s heavy-metal-with-black-roots music." A live concert performance is essentially what Islam attempted to capture on tape. It was a move that he argued made sonic sense because, "Body Count was made to be a performance band for Lollapalooza. So it made sense for the band to record pretty much live off the floor: number one it was a lot of fun, and number two it was loops upon loops and eventually picking the right loops, and putting all that together. We were celebrating influences like Hendrix, Buddy Miles, Baby Huey, Little Richard, Chuck Berry, Living Colour's Vernon Reid, and Doug Wimbash. We were responding more with a concern for holding up the fort the rock concept. A lot of riffs went down the drain, but the ones that got chosen seemed to hold up for the test of time."

Always controversial, Ice would rock the establishment literally when he released the single *Cop Killer*. Causing L.A. riots-hot fire throughout the political, corporate and law enforcement communities which raised both Ice-T and *Body Count*'s profile and position in the Top 40 when *Entertainment Weekly* reported that constant press by it and hundreds of other mainstream media "Boosted *Body Count* from #73 to #26 on the

Billboard pop-album chart." Blaming the song's firestorm in part on circumstance – although one could argue Ice had been predicting it for years in his gangster raps – with the fact it dropped right before the Rodney King verdict, Islam reveals:

> I think we recorded that song a year and a half before the riots hit. Ironically, that wasn't a single off the album for all the attention it got. The single was *The Winner Loses* and was an anti-drug record. But then when the riots happened, *Cop Killer* became a right-time/right-place type anthem. That shit shocked everything, because it was shocking for standard society to hear brothers speaking loud, like, "Here's one from us that's a psychopath that says, FUCK YOU!"

Throughout his studio successes, Islam has never lost touch with his b-boy roots, touring the world where his DJing legend preceded him globally. Teaming up with techno turntable wizard Westbam as a touring duo, they released their first single *Nite Of the Tschuldigungs* in 1996 followed by *Free Me, What's Up at the Brotherfront,* and *Viva la Revolucion,* before dropping their debut album, *New World Order* in 1999. The producer – who performs behind the wheels of steel with Westbam under the pseudonym Mr. X and Mr. Y – feels his current spin around the Technics is something of a full-circle:

> The proud part for me comes from other people realizing and going, "Oh shit, I didn't know you did this!" It's a hard thing for people to make the jump where they go, "Yo, you've been playing EDM," and I'm like, "Nah, I'm kind of one of

the ones that helped invent that too," and they're going, "I didn't see your name," and I tell them "I did it under Mr. X." And when I get asked why I went under a pseudonym, I say, "Because I wanted to challenge myself again." I didn't want to reinvent myself, I just wanted to challenge myself to twist electronic music into hip hop. There were a couple different things when X/Y shit hit. We did a *New World Order* record, and it hit all over Europe, and *Viva la Revolucion*, hit in Argentina. Then, we're getting up to play, and there's 100,000 people outside because it's their theme song from jail. So yeah, a couple of times that shit fucks you up.

So the double-man group of Mr. X and Mr. Y was born with me and Westbam. It was four turntables, all live, scratching, a mic, and echo chambers. The next thing I know, you have groups coming out and EDM is getting bigger and there's more money being made. And it's stretching the rubber band. I'm reaching back to all of my other DJ brethren going, "You don't really just have to play that. You're a DJ first," and any time you just say, "I'm a hip hop DJ," you're still limiting yourself. Because that's your craft and your craft goes everywhere. That's just the music that's on your turntable right now, and you're not selling out. You're expanding the universe, and that's what I do – more like a farmer planting seeds, and taking it around the world because I know I've influenced a lot of people around the world.

Bringing the Zulu revolution into its next generation courtesy of a new label he's co-founded recently with longtime collaborator Ice-T, Afrika rises each morning with sights on the next sonic boom that he hopes will flatten all genre boundaries when it drops. Describing his vision as one where, "Our record label Electronic Beats Empire is like the no limitations." When seeking to inspire the same boundless ambition, or answer a next-step question from an aspiring up and coming producer he's already set off marching that direction to his beat. Islam recommends keeping your eyes and ears first and foremost with how the rap artist presents himself:

> If you're producing a rap artist, that's the thing you gotta deal with. If you've got a great rapper, like a Tupac or a Biggie or a Rakim or a Kool Keith or Chuck D who can jump on anything and make that better, then you're blessed. Because they can turn any beat – even something that may not be up to their par – into something great. If you've got a rapper that's less and you've got a beat that's fire and he can't get down on top of that fire, then you're wasting a beat because hip hop is all about the beat. Rap is a different thing. Rap is just a part of hip hop. But hip hop is all about the beat...straight-up! A dope beat can live on its own.
> *https://twitter.com/afrikaislam*

CHAPTER NINETEEN
The Preacher's Son– Wyclef Jean

Hip hop has always offered the greatest opportunity within any music genre to open musical minds to new infusions of styles interplaying on the same track for the first time. One of its bedrocks of invention, from the always-fresh ways in which samples were pulled from R&B, soul, jazz, pop, classical, and beyond. And then re-invented into a new sound altogether. There have been many scientists of this sonic artform, but few as responsible for the introduction of World Music into hip hop as the internationally revered and respected as Wyclef Jean. Hailing from abroad himself, Wyclef's roots in world music are as natural as they come, born in the slums of Haiti. Jean first heard the beat of the streets enter his ear as organically as the sounds of nature:

> For me, it started in Haiti, I was in a village, and I remember my introduction to music was listening to the birds and the wind. We were in a small village in the town of Croix-des-Bouquets. And there was a small Nazarene church that we would go to every Sunday. That church would be like banging bongos, all types of stuff, and naturally we felt at home.
>
> I would say my first experience with music was more of like a tribal one. Just a one with nature vibe. Because in the village you had no electricity, no nothing, so my first 808 sound I heard was the sound of thunder! My first treble was the sound of lightning, that's like fact.

Long before revolutionizing hip hop forever when he co-founded The Fugees, Wyclef's musical journey would become Americanized after his family emigrated to New York City in the dawn of a new decade in 1979, right as Rap's own sun was first rising. Hearing a different kind of beat on his block, this time the electronic kind blasted through the sonic frame of a boom box, Clef had already begun to follow his ear to the source, physically sounding out the patterns he heard on the bongos with his own hands on whatever he could get his hands on around the house before the church became a catalyst for his first real instrumental discoveries. Quickly revealing himself as a prodigious talent, able to wrap his musical mind around any instrument he could get his hands on, while other kids his age were out running around on the playground, thankfully, his father's church had a whole music room for Clef to - quite literally - *play* in as talent took over his self-study on an accelerated learning course:

> I got to the projects of Brooklyn when I was ten years old, the Marlboro Projects in Coney Island, and my dad was a Minister - similar to Marvin Gaye's father or Aretha or Whitney, just different people from the church - so you're naturally influenced by that culture, and I just found myself loving instruments at a young age and wanting to play multiple instruments.

> My early instruments in the church were as follows: accordion, trombone, organ, piano, then it led into guitar, bass, and drums. Those were like the structures of the instruments, and the idea of where producing came from, that just came from being a choir director at a very young age. I had to put the songs together, the parts together - soprano, bass, alto, "Bassman, this is what you wanna do, drummer, this is what you wanna do," at a very young age. It was key for every Sunday morning, and I remember one Sunday just running out of hymns in the church book, and I was like, "Dad, we don't got no more hymns," and he was like, "Well, go make

up some songs, those are gonna be the new hymns." (laughs) So I guess that's maybe where my whole production/composing chops started out.

When he wasn't in church, growing up in the projects where hip hop was the official soundtrack, Clef took musical direction from the block as well. It was here he discovered a key personality within his voice via the unique cheering section of the hustlers on the corner who – clearly aware of young Wyclef's gift and distinct Caribbean accent – paid him not to be a 5-0 lookout or drug runner, but rather an entertainer. Hiring Clef to serenade them with his acoustic guitar and voice playing Bob Marley, Peter Tosh and other reggae favorites, he became part of that urban soundtrack. An extraordinary compliment of encouragement that reflected just how brightly Clef's potential inspired those around him, he humbly recalls:

> I just consider myself a viber, like Sting, like Bob Marley. Just a soul viber. I always considered my sister the singer, but I think I discovered my voice when I was probably like fourteen, and I would just be singing with the guitar. I remember like dudes, if they had a problem with they girlfriend, they would be like, "Yo Clef man, come sing something with this guitar, put my name on it," and then they got back with their girls after I did that. So I was like, "Yo, there must be something going on with my voice." (laughs)

It felt kind of cool. Then it was cool for me because you're on the block, right, and the fact that sometimes like a drug dealer would give you like, "You shorty, you don't wanna be on this corner. Take that guitar and make something of yourself." You know? Or they'd be like, "Yo man, play us Bob Marley." So now you become like this voice of the streets. So whatever you're doing, it's based from this whole urban-type street thing. And you don't know what it is yet, but you validate it. So by the time you get to pop culture, that thing that they're feeling is that thing that is built from the gutter.

When he wasn't singing, Wyclef soon found another important voice within his musical personality on the block. When he got in on an inner-city teenage past-time as all-American as football or roller skating. "At probably thirteen or fourteen, I fell in love with battle rapping, and battle rapping for me was very important because I was coming from a place where I didn't know how to speak English. So automatically when you get to America, it's a culture shock. So you're automatically trying to be a part of something. Within our communities, you are going to be a part of a gang, so you need to figure out which gang you're going to be a part of? Luckily, we had the hip hop gang, and within that battle culture was very strong. I felt this was a way for me to get in and communicate my feeling towards a place that I felt was like a new entry for me, and remember myself being obsessed with battle rap."

Reflective of Clef's eclectic tree of stylistic roots, as seeds were planted, and his multi-talented ability to translate his ear to instrument fluently came into fuller bloom as he made his way through high school. "By fifteen, a music teacher in my high school saw me playing crazy chords on a piano and asked me, 'Where did you learn this?', and I said, 'I can just hear it. It's my daddy's church.' And that teacher, Valerie Price, dragged me into class, and forced me to be in choir. Then, forced the jazz teacher, Mr. Hayes, to take me in." While the swing of jazz would become an instant part of his pedigree as a player, Wyclef was drawn even more strongly to shape himself as a performer and producer in the mold of his Island music roots. Musing in reflection:

> At the same time, I was obsessed with sound system, and in reggae sound system, we have what are known as "dub plates," so as I'm going through these sound systems and all of this Reggae, I just started discovering, then I saw this dude named Bigga Haitian, and the way the dude was sounding, he sounded Jamaican but then he was Haitian, and he was rapping in Creole too, so now I found this stuff fascinating even more. Because it's always good when you see there are those that are doing it before you, so you don't feel alone. So I just started researching a lot of that stuff and I could identify with it. I was listening to Tiger was a Reggae DJ, all of this was very dance hall-influenced stuff, and he was definitely an influence, a lot of Reggae: King Yellowman, Ninjaman, early Supercat was an influence, and the Sound System, Stone Love, stuff like that.

I think what separated me from everybody at the time was I was the only one who was rapping and singing, so like what you see Drake doing now, I was doing that when I was sixteen, seventeen, and even coming out with the Fugees and *Gone to November*, that's rapping-singing. So we have this thing called *Monotone Rap* that's just like you don't hear notes, and I always had notes within my raps, there was always melodies coming in, and I definitely credit that to the reggae influence.

Turning his bedroom into his first recording studio at age sixteen, Wyclef soon, "Started tinkering with electronics. I used to go to Sam Ash, and the cool thing about Sam Ash was then, even if you couldn't afford it, you could walk around the store, play with the stuff, and read the manuals. So I used to constantly read the manuals, and the first person I ever recorded was my girl – whose my wife today (laughs) – and I charged her, so we always make fun of that." The original engines of invention for hip hop's first generation, Roland's drum machines were the gateway for urban prodigies like Clef to translate the drums he was hearing in his head into real beats, mapping out a rhythmic revolution that began with the R-8 Human Rhythm Composer:

My first beat as a battle rapper was banging in the cafeteria. So it goes from banging in the cafeteria to what would be the coolest drum machines. My first drum machine was an R-8, a very cool drum machine. I started doing beats on the R-8 but what I discovered was like, I could trigger live drums to the R-8, and it was insane.

So for me, I was like, "Hold up, I can actually trigger a live kit with this R-8?", and that opened up my brain to a different style, and I was like, "Oh, I can probably produce like Quincy Jones or Kurtis Blow and those guys and mix live music with electronics. So in the very beginning, my idea was, *How can I make man meet machine?* You know what I mean?

So from the R-8 generally comes the SP for me, and the MPC-60. Those were some of the early machineries. But as far as like sequencing, my Pro Tools or my Logic or my Ableton at the time was a drum machine called the Linn 9000. Only nerdy producer geeks know what I'm talking about. That was the original Ableton for us, and that machine I discovered working with a producer named Ronald Bell. Now known as Khalis Bayyan, who played saxophone in the band Kool in the Gang and is the brother of co-founding member/lead singer Kool. He put me up on the Linn 9000.

As the buzz on the block about Clef made its way around the neighborhood's musical network where even the stars who had made it out still kept their ear to the street, often providing the next generation from their home hoods their first foot in the door. A true New York rap pioneer would do just that for Wyclef when the one and only Kurtis Blow took an interest in the teenage wunderkind. Knowing he was home the moment Kurtis gave Clef his exposure to a real recording studio, the producer still fondly recalls:

My first time working in a proper studio, which was with Kurtis Blow when I was like fifteen in New York City. That was my first exposure to a proper recording studio. The first question I remember asking was, "What's this big thing?", and they told me, "It's called a Neve console," and I was like, "Huh, all these buttons, what does it do?" (laughs) At the time, Kurtis Blow was producing the group I had before the Fugees called Exact Change. But I was one of those kids who was watching, and asking questions. And when I saw what he was doing, I was like, "Man, I'm going to get my equipment, I'm going to go to Sam Ash. I can't buy a Neve, but I'm gonna buy something," and it starts there.

As he grew up against the gritty backdrop of Newark, New Jersey in the 1980s, DJing was as much a material part of the hip hop fabric as the boombox or b-boy breakdancer. Pretty soon, as with every other instrument, Clef got his hands on a set of turntables and began spinning, confidently recalling that, "It was a natural thing. With us, it's called Sound System, which is when we're juggling. There's two of us, so my DJ – his name is DJ Leon, original DJ of the Fugees – so it would be me and Leon doing parties together. I would be toasting, which is when you get on the mic onto the next record, we trade off, and we play records. I used to love to do the reggae set." By then, he'd graduated from Vailsburg High School and turned his bedroom into a larger basement studio, "That consisted of an SP-1200 and a VFX keyboard. The SP was definitely a tool that opened your mind to know you had this amount of seconds and you could pull up a loop, and past the SP, there's another one called the

S900 Akai that I really used to sample with. The imagination for that, I just felt like as long as I had the parameters, I felt it was insanely great for me." There, he and cousin Jerry Duplessis began recording local talent including future Fugees band member Lauryn Hill, who even back then Clef instantly recognized was a star, mentoring her from her early teens on:

> Keep in mind, I was recording Lauryn at a young age, so I had time to experiment. I met her when she was fourteen, and for me, she was just soul music. It was like you heard a kid singing and was like, "Holy crap, this sounds like soul music." Like the vinyl she was playing for me, she was sounding like those kind of people. Those voices didn't exist no more, because it was sort of like if someone was singing R&B, it was like clean. So very few, Lauryn, Mary J, there was just something going on with these voices where people can feel something, whether it was struggle, happiness, or pain, they brought that soul out. That came at a young age.

The Fugees were the first true alternative hip hop phenomenon of the 1990s, a pop culture explosion that needed no time for cross-over warm-up. The super-group fit their time perfectly, one where East Coast producers were riding their own new experimental wave through a galaxy of soundscapes that *Rolling Stone Magazine* correctly called "A neopolitan treat, sweet in three layers: rhyme, sample and groove." From their earliest incarnations, those sensibilities were already naturally at play. Producing a sound the world hadn't heard before the Fugees invaded radio from their remarkable beyond exotic form of futuristic-sounding beats to the cosmopolitan musical vibe that Wyclef as the group's lead producer on *The Score* first introduced to hip hop. He matched the album's planetary pallet of musical styles with the equally-universal lyrical panorama. A dizzying, tongue-twisting interplay that the producer traces all the way back to:

> The first group I was ever in was called Exact Change. Then the group became Translator and the idea of Rap Translator was we used to do rap in multiple languages. So it was like rap-linguists. We can translate any form of music to you and however you want it. So that's where Translators came in and then they became Refugee Camp. Originally we wanted to call the group Refugees but there was a rock group with that name. So we were like, "We'll call it Fugees, and people will identify it with Refugees."

Later praised by *Entertainment Weekly* for the fact that, "Unlike much East Coast rap, *The Score* feels warm and intimate – partly because the instruments are live." Wyclef agreed that, "I felt like we could have been like the first hip hop band. And when we say band, the guitarist is singing. You know what I mean? The group is actually playing the instruments, because a lot of artists have hip hop bands but someone's playing the instruments for the band. So I think the Fugees and the Roots had that vibe where it was like a real band. That's really where it starts for me." Something of a testing ground for the world-rap genre that the Fugees would introduce to the world on their break-out album *The Score*, with their 1994 debut *Blunted by Reality*, which *The Source* hailed as, "An eighteen track boom bap classic." Clef – who co-produced the record – considered it an education that he still regards as:

> Important historically because *Blunted on Reality*, the combination of the production was mostly coming from Khalis Bayyan. The concept of all of the records was coming from my brain. Right? So in my brain, I wanted to do *Boof Baf* and wanted it to sound a certain way. *Vocab* was coming, in my brain. Now, this is my brain thinking as a producer, but I'm still not in the forefront yet, you see. But in my brain, I'm already creating *The Score* in my mind, which was ill! Like you're a little kid sitting in there with these bigwigs, and you're like, "Well, I got a concept for this one. It's gonna be called *Vocab*, and here's my guitar riff. This is how it's gonna go." You know what I mean? Usually, the way that it worked for *Blunted*, I came in with all the concepts, like, "This is the theory. This is what we're gonna talk about."

The Score was a tour-de-force that the *BBC* argued took the world of hip hop by storm so successfully because "The Fugees wear their influences on their sleeves both musically and lyrically. Name-checking Santana and Bob Marley, artists who, like them, took their culture mainstream. At a time when communication and travel were going global, this was the ultimate eclectic post-modernist album – of Chinese food, cognac, Westerns, Kung Fu, sitars and reggae. No wonder it went multi-platinum, leaving its creators with the world at their feet." As the mastermind behind the album's sci-fi sounding sonics, Clef remembered channeling as muse a true master of the concept record as producer of the mother of them all, Michael Jackson's *Thriller*, sharing that conceptually:

> I used to love the way Quincy Jones had all of these layers in the records, and then it always came back to the funk. So for me, I would say that's where my hip hop/jazz brain kicked in. I wanted to make something sound sonically different from what anybody was doing out there. We knew that there was a group of people who would fully understand what we were doing because they were just like us. They were looking for that natural mix. Like there were people who loved hip hop. But at the same time were rock heads. Real big hip hop heads, but people were big jazz heads. So the whole thing was: *how can we cook up something for them?* That was the thought.

Setting up a sonic laboratory in the basement of his uncle's house in New Jersey, Clef remembered, "I had my SP-1200, I had my MPC9000, and I've always been practicing. So I felt like I was ready!" Booga Basement Studio was born in the summer of 1995 after Wyclef, Lauryn and Pras talked Ruffhouse CEO Chris Schwartz into taking a gamble on letting the group produce their next album. Bringing out colors that hip hop had never heard musically blended before. Clef breaks down the composition of the group's individual influences, beginning with his own:

> Me, I was very eclectic: I came from the Caribbean. I didn't forget my Caribbean roots,

and at the same time, I was influenced by certain styles of music. Pras was more like an 80's head, he was like a rock head. I think he thought he was Axl Rose or something! (laughs) He could tell you every rock record and how it was coming. Then you had Lauryn who's straight soul music. And I think that algorithm collectively together is the scientific component of the Fugees.

Producing a sound truly heard around the world, including atop the UK Singles Chart when the international warning *Ready or Not* introduced the Fugees to millions of new fans, cracking the Top 10 around Europe in Germany (#8), Belgium (#6), Finland (#2), Ireland (#2), the Netherlands (#3), Norway (#8), Sweden (#3). Reflective of Wyclef's genius for flipping samples into their next dimension as he did when he interfused space rock with psychedelia and jazz with old-school R&B, in revisiting the creative headspace where they sounded sensible to mix he reasons because:

I'm a fan of the Grateful Dead, I'm a fan of *The Wall* by Pink Floyd, so I'm all about that space. I'm a fan of Miles Davis' *Bitches Brew*, so I was like, "Wow, look at this long sample stretch with just a hollow beat in the middle, and this space is completely open!" And once day Lauryn walks in and she's just like, "Ready or Not, here I come." And she's influenced by the Four Tops and Aretha Franklin. So you see how the influences vary? So to me, the chemistry of *The Score*, the reason why I think it came out like that was because you had three different kids from three different boroughs that connected together.

I knew that this would be different because of the vastness of what we were listening to. Like I knew that Enya lived in a castle in Europe and I knew what she did musically. So when you have a thirst for music, you're searching for those things, and you live in eclectic space. One day I was watching a movie called *Sleep Walker* and an Enya sample came in. And I was like, "Holy shit! I'm about to sample Enya. And then I'm gonna put her over an SP drum."

With a musical mind the metaphorical size of a concert hall, Clef confirms the need for that much room to stretch out as he sketches out an entire song's instrumental scope, revealing that "The orchestra lives in my brain. You know? Just like the choir thing I was telling you about. It's sort of like, I can hear the drums. But maybe they come from the cafeteria banging out. You know? Sometimes the writing process can just come from a piano lick. But my main thing is, I believe in simplicity. I believed the simpler the sonics were, the cooler it would sound. This generation right now, sonically, there's five sonics on a record. So you can listen to any Drake record and there's really no more than five sonics. He would have the 808 sonic, which is the main sonic, then you would have the vocal sonic – which plays in two spaces, it plays within the lead space and it plays in that Auto-Tune space. That Auto-Tune space really is Roger Trautman and Teddy Riley. They created all of that space. And then you would have one more space where like a keyboard sonic might go. So when you're listening to *The Score*, you're not hearing more than five, six sonics, because the MP was so strong that it just covered like 20,000 drum kits in one. So it was shit like that going on."

Taking their globe-hopping atop the charts to the next level for hip hop as a genre when their reinvention of the Roberta Flack classic *Killing Me Softly* broke records the planet over, hitting #1 in Australia, across Europe from Italy to France and on the Eurochart Hot 100 and of course back home on the Billboard Hot 100 Singles chart. The Fugees reigned supreme. Decoding the brilliant construction of the production, Clef points first and foremost to, "What made that record incredible: the amount of vocals Lauryn got on there! I kid you not, I think Lauryn has at least three thousand vocal backgrounds on that record, literally doing *Killing Me Softly*. I think she spent like six, seven days just doing backgrounds." When his ear turned to creating the ambient atmosphere surrounding Lauryn Hill's elegant lead vocal performance, Wyclef chose a reverb that became a signature part of the singer's sound throughout the album:

> The verb we used on her for that song and throughout *The Score* was the XB80. I used a very small room verb because the key to recording a vocalist who sounds so raw and so real, is less is better. So you have to find the right amount of room to put in within the verb or you're basically gonna put her in a situation of space and it's gonna be missed. So the trick was to put her vocal in the front and just wet it a little bit. And we captured that.

I used a Neumann microphone mostly on Lauryn. That was a very cool mic. It sort of gave me that old-school vibe. Like when you put it on Omni, and it gives you that warmth. The way those Billy Holiday standards used to be recorded. You know? Where it was all about the vocal and the vocal being in the front. I liked that mic, it was good for drums, etc.

Floating overtop Clef's day-dreamy instrumental, versus putting slaving for days in the studio over the track, the producer remembered taking an approach as relaxed as the song's beat, confessing that, "I guess I probably thought it was going to be a mixtape record, so I didn't do much to it. I played the keyboard, and when you hear *Killing Me Softly*, and you hear that Fender Rhodes. That's not even a Fender Rhodes, it's an Akai S900 Oscillator 448 tone. I sampled the break beats from A Tribe Called Quest, and Jerry Wonder played a bass on it." Ironically, alongside producing Lauryn's lead vocal performance, for which he'd win a Grammy for Best R&B Performance by a Duo or Group with Vocal, throughout the album Wyclef produced himself in the studio, a fascinating process he broke down to begin with an arrangement approach:

I guess that's similar to Lauryn, because if you've heard my music through the years, you can hear all these layers of harmonies. So the best way to record it is, I like a little bit of verb, but the first vocal – which will be the lead – is in the front, then harmony one goes to the left ear. Then once I was done with harmony one, it stays on the left ear, and harmony two goes on the right ear. Once I'm done with harmony two on the right ear, you push that harmony to the left ear, and I continue with harmony three on the right ear. And this is an algorithm that we use naturally to stack and to build incredible harmonies. That's remained that way throughout my career.

To all of the young producers and different producers coming up, I would say my secret to you all is: as a producer, we're here to serve. Right? And to make sure the final product is right. So a vocal booth is not necessary. Better to use the mixes within the headphones, and constantly make the person that you're recording feel free. "Feel free," just means being in an open space where you're being recorded. So I think investing in keeping everything within the same room is kind of like a cool thing, and it brings a certain energy. Even though we're using software plug-ins, which we all do now, at the same time it's great to have three or four pieces that are analog. So the best thing is when you can mix the analog with some of the software that you're using. It creates a sonic fusion that is the best fusion of when man meets machine. If you know what I mean?

Declared an, "Instant classic" by *Spin*, *Billboard* joined what would be a chorus of celebration of *The Score* as "A rap album for everyone," while *Rolling Stone* singled out the popular knowledge that, "Led by Wyclef Jean, the Fugees created eclectic, politically aware R&B hip hop." A formula he would prove wasn't a fluke when he produced another world-wide chart-topper with *Ghetto Supastar* a year later in 1997, with the smash single and title cut from Fugees' member Pras' debut solo LP. Clef took the emcee on a ride along with Wu-Tang star Ol' Dirty Bastard and Mya to #1 in Austria, Belgium, Denmark, Germany, Ireland, the Netherlands, New Zealand, Norway Switzerland, the UK R&B Chart and Europe's Eurochart Hot 100, while it peaked just shy of #1 in Australia and the UK Singles Chart, and scoring another Top 20 hit on the Billboard Hot 100 Singles Chart. The song's infectious chorus hook was one creative contribution Clef credited to the legendary head of Interscope Records, confirming that, "The idea of the *Islands In The Stream* came from Jimmy Iovine. At the time, he gave me a call and he knows that I'm known to flip records – that I could take old records and make them sound modern – and he was like, "Yo, I got this girl named Mya, and I need you to make her a superstar. You do it for all of the other girls." So I was listening to *Islands In The Stream* thinking, *Okay, how can I make this cool?* And I just dug in and it just came out the way it did."

Electrified by a propulsive beat that sounded like a Ferrari engine revving up each time a new bounce dropped, guitar riffs chugging along overtop as part of the song's rhythmic pulse. Along with sampling country with Kenny Rodgers and Dolly Parton, Clef channeled one of hip hop and rock & roll's great big bang moments when he injected Aerosmith up in the mix, bringing the experiment current when it first hit him that:

> The thing that makes that record stand out are the rock guitars. I was inspired by Run-D.M.C.'s *Walk This Way*, and if you hear the guitar riff in *Supastar*, I wanted it to have like an Aerosmith

vibe – like a really modern, *Walk This Way* kind of energy. You know, where you're hearing the guitars crossing through a straight hip hop break beat. I felt like that was the kind of energy we were searching for in a record like that. The Juno-106 was the primary keyboard on that one for some of the bass-heavy sound. The drum machines were a mix of MPs and then a mixture of live drums too. So that rhythm track was very heavily layered – that was a multi-tiered, overdubbed instrumental. So the guitars were overdubbed, and the drums were overdubbed, etc.

An equally important source for the song's animated energy came from the explosive presence of Ol' Dirty Bastard on the track, stealing the show lyrically back and forth from Mya's candy chorus during his verses, where ODB's performance – as coached by producer Wyclef personally – captured a, "Personality and ostentatious demeanor," that "Were representative of the soul of hip hop." Knowing from the first thought of the flamboyant rapper that his presence would provide the perfect extra boost of lyrical fuel for the song's fire, Clef recalled that, "For me, Ol' Dirty Bastard, it was important that I had him on that record. That was my church/choir director brain thinking like, 'ODB's going to bring an element of funk that don't exist on that record.' I needed that, 'Oh baby come on.' I needed that guy to bring that thing. I think this is what separates like pilots from co-pilots. Because you have to be able to fly the plane, and with someone like ODB, you *have to* fly the plane. So flying the plane means he comes in, and I let him do exactly what's in his head, and then I express to him,

'Look, this is where we're going, let me get more.' So I got as much as I can out of him without disturbing his energy. And then after he left, I took three or four hours of material and cut it down into the best three minutes that you heard on the final track."

Well before the end of his first decade in the game – the traditional point where "influence" labels start to attach themselves to a catalog of music. Usually, in acknowledgement of what critics are excited about with expectation of what is still to come – Wyclef's students in the media were already looking back at what he'd already accomplished! With his influence spreading around the globe like a new musical awakening, *Time* – arguably the world's most purest-in-motive reporter of social phenomena – would add to their analysis of Wyclef Jean's immediate grip on the earth's musical eco-culture that it had spread so swiftly on the wind of, "His sonic curiosity has broadened since *The Carnival*, and his songwriting skills have sharpened. He's like a pop-music search engine, filtering through genres, highlighting what's melodious and spirited."

A fitting title for the jamboree of music playing throughout the album, Clef's vision was revelationary enough to inspire critics like *Entertainment Weekly* to muse allowed, "Is there no end to the talents of Fugee member Wyclef Jean?" Decorated with twenty-four songs that might as well have been their own country with the unique cultural focus of each musically. The personalities that expressed themselves so beautifully throughout this masterpiece were all part of a concept where the producer solidified his signature stamp on world music within hip hop, sharing a creative headspace heading into recording where:

> With *The Carnival*, I was thinking about creative
> freedom. I didn't have to talk to Lauryn, I didn't

have to talk to Pras, I didn't have to talk to nobody. And then I never really wanted to be famous. Right? Because *The Carnival* is not a [CD] where anybody's trying to be famous. It's purely a piece of art, which is hieroglyphics on the wall. Depending on what mushroom you take during the day. That [CD] represents to me what I call, "World hip hop," sonics. Because the idea with that would be to now explore into my natural being, which is coming from the Caribbean. And being a natural Pan-African thinker in my brain as far as drums and percussiveness, I could try things I would not be able to chance with the Fugees. Because we were coming from a 15 million album space, and I was like, "Well, I'm just going to do that in my head for *The Carnival*."

Wearing many hats at once as an artist recording himself, *Spin* put him on the rare level of his West Coast peer, crowning him, "A master producer and Dr. Dre in any genre," and as Clef invites fans inside that 3D frame of mind at work, he selects the creation of one of the album's true gems, *Gone Till November,* as an example. A remarkable Top 10 hit that gave visibility with its chart position to show just how fully into bloom hip hop had grown as a credible music *genre*- with arguably some of those leaps forward made courtesy of the Fugees – on this symphony-backed solo ballad, Clef confirmed he was indeed seeking to make a statement of musical sophistication in that same spirit. One where he had ambitiously planned:

For myself, I was like, "Okay, I want *Gone Till November* to be like hip hop Amadeus," in one sort, then I was like, "Okay, now I have to go back to my jazz/classical brain, and Philharmonic Orchestra. These are the layouts, these are the parts," then bring a composer in to work with me that understands what I'm trying to do and put it in institution form for the orchestra. If you notice, everything was overhead mics, so it was like the orchestra was recorded like the old-school big band.

The trick when you're producing for yourself is you think more, because for other people, you know exactly what they want. They come to you like, "Yo, I'm looking for this," and you give it to them. That song was definitely inspired by the Beatles in the sense of the album where they used the orchestra. So sonically, it played part of the same tier. Once again, the drums were basic to a MPC and all of the instruments were completely live. My mic of choice is always a Neumann. And I also like Binaural microphones.

Reflective of the universal respect Clef held in both the streets and the suburbs with consumers as well as his peers at the highest levels of rock & roll royalty – evinced by Bob Dylan's cameo in the hit video – *Gone Till November* would peak at #2 on the Billboard Hot Rap Singles Chart and garner a Grammy Nomination for Best Rap Solo Performance. On the same album, he traveled from the Caribbean to Cuba with another of the album's eclectic singles, *Guantanamera,* where the producer felt he best summed up the records' conceptual essence in a single musical statement. Reasoning that, "The whole idea with *The Carnival* was to give you a world journey to places you might not necessarily be but that can make you feel time travel at the time. And all of the carnivals do that. It's all time-travel, so for me, *Guantanamera* was about, *How can I keep a hard hip hop groove and undertone?* And then the top, we can start to introduce some of the Pan-African layers, and it worked out cool. *Guantanamera* – is a Cuban poem, and Celia Cruz, who I was obsessed with, came and flipped the poem into what became the song."

Musician Magazine in a stellar review bumped happily along to the, "Dizzying, invigorating midway of thick rhythms, canny arrangements, comic set-pieces, and a winning blend of song styles from all over the Western hemisphere...nearly every track mixes some sounds of tradition with thoroughly modern hip hop sonics." Within that spectrum, the rhythm beds Clef laid down were as percussively cosmic as ever. Designing his studio production to re-create a live show's vibe, Clef spills the secret:

> If you haven't caught a live Clef show, you can catch the show, because it shows you real-time. On stage I show you exactly how I do it real-time. And in the studio, we would always mic the percussionist live overhead. The key is he would just have to super-lock into the sample. Right? Once he locked into the sample, the key is within the mix: *how can we EQ it so it all feels like one thing?*

JAKE BROWN

Where so much of hip hop's focus by the late 1990s and early 2000s was centered on material bling, Wyclef continued to enlighten with his sophomore solo LP, *The Ecleftic: 2 Sides II a Book*, where *Rolling Stone Magazine* found itself marveling at the feat that, "Clef continues to do tricks others can't: Part world music, part pop, part rock, part righteous message, and part braggadocio. Wyclef's sound reflects his Haitian roots as much as his Brooklyn and New Jersey roots." As the millennium advanced, Clef's next couple musical statements would be of a more personal than political nature, musical therapy as he worked his way through the devastating loss of his father, *Reverend Gesner Jean.* Opening up candidly about the way art imitated life, he began with the way he wore his sorrow on sleeve on the album's cover art, confirming that, "I mean, if you see my two hands in front of my face, I was confused, it was a masquerade. My father had just passed away, and if you go through that, you can see just confusion in just trying to find my way back. And at the end of *Masquerade*, you'll hear I did a song for him called *Daddy* and that [CD] was like hiding inside of a masquerade, just trying to find a way back. That's why you hear like *Peace God*, the intro took it back to the essence of where it started for me. And the ending was my dad. That's one of those things I think when people go back now and analyze and listen, they be like, 'Woah! Okay. This is the one he did right after his father died and he had to bury him.'"

Returning to the refuge of the studio to mourn, he returned in 2003 with the tribute, *The Preacher's Son*, which featured the hit single *Party to Damascus*, and personally stands as among the rapper's proudest musical accomplishments to date, affirming his belief that, *The Preacher's Son* is one of the most underrated Wyclef albums. I think when I leave the earth, it's probably going to be one of the top three Wyclef albums. On that album,

I got a chance to work with Clive Davis, which was incredible. The whole idea of that record was one of celebration, 'It's gonna be alright. You know what I mean? Life is good, everything's gonna be okay.'"

Proving he still had the hit-making mojo and club-floor cred as a producer he'd firstheld back in the Fugees heyday, in 2006, Clef would return to #1 in eighteen countries around the world. This astonishing list included the US Billboard Hot 100 Singles Chart, France, Columbia, Italy, Switzerland, Australia, Czech Republic, Hong Kong, Germany, Belgium, the U.K., Romania, the Netherlands, Ireland, New Zealand, Greece, India, Singapore, Lebanon, Portugal, Romania, Venezuela and South Africa, and #2 in Japan, Canada, Austria, Finland, Brazil, Hungary, Poland, Norway – after he produced the global smash *Hips Don't Lie* for Latin pop superstar Shakira. Inspired as an offspring of another creative avenue Clef had begun pursuing when Hollywood came calling, inviting him into the elite world of film scoring:

> That song was inspired actually because one of the early scores I did in my career was *Life* starring Eddie Murphy and Martin Lawrence. I did the entire score for that movie. So it was a part of Hollywood that was looking at me as the guy who can do music for movies. And I was approached to write a song for another film called *Havana Nights*. The song that I wrote was originally *Hips Don't Lie*, but that wasn't the title of it. I had another singer singing it and it was purely for the movie. The movie came out and did great. Two years later, Donnie Ienner called me up and says they need a song for Shakira, and

I said, "I have this song that was sitting on the *Havana Nights* soundtrack and I think it would be perfect if she cut the song." She cut it and it became a hit.

My scoring, I credit it to my jazz teacher, Mr. Hayes. My process is purely institution in creativity when I deal from a level of scoring, because there's rules, there's laws, there's emotions people have to feel. You're building something that already exists. Right? So my process is to watch the movie from beginning to end to get the emotion. Once I watch it from beginning to end, then I like to score the parts. And I usually start with the danger parts first because it takes a lot out of me emotionally. Then I do the love scenes, and the heavy stuff last.

Moving over 10 million digital downloads, the song became a genuine phenomenon, winning awards around the world, including the International Dance Music Awards for Best Latin/Reggaeton Track, the Latin Billboard Music Awards where it took home the trophy for Hot Latin Song of the Year-Vocal Duet or Collaboration, Song of the Year at the Los Premios MTV Latinoamérica, and BMI Urban Award - Billboard No. 1s at the BMI Awards. A veteran of the red carpet world after his trophy shelf began filling up with Grammys in the 1990s, including two wins with the Fugees and again in 2000 when he won an Album of the Year statue for his work on Carlos Santana's *Supernatural* album out of Clef's ten total lifetime nominations.

Reteaming with Santana, Avicii, and Alexandre Pires in 2014 when he was asked to perform at the closing ceremony of the 2014 FIFA world cup, watched by over 43 million people, whereafter their single, *Dar um Jeito* became the official World Cup anthem. Jean has remained as popular on the world stage receiving awards that in recent years have begun to reflect the sheer sphere of his influence around the globe. These prestigious recognitions have included highlights like the 2005 Satellite Award for Best Song by the International Press Academy, 2009 BET Humanitarian Award, and the 2010 NAACP Image Awards' Vanguard Award. Arguably the most personal prize to the producer's accolades is, in 2011, his home country of Haiti donned Jean with the rank of Grand Officer, "As a sign of high consideration national for his dedication to the promotion of Haiti around the world." In 2017, after he was inducted into the New Jersey Hall of Fame, Wyclef took a moment to appreciate the props, admitting that from a purely artistic point of view:

> Awards definitely make you feel like you're a part of a musical institution and that people appreciate your art and what you do. They're definitely a great thing. But for me, knowing that so many musicians are playing in the train stations, on the streets, and all of that, it's great when they acknowledge musicians who actually play instruments – real keyboards, real pianos, things in the studio – so for me, that's always a great accomplishment. So when I get these awards, I always like to encourage people: "This is all for us."

Bringing the world festival back to town with the *Carnival Vol. II: Memories of an Immigrant* LP in 2007, where he stayed as musically colorful as ever, both in styles and cast of players, inspiring *USA Today* to applaud, "The often-exuberant blend of politics and eclectic musical styles is bolstered by such diverse collaborators as Sizzla, Akon, Lil Wayne, T.I., Shakira, Norah Jones, Chamillionaire, Will.i.am, Serj Tankian, Mary J. Blige, and Paul Simon. But rather than simply bristling with big stars, the album deftly uses their unique talents to push his art forward." Slipping into alter-ego Toussaint St. Jean – where he was channeling Haitian liberator Toussaint Louverture – on his seventh studio album, *From the Hut, To the Projects, To the Mansion*, Clef handed the musical reigns for a change over to DJ Drama, who he co-produced the project with, "Because I wanted to do a mixtape and I wanted to do something unique. Toussaint was one of the revolutionaries in our country, so based on that, I wanted to create a mixtape with Drama, and wanted on that [CD] to take you on a lyrical journey. That [CD] was definitely one where sometimes you're doing so much people forget the foundation of some of what you do is rap. And that album took me back there."

Clef made global headlines again in 2010 when he announced he was considering running for president of his birth country Haiti. A campaign that was taken seriously enough that it garnered coverage on CBS News, where it was reported, "Jean could be in a good position to battle the rampant corruption of his Caribbean homeland since he's already wealthy." For the producer personally ahead even of politically, the opportunity to be considered in and of itself made him proud, as well as the international spotlight it kept on his impoverished homeland. Reasoning that, "You should never forget the village you came from. I think for me that's just a natural thing. Similar to Bob

Marley, Africa plays an important part in my music, and if you listen to my different albums, there's always an undertone about Africa somewhere, similar to Haiti. Bob Marley does that for Jamaica, for people. And the idea to be able to give back is always the greatest thing."

Ultimately, the Haitian government ruled the raptivist wasn't eligible to run because of residency restrictions. But he inspired the social media hit single *If I Was President*, which – has almost 4 million YouTube views and counting. To date the political protest anthem remains one of Jean's proudest successes because, "You can see through the course of my career, even if you listen to *If I Was President*, which online is as big as *Gone Till November*. So it's weird. And I try to tell people, I don't think of commerciality." Driven to make as powerful a political statement as ever, Wyclef pointed within his motivation as a composer writing the song to the fact that:

> There's always a social undertone with me as a reader. And I just used to look at JFK, Lincoln's luck, and Martin Luther, like man, these dudes really put in their time. But then everybody just disappears and gives them a holiday and keep on voting like they didn't kill these people. You understand? So I just put myself in that role, and the song resonates because it's truth, "Oh, that's what happens: they'll assassinate you and then go back to work as if nothing happened."

Championing the millennials who have embraced YouTube as their generation's MTV, Wyclef has stayed connected with a global fan base that after almost a quarter-century, includes not only his fans, but his fans' kids as well. A family affair that Clef feels, "Is just beautiful, because you can drop a record like *If I Was President*, and then be like, *Radio won't play this, They call it rebel music. How can you refuse it, children of Moses?* Like, you can say this, and you wouldn't be able to do that if you didn't have channels like YouTube that allow us to. And the analytics and data, if you look at it, *Gone Till November* and *If I Was President*, they're sitting on the same data analytically. And one was one of the biggest songs of all time ever with an orchestra and then the other was, 'Let me do this song on Dave Chappell real quick!', and 3,721,125 views later..."

Clef regularly racks up astonishing numbers of plays in the streaming world, including the digital single *Divine Sorrow*, a collaboration with wildly popular Swedish producer/DJ Avicii from his 2014 studio album *Clefication*, which has racked up a head-spinning 50+ million streams on Spotify alone, or *Sweetest Girl (Dollar Bill)* featuring Akon and Lil Wayne, which has over 28 million plays and counting. And his most recent single, *Hendrix* off the 2017 EP *J'ouvert*, which is already up over the 10 million mark.

Reflecting his relevance with today's youth around the world, and aware of the responsibility of being an influence, Clef muses that, "What I'm most proud of is, within this generation, I'm able to give my country a voice, nothing beats that. That's just history, long after me, that will always be there." When the aspiring producers among those fans hit him up on Twitter – where the producer has roughly 4.3 million followers –to ask for advice on how to follow in his footsteps, Jean routinely drops the following jewels of wisdom on them:

> For all of my hip hop producers, everyone says
> that they're great, and everyone tells you that
> they're the best. And that you should listen to

their music. So the only thing that can separate you is: do not create hits, because if you create hits, you're gonna be out there and disappear. Focus on creating cultural phenomenons, because a cultural phenomenon is gonna outlive you. And that's when you're really in the game.

Drawing his latest inspiration for the forthcoming trilogy of the *Carnival* series from, "My daughter, she's eleven-years-old, so all that energy is coming from her." Wyclef Jean has his eyes and ears set on bigger ambitions than ever where, "The thing right now is, I'm forty-six, so I think I'm in the process of where I'm probably going to create *Thriller* and a bunch of crazy stuff like Quincy Jones did when he created all that crazy stuff. So I just keep moving forward. I look at all of them as great bodies of work, and honestly, I've never heard them back-to-back-to-back-to-back. Maybe I'll do that when I get to be seventy. But for now, I'll just keep pushing."

While some could argue Clef is the Quincy Jones of hip hop, he has his own designs on, "Sharing the same space as Thelonious Monk, because I'm part of the institution. And I'm able to take the institution and modernize it. So our idea was to bring modern fusion to a generation where at times the music was separated." Looking back, as he looks ahead to his next act, Wyclef Jean remains as cutting edge as he does old-school, striking a balance that in closing he argues – as many do – crowns him:

The most eclectic producer that ever lived in my generation. I can go from Johnny Cash to T.I. And all of this is documented, which is crazy. I think that just comes from that digging-in-the-crates mentality.

www.wyclef.com

CHAPTER TWENTY
BASECAMP - Aaron Harmon

Very few groups ever made it onto Billboard's radar, and those who do usually are headed for the stars, and hopefully the top of the charts too, and when BASECAMP first turned up on the Top 40 of *Billboard*'s Twitter Emerging Artist Chart in 2014 with the single *Shutter,* which peaked at #35. While music business old-heads might have dismissed the notion of social media being worthy of its own chart in the legendary industry bible, it was a sign of the times and how hot something in fact was among the digital generation of millennial streamers and downloaders that were hipping the world to the arrival of a group. In describing the group's eclectic sound, the magazine seemed to find amusement within the irony that though, "BASECAMP hail from Nashville, Tennessee...their sound has little, if anything, in common with most of the music typically associated with the city. Instead of country music, the trio (consisting of Aaron Miller, Aaron C. Harmon, and Jordan Reyes) creates moody electronic pop songs with subtle, glitchy production effects, haunting cello and guitar, and R&B-inspired vocals. Their measured, detailed beats – reminiscent of U.K. garage/post-dubstep artists such as Mount Kimbie and SBTRKT – typically keep to a slow tempo but occasionally quicken their pulse to emphasize particularly dramatic moments."

Word has been traveling fast around Nashville in circles – first small and now larger and growing by the next new buzz – about Harmon's production chops for years now. In 2016, it made enough noise to wind up on Revolt TV, one of the hottest hip hop cable networks on television. The network took notice of one of Harmon's most frequent studio collaborators outside of BASECAMP when they spotlighted music city rapper Chancellor Warhol for pulling off precisely what Harmon had achieved with his own sound: "Doing the unordinary: leading the hip hop renaissance within the country music capital of the world, Nashville, Tennessee." The duo would earn enough respect from the West Coast on a 2011 Dr. Dre Tribute to catch the ear of the *L.A. Weekly*, congratulating, "Tennessee mc Chancellor Warhol," for "Dropping a verse that Dre would be proud of. This single...was stone cold, and Warhol, inhabiting the big-balled persona of Dre on the first verse, does it justice."

These days, Warhol is widely regarded as Nashville's equivalent of L.A.'s Kendrick Lamar or Toronto's Drake. He flowed around Harmon's spacey musical landscapes for years laying every lyrical color possible overtop the musical moods that Harmon sets for Warhol throughout their almost decade-long studio collaboration. In doing so, the artist has become Andy himself with the vivid way his lyrical illustrations have routinely highlighted the producer's musical canvas. Their first collaboration together, 2010's *Japanese Lunchbox*, where Harmon produced standout cuts like, *I'm On, In a Dream, Falling Through Clouds, Fame Kills,* and *Comatose* was voted Best Rap Album by the Nashville Scene, who decided the rapper was *IT* after delivering, "A record that's setting a new high-water mark for Nashville's dance and hip hop scenes...*Japanese Lunchbox* is the product of a scene that's reaching maturity and finding its own sound on its own terms!" That scene is where producer and artist first heard something unique in each other and the way those elements fused together on record:

Aaron Harmon: We've worked together a really long time. I first met Chancellor Warhol when he came to one of our *Enjoy the Zoo* shows. From what he's told me it really inspired him to start performing live, because he was always rapping but kind of keeping it to himself. And we became friends and started talking. He said, "I want to do a record," and he and his partner Ducko McFly – who is now signed to Mike Wills' EarDummer camp – were in a group called the NoBots at the time. I was a big fan of his lyrics. They were cool and hip in our world. Not like your typical rapper's lyrics. It was more our scene. So I knew what he was looking for musically, and we've done every record together since then.

I feel like why we've always worked well together and to this day, other artists I work well with, is they're the ones that have no boundaries, in a sense. So I would either play Chance a beat that I'd made that sounded like *Final Fantasy* or something. And I wasn't expecting anyone to like it. It was just something I'd made because it was super weird. And he'd say, "This is dope!" Then I'd make him stuff I thought he'd want to hear. Like a certain style of beat, and he just wouldn't feel it. So I think he's attracted to out of the box creative ideas. That's always been my headspace as a producer. I don't want to do something that I've already heard. I try not to anyway.

After setting Nashville afire, the duo's buzz blazed its way into the pop culture with recent high-profile placements everywhere from the Kardashian world to a car commercial running during the NBA finals. Warhol's producer proudly cheers on the rapper's most recent single, *Elvis,* one he highlights as, "By far the biggest song Chance and I have ever done together as far as synchs go. Like we just got a Kia NBA synch, which is huge. It's crazy! We've gotten synchs fifteen times over the years with like *Keeping Up with the Kardashians*, the *Teen Wolf* TV show on MTV, and ESPN. But the NBA was definitely the coolest for me!" No doubt his parents were rooting him on too, as they used to back when during his early days as a bar band guitar player growing up back in Las Vegas, Nevada:

> My bandmate, producing partner and best friend Jordan Rayes and I started out as bandmates together back in Vegas as Beginner's Mind. And for two years before moving to Nashville, while we were still teenagers, we gigged every place that Vegas had to offer, even dive bars. Back then, we'd play to our parents basically, and the sound man. Our parents were just at the bar throwing 'em back, yelling, "That's my boy!" They came out to every single show.

The winning incarnation of the band would wind up becoming BASECAMP once Harmon moved to Nashville in 2005. Evolving out of what the producer jokes have been several monumental and consequential happy accidents of Harmon and producing/writing partner Jordan Reyes' adventures in recording where, "From working with Chancellor, we then started working with Drupy, who used to be in a group with Chance. Then, when BASECAMP got together, we signed with Dr. Luke. Basically, once you have a deal, your publisher kind of becomes your manager and finds you writing gigs. And puts you in a room with all these different people they think you'll have good chemistry with. And ultimately, they hope, write a hit with. So the biggest opportunities for us that definitely came up from it was exactly that. Getting to meet and write with pop and hip hop names like Baby E and Doja Cat." Recognizing Harmon and Co.'s potential immediately as one of the most promising production teams to bump onto his radar in years, Prescription Songs soon began tapping their musical medicine in an almost accidental creative exercise that became permanent as the trio creatively gelled:

> At first, we weren't trying to make a band. We were just writing songs for TV, and we did a lot of really cool sampling on that record. We'd be banging on the walls, sampling picture frames bouncing off the walls, and I remember slamming a garbage can on that song. The chorus was played on an instrument Jordan's dad brought him back when he went to Africa. It was all out of tune, but we just sampled it and tuned it in Melodyne. Then we played it for the chorus. There were a lot of live guitar samples, live bass samples, and a lot of live percussion smacks.
>
> I always thought I was going to be in a band so that was a huge thing for me. But when Enjoy the Zoo broke up, producing felt like a natural thing to go into next. My attitude was, if I couldn't be in a band, I would work with bands. That's when me and Jordan started Boy Genius, producing pop music of all things. To get a foot in the door, we decided to write a bunch of songs for kid TV shows, and it came really natural. It was never difficult and we had fun doing it. Writing those kinds of songs as a producer is more like a job, because you have a goal, "We have to write a song about *THIS*," and the first thing that pops in my head is when we wrote a song called *Adhesion* for *Blaze and the Monster*

Machines on the Nickelodeon Jr. network. That was literally a song about science, technology, engineering and math. So you're teaching kids with the lyrics about *Adhesion* but you're doing it in a catchy pop song so they remember it.

Once BASECAMP's members weren't writing under the Boy Genius moniker for other artists, they were busy grinding it out in the studio producing their own record in a, "Bedroom studio," that Red Bull Academy quipped after hearing the music they produced there wouldn't be, "Their 'typical situation' much longer." One of a handful of mainstream music critics with an opinion on the subject, the esteemed Red Bull Academy followed through on their prognosis for the Dr. Luke protégés with the follow-up report in late 2015 that, "Their simmer turned into a full-blown boil this summer when the electronic-meets-R&B group that has no problem glossing say, an 80's Genesis slow jam, with their slinky sheen signed to Skrillex's OWSLA label."

Hypebeast.com would warn soon after that, "If BASECAMP hasn't been on your radar, they definitely should be." Locally, the *Nashville Scene* – a longtime fan who years earlier had first helped discover Harmon through their coverage of his work with Chancellor Warhol – realized their recognition of that potential full circle circa with a review of the group's EP *Greater Than* when they correctly captured Harmon's sound as, "Smooth and cool, but it's in constant motion." Describing what the band's music has organically become in his own terms. The producer brings his studio journey full-circle from his hip hop roots to his next musical evolution in what he describes in its simplest definitions as:

Electronic music. BASECAMP actually formed through meeting Chancellor Warhol, because that led us to meet Aaron Miller, who was singing hooks for Chance on his songs. Me and Jordan were making the beats, and I was recording and mixing all of Chancellor's songs, even the ones I didn't produce. So we were in the studio all the time, and I was recording Aaron's vocals. But it wasn't until a couple years later that one of us overheard the other talking about James Blake or Subtract. One of those artists, decided to write a song together and see what happened. The first thing us three wrote happened to be BASECAMP's first single, *Emmanuel.*

On another of our singles, we had this one song where my amp's speaker was blown and would only make this horrible fuzzy noise. We were recording it that way and there was a moment when it got so bad that when I played it back and began listening to it, the smack sounded really tight. So we chopped it up and used it as the snare drum. We do that kind of stuff all the time in our productions. We count on those kind of happy accidents where you go, "Woah! That's kind of tight," and all of a sudden it's part of a song. The coolest thing we've gotten to do so far is work with Del the Funky Homosapien, which was a dream come true for me personally as a producer. I grew up on his voice, we all did. So it was a dream come true for all of us being able to hear his voice on our production and song. It

was crazy. Even still listening to it weirds me
out.

So hip that super horror producer Jason Blume recently took
note of Harmon's sound recently when a side-project, *The Future
is Pointless*, appearing to be a fan of as his website,
Blumhouse.com, remarked in a review of their first release that,
"Sometimes, a band comes out of nowhere that combines various
elements of different genres in a way that's unique, exciting and
just rockin'. THE FUTURE IS POINTLESS is one of those
bands. The group features Villz, as well as Aaron C. Harmon
and Jordan Reyes from BASECAMP." Taking it all in stride,
Harmon remains as laid back as the Nevada desert he grew up in.
Fortunate enough to count himself as one of a few among a club
of on-the-rise millennial producers who haven't held a day job
since they decided to start producing music full time.

One of the hippest hip hop/Electronic fusion producers to
ever come out of Nashville, for the droves of millennial kids to
come up to him at shows in town or on the road these days to
solicit advice on how they can wind up on the answering end of
that question. He sums up ten plus years of accrued acumen this
way:

> Just work hard and practice a lot. That's the only
> tip I can give because I started when I was fifteen
> and picked up a guitar. And as soon as I did, I fell
> in love with music instantly. That's what I
> wanted to do with my life. I tried to do that with
> my life till I was twenty-seven or twenty-eight
> when BASECAMP finally got some actual
> success. So that's however many years of really

trying hard. Doing it full-time...breakfast, lunch, and dinner every day. NON-STOP! *www.BASECAMPmusique.com*

Award-winning music biographer **Jake Brown** has written 45 published books since 2001 featuring many authorized collaborations with some of rock's biggest artists, including 2013 Rock & Roll Hall of Fame inductees **Heart** (with Ann and Nancy Wilson), living guitar legend **Joe Satriani**, country music legends **Merle Haggard** and **Freddy Powers**, heavy metal pioneers **Motorhead** (with Lemmy Kilmister), late hip hop icon **Tupac Shakur** (with the estate), celebrated rock drummer **Kenny Aronoff**, legendary R&B producer **Teddy Riley**, country rap star **Big Smo**, late funk pioneer **Rick James**, superstar country music anthology *Nashville Songwriter*, all-star rock drummers anthology *Beyond the Beats*, all-star rap producers HIP HOP HITS anthology, and the all-star rock producers anthology *Behind the Boards*, among many others. In 2012, Brown won the Association for Recorded Sound Collections Award in the category of Excellence in Historical Recorded Sound Research. Brown is a regular contributor to Tape Op (including the 2016 AES Cover Story with Smashing Pumpkins mastermind Billy Corgan). He has also appeared as the featured biographer of record on Fuse TV's *Live Through This* series, Bloomberg TV's *Game Changers* series, and received national press in *Rolling Stone Magazine*, CBS News, *USA Today*, *MTV.com*, *The Hollywood Reporter*, *Parade Magazine*, and *Billboard*. Jake will also be featured in the BET Death Row Records docuseries airing in 2018.

www.twitter.com/jakebrownbooks

CPSIA information can be obtained
at www.ICGtesting.com
Printed in the USA
BVOW09s1922081017
497055BV00001B/1/P